MW01047129

An
Introduction
to

CLASSICAL
BALLET

An
Introduction
to
CLASSICAL
BALLET

CAROL LEE

LEA
LAWRENCE ERLBAUM ASSOCIATES, PUBLISHERS
1983   Hillsdale, New Jersey   London

Lawrence Erlbaum Associates, Inc., Publishers
365 Broadway
Hillsdale, New Jersey 07642

Library of Congress Cataloging in Publication Data

Lee, Carol, 1936–
     An introduction to classical ballet.

     Bibliography: p.
     Includes indexes.
     1. Ballet.   2. Ballet—History.   3.Ballet dancing.
I. Title.   II. Title: Classical ballet.
GV1787.L3195   1982   792.8   82-16398
ISBN 0-89859-279-8

Printed in the United States of America
10   9   8   7   6   5   4   3   2   1

CONTENTS

FOREWORD BY
VIOLETTE VERDY

Never has an art form enjoyed greater popularity and a more rapid growth than that of the classical ballet. The ubiquitous presence of ballet has been everywhere instrumental in breaking down social and cultural barriers from the great international opera houses to the small neighborhood dancing schools here at home. Each year its growing presence can be found thriving in new circumstances. Even the exotic East has joined in embracing this Western dance style in the firm establishment of its practice in China and Japan. Recently our own Boston Ballet has had the honor of dancing in the ancient city of Peking to enthralled audiences.

A few decades ago, only New York City could provide a steady diet of dance for the dance lover, top-notch training for those with stars in their eyes, and dance jobs for those who excelled. Today in the United States touring dance companies bring exciting entertainment to almost any town which has a theatre big enough to hold full-blown ballet evenings. Young people, home-trained in states from Massachusetts to Texas, from Georgia to California, go on to become our brilliant native dancers. Currently there are more jobs in regional ballet companies for highly skilled dancers than can be filled.

The development of the communications media has been an enormous factor in aiding the growth of the art. Wonderful evenings of classical ballet are frequently at hand with the turn of the television dial. Millions upon millions of people witness the PBS performances of the best this country has to offer. These performances in turn inspire American youth and enrich the cultural life of the adult viewer. And so the whirlwind of ballet continues to sweep across the country, enshrining itself in the national artistic conscience.

This national interest in classical ballet has coincided with its enthusiastic presence on hundreds of college and university campuses. Whether for dance majors or for the general student, classes in ballet abound. With the arrival of ballet on the campus, a broader need for dance literature has emerged. A number of excellent critical essays and collected vignettes written by a new breed in America—the dance historian—now complement the many beautiful picture books that proliferate library shelves. The publication of scholarly dissertations on Noverre and Didelot, ballet's founding fathers, has begun to create a significant body of ballet literature for the researcher, and translations of European ballet histories have gone hand in hand with the rediscovery of books on technique dating back to the Renaissance. There has also been a flourish of English language reprintings of many technical manuals dating from the 1940's. Still missing, however, is that basic tool intrinsic to any college course, a substantial textbook to inform and stimulate the ballet student. A major textbook on classical ballet designed specifically with the college adult in mind is long overdue.

Introduction to Classical Ballet presents material designed to meet the dancer's early quest for knowledge in the field. The historical survey of ballet's exciting heritage in the first part of the book illuminates and enriches the student's practical efforts in the ballet class. A scintillating gallery of dancers and dance-makers glide across these pages to recreate the glittering history of America's foremost performing art. Fascinating is the story of the continual contest for ascendancy between form and content, technique and expressiveness, ballerina and choreographer. From the splendors of the Renaissance *balletti* to the Versailles court of the dancing Sun King, from wilis and sylphs to the Imperial Ballet of old Petipa and the art nouveau spirit of Diaghilev's Ballets Russes, we arrive in today's dance world which bears witness to the ballet art—fully ripe and yet without any sign of decline.

In the second part of *Introduction to Classical Ballet,* the detailed analysis and discussion of the technical foundations of classical ballet provide a tangible learning tool to complement and reinforce the many hours of physical effort required of the student. Frequent references to a variety of pedagogical approaches illustrate the American eclecticism, a happy result of the diverse international influences that have contributed to our native ballet. The brief glossary serves to further assist the beginning student by providing clear and concise definitions for the most important terms in the technical vocabulary of ballet.

Many ballet teachers have observed that the more interested their dancers become in technique, the more fascinated they become with the entire profession. Consequently, teachers of dance at the college level will find *Introduction to Classical Ballet* an indispensible text for their students. This book contains, in a most organized fashion, a distillation of a vast amount of information pertaining to the dancer's centuries-old heritage and classroom practice. A wealth of information pertaining to ballet's dynamic history is presented with enthusiasm and a sensitive understanding of its evolution as a major artistic force, which cannot but help spur the students' effort and interest in classical dance and kindle a deep appreciation for all that surrounds it. The myriad of "do's and dont's" that are a part of every teacher's presentation are taken into account. Consideration is also given to matters such as the purpose of the traditional sequence of exercises, the significance of movements ranging from *pliés* to the *petit* and *grand adage,* and why and how particular steps and positions have evolved into aesthetic expressions. Much rewarded will be the teacher and student who supplement the classroom work with this beautiful contribution to the literature.

College classes in ballet must be tightly fitted into the curriculum, and most teachers are hard-pressed with the brief time alotted for giving the barre and center work and keeping the student involved in old and new movement challenges. Moreover, the teacher must put out enormous energy in instructing, encouraging, and cajoling the student who in turn is struggling and straining with the physicality of the exercises and steps. Therefore, a book that provides the ballet class with an intellectual structure will be a welcome teaching aid supporting the teacher's work. By providing historical and technical information to supplement the teacher, this book can contribute to classroom work. College students are trained to learn quickly and the sooner a dancer grasps the concepts behind the technique, the sooner and the better they will absorb the skill.

Teachers associated with private dance studios will find *Introduction to Classical Ballet* an invaluable source of information. Constant search for novel approaches and renewed inspiration in the preparation of daily classes are part and parcel of the teaching profession and while the Muse comes in many guises, these pages are convenient for a refresher course in ballet history and as a storehouse of ballet fundamentals. Teachers may also wish to recommend this book to their adult students as well as their more mature high school age dancers. Adult ballet students have a healthy curiosity about the underpinnings of ballet and they will find the chapters of history absorbing reading. Teenagers will benefit from *Introduction to Classical Ballet* in that a whole new world is condensed for them, explaining what came before them as well as the prospect ahead.

No one, it seems to me, is better qualified to write this unique dance book than Carol Lee. The author's rich and diverse background provides her with an invaluable perspective to present ballet as a precious form of cultural expression. Her academic training in history and aesthetics, integrated with an artist's life as a dancer, teacher and choreographer, all contribute to her ability to illuminate our marvelous ballet heritage and its fundamental technical details.

Every page in this volume is imbued with the author's first-hand experience of the dance world and its many aspects. From her first *plié* as a child to that special performing "high" that only those who have worked in ballet companies can understand, from the writer's desk to the crystallization of artistic insights, Carol Lee's broad dance experience gives credence to the book's wealth of content. Particularly sensitive, from a dancer's point-of-view, is her presentation of pre-Romantic and Romantic ballet as it bloomed in Paris, and later in the halcyon days of Diaghilev, with all its drama and excitement. In Part II, her wise ordering and categorizing of ballet exercises, steps, and positions pleased me much from a pedagogical standpoint and her careful attention to the spelling and grammatical accuracy of the French terminology is most laudable.

Best of all, for students and teachers alike, the author has concisely organized these vital topics within the confines of a single volume, enhanced by a pleasing array of prints, photographs and drawings. Ballet literature has at last received a substantial book, geared essentially to the thousands of young people who so beautifully enrich the quality of campus and community life.

PREFACE

Classical Ballet in the United States has experienced extraordinary growth since the end of World War II. Although the presence of ballet in this country can be traced back to the days of the American Revolution, its surge of popularity in the past few decades is truly remarkable. Indeed, it would sometimes seem that "all America is dancing," to paraphrase Agnes de Mille. Not only has our national prosperity increased the enrollments in neighborhood dancing schools around the country, but federal and private endowments to national, state, and local ballet companies have supported their continuing presence in our society.

Ballet is now taught at all levels of public and private education, from elementary school to graduate dance programs in universities. The Regional Ballet Movement throughout the United States has not only contributed to improving the quality of ballet, but by its own philosophy also provides young students with the opportunity to continue to dance at home when they mature. After many years of being considered an aristocratic art, even in this country, ballet is enjoying popular acceptance. Ballet is now highly visible in movies and television, professional ballet companies perform in communities and on campuses, there is growing awareness of the presence of regional ballet companies in our towns and cities, and visits by foreign ballet companies to our shores are more frequent and often create a sensation.

One force that contributes greatly to the popularity of ballet in the United States is the presence of the "ballet class" in numerous colleges and universities. Many college programs offer a major concentration in ballet while "ballet," as a course offering in liberal arts programs, serves thousands of interested students every semester. Who can say exactly why this most difficult, complex, and even masochistic form of the performing arts is so popular on campus? Whatever the reasons may be, passion for, and delight in, participation in this marvelous kinetic mode of expression is an observable phenomenon in youth on our campuses.

The time-honored structure of the ballet class demands "doing" rather than "talking" about dancing. Consequently, the college student's ballet experience typically does not provide an academic and intellectual foundation for ballet. In order to convey the rich cultural and historical heritage of ballet in the context of the liberal arts idea, it would seem essential for the ballet student to obtain an intellectual grasp of the philosophical, technical, and aesthetic aspects of ballet within their historical context.

This book was conceived with the idea of supplementing the college student's overall grasp of the art of ballet. In the hour and a half that is usually allotted to the ballet class, the teacher only has time to impart the correct manner of performing the barre and center exercises, and the *adagio* and *allégro* movement. There is not adequate time to discuss in depth the aesthetic, philosophical, historical, and technical aspects of ballet because the "warmed-up" body must keep moving. I have always felt my own teachers had so much accumulated knowledge that was never shared because there was no opportunity in the ballet class itself. Consequently, I hope this book will supplement and complement the joint efforts of the teacher and the student in the study of ballet.

In essence, the book covers the historical and technical foundations of the classical ballet. Intermingled throughout are philosophical and aesthetic discussions that, hopefully, will enrich and augment the student's physical activity in the study of ballet. I have endeavored to make the history section comprehensive, but not overly detailed. The technique section departs from the classical manuals of Vaganova, Craske, and Stuart in that it is directed to the college student's need for technical information about the first years of ballet study.

Hopefully, the technical material that is included in this book will aid those dance majors who plan to teach ballet. Toward this goal, I have included the pedagogical explanation of the ballet exercises and classical steps gleaned from countless schools and teachers. The French terminology is based on the manual of Gail Grant. The glossary of terminology, which is based on the writings of Grant, Vaganova, Mara, and Kasavina, is designed to provide a quick and ready reference for the beginning ballet student.

ACKNOWLEDGMENTS

I wish to extend my sincere thanks to those who have so generously helped me in the realization of this book. For the inspiration that has permeated my career I thank all my former teachers but wish to acknowledge a special indebtedness to Ben Harkarvy for his wise guidance and superb training, to Antony Tudor, Felia Doubrovska and Muriel Stuart for their stimulating and lyrical classes, and Madame Nora Kiss who groomed me for my early professional work. I am also grateful to the artistic staff of Netherlands Dance Theater whose talents supplied me with renewed aesthetic vision during my 1979--80 sojourn in The Hague as this volume was being completed.

I wish to thank my colleagues at The Tampa Ballet who have provided me with an artistic base and a creative lifeline, and especially, Anzia Arsenault, for her unfailing support and eternal smile. I would also like to express my appreciation to Violette Verdy for taking time out of her busy schedule as Co-Artistic Director of the Boston Ballet to review the manuscript and prepare the Foreword for the book. Special thanks are also due to Genevieve Oswald, Curator of the Dance Collection at the New York Public Library for the Performing Arts, and her staff; to the respective staffs of the Bibliothèque et Musée de l'Opéra, Paris, and the Victoria and Albert Museum, London, for making their treasures available for my research; and to Madame Gilberte Cournand for her guidance on the French Renaissance period.

To Linda and Jack Vartoogian I am indebted for the use of their wonderful photographs, and to artist Ralph Castânet, for his technical contribution in the drawings for Part II. I wish also to thank Susan Frei, whose integrity as an editorial assistant is exceeded only by the quality of her beautiful dancing, Diane Gregg whose efforts were truly heroic over several years in typing the countless drafts of the text, and Dwight Strawser for his invaluable assistance in reproducing the entire manuscript.

Finally, I must thank my dear husband, Charles, for the initial push, constant encouragement and expert guidance without which this book would not exist; and my son, Nicholas, for all the patience of his childhood years which touch every page.

Carol Lee

An
Introduction
to
CLASSICAL
BALLET

I. A Brief History of Ballet

CHAPTER 1

The Nature of Dance

Movement is central to our concept of life. In fact, movement and life can be viewed as synonymous from the instant of man's conception. Clearly, man moved before he did anything else when viewed from his initial two-celled existence.

A study of anthropology and the earliest available historical records establishes the fact that man's emotions found a channel of expression in his natural disposition to move. Even in prehistoric societies, it seems likely that prehistoric man knowingly experienced feelings of love, hate, fear, hope, and the like, and that these emotions found expression in spontaneous movement.

Man's spontaneous tendencies to express his feelings in movement eventually took on formal characteristics. When stylized into certain formats and designs stipulated by tribal leaders, these movements became dances that were performed in relation to the various social needs of the group. Entire tribes responded to their emotions when they danced to appease the wrath of the gods or to invoke from the gods the blessings of fertility.

At its roots, spontaneous human movement is so fundamental that John Martin, the noted dance critic of the *New York Times,* refers to it as "basic dance." According to Martin, basic dance is simply the result of emotional states expressed through physical movement. Such expressions of movement or "dance" were present in the lives of earliest man before activity became ritualized and used for specific purposes. Even today we can see fundmental movement, almost dancelike in character, in the wildly cheering fans who participate in the excitement of a sports event. While there are certain learned gestures, the movement patterns observable in a cheering crowd are spontaneous and propelled by emotion rather than intention.

At a certain point in prehistoric time, tribal leaders or priests took over the function of dancing in religious ritual while the remainder of the tribal community participated only as respectful on-lookers. Once

3

Fig. 1 Grecian Dancer with Symbols. Courtesy of the New York Public Library for the Performing Arts.

4

the role of spectator was established in ritual dance, the concept of performing for and communicating to an audience began to evolve. Two kinds of dance have subsequently emerged. These may be referred to as group participation dance and theatrical dance. The latter, like ritual dances, involved both performer and spectator.

In primitive societies, group participation dance arose out of fundamental movement that occurred in response to emotions. That is, stylized primative movement served as the medium to express social and religious feeling. Dance was also a desirable activity for the sheer kinetic pleasure movement gave. Socio-religious needs and kinetic enjoyment were the chief elements of the Dithyramb, an early dance form created by the ancient Greek civilization. This was initially an improvised music and dance festival in honor of Dionysus. In time the Dithyramb became more structured and it evolved into a competition where highly skilled performers competed for prizes before an audience.

Through the centuries dance as a participation activity has taken many forms. The early Church incorporated group dancing as part of the Christian Mass. The peasant dances of the early Middle Ages evolved into the national or folk dances that are still performed today. Court dances of the later Middle Ages, which were indoor refinements of the peasant dances, relate to our own concept of ballroom dancing and, more recently, discotheque dancing.

The second kind of dance that has evolved from the natural instincts of basic dance is that which is performed for onlookers, and it is theatrical in essence. Because the viewing of dance is pleasurable, dance has evolved as a spectacle or theatrical art. The ancient Greeks and Romans considered dance to be an important contribution to their games and circuses.

The Middle Ages also enjoyed the theatrical spectacle of tournaments, dancing acrobats, *jongleurs,* and troubadours who were part of the daily scene. Later, the nobles of the Renaissance enjoyed the extraordinary spectacles called "triumphs" which were devised as political propaganda. Barzini relates that 15th century Italy made full use of such grandiose and gorgeous spectacles, called *balletti,* which served to divert the attention of the starving masses from their helpless plight.

With the timely establishment of dance in France by Louis XIV, in the *L'Academie Royale de Musique* in 1672, the concept of dance as a performing profession was secured. This newly formed discipline of dance, which eventually came to be known as classical ballet, developed and refined itself into a profession in which individuals were specifically trained to participate. Many talented people have subsequently contributed to the evolutionary process from which dance has emerged as a contemporary art form.

BALLET AS AN ART FORM

That grand lady of contemporary philosophy, Susan K. Langer, succinctly states that an art work may be regarded as the objectification of subjective life. A work of art is the human experience of an artist, selected and crystalized according to his unique vision, and created primarily for the perception of others. Essentially, the process and product to which Langer refers in philosophical language is what occurs in the making of a ballet production.

Since the establishment of the French academy for dance and music in 1672, the creators of ballet have been developing and expanding the body of balletic material. These creative artists of the ballet are called choreographers. Ballet choreographers work consciously or instinctively from the premise that their artistic intentions—based on experiences, feelings, thoughts, and emotions—are objectified through the medium of human movement.

The instruments of the choreographer are the dancers whom he uses to concretize his creative intentions and inspirations. The choreographer molds and then incorporates the movement generated by dancers into the dimensions of time and space. Dancers are the interpretative creators of the ballet and under the artistic direction of the choreographer, it is the dancer who resides at the very heart of the ballet.

The particular subject matter of ballet may range from feelings which escape discursive articulation to ideas that are explicitly narrative. For example, the exquisite feelings and moods portrayed by the ten dancers in Robbins' *Dances at a Gathering* defy verbal description, so subtle and delicate are these moods. In contrast, the choreographic rendering of the role of Hagar in *Pillar of Fire* is given to some literal meaning while the pantomime scenes and choreographic passages in *La Sylphide* make the stage action as clear as if it were being read to us. The point that must be understood is that the ballet, whether totally non-discursive or predominantly narrative, impresses itself on the hearts and minds of the audience.

Ballet is distinguished from the social, religious, and recreational forms of dance in that it is, essentially, a theatrical art. By its very nature, ballet is meant to be performed for an audience. Within the meaning of all of the performing arts is contained the concept of the fleeting, the momentary, the ephemeral existence. A performance of dance, music, or drama only *is* as it is being performed. If a certain performance lasts 42 minutes, that is the extent of its existence in a given time and place, until its next performance.

The concept of ballet as an art whose existence depends upon the actual performance permeates the total conception of the study of ballet. The balletic arrow, so to speak, points to performance. Performance and spectacle were at the root of the development of ballet even in its 16th century infancy; performance has been at the center of its evolving history. The major thrust of ballet today in the international conservatories, in private dancing schools, and in colleges and universities where it is studied, is performance.

Balletic movement is symbolic expression created out of man's natural disposition to move. In logical definition, a symbol stands for, or is expressive of, something else. Symbols in art are devices for formalizing, transferring, stylizing, and expressing the artist's impression of his inner experience. Symbols are created from nature in order to express, in a new and sensory way, the subjective experiences of thoughts, feelings, and things. Symbolic creations that exist solely for the delectibility of man's perceptions are an integral part of the art experience.

In ballet, symbols are kinetically expressed feelings and ideas, that is, the stuff out of which balletic symbols are made is *kinetic*. The word "kinetic" refers to the movement of human bodies and the force and energy their action and interaction creates. Kinetic symbols are perceived by the audience via a combination of the viewer's visual and auditory senses, coupled with his empathic kinesthetic awareness. Thus, kinetically expressed symbolic forms are presented to the viewer through the essential elements of space, time and energy.

THE EVOLUTION AND DEVELOPMENT OF BALLET

The evolution and development of balletic art reflects kinetic symbolic forms which arose out of specific historical contexts. Various elements which comprised the ballet as it emerged in 15th century Italy can be traced to earlier times. The ancient art of mime, medieval folk and court dances, and the morality plays of the early Christian church, are but a few of the forces that contributed material to the development of the Renaissance theatrical spectacle known as *balletti*. Three general stages of historical development can be identified. They are as follows:

1. 1400–1600. In its earliest stage of development, ballet served to represent Italian, and later French, power and wealth. The principal purpose of dance was to provide amusement at luxurious court entertainments.
2. 1600–1700. Ballet developed as a theatrical profession that was unique and complimentary to the flowering and embellishment of French civilization.
3. 1700–present. A formal body of knowledge evolved that allowed for the technical and artistic grooming of great individual talents who were instrumental in raising ballet from a theatrical form of entertainment to an art.

Origins of Ballet: 1400–1600

Prior to the formal establishment of ballet in the court of Louis XIV, the Renaissance court spectacles were primarily pictorial. Dance pageantry served as a means of entertainment for the court and on special occasions, the entire populace. In Italy, these so-called *balletti* or ballets represented political and economic power on the occasions of great marriages, visits from foreign dignitaries, and the celebrations accompanying peace treaties.

The term *balletti* was derived from the Italian word *ballare*, meaning "to dance", and it is from this etymological root that we have the word, ballet. The *balletti* were stupendous entertainments, gorgeous in detail and complex in overall construction, that were extremely popular with the Renaissance nobility who paid for their production. They involved contemporary music of the times, large numbers of dancers executing relatively simple ballet steps, and poetic and mythological dramatizations.

The early *balletti* employed the use of noblemen and members of the court who performed the dancing and singing, foot soldiers, cavalry, jesters and buffoons, horses, wooden machines which resembled floats, fireworks and other exotica. They were often designed by such great artists as da Vinci, Raphael, and Botticelli for the enormous outdoor spaces that were provided by a fortress or palace courtyard.

Such spectacles served to express military might and enormous wealth. At the same time, their impressive display enkindled delight and admiration in all who viewed these extravagant royal showings. So much so, in fact, that the popularity of these entertainments ensured their continuation even when such dazzlement crippled family fortunes and city-state treasuries.

The Renaissance and the Court Ballet: 1600–1700

The Italian-style spectacles or so-called ballets were introduced into the French Court around 1533, during the reign of Henry II. The ballet was a way of demonstrating wealth and power, and its tremendous visual appeal proved to be irresistibly attractive to the pleasure-loving French. Thus, ballets as court entertainments steadily increased in refinement and popularity, and the tremendous pleasure they gave insured their continuing presence at Court.

Ballet as entertainment and a royal activity was one of the French Court's central pleasures. These entertainments typically included a combination of opera, recitation and dancing. The subject matter of the opera-ballets reflected the precepts of those literary people charged with producing them. Opera-ballets were based on allegories which were presented according to a pre-stated formula. Some years later, in the rarified atmosphere of Louis XIV's palace at Versailles, the function of the ballet became less representational of political power and more and more aesthetic in character. The composition of the ballet increasingly suggested a growing attention to the incorporation of literary ideals and the perfection of French tastes as important ends in themselves.

The growing self-awareness of France as a unified nation and a European power culminated in the blossoming of French artistic concepts that are still, in our times, generally considered to be guidelines of taste. Apollonian or formal concepts of harmony, balance, and symmetry, executed with exquisite detail and superb workmanship, were reflected in the literature, music, architecture, horticulture, interior decoration and fashion of the times. The court ballets gloriously symbolized these refined and elaborate tastes in the process of their theatrical realization in performance. Indeed, these court ballets kinetically symbolized an entire way of life for the noble class.

Even when the professional dancer replaced the courtier in the role of ballet performer, allegorical subject matter, style, and techniques of production did not radically change. Professional dancers and ballet masters continued to strive for a degree of perfection which, in essence, attempted to improve on nature. The final result was one of the most amazing artificial constructs aesthetic man has yet produced, the classical ballet.

Ballet and the age of Enlightenment: 1700–present

Louis XIV was himself an accomplished dancer who is said to have practiced daily for twenty years. He clearly realized the dance would further develop its theatrical possibilities if it were formally established and he may be credited for achieving this goal. Upon Louis' retirement from dance activities, the courtiers followed suit and court ballet, so to speak, was dead. Upon the advice of his great minister, Colbert, Louis founded the *L'Academie Royale de Danse* — a group of scholars who were authorized to reform and improve the status of dance. A new era began with trained dancers moving to theatres to perform for the public.

The steady development of ballet techniques in the late 18th century eventually reached a point where certain extraordinary human beings were able to use the medium of ballet technique to uniquely project to others their especially sensitive vision of the human condition. In due course, talented individual dance personalities carried this carefully developing body of knowledge to a new level of symbolic function. The particular genius of these dancers, choreographers and teachers found in ballet a new and lofty means to express the inner life of human experience.

The literary accounts of the early 18th century speak of the talents of Sallé and Camargo as dancers who possessed the powers to move the hearts of men. At the same time in history, the writings of their colleague, the great theoretician, artist, and teacher, Jean Georges Noverre, describe for us the dawn of dance as an art form, and the unique contributions of dancers as artists. Through the miracle of their artistic sensitivity and intelligence, these great dancers were able to penetrate and influence the inner life of those who saw them perform.

In this sense, the ballet functioned as a mechanism that served man's urge to re-create his inner experience in objective and concrete ways. Thus, the ballet historically emerges as a Western art form.

To summarize briefly, ballet in its historical development has evolved through three distinct stages which still play a role in its current conceptualization. At first, ballet in its infancy was used to symbolize the power of families, city states and kingdoms. In time, ballet came to symbolize the aesthetic ideals developed by the collective artistic minds of the French court. Finally, the ballet itself developed into an art form which, in the context of its kinetic medium, is capable of uniquely symbolizing the innermost subtleties of the human spirit.

THE PURPOSE OF HISTORICAL STUDY

No one questions the fact that dancers, dance teachers, students and choreographers participate in ballet out of sheer and undying love of the art. The many years of study, the unflagging dedication and almost inhuman effort required by this art form rarely justify the comparatively small remuneration or public acclamation received by thousands upon thousands of dance aspirants. In this sense, the ballet is truly an extraordinary phenomenon. Vast numbers of people actively participate in ballet or involve themselves in the very serious role of the balletomane.

Once the delights of participating in the art of ballet are experienced, its surface attractions often turn to a deep and abiding personal commitment. The surface attractions of the ballet performance are commonly known. They are described by such adjectives as elegant, glamorous, ethereal, exciting. Phrases often used to describe the classroom experiences of ballet are the kinetic awareness of one's own body, a novel and eloquent kind of physical and psychic freedom, an urge to remake the natural body shape according to traditional balletic forms, the pure joy of movement and its retrospective kinetic remembrance.

Love is merely a broad clue to the ballet's phenomenal attraction to so many. Yet, it is sufficient to serve as a springboard for an interest in the study of ballet. To dance is to love it, and implicit in loving anything is the desire to know more about it.

Ballet is a traditional art whose major body of information has been very personally handed down through many generations of dancers. Therefore, ballet history ought to be studied because today's dancers are the heirs of all the dancers who went before them. Those experienced dancers who turned teachers to young dancers continue to live through many generations of students. To be a part of ballet is to belong to a very honored and ancient family. To know one's own genealogy, then, is a matter of family pride and personal responsibility.

All dance students should have a particular reason for studying ballet history. A rich knowledge of ballet's past will enhance, in countless ways, the student's work. This is true for students who are interested in pursuing a dance career, or who desire to have a knowledge of ballet for its own sake, or who plan to work in another field. Imbued with a strong sense of ballet history, one's current involvement can take on deeper dimensions of appreciation of ballet as an art and greater satisfaction with one's own achievement. Thus, it follows that if the present work of professional dancers, as well as ballet lovers, is enriched with an understanding of its fabulous past, the future will host a continued and enlightened growth of ballet.

The ballet history which follows is based on original and translations of primary source materials, and secondary sources that are indicated at the end of each chapter. This history has been considerably condensed, and is not meant to be definitive. Rather, it should serve to complement the technical work of the ballet class at the beginning or intermediate college levels. Hopefully, it will entice the ballet student to delve further into the extensive historical literature on the dance which yearly beomes more abundant. Without further deliberation, then, let us embark on a brief historical tour of this beloved and extraordinary art.

REFERENCES

Barzini, L. *The Italians.* New York: Atheneum Publishers, 1964.

De Mille, A. *The Book of the Dance.* New York: Golden Press, 1963.

Kraus, R. *History of the Dance.* Englewood Cliffs, New Jersey: Prentice-Hall, 1969.

Langer, S. K. *Problems of Art.* New York: Charles Scribner's Sons, 1957.

Lawler, L. *The Dance in Ancient Greece.* Seattle: University of Washington Press, 1964.

Martin, J. *John Martin's Book of the Dance.* New York: Tudor Publishing Co., 1963.

SUGGESTIONS FOR FURTHER READING

H'Doubler, M. *Dance, A Creative Art Experience.* Madison: University of Wisconsin Press, 1966.

Read, H. *The Meaning of Art.* Baltimore: Penguin, 1931.

Sachs, C. *World History of Dance.* New York: W. W. Norton & Co., 1965.

Sheets, Maxine. *The Phenomenology of Dance.* Madison: University of Wisconsin Press, 1966.

CHAPTER 2

Origins of the Ballet

The reason that the ballet exists derives naturally enough from the fact that people enjoy watching others dance. This simple fact is what creates an audience for dance and provides, at the same time, greater impetus for those who love to dance and to perform for others. While people have loved to dance for others since time immemorial, there are certain elements in ballet today that can be traced to ancient times.

EXPRESSIVE GESTURE AND THE PANTOMIMI

The techniques of expressive gesture are at the heart of ballet which is richly endowed as a form of non-verbal communication. These techniques originated in the ancient Greek dramas. As Rome conquered the ancient Greek civilization, its need to communicate through the language barrier prompted her to call on actors from the Greek theatres who were skilled in pantomime. These men, called *pantomimi*, possessed the technique of theatrically expressive gesturing which made them excellent interpreters. At the same time, this practical employment gave the *pantomimi* opportunity to continue to develop the subtleties of their art.

In later times, the Church, fearing a return to the decadent ways of Rome, condemned and exiled the *pantomimi*, scattering them over the face of medieval Europe. However, their valued skills were absorbed into the many provincial courts of the sprawling Roman Empire. Within these courts, they were useful in providing a form of entertainment that could be understood without the use of song or spoken word. The theatrical traditions established by the *pantomimi* in the Roman Empire were subsequently absorbed into the activities of itinerant troubadours.

Fig. 1. A Roman Bacchant providing entertainment for the ruling class prior to the establishment of Christianity. Courtesy of the New York Public Library for the Performing Arts.

DANCING AND THE EARLY CHURCH

Upon the collapse of the Roman Empire in 476 A.D., the Christian Church gained total dominance over the secular as well as the religious lives of its members. Little by little, the barbarians were assimilated as the early Christian culture was gradually extended to the borders of what we now call Europe. The church fathers felt that in order to save what was left of humanity after the barbarian invasions and to firmly establish the spiritual power of the Church, they would have to counteract the remnants of the degenerate pagan ways rampant during the Roman Empire. A new philosophy in life was called for; one in which the new religion was based on the novelties of faith, hope and charity. These fresh ideals, expounded in the works of St. Augustine, would give man a view of himself as being primarily created for a future life.

A protected and organized way of life would be necessary if mankind was to hold itself together after the centuries of barbarian desecration of Roman Civilization. Thus, Augustinian philosophy as adopted by the early Church was a complete contrast to the physical and material views of the Romans. Where there had been an overwhelming emphasis on epicurianism, hedonism, and stoicism, St. Augustine fostered a platonically derived philosophy which emphasized the subjugation of the body for the salvation of the soul. Beginning in the 6th century, and for the next 400 years, the Christian concept of a better life after death instilled the light of hope in an unstable world. This period, sometimes called the Dark Ages, was one of transition between great civilizations. Generally speaking, human development was at a low point. Economic structure was minimal, while social structure suffered from a world harsh with disease and poverty and one that was often filled by a sense of futility.

The consequence of all this for dance during the Dark Ages is most interesting. Dance and pantomime had been an important part of the revelry of the pleasure-loving Romans as well as that of its conquered peoples. It was still a part of the natural character of their newly Christianized progeny. The church fathers recognized this fact, and instead of suppressing altogether the pagan practice of dancing, they wisely modified and included dance in church services. For example, the expressive powers of the old Roman pantomime naturally lent itself to explaining to newly converted Christians the various rituals included in their worship which were chanted or spoken only in Latin.

Professor Kraus points out that there is much historical evidence that suggests that an appropriately pious form of dancing during church services was encouraged. The form these dances took was often simple circle dancing in which formalized gesturing was accompanied by singing. Psychologically, and a credit to the genius of the Church in the Dark Ages, the sense of community and security in a common belief was heightened by participation in such collective dance movement.

The Roman circuses and games held in the great stone amphitheatres no longer existed as public entertainment in the Dark Ages, and so the secular form of dance lost its showcase for mass spectacle. Furthermore, any non-religious use of dance was officially forbidden by the Church as sinful and reminiscent of Roman degeneracy. This is not to say, however, that secular dancing in some form or other did not exist in the Dark and early Middle Ages. There were always the mime and the dances of the wandering acrobats, poets, jugglers and musicians from the East. These popular entertainers performed in village squares throughout Europe and were variously called *spielmänner, jongleurs,* and *troubadours.*

During the Dark Ages, festival days of earlier pagan times were made to coincide with those of Christianity. As long as there were people getting together, there was the opportunity for spontaneous expression through movement. Simple outbursts of dancing by the common people erupted into a lively catching of hands, circling and rhythmic stamping. Eventually, such group dance activity emerged as a more formalized product of peasant society. Over time, there developed the peasant dancing which is the basis for today's European folk dances.

FOLK DANCING: ROUND AND COUPLE DANCES

Whenever possible, the common people of the Middle Ages lived their daily lives outdoors. In cases of war or natural catastrophe, they took shelter in their feudal overlord's walled and moated castle. Only the harshest weather could contain them in the typical, tiny and miserable huts that served as their own shelters. Although dancing was frowned upon by the Church as the devil's advocate, the common people still reveled in it when they got together on days of religious celebrations. Martin provides insight into the history of this form of dance when he suggests that the feeling of oneness with others, which comes with collective dancing, is one of the principle reasons for the persistence of folk dance. Man, then as now, was a social animal and, considering the fearful times in which medieval man lived, his dances must have been a consolation. There were two basic forms of these peasant dances, the round dance and the couple dance.

In the round dances, which were called *carole,* a leader commonly led a chain of dancers in line and circles. The dancers sang their accompaniment to marching rhythms that caused feet to beat together and advance forward and backward. Occasionally, the dancers performed hops and leaping movements. Kirstein comments that the dancers also made rhythmic sounds with their lips and tongues, and yodeled or imitated sounds of bagpipes, flutes and drums. The maypole dance, still performed today, is an example of a *carole*. It is a carry-over from ancient Druid times in which it served as a magical fertility dance. The Middle Ages, having forgotten the full pagan significance of this ceremonial dance, retained and adapted its colorful external dance forms.

Couple dances were unbashed courting dances. These dances shared the same musical characteristics of the round dances, but were performed less often since they were only danced by men and women seeking mates. Like the folk who performed them, these dances were often ribald, lusty and abundantly energetic.

To form a clearer idea as to the sights and atmosphere which peasant round and couple dances created, one can observe various extraordinary paintings by Bruegel the Elder reproduced in art books that are available in most libraries. These paintings vividly suggest that such dances were generally noisy, lusty and earthy. Because they were danced on the grass, the vigorous movements of the participants were coarse and incorporated large steps. The peasants' clothes were rough and bulky and lacked decoration, a characteristic which lent a special rustic quality of movement to the total effect. In addition, their animal-skin boots or bare feet probably did not permit much pivoting or spinning. Underlying these elements that contributed to the movement quality of folk dances was the peasant body itself; short, squat and hence given to much stamping, thumping and skipping. Peasant dances were numerous and, for the most part, those which retained their popularity were handed down through generations. These folk dances remain essentially unchanged in floor patterns, footwork and musical rhythms, and are still lovingly performed in Europe today.

Danse Macabre

The medieval peasants could not resist participating in a curiously morbid type of round dance called the *danse macabre* or dance of death, despite the fact that the Church attempted to forbit it. While the *danse macabre* provided a popular theme for pictorial and literary

Fig. 2. Two examples of social dancing. The boistrous fun of the *branle* contrasts with a refined and stately version of a *carole* from a later period. Courtesy of the New York Public Library for the Performing Arts.

forms, it is known that it was also observed as a dance form on occasion.

When the black death swept Europe in 1347, half the population was ravaged within a few years by its appalling presence. The mentality of the peasant population in the Middle Ages had always been one of a preoccupation with death and now death was the great leveler of mankind. No one could be sure of escape from its jaws, no holy prayer or pious living was assurance of deliverance from the plague. Such notions were infused with lingering primitive beliefs that the dead return to haunt the living. It was thought by many that the dead danced nocturnal dances themselves until the cock crowed.

The upshot of all this was that people, including the elderly superstitious and the youthful pranksters alike, gathered in the graveyards. There, they performed game-like round dances at wakes for the dead. Wild gaiety preceded a mimed death which occurred at a given musical signal. The mood of the dance would become somber as one of the male participants sank to the ground feigning death. The other female dancers would then take turns kissing the deceased back to life, whereupon all would celebrate in a general round dance. The make-believe scenario was then repeated with a female dancer feigning death on a certain cue and the male dancers in turn reviving her with a kiss. Kirstein points out that the kissing part of the dance was always popular, but the modern mind cringes at the terrifying thought of passing germs from mouth to mouth in times of plague.

It is an interesting but jarring thought that this macabre practice of kissing the dead back to life is probably the original inspiration for the central moment in Petipa's grand ballet, *The Sleeping Beauty*, when the prince revives his princess with a kiss!

A further outcome of the medieval mind's preoccupation with death was another form of the *danse macabre*. From gothic times it was thought that the dead returned to lure the living into a dance of death, signifying that the living really dance toward their deaths in the course of living. This is especially interesting because it is precisely this ancient legend upon which Gautier based his scenario for the great 19th century narrative ballet, *Giselle*. The second act of this ballet depicts maidenly ghosts, including the story's heroine, as returning to the real world to dance to death the lovesick hero who had been the reason for Giselle's dancing herself to death in the first act.

The reason for the persistance of the *danse macabre* was the waning of the Middle Ages, the collapse of the entire feudal system, and the dawning sense of human equality. The concept of personified "Death" stalking its prey in the common man's mind was a sweet revenge on the wealthy class. Death leveled kings, bishops and the poor alike, and all men were equal in the clutches of death. Martin gives further insight into this strange practice when he claims that death dances were desperate statements of the common man's disillusionment with the entire social, political, and religious setting. Death disregarded the loftiness of rank or station and proved them ultimately vain.

Another sinister phenomenon known as *danseomania* occurred at this time in history. It was characterized by large numbers of people, often entire towns, taking to dancing until they collapsed or even died of exhaustion. For the most part, this dance was formless in the usual sense of organized dancing. It would appear that this nature was one of hysterical improvisation urged on by the effects of mass psychology. It was thought by many that this mania for dancing was the result of witchcraft, the bite of the tarantella spider or the devil. More enlightened men, however, diagnosed *danseomania* as resulting from mass-hypnosis, sexual excitement or hysterical symptoms of merriment. In any event, man was again expressing his discontent and fear in the most instinctive manner known to him—movement. It is worth mentioning here in the interest of ballet history that the Hans Christian Anderson fairy tale which inspired the beautiful film, *The Red Shoes,* tells, albeit enchantingly, the tale of a victim of *danseomania*.

Folk dance is not a dance form directly related to the theatrical performance of ballet. It has been discussed here for two basic reasons. First, folk or peasant dancing represents the continued human interest in dancing as an amusement even when it was not sanctioned by the official body of the medieval Church. More important, however, peasant dancing lent its round and couple dance patterns to the crude, but developing, courts of the feudal lords. In keeping with the advent of chivalry, the troubadours refined and transformed peasant dances for indoor dancing. Hence, they found their way into the great stone fortresses of Christendom as court dances. These medieval court dances represent the popular presence of dance in the lives of the nobles. Conversely, it signified that dance contained educational values and in itself represented ennobling characteristics. Thus, its courtly existence was assured of a permanent and honored place in the houses of the mighty.

COURT DANCING

In the early Middle Ages, power of the sword was the only actual distinguishing mark between the common man and his lord. Feudalism was organically a fighting body held together by common socio-economic bonds necessary to survival. Early medieval life boasted no luxuries, delicacies or refinements which we usually associate with the good life. The so-called nobles were as uncouth, uneducated and unpolished as their serfs. The overlord's primary concern was to maintain the hierarchical structure of his feudal kingdom, to see it functioning well and to keep his feudal neighbor from stealing it from him. In time, however, as a matter of pride and ambition, the overlord wished to improve and embellish his court. Consequently, outsiders became attached to the feudal courts with the responsibility of instructing the nobles in etiquette, comportment, the skills of music, dancing and poetry. The most common of these court *attachés* was the troubadour.

Troubadours

The troubadours were itinerant poets and songwriters in southern France and flourished from 1100 A.D. onwards for several hundred years. During their wanderings, the troubadours absorbed much of the classical learning and other marks of civilization from a number of Eastern scholars coming from the Byzantine at the time of the Crusades. Lawson points out that the troubadours were generally learned men and they enjoyed deliberating the classical writer's views on education. Since the value of dance in society was much discussed, the troubadours gave instruction in dancing and courtly manners as part of their profession. As knowledgable men who composed music and poetry, they were also credited for setting down rigid rules for their compositions which was much later reflected in the structure of the Renaissance court ballets.

The troubadour in his role as a dancing master, had quite a challenge considering the ungainly state of his noble pupils. He borrowed the rowdy peasant dances as the choreographic basis for his courtly versions so that they basically included the same floor patterns and foot steps as the peasant dances. However, the dancing master was confronted with redesigning the dances for hard stone floors inside the fortress. Before he could make much headway teaching the court these refined versions of the peasant dances, he had to teach the men how to behave in a mannerly way and even how to step in their curiously curled-toe shoes. The ladies had to be taught how to manipulate their trains and unwieldy head dresses. Refinement in all things became the objective of court life and so these dance activities developed more and more artifice. Due to the emphasis on refinement, this contrived elegance in the dancing tended to become stylized so that court dances became conventional and devoid of most of their spontaneous emotion.

Court dances had two chief concerns, that of showing off one's self and of courtship. The round dances certainly led themselves to the first concern with the characteristics of preening, parading and posturing movements. The couple dances were convenient vehicles for purposes of courtship. They also derived from the peasant forms of courtship dances but were accordingly more refined and haughty in manner.

Court dancing was part of the life of chivalry insofar as the dances stressed elegance of bearing, precision of execution, and coquetry on the part of the ladies. The earliest dances were called *basse* (low) dances because they involved low, close to the floor stepping and gliding movements. It is possible to observe a chain of kinship between our classical ballet *terre à terre* movements and their mannerly executed ancestorial steps described by scholars explaining the characteristics of the *basse* dance. Although stately and ceremonial, Sachs

Fig. 3. Artist's version of a 13th century *basse danse*. This dance was performed to express one's studied manners as well as to display material refinement. Note the haughty style of the dancers with that of the humble servant doubling as musician. Courtesy of the New York Public Library for the Performing Arts.

notes that the earliest *basse* dances did not have a prescribed order of steps. Rather, it was necessary that the courtiers rely on memory to endlessly combine anew the individual steps of the *basse* dance.

Peasant dances continued to influence court dancing and their rowdiness eventually lent a more lively air to the newly devised dances at court. These were *haute* (high) dances or *balli* and incorporated jumping or leaping steps which might be considered the courtly roots of our ballet steps of elevation. Due to the women's heavy dresses, they probably left the performance of the *balli* up to the men.

The Dancing Masters

The earliest dancing masters known to us by name lived in the second half of the 15th century. They were William the Jew, Cornazano, and Domenico Piacenza. These men had been trained from youth in the arts of dancing so their experience and knowledge of dance was certainly superior to that of the earlier troubadours. Attached to powerful courts in northern Italy, they were responsible for teaching and rehearsing the nobles for the courtly balls where they had to perform the precisely executed steps for which each dance called. These three dancing masters arranged a great variety of dances to newly introduced musical forms and the product of their efforts became the rage of the upper class, all wishing to learn them. William wrote *Treatise on the Art of Dancing* in which he instructed his readers in the various requisites of a dancer. His contemporary, Cornazano commented extensively on the manner of execution and relative merits of the various new *basse* and *haute* dances. Domenico Piacenza also left a treatise on dancing wherein is found the first collection of individual steps independent of any specific dance. Here we find mention of *battement de pieds, pas couru,* and *changement de pieds* which still persist as names of movements in today's ballet. Hence, in the 15th century there was a body of independent, codified dance steps which could be used in various contexts and in this sense it fostered the birth of choreography.

While there are written descriptions of court dances of the late Middle Ages, it is often difficult to gain a precise idea of what they were really like due to problems of manuscript interpretation. As research in early musical notation and musical instruments continues, however, it is possible to experience the sonorous elements of these dances and fascinating to speculate on the qualitative aspect of the movements.

MEDIEVAL SPECTACLE

While chivalrous knights were expected to be accomplished in these courtly dances inside the castle walls, the high Middle Ages saw them excel outdoors in the tournament. Tournaments were elaborate mock-combats and were almost game-like in spirit. The root of the term tournament is probably the French *tourner* which referred to the mounted knight's charging past the mock foe and rapidly "turning around" his own horse for another go at unseating him. In time the tournament as a public spectacle became a ritualized display of wealth and was a means for impressing all who attended. The aspect of ritual naturally brought to the tournament tremendous heraldry which ultimately became their chief and lasting attraction. With the great popularity of the tournament in these times, the Church eased its prohibitions of non-religious public spectacle. The Church's more lenient attitude toward the popular tastes paved the way for the growth of various types and styles of public display, each of which became more theatrical in essence.

Moresques and Religious Plays

In the 12th century, there appeared a dance form called the moresque in Italy, France and Spain. The moresques were danced stories which related the century-old religious and territorial struggles between the Moors and Christians. The earliest type of the moresques were motivated by religious ideals and they were performed on festival days. The participants were made up of townspeople and ubiquitous troubadours, acrobats, and musicians who were accompanied by the fife and drum. The ingredients of the moresque varied little. There was the danced and pantomimed reinactment of the black-faced moor giving battle to Christian soldiers. The inevitable defeat of the Moor resulted in a jubilant finale. In time, the nature of these moresques changed by becoming less religiously inspired but more entertaining. Additional attractions such as interludes of singing, dances by satyrs, nymphs and savages, and the use of elaborate tableaux increased their sophistication and popularity, especially in the great northern Italian towns.

Besides the moresques, there existed in as early as the 10th century miracle and mystery plays or "sacred representations" as they were called in Italy. These were dramatic reinactments devised for the purpose of teaching biblical history and Christian dogma to the illiterate masses. Both forms of plays were often elaborately performed with singing and dancing and were popular fare on religious feast days. Miracle plays often took the form of processional dancing to commemorate the miracles which had been attributed to the holiness of certain saints. During celebrations, relics of the saints would be piously paraded through the streets amidst much holy regalia. Cloaked in brocade, and leading the procession, priests and deacons bore the gold-encased relics while billows of incense, Gregorian chanting and rhythmic stepping all contributed to this devout spectacle. The populace, including children, were encouraged to join in these processions which, due to the musical rhythms of the singing, produced a swaying-like dance as it advanced through the streets from church to church. Mystery plays likewise illustrated in colorful pageantry the non-rational aspects of Christian dogma called "mysteries". Thus, the sense of spectacle was still present in the lives of men, but in a religious guise. Anyone fortunate enough to witness the Holy Week services today in Seville will gain a good notion as to the atmosphere and character of these medieval plays and processionals.

Pageants

The medieval pageant brings us closer to the beginnings of the ballet. In fact, the pageants contained many elements of the dinner ballets and the theatrical traditions which were firmly established by the court of Louis XIV.

The pageant was an ambulant spectacle which retained certain aspects of the structure of the miracle and mystery plays, but in essence less genuinely religious. It consisted of a parade of elaborate floats constructed by the various trade guilds of the town. The guilds competed in devising these ornate, mobile scenes in order to pay homage to their patron saints as well as to provide splendid advertising for themselves. These floats displayed allegorical themes enlivened by dancers and singers and were based on any and all aspects of medieval life, thus proclaiming something to please every onlooker. The floats with their living *tableaux* were pulled through the streets and as the pageant drew to a close, the participants would end their parading for some welcomed nourishment. This was simply an invitation to devise further fantasies of a culinary nature. These pageants, followed by banquets, where it was often difficult to find the food amidst its ornamentation, often preceded Crusades or celebrated political alliances. They are significant in ballet history in that they were the predecessors of the dinner ballets of the French court.

Kirstein throws further light on the pageant's direct relationship to the ballet in that he points out that the ornate floats were the forerunners of theatrical scenery. Such extravaganzas were seen to hide the facade of the city buildings and, in so doing, they could provide unique atmospheric effects. From this juncture, it is but a small step to understand the origin of the concept of the traditional ballet scenery.

In summation, it is significant that the ancestral dance roots of the ballet from Greek times throughout the 16th century were inextricably related to the development of the European civilization. During its social, religious, political, and economic formation, Europe was infused with the presence of dancing. From the days of the *pantomimi,* the troubadours, folk, and court dancers, various human purposes were served by dance and, therefore, diverse forms of dance evolved to fit each need. Dancing in the early Church was used to divert the proverbial Roman energies for revel and bacchanal toward group participation in pious religious ceremony. The troubadour served as educator and entertainer, spreading the presence and instruction of his dances throughout western Europe. Moresques, mystery plays, and pageants brought with them an ever-increasing presence of the dance as a spectacle while folk dancing and court dancing developed as social custom. As a result, the popularity of various forms of dance activity in Europe up to the 1400's contributed to the Renaissance concept of the "dinner ballet" which would develop into the 16th century *Ballet Comique de la Reine.*

Central to the development of the dance throughout the Middle Ages and into the Renaissance was the "dancing master". When the steps of favorite dances began to be recognized as individual movement patterns which were separate from the dance itself, a composite of steps or *pas* came into existence and, hence, the science of choreography was born. The work of the "dancing master" was considered a serious profession and much time and effort was devoted to it so that dancing became an "'official" part of life as well as natural human pleasure.

REFERENCES

Burdick, J. *Theatre.* New York: Newsweek Books, 1974.

DeMille, A. *The Book of the Dance.* New York: Golden Press, 1963.

Horst, L. *Pre-classic Dance Forms.* Brooklyn: Dance horizons, Inc., 1968.

Kinkeldy, O. *A Jewish Dancing Master of the Renaissance: Gugielmo Ebreo.* Brooklyn, N.Y.: Dance Horizons, Inc. 1972.

Kirstein, L. *Dance, A Short history of Classical Theatrical Dancing.* Brooklyn: Dance Horizons, 1969.

Kraus, R. *History of the Dance.* Englewood Cliffs, N.J.: Prentice-Hall, 1969.

Lawson, J. *History of Ballet and Its Makers.* London: Chameleon Press Ltd., 1973.

Reyne, F. *A Concise History of Ballet.* New York: Grosset & Dunlap, 1965.

SUGGESTIONS FOR FURTHER READING

Wood, M. *Historical Dances, 12th to 19th Century.* London: Lowe and Brigdone, Ltd., 1972.

Sorell, W. *Dance in its Time.* Garden City, N.Y.: Anchor Press/Doubleday, 1981.

Tuchman, B. *A Distant Mirror, The Calamitous 14th Century.* New York: Ballantine Books, 1978.

CHAPTER 3

The Renaissance Ballet

Unwittingly, the Crusades and the eventual collapse of the Byzantine Empire precipitated the revival of classical learning that occurred in the period known as the Renaissance. Returning crusaders carried home with them classical ideas and attitudes long since forgotten in Europe. From 1100 onward, contact with Eastern civilization also opened up an unknown world of ancient Greek mythology and philosophy for the Christian scholar who in turn seized upon the rare antique themes and re-interpreted them with an embellishment of Christian ideology. Slowly but surely classical ideas became absorbed into European culture. When the Byzantine Empire, bastion of Greek thought, Roman traditions and Christian religion fell to the Turks in 1453, the upheaval sent hundreds of Eastern scholars scurrying to the West where they were welcomed in the awakening spirit of the times. Hence, the availability of rediscovered ancient knowledge provided the keystone for the European Renaissance, supplying new concepts of the individual, his unique worth as an individual and his superior place in the universe.

Due to various circumstances, Italy was the principal locale for this influx of men and ideas. And so, after a thousand austere years, the homeland of the ancient Roman Empire became the cradle of a massive intellectual rebirth. Classical ideas mingled with Christian values to produce a vibrant awareness labeled by historians as humanism. The influence of classical writings reshaped man's self-concept which resulted in the notion of a man-centered universe while humanistic values tended to emphasize the dual nature of man. Whereas a medieval Christian's greatest hope was for a life beyond the grave, Renaissance man believed that man's earthly existence could be indeed significant and even joyful in helping him achieve heaven. Such abrupt changes in man's thinking underscored the Renaissance's proclivity for the sensuous and material aspect of existence.

The new thinking, which was the foundation of the age's massive creativity, had a direct influence on man's attitude toward his own personal creative urges and his desire for spectacular entertainments. One of the earliest examples of meshing classical themes with the pageants or "sacred representations" as they were called in Renaissance Italy, was in the court of the great Medici Family of Florence. Lorenzo de Medici was the most celebrated member of this noble clan and he used his lofty station to patronize the arts as well as establish an academy of learning devoted to a study of ancient Greek thought.

Trionfi

The Academy's understanding of ancient thought, life and theatre, while not always accurate, did supply a wealth of inspiration for the sacred representations which Lorenzo ordered to be held at carnival time. These sacred representations tinged with classical pagan themes, came to be known as *trionfi* (triumphant parades). They were essentially like the pageants in that they were elaborately masked spectacles mounted on chariots, but they also incorporated the additional dimension of classic knowledge. The allegorical themes of many of these *trionfi* were often well suited to contemporary happenings of the Medici court. In time, the holy themes lost their religious purpose and the *trionfi* became more and more filled with pure fantasy for its own sake. Eventually such spectacles become standard fare for welcoming dintinguished personages of foreign states and we see history come to a full circle. The effect of the entire spectacle was reminiscent of a visual reënactment of pagan Rome welcoming home her victorious generals.

Basically, the average man of the time had little patience with a strict revival of ancient Greek drama. He demanded interludes of singing, and dancing, and general entertainment between the scenes of revived Greek tragedies. In fact, no distinction clearly defined the one art form from another. Emphasis was on the elaborate spectacle which included all sorts of diversion and, hence, pleasing at least in part to all levels of the population. In keeping with the spirit of the times, the Church often encouraged such official public spectacles.

ITALIAN DINNER BALLETS

The fame of the Medici Court extended far and its life style was eagerly copied by other powerful nobles such as the Sforzas of Milan and the Estes of Ferrera who contended for similar greatness. The Academy at Florence was one of the most emulated institutions of the Medici Court since it was with learned men of the Academy that the highly valued classical knowledge lay.

One of the chief responsibilities of the Renaissance academies was to produce dinner ballets which were not ballets in our sense of the term but rather, they were elaborate feasts with entertainments that presupposed extensive knowledge of ancient myth and allegory. Originally, the dinner ballets were complex dramatizations which, under ideal circumstances, were filled with erudite notions that only a carefully educated class of people could understand. The purpose of these productions was twofold. These lofty spectacles, soon to be composed all over northern Italy, served as political propaganda since current events could always be found to have some half-hidden, but richly cloaked, allegorical parallel in the ancient literature. Such intellectual extravaganzas were also meant to serve as appropriate vehicles for the moral edification of the Renaissance courts. While it pleased the scholars that the dinner ballets should employ the use of complex symbolism and allegory, this aspect was probably not duly appreciated or even important to the general audience of the time. Kirstein suggests that while the court clamored for sumptuous and ingenious display, it possessed precious little critical faculty, having no basis for comparison for such lavish and successfully novel productions.

The Italian dinner ballets, and later their French counterparts, were given in the immense halls of princely palaces. These were actually enormous rectangular-shaped rooms whose walls were adorned with massive paintings framed in ornate classic-styled carvings. Windows were set off with splendidly carved stone casements. The floors were highly polished, multi-colored marbles arranged to create splendid floor designs. But most amazing were the extraordinarily wrought ceilings. They consisted of dazzling voluptuous amounts of gilded carved beams and polychromed pictures of allegorical figures peering down from painting heavens.

For a dinner ballet, it was often the custom for the banquet to take place in one room and the entertainment in another. The hosts and the guests of honor were placed on a dais at one end of the room with other guests seated at long tables. These were set with elaborate decoration of amazing artistic fantasy and invention. Plates and wine goblets were fashioned of gold, silver and rock crystal; exquisite two-pronged forks and stilleto-like knives were of silver and carved ivory. In keeping with the Renaissance lust for life, 30 to 100 garnished dishes of food which were served in numerous courses were not uncommon. After the feasting, the guests would move to a similarly ornate hall arranged for the ballet. Here the performers occupied the main portion of the floor and the guests observed the performance from the sides of the room or from galleries.

In principle, dinner ballets boasted a more weighty intellectual basis than the out-of-doors *trionfi*. Lavishly designed by artists such as da Vinci and Botticelli, they were explicitly created to enhance luxuriously decorated ballrooms of the Renaissance palaces. Forests, nymphs, fountains, rocks and satyrs were dispersed throughout the great hall and the dramatic action would move from one area of the room to another embellished with the geometric patterns of heavily costumed dancers. Accordingly, the performers were carefully selected in that they had to be skilled and disciplined to conform to the complex and exacting directives of those responsible for the spectacle. Kirstein illuminates the historical setting in the following quote:

> The apogee of these arrangements for eating and dancing occurred in Milan in 1489, and has been sometimes referred to as the 'first' ballet. More truthfully, it was a banquet-hall, but all the entremets were related to (danced interludes) one another in a consistent pattern, and the *féte* was designed as an artistic entity, though the dramatic action was fragmentary and any expression of emotion merely a literary device for seemly display.

The nobles attending the dinner ballets found in them one more opportunity to indulge their insatiable Renaissance appetites for sensory beauty. Not only did these fantasies include magnificent sights and sounds in their allegorical displays, but interludes of elaborately costumed dancing augmented these productions which sometimes lasted for days!

Catherine de Medici, a scion of the great Florentine family, married Henry II of France and became Queen in 1547. As a child she had been nurtured on the great Italian dinner ballets and later grew to understand their potential political use as much as she loved dancing in them. From the earliest years of her reign as a French Queen, she saw to it that her introduction of the Italianate spectacle would be wedded to the glittering French court masquerades. Many court ballets were produced during her reign, but none of them achieved or exceeded the artistic success of the *Ballet Comique de la Reine*.

True to the art-loving life style of her ancestors, Catherine as the French Queen proceeded to patronize the literary and musical academies in Paris. The literary academy of *Pleiade*, as it was named, was headed by Jean de Baif whose theories on song, verse and dance were later synthesized into the structure of the *Ballet Comique de la Reine*. His major contribution to the development of ballet proposed that the duration of the musical, danced and spoken phrase, should all dovetail to form a harmonious and pleasing organism of artistic expression. While Jean de Baif's aesthetic concept of unity was novel in the 16th century court circles, he intended it to epitomize the classical age of Greek art. On the other end of time, the aesthetic concept of unity is seen as acceptable orthodoxy in most dance composition classes.

BALLET COMIQUE DE LA REINE AND THE "CIRCE"

Alas, the year 1581 witnessed the presentation at the palace of Fountainbleau what history generally considers the first authentic ballet. Under the general title of *Ballet Comique de la Reine,* the production of "Circe" was presented to the court on the occasion of a royal wedding. The *Ballet Comique de la Reine* was so named "Comique" from the fact that the themes chosen for the production were light-hearted as opposed to tragic, and the term "Ballet" referred to the geometrical arrangements of many people to diverse musical harmonies. The central responsibility for the entire production resided with the Queen's Italian-born dancing master, Beaujoyeulx, whose genius magnificently coordinated de Baif's ideals in aligning the components of music, verse and dancing into a unified whole. The thematic material of "Circe" which Beaujoyeulx and members of the academies chose for the *Ballet Comique* was the amusing and classical tale of the enchantress Circe who overcame Apollo, but in the conclusion she and the other gods happily paid homage to a greater diety, the King of France.

The *Ballet Comique* has been summed up as an original and clever mixture of French taste and Italian Renaissance theories on classical drama. Its creation represents the first theatrical production in which a central theme coordinated the various elements of dance, music and verse to form a meaningful whole. Practically speaking, the "Circe" production resulted from ideas which had been fermenting for some 15 years, but it took a talented individual, namely Beaujoyeulx, to successfully harvest them. It was through his efforts, based on the concepts of de Baif, that the context of the sung verse was perfectly unified with the dancing and organized into a harmonious organsim.

One novelty developed in the "Circe" was a special kind of dancing interlude called a pastoral. Its characters were rustic in nature and they performed folksy dances which contributed a touch of the bucolic to contrast with the rest of the ballet's contrived magnificence. The added touch of dancing shepherds and arcadian nymphs completed what the Renaissance considered to be authentic classical Greek drama. As to the dancing in the *Ballet Comique,* aside from the pastorals, it is difficult to say exactly what it was like since it would not have resembled what we know as ballet dancing today. From the tenor and cadence of the music of the time, however, the dancing probably consisted of elegant and geometric marching, poising and gesturing which surely pleased the eyes, ears and mind.

A prime factor which contributed to this production's astounding artistic success was the recent development in music. The great composer, Palestrina, had opened up the complex mechanics of sung drama, hitherto thought to have been lost in antiquity. Certainly, the knowledge of his operatic techniques was skillfully employed in the singing of the dramatic action in "Circe."

All accounts of Catherine's *Ballet Comique* attest to its magnificance. However, the cost for this extravaganza was indeed a king's ransom. Foreign and domestic opinion derided such expense and a reaction set in at court. Instead of sparking further enrichment in the development of the ballet in France, the "Circe" stands alone and is immediately followed by an artistic decline. Thereafter, and until the advent of professional ballet in the time of Louis XIV, nobles contended themselves with affairs of less artistic significance.

COURT BALLET

In the years to come, the French love of masquerades sufficed to be joined to simpler ballets which consisted of unrelated entrances. These ballet masquerades, called *ballet d' entrèe,* were vital and amusing, though of little artistic import. It has been suggested that the artistic decline was due to an increasing lack of subject matter since there was a limited amount of ancient mythology, which was considered the only appropriate source material. But there were additional reasons marking the decline of creative ideas such as the Civil Wars which kept France in a state of bankruptcy. Also, the producers of the ballets were still a combination of literary men and amateurs who lacked a meaningful knowledge of the nature of dance as an expressive form. The dance as a means to communicate emotion was unthought of. Literary men used the court ballets for the effect that its outward display would have on the audience and the amateurs still looked on dance as part of their aristocratic lifestyle.

Equestrian Ballet

Along with the return of the elegant pastiche of the *ballet d' entrèe,* was the appearance of equestrian ballets during the 16th and 17th centuries. The pageantry and excitement of the medieval tournaments were combined with the visual design and musical grace of the court ballet to provide a form of outdoor entertainment perfect for the vast square courtyards of Renaissance palaces. Equestrian ballets were, without question, beautiful to behold. Countless illustrations of their symmetrical ground patterns remain to assure us of their entertainment value. Not only were these ballets recorded with special notation (since horses have four legs), but the vocabulary of the steps such as jumps, cabrioles, gallops and turns are shown to relate to the musical accompaniment. The dancing horses were made to follow fairly complex patterns and rhythms which underscored the balletic aspect. These dancing segments were interspersed with mounted duels and chases which lent bravura and *élan* to the proceedings. We are told that actors and singers outlined the general plot before the spectacle began and that the proceedings ended with a grandly staged finale in the form of a battle.

Fig. 1. Designers of equestrian ballets followed formal grand patterns in arranging choreography for horses. Courtesy of the Author.

38

Due to the opening of public theatres and the popularity of opera in the early 17th century, the French interest in horse ballets all but disappeared. In the 18th century Viennese Court, equestrian ballets found such favor, however, that they became permanent to some degree. The famous Lipizzaner horses are one of the indispensable tourist attractions in Vienna today. To a large extent, the theatrical heritage of these dazzling animals is traceable to the equestrian ballet.

Masks and Masques

While the equestrian ballets provided out-of-door spectacle in the reign of Henry IV (1589-1610), numerous *ballet d' entrèes* were given at court in addition to the masked balls known in France as masques. Wearing masks had been an ancient and time-honored device used to heighten the theatrics and amusement of celebrations since the dawn of man. The use of masks was probably carried over from ancient days into the medieval religious plays via the ubiquitous *pantomimi*. In the late Middle Ages, a courtier could leave the stuffy atmosphere of the court balls and, provided he followed the formality of wearing a mask, would descend to the street to dance and carouse with the high-spirited townsfolk. In the early court ballets masks were worn by all and in particular by men *en travesti* (those who took female roles), since women did not generally dance in public or court spectacles. Masks were also useful in aiding the intrigue and coquetry at court functions and were considered a necessary part of one's wearing apparel at court balls. Masks were functionally elemental in extending the allegoric fantasy throughout the Renaissance ballets. Concurrent with the development of the style of the *Commedia dell Arte,* masks were kept well into the 18th century.

SIXTEENTH CENTURY WRITINGS ON BALLET

The Renaissance has left us with many detailed literary and pictorial descriptions of its ballets. Three of the best-known authors on the ballet were dancers themselves and their works remain to give us a special insight into the evolution of stage dancing. In 1581, Caraso's *Il Ballerino* was published, substantiating the fact that there was already an established Italian style of dancing at that time. The book lists numerous rules which indicate considerable technical progress since the time of William the Jew in the previous century. Some years later, Negri, an Italian contemporary of Caruso who spent an active career in France, wrote a book in his old age entitled *Nuove Inventioni de Balli* which logically lays the foundation of classical ballet. It includes general advice about dancing, fifty-five technical comments and his directives for a number of dances. Both the manuals of Caruso and Negri attest to the technical progress of dance. They state that the virtuosity of beats and turns existed and were the domain of the male dancer. According to Ivor Guest, Negri's treatise contains the earliest mention of a *plié*, which was given as advice for the proper execution of jumps and *capriolles*.

In 1588 Arbeau's *Orchesography* appeared in the form of an engaging treatise written as a dialogue between the author and his young dance pupil. The book was to have an even greater influence on the development of dance than the *Ballet Comique* and is perhaps our most important heritage of the 16th century. The *Orchesography* was chiefly concerned with discussion of dance steps and rhythms such as the *pavanne, allemande, gaillard, courante, gigue,* etc. While these dances were originally social dance forms in the sense that Arbeau and young Capriol discuss them, they became ballet movements as the art continued to develop. Arbeau incorporated in his instruction on executing the various dances many practical hints for solving technical difficulties. The book's illustrations complemented his ideas on basic positions of the body, the transference of weight from one leg to the other and the uses of the arms.

The historical importance of the *Orchesography* cannot be underestimated, since with its publication, the French become preëminent in the growth of ballet. As we have seen, up to this time the clever and charming Italians were the dancing masters sought after for their great knowledge and tradition. But, by the end of the 16th century, Italianate know-how became assimilated with French taste. Under the aegis of an increasingly powerful and centralized monarchy, France was able to provide a breeding ground for the infancy of the ballet.

RENAISSANCE THEATRES

The developmental period of a theatrical dance form which evolved into the later court ballets covered the centuries from the late Middle Ages and its out-of-door pageants to the high Renaissance. Yet, dur-

ing this time, the growth of theatrical dance was fragmentary and often accidental in nature. The greatest contributing factor explaining
the slowness of this evolutionary process was probably the lack of a
permanent home for the dance. Since there was no specific location
for theatrical and festive activities, every pageant or *trionfi* had called
for original plans, places and people. Every dinner ballet had assumed
a new creation forged from all the necessary elements and the temporary adaptation and adornment of a palatial banquet hall for the performance. A most significant concept which the Renaissance revived
from antiquity, therefore, was that of a special place for
entertainment—a theatre. The last to build theatres had been the Romans and the early Church's ban on theatres saw to it that the idea
was nearly lost.

In 1446, the publication *De Architectura* by the ancient Roman
builder, Vitrivius, proferred directives for construction of indoor theatres which were swiftly incorporated into the building plans of many a
Renaissance noble. This book received a monumental commentary
by Sebastiano Serlio around 1560 and subsequent theatre architects
used this work as a guideline for the next 150 years. Serlio's theatre
included a general rectangular shape for a roofed building, a raised
stage, a staged area, semi-circular seating arrangement and typical
Roman vomitorium exit and entrance ways for the audience. Many of
these theatres such as the 16th century Teatro Olimpico in Vincenza,
incorporated permanent wood scenery. The keen desire for the illusion of deep perspective or three-dimensional space in a limited area
called for precisely constructed sight lines which focused on one or
more vanishing points. The Olimpico is noted for three doors in the
permanent stage opening. The three doors frame streets which recede in false perspective to three different vanishing points. While
scenery such as the Olimpico stage was often built in finely carved
wood it was also created by means of beautifully painted panels or
flats.

Later in 1638, Niccolo Sabattini made many improvements in the
theatre designs of Serlio in that movable scenery became essential,
painted stage details replaced constructed ones, painted perspective
and other illusions replaced those in wood. Sabattini was also responsible for improving medieval devices for flying both actors and large
set pieces. Many of these innovations are important to us in that they
would be used by the French court ballets which were ultimately
housed in palace theatres.

The Renaissance theatres were designed to house the performance of actors and dancers. The only dances performed in them, however, were the specially choreographed interludes in between dramatic acts. The stages of these theatres were not designed to hold the large spectacles that comprised the dinner ballets and later court ballets. At the same time, the Renaissance concept of stage space did exert considerable influence on dancing masters who arranged these danced interludes accompanying the plays. The dancing master had to essentially direct the action through the stage opening toward the seating areas. His dance configurations had to be arranged so that pleasing design would be seen by the audience and the most effective presentation of a solo performer had to be considered. During the Renaissance it was not uncommon for the production to move out into the house of the theatre. Since there were no stationary chairs in what we call the orchestra seats, the more elaborate parts of the production could easily move into this space.

The Advent of Public Theatres

Louis XIII, like his royal predecessors, was a devoted lover of court ballet. His nobles were accomplished in the art, and they not only performed at court ballets devised for them by professional dancing masters and musicians, but often repeated these performances out of doors for the common folk of Paris. As the 16th century waned, growing middle-class tastes invited the presence of public theatres and, in their own way, encouraged various aspects of theatrical development in general.

During Louis XIII's reign (1610-1643), his brilliant and crafty master, Richelieu, had built in Paris at the Palais Royale the most advanced theatre of the time and it is particularly notable for us in that it had a proscenium arch. It is commonly believed that during this period the action of the ballets (*ballet d' entrèe*) was confined to the stage area whereas it had previously extended into the house. Here, and into the regency of Louis XIV, the public could, on occasion, attend operas and plays laced with dancing interludes. By the end of his life, Richelieu had also added to the three public theatres already existing in Paris and built several large and well-equipped auditoriums for the growing Paris audience.

The regency of Louis XIV witnessed an emphasis on the predominantly musical or melodramatic ballet where expressive singing re-

Fig. 2. Strict adherence to symmetry typifies the Renaissance aesthetic in this early ballet staged for a proscenium arch theatre. Courtesy of the New York Public Library for the Performing Arts.

placed spoken verse and the dancing element was minimized. Another great minister, the Italian-born Mazarin, who succeeded Richelieu, wished the musical predominance of the court ballets of his native land to be developed in France. Therefore, he greatly encouraged the production of operas to be given for the Parisian public.

A new challenge for the choreographers in charge resulted from productions in these theatres. Because of the proscenium and the elevated stage, dance became more space oriented. Not only was it important for the dancers to skillfully move sideways, which gave further impetus to the functional necessity for turned-out legs, but dancers could advantageously jump, thus starting the vogue for elevation steps. Insofar as the proscenium provided a definite separation of performers from the audience, the spectacle became more theatrical and less of a social affair. Eventually, when courtiers began to hire professionals to dance their increasingly difficult roles, the proscenium served as a convenient social barrier in the class-conscious atmosphere of the 18th century. De Mille further supports this idea when she suggests that masks were used to suitably disguise a noble dancing next to his lackey or perhaps a professional dancer, both his social inferiors. Such social stigma attached to the theatre people has lasted well into this century and probably is directly traced to the days when aristocracy did not mix under any circumstances.

In summing up the origins of the ballet, history looks to 15th century Italy and France. The revival of learning which was the hallmark of the Renaissance, also revived men's spirits. The new learning or humanism as it was called, gave man the novel concept of "self". Clearly, man recognized his desire to enjoy his new views of life and the living of it. In a man-centered universe which the new knowledge established, the human creative psyche flourished, exploiting numerous avenues of expression.

Renaissance man desired and relished all forms of display. Outdoor spectacles, such as the sacred representations and the trionfi displayed both sacred and profane subject matter for the delectation of the nobility and common people alike. The dinner ballets were indoor entertainments which were more confined in terms of space but exceeded outdoor spectacles in their quality of conception and refinement of production. The Italian, and later, French dinner ballets were highly complex creations involving dance, myth, poetry and song which were assembled by skilled artisans under the direction of court scholars. The most celebrated example of the dinner ballets occurred at Fountainbleau in 1581. The Ballet Comique de la Reine presented "Circe" to celebrate a royal marriage. No expense or detail was spared to prepare this sumptuous feast and entertainment. While it was a huge success, it did not start a new trend in artistic entertainment however, because of its staggering costs. Consequently, it stands alone as the only first-rate example of a Renaissance dance and music production.

Those courtiers responsible for the various Renaissance entertainments frequently recorded the specifics of their work. Fortunately many of these manuscripts which deal with the dance of the period still exist. The most important document remains Arbeau's *Orchesography* in that it dealt with a variety of pertinent dance information. Upon its publication, France succeeded Italy as the center of theatrical dance, having assimilated the precious Italian know-how with its own inimitable taste and style.

The Renaissance craze for building further aided the growth of dance as an indispensible part of life by constructing the first theatres to be built since antiquity. In time these theatres would provide a permanent home in which to house the practice and performance of theatrical dance. Thus, while ballet, as we understand the term, was not yet born, the 1500 years from Rome to Renaissance established the significance of dance as religious and social tradition as well as an important means of entertainment. The Renaissance with its fresh view of man as the pivotal force in the universe was to be the turning point in dance's evolutionary advancement. The power and might of dynasties could be reflected in the *trionfi,* the dinner ballets, and even in the popular equestrian ballets so that their support became a political necessity. From this fertile and healthy soil would spring the rarefied art form called "classical ballet" to be born in the reign of Louis XIV.

REFERENCES

Arbeau, T. Translated by M. S. Evans. *Orchesography.* New York: Dover, 1967.

Burns, E. *Western Civilization.* New York: W. W. Norton & Co., Inc., 1958.

Cameron, M., & Hoffman, T. *A Guide to Theatre Study.* New York: MacMillan Publishing Co., 1974.

Horst, L. *Pre-Classic Dance Forms.* Brooklyn: Dance Horizons, Inc., 1968.

Kinkeldey, O. *A Jewish Dancing Master of the Renaissance: Guglielmo Ebreo.* Brooklyn: Dance Horizons, Inc., 1972.

Kirstein, L. *Dance, A Short History of Classic Theatrical Dancing.* Brooklyn: Dance Horizons, Inc., 1972.

Kristeller, P. *Renaissance Thought.* New York: Harper & Row, 1961.

Lawson, J. *A History of Ballet and Its Makers.* London: Chameleon Press, Ltd., 1973.

Maurer, A. *Medieval Philosophy.* New York: Random House, 1962.

Roeder, R. *Catherine de' Medici.* New York: Alfred A. Knopf, Inc., 1969.

Sachs, C. *World History of the Dance.* New York: W. W. Norton & Co., Inc., 1965.

Tafuri, M. *Teatri E Scenografie.* Milano: Touring Club Italiano, 1976.

SUGGESTIONS FOR FURTHER READING

Cohen, S. *Dance as a Theatre Art*. New York: Dodd, Mean & Co., 1974.
Kirsten, L. *Movement and Metaphor*. New York: Praeger Publishing, 1970.
Plumb, J. *The Renaissance*. New York: American Heritage Publishing Co., 1961.
Wood, M. *Historical Dance, 12th to 19th Century*, London: Imperial Society of Teachers of Dancing, 1972.

CHAPTER 4
The Baroque Ballet

Baroque is a term applied to a European style of art which originated in Italy in the late 1500's. The richly dramatic style of the baroque era reflected an aesthetic reaction to the order and symmetry slavishly adhered to in the Renaissance style. The baroque style expressed itself in the French theatre arts by presenting allegorical subject matter with a distinctive voluptuousness of form, color and texture.

THE COURT OF LOUIS XIV

The pinnacle of French baroque coincided with the lengthy reign of Louis XIV (1643-1715) during which the ballet was firmly established as a theatrical form. Louis' father (Louis XIII) had been a fine dancer. It is said that when he was not in the field enjoying the equestrian ballets of his cavalry, he and his noblemen were amused to appear as guest stars in his own court theatre in Paris. Thus, Louis XIV quite naturally inherited a genuine affection for the ballet. Moreover, he used it as an instrument to help centralize and stabilize his war-weary country. Louis built the stupendous chateau of Versailles to house himself and the landed aristocracy in appropriate splendor. At Versailles the wealth and energy of the nobility was devoted to pleasures, not the least being the court ballet. Living off the King's bounty, encouraged to enjoy such diversions as the chase, cuisine, boudoir and ballet, the nobles neglected their distant estates. Thus, with their political power so painlessly sapped, serious intrigue against the crown, accompanied by the threat of civil war, was dissipated and Louis emerged as the supreme monarch.

Louis XIV was not only a keen ballet patron and practitioner taking daily lessons, but he was surrounded by a cluster of artists without whose varied talents no significant development in the ballet would have occurred. The first twenty years of Louis' reign witnessed rapid

Fig. 1. Louis XIV lived his long life in character with his most famous dancing role, that of "The Sun King," performed when he was 15 years old. Courtesy of the New York Public Library for the Performing Arts.

artistic and technical advancements in theatrical dance. Everyone at Versailles seemed to be concerned in one way or another with the elaborate and lengthy ballets, whence the aristocracy would bask in the proximity of their dancing king. By the time the increasingly portly Louis retired from dancing in 1670, the royal productions were demanding a level of competency which was more than the amateur courtier could achieve. Fortunately for ballet and in accordance with court protocol, the courtiers retired along with the king. The creation of ballet performances was, therefore, entrusted to the hired dancing masters, their students and to professional musicians, designers and librettists. The profession of ballet thus replaced dancing as an elegant pastime for the French nobility.

At the close of the baroque era, several public theatres had opened, exposing a segment of the population to ballet. Its popularity readily created a demand for more ballet performances with more theatres to house them. Hence, from this time onward, the continued existence of ballet as a unique offspring of European civilization would be insured through royally subsidized ballet schools, professional companies and theatres.

Lully

Music has always been closely linked with all aspects of the earliest ballet, but never before had it occupied such a significant place as in the baroque era. The consummate artistic personality, serving the reign of Louis XIV, who was most responsible for the general direction that the ballet would take in its first 100 years was not primarily a dancer (although he danced and performed excellently), but was a wonderfully talented, clever and altogether unscrupulous musician by the name of Jean Baptiste Lully. As a native Italian in the French court, Lully brilliantly used his extensive talents as producer and composer in conjunction with his political astuteness and boon companionship with Louis XIV. The King, like many of his forebearers was a great patron of the arts but, better yet, history relates that he was a competent dancer who performed and was wholeheartedly involved with numerous ballets from their inception. Louis XIV not only genuinely admired Lully as an outstanding and creative master, but supported and favored his prodigious work throughout the artist's life. It was through his participation in one of Lully's inspired dance productions that Louis XIV earned forever the title of "The Sun King", a part he danced well and a role in life in which no monarch before or after him has emulated.

Lully should be remembered for his intimate knowledge of the problems of ballet music. As an experienced dancer himself, Lully understood the body's natural rhythmic flow and how its phrasing, within the balletic mold, could most successfully be accomplished with similar musical phrasing. Lully saw to it that his ballet music was precise and without undue ornamentation. That is, his compositions reflected a lushness in their very structure so that secondary embellishments were unnecessary. His music was baroque in the purist sense of the term. It was full of lyrical melody and, at the same time, sustained by simple counterpoint. The musical scores for his ballets followed a set structure wherein the pre-classic dance forms suggested the musical form so that *gigues, pavannes, minuets, allemandes,* etc. were always set in between the solemn musical introductions and triumphant finales. But most of all, Lully's music was the perfect complement for the quality of movement emerging from the newly evolving ballet steps of which he himself had first-hand practice. Lully further extended his ideas on the sensitive unification between the quality of sound and the quality of movement in that he saw the necessity of creating productions which had the theatrical coherence of one choreographer, one composer, one designer, and one dramatist. It must be pointed out that Lully's insistence on unified collaboration was novel at the time since it had always been the custom for many composers, poets, and choreographers to work on one production. Up to this time, too many cooks had usually spoiled the artistic soup. It is a tribute to Lully's foresight and aesthetic insight that he forbade such top-heavy collaborative arrangements which produced, at best, mediocre disorganization.

In 1661, Lully had the good fortune to collaborate with the great French playwright, Molière who was writing *Les Facheux.* Lully was assigned to compose and choreograph a separate ballet for insertion into the dramatic piece. But there were very few good dancers available since the ballet school of the Academy was not yet in existence. Bearing this difficulty in mind, Lully and Molière agreed that the dancing should relate to and extend the plot of the play, thus providing a structure which would allow for an unprecedented amount of dramatic and balletic integration. The small number of dancers at their disposal were woven into the plot and their dancing was meaningfully merged with the speeches into a very successful whole.

Lully and Molière continued their collaboration and eventually as-similated the ever-popular style of the *Commedia dell'Arte* into their work. This style of theatre had originated in Italy and had come to France in the 16th century. Its standardized characters of Harlequin, Pierrot, and Colombina with their improvised comic bits called *lassi*, provided a mine of comic devices for the divinely funny Molière to shape and adapt to his scripts. Molière was further able to offer Lully the special kind of inspiration which springs from brilliant collabora-tors in that the playwright was also an experienced dancer. Accord-ingly, Molière's characters were made to move in a style that reflected their zany lines. Lully, in other words, was able to stylize his music to suggest the antics of Molière's individual characterization. And, thus, was born another level of artistic oneness that would, in time, contrib-ute to the birth of our contemporary concept of ballet.

Lully's influence on ballet did not stop with his dance-sensitive mu-sical compositions. In 1661 Louis XIV had authorized a group of dan-cing masters to organize under the title of the Royal Academy of Dance for the purpose of re-establishing the art of dance in its original perfection, but this group apparently did little more than theorize, having left no concrete record to the contrary. In 1669 the Royal Academy of Music was founded to develop music throughout France. This body was more successful at achieving its aims and still exists to-day as the Paris Opera. In 1672 the King authorized his well-loved Lully to take over the Royal Academy of Music and add to its scope equal attention to dancing. Naturally, Lully relied on advice from the King's personal dancing master, Pierre Beauchamp who had been a member of the disbanded Royal Academy of Dance.

From childhood on, Louis XIV had grown up obsessed with his greatness and so desired that the world should see him that way. Ac-cordingly, he insisted that those who worked to enhance the magnifi-cence of his reign were also first-rate talents. Upon his retirement as a dancer, there still remained his inspired and competent professional dancing masters and their students to keep alive the King's ballet. Soon dancing masters and students alike were absorbed into the Royal Academy of Music where they were to flourish in a permanent home. Alas, the court ballet is dead! Long live the professional ballet! And that is exactly what has happened from 1670 to this day. Ballet became the metier of professional dancers, teachers, choreographers, and aspiring students and never again would its great creative talents be subject to amateur whims of court life.

Beauchamp and the Danse d'école

The artistic gifts of Pierre Beauchamp figured significantly in the rapid development of 17th century dance. He was reported to be a masterful choreographer and dancer who excelled in the execution of turns or *pirouettes*. Historians generally credit him with the formal innovation of the five classical positions of the legs, twelve positions of the arms, the mandatory use of turnout, the development and codification of new ballet steps, and new concepts in ballet choreography. This last point is perhaps his most significant contribution although there is no record of how he specifically dealt with choreographic problems presented by a proscenium arch stage.

As we have seen earlier, Richelieu had built a magnificent theatre in which Molière presented plays for the Parisian public. Lully took over this theatre when Molière died in 1673, and it was here that he installed Beauchamp who worked out the problems of ballet as seen from the audience's focal point. Beauchamp's efforts resulted in numerous advancements in ballet creation and production. No longer was the grand floor pattern uppermost in importance as when audiences sat around three sides or viewed ballets from overhead galleries. Beauchamp revealed the novel aesthetic of the vertical line of the dancer's body with its complementary *port de bras* and turned-out legs. The richness of the body's design potential became apparent when presented in full-view on an elevated stage. From the raised stage, dancers themselves could likewise revel in the challenge of the illusory effects of an elegant posture. Due to the large stage area, dancers could sweep up and downstage creating their own dimensions of spacial depth. Under the aegis of Beauchamp, the presence of adequate stage space and the growing emphasis on technical nuance eliminated once and for all the need for the ballet to descend into the house itself.

From 1670 to 1687 Lully and Beauchamp, along with Berain, the great 18th century stage designer, and Bensarade who was their librettist, created works of unsurpassed baroque elegance. The professional dancers appearing in these ballets were private students of Lully and Beauchamp or the skilled commoners who, prior to Louis' retirement, had danced along with the courtiers. In 1681, one of their students and the first professional ballerina, La Fontaine, appeared and rightfully claimed female roles which, up to that time, had been performed by men, thereby initiating another welcome and meaningful reform in the ballet.

From the time of Beauchamp to 1714, the Royal Academy of Music and Dance had been the official and active body in regard to the theory and production of ballets. In this year, a training school was added to teach and give classes to professional dancers, but not until 1784 did the Academy add a school for children. Owing to Beauchamps' interest in the development of the individual's dance technique, the concept of *danse d'école* emerged. It is important to remember that the roots of these movements which formed the body of knowledge called the *danse d'école* resulted from an accumulation of dance ideas stemming from the medieval and Renaissance times. Beauchamp is historically credited with the introduction of a precise manner of dancing these movements for which the performers needed exact instruction. There were specified steps, poses and positions to be learned along with their special terminology and rules for correct execution. Turnout of the legs (although not the 180° expected in our century), and stylized arm movements called *port de bras* were also part of the body of material to be mastered by all dancers working under Beauchamp.

EIGHTEENTH CENTURY WRITINGS ON THE BALLET

Feuillet

The most important writing to emerge from the first years of professional dance was done in 1701 by the dancing master, Roaul Feuillet who previously had served as grammarian in Beauchamp's school. His work was widely disseminated and in 1706 was translated by the English dancer John Weaver under the title of *On the Art of Dancing*. Feuillet's writing was essentially a technical manual based on the work of Beauchamp. As written information, it served to stabilize the French ballet terminology, codify existing ballet steps and define the five classic positions, although these were in part reminiscent of those presented by Arbeau a century earlier. Feuillet also invented a system of dance notation, but his chief legacy to dance was that both his technical manual and dance notation were concerned with theatrical ballet and not social forms of dance.

Interestingly enough, the notation and accompanying scores for theatrical dances of the 18th century were published just as sheet music is today. Although it takes a special skill to interpret these beautifully drawn dance notations in our time, they did include a considerable amount of information. For instance, the notations of Feuillet indicate the nature of the steps, which were generally walking or springing movements, and their rhythms. The spacial design of the dance was conveyed by drawing the path or track which the dancer followed, graphically suggesting the overall patterns created in the dance. Special symbols were used to mark the movement for a bow, turn, jump, rise or fall. What is not stressed, however, is the carriage of the head and body. The quality of the movement derived from the posture of the head and spine was the same as the everyday deportment acquired by the 18th century person of quality.

Following on the heels of Feuillet's publication was that of Rameau's *The Dancing Master* in 1725. While this French work was concerned with social dances, it did contribute to stage dancing of the day in that it carefully explained movement style of various social dances with reference and timely examples relating to leading ballet dancers. Whereas such previous writings were more concerned with the floor patterns or steps themselves, Rameau discussed quality of movement in dancing based on his personal experience and acknowledgement of his association with the great dancing masters of the time. Rameau's treatise considered in detail the five classical positions and the proper forms of etiquette, social gesture, and court protocol. He expounded on such steps as *balancé, jeté, entrechat,* and *sissonne,* but as Kirstein notes, these steps were more like the primitive roots of those we perform today by the same names. In addition, Rameau followed the ideas of Beauchamps in discussing *port de bras* at length. He was the first dance writer to present the notion of oppositional movement of the limbs. Treating the notion of opposition from two points of view, he regarded it as necessary to the design of the body and when opposition is used correctly, he points out that it aids in technical accomplishment.

It is clear from reading such accounts as that of Feuillet and Rameau, that the structure of a progressive ballet technique was steadily evolving despite the temporary loss of artistic standards. As one looks back over the three centuries of ballet's growth, it appears to be a persistent and steady climb into the present. Yet the dancers, teachers, and choreographers who lived through these years, day by day experienced the gamut of emotional trauma in their work. Glorious years led by genius usually fell into rigidity and decadence. On the other hand, innovative reactions to dry but honorable tradition caused riot, scandal, and sometimes broken heads, and emphasis on brilliant technique was inevitably at war with artistic expressiveness. The period which followed the splendid years of Lully and Beauchamp coincided with the dimming of the long reign of the Sun King. At the same time, this period should be thought of as one of artistic incubation. Creative forces recede only to regroup and regenerate, synthesizing past experience into new artistic life.

ARTISTIC DECLINE

At the beginning of the 18th century, a set formula had been established and adhered to for the creating of classical ballets, so revered and influential had been the impact of Lully's life work. There were still the themes from mythology which symbolically and allegorically related to the occasion of the production; there were still the musical and dramatic sections interspersed with dancing. From the theoretical work of the Academy, a pedagogical system, called the *danse d'école,* had evolved in which pupils maintained the technical standards of excellence of their masters. But, sadly, the most inspirational aspects of the works of Lully and Beauchamp gave way to the less taxing formula of the old *ballet d'entrées* and the opera ballets. As the times changed, so did the taste of Paris and the paying public set the trend. Dramatic plots were minimized, logical sequence became irrelevant and music merely served the decorative dancing with a beat instead of merging with expressive movement to form an artistic whole. Previously, ballet names of *Loves of. . .* or *Fêtes of. . .* served as generic frames in which divertissements could have some thread holding them together, but now they lost even that element of cohesion. This fragmentation of creative effort actually came to be called *Fragments of. . .* whatever style or composer who happened to lend bits and pieces to such a production.

As to the creative activity of this period (1690-1740), it is only remarkable for the musical and dramatic collaborative efforts of Voltaire and Rameau which resulted in the opera, *Les Indes Galantes* (1735). Unfortunately, there was no dancing master of comparable talent to devise memorable ballets for this or other productions. Instead, various mediocre dancing masters who dared not attempt to violate the Lullian formula of opera ballets were charged with the choreographic responsibilities of these operatic works.

THE PROFESSIONAL BALLET

The early 18th century prepared the way for the technical brilliance of the individual dancer while it briefly overshadowed the possibility of choreographic creativity. By 1730 the stately *terre à terre* movement of the *basse* dance which had been the predominant style of Beauchamp gave way to the *danse en l'air*. All manner of beaten steps and leaps were *de rigeur,* so much so that those who favored the old days, critically remarked that "once there were dances; now only jumps". The theatrical adaptation of social dances and their emphasis on floor pattern gave way to improved execution of *pirouettes, entrechat quartes, sissonnes* and *cabrioles.* This occurrence was in part due to the recently acquired professional status of ballet. At this time a small nucleus of professional dance personnel staffed the Academy, later known as the Paris Opera. They consisted of ten women dancers, twelve male dancers, ballet master, choreographer, designer and costumer. The choreographer, however, seems to have arranged dances out of previously existing choreographic ideas instead of inventing new ones. The dancers, no longer minions of the court, were free to mingle with other theatrical influences in Paris as well as at Versailles. For example, the players of the *Commedia dell'Arte* borrowed from the Academy but also invented new steps to add to their own repertories of virtuosity which served their highly skilled art form of comedy and pantomime. At the Academy, the objective of those trained in the *danse d'école* was also to entertain, so what better technical influence could they have than these amazing and popular entertainers of the *Commedia* who frequently appeared in the Parisian theatres?

Ballet in England

The development of ballet during these years persisted in Paris, although it was never totally cut off from foreign influences. And, as one would imagine, the proximity of London and the special English character did not preclude an interest in French ballet. Tudor England had included dancing in its Renaissance masques earlier than other northern countries. Dance and mime had been a popular form of entertainment in the days of Henry VII and Henry VIII and later social dancing enjoyed the loving dilettantism of Queen Elizabeth. London had a vital theatre wherein the plays of Shakespeare centered around the dramatic action, while thematic symbolism was secondary. The English theatre was noted for its rich variety, even on a single program. In short, England had its own brilliant artistic Renaissance.

During these years the arts in England did not have the institutionalized patronage of the monarch. This lack of official direction happily allowed for the freedom to experiment and England's heritage of a public theatre provided an audience tolerant of innovation. As to the ballet, however, there had never been opportunity for dance to develop there as it did within the gilded coffers of the Bourbons. Consequently, English theatrical dance grew on a smaller scale, but its public was ever eager for the visits of dancers from France and Italy.

Weaver

At this time, the Englishman John Weaver stands out as the dominant figure in the profession. He worked in London from 1702 to 1733 as a dancer, teacher, and choreographer. As we have seen earlier, he translated Feuillet's treatise *On the Art of Dancing* in 1706, thus giving the English the benefit of Beauchamp's technical knowledge and the codified French terminology for ballet steps. Weaver knew and worked with visiting French dancers so there was continuous artistic exchange and undoubtedly he had real, if unknown to us, influence on the French dancers. During his busy career as a choreographer, Weaver found time to write on dance theory and history. Perhaps his most amazing writing was *Anatomical and Mechanical Lectures,* the first scientific treatise to relate the structure of the human body to the demands of classical ballet positions and steps.

Weaver felt very strongly that dance was an expressive medium and that virtuosity should support characterization rather than exist for its own sake. The idea that a story could be expressed in mime and movement without sung or spoken explanation was taken from classical literature and revived by Renaissance commentators. But this was an idea only, for it had never been successfully achieved.

Weaver's most famous ballet, *The Loves of Mars and Venus* (1717) embodied his theoretical ideas on what a ballet could be. His was the original, if imperfect, *ballet d'action* wherein the dancers conveyed the dramatic plot during distinct sections of dance and mime. This work marked the first time in a full-length professional ballet that there was no recitation of verse to advance the story line.

A singular such entertainment prior to Weaver's *ballet d'action* was arranged for a party given by the Duchess of Maine at Seaux in 1708. She commissioned a composer to set music to dramatic verse but then had the lines mimed by two professional dancers rather than spoken by actors. Contemporary accounts of the evening indicate that the dancers, Balon and Prévost, were skilled and expressive enough to bring tears to the eyes of their audience. Although the duet was a great success at the party, it was an isolated artistic event born before its time. The idea failed to find fertile ground in the professional ballet world where it might have flourished prior to the advent of Noverre.

In addition to John Weaver, there were several other precursors of the full blown *ballet d'action* who worked not altogether independently of each other in various parts of Europe. By way of certain productions of the Italian Theatre in Paris, some of the English style crept into Paris. The naturalness and lack of affectation in English dancers was noteworthy for many a continental visitor. Furthermore, the French dancers visiting London were intrigued by Shakespeare's plays which dealt primarily with the human condition and not, alas, Greek gods with Bourbon counterparts. English theatre was fresh and vital without official direction and this element in London's theatre even encouraged touches of democratic thinking in French dancers. As a consequence of this artistic channel crossing, the Paris Opera occasionally presented primitive forms of *ballet d'action* but so unusual were these productions considered that they were announced to the public at curtain time as ballets played in mute scenes.

Sallé

Marie Sallé, who had been a pupil of Mlle. Prévost (a contemporary of Beauchamp), was extremely interested in the expressive nature of dance. As a child prodigy she had enormous success in London. Later she returned to triumph there in her own dramatic ballet *Pygmalion* in 1734. During this time she discarded the pannier worn by all female

Fig. 2. This early 18th century dancer must have specialized in *terre á terre* dancing because her plumes, pannier and heels would not have allowed for much variety of movement. Courtesy of the Author.

dancers and appeared in a simple flowing dress with her hair loose about her shoulders. Although Sallé was French and spent much of her career working in Paris, she found a greater creative freedom outside the official shackles of the Paris Opera. Sallé was said to command an extensive range of emotions while dancing in each of her many roles. It is an everlasting compliment to her honored place in dance history that the great composer Handel paid tribute to her musical sensitivity. While she was never especially acclaimed for brilliant technique, she must have been a supreme actress, imaginative in her rendition of dances, and creative in her poses to the extent that they metaphorically became meaningful gestures. Mlle. Sallé was a living example of those artistic notions of Lully which pertained to unity and expressiveness in dance. She was particularly deft at creating her own *pas de deux* and, for the first time in classical ballet, a duet became a true conversation in movement. Although lifts and intricately supported poses were not yet invented, the expressive interchange of gesture between Sallé and her better partners gained appreciable attention from the public. During her lifetime, she enjoyed royal favor and after her death she was revered for her gentleness of spirit.

The Ballet in Vienna: Hilferding and Angiolini

Sallé's contemporary, Franz Hilferding, was an Austrian choreographer who returned to his native Vienna after a sojourn of study in Paris. At home he created ballets based on the works of Racine and Voltaire which were in essence pantomimed dramas and pastorals. He eventually designed works in which the dancers carried the entire dramatic line while the story was reinforced with meaningful gesture. His productions were examples of the ever-growing trend to rid ballet of its superfluous conventions such as helmets, masks, wigs, and hoop skirts. One innovation attributed to Hilferding was the creation of a kind of character dancing. That is, instead of using stock characters from the *Commedia dell'Arte* for comic roles, he modeled dances on people and occupations found in everyday life.

In 1757, Hilferding accepted an invitation from Catherine the Great to work in Russia. His pupil Gasparo Angiolini assumed his duties at the Vienna Opera. Angiolini's ballets were not unlike those of his master. He used scenes from everyday life as well as ethnic and national themes to design his scenarios. His successes led him to produce a version of Molière's *Don Juan* in which the story line was logically wrought and then enhanced by Gluck's innovative score. For the first time in dance history, a first-rate composer who understood the needs of a dramatic ballet, wrote a musical score which matched the dramatic and emotional content of the plot. Whereas Lully's music was always framed in the pre-classic dance forms employing *gigues, passe pieds, gavottes,* etc., Gluck's music underscored and meshed with the dramatic action. As a result, the descriptive power of Gluck's music alleviated the need for a sung explanation of the dramatic sequences. Most important for the quality of future ballet music was the fact that Gluck did not compose a series of dance numbers as typified by Lullian standards, but rather the music followed the dynamic rise and fall of the danced drama. Apparently Angiolini and Gluck mutually benefited from this collaboration because they again worked together in Gluck's opera *Orpheus.* It was during these years that the term "ballet" once and for all time came to replace the word "opera" which had been used to connote a work of music and dance. And so the concept and direction of ballet took one more turn toward its evolution into the future.

Two French Dancers: Le Grand Dupré and La Camargo

A number of dancers during this period emerged to catch the public notice and are still remembered today for their style. Two of the most extraordinary are Le Grand Dupré (1697-1774) and La Camargo (1710-1770). The "inimitable Dupré," as Casanova wrote of him was still dancing in his fifties. Dupré was a successor of Beauchamp at the Opera and apparently was famous for performing the *terre à terre* movement of the previous generation with enormous elegance and gravity of manner. He had spent time in England and had danced in Weaver's *Loves of Mars and Venus.* Dupré, in his many years as a dancer, experimented with improvisation in order to seek out the relationship between dance steps and their musicality. Undoubtedly, this led him to add to the variety and richness of ballet steps as well as ascertaining their most economic means of execution. His illustrious pupils, namely Noverre, Gaëtan Vestris, and La Camargo, attest to his reputation as a discerning teacher in that their own contributions to ballet reach well into our century.

La Camargo with her vivacious personality, enjoyed and surely helped carve the stereotype of the ballerina. She exhibited a fiery brilliance in her dancing, no doubt due to her Spanish ancestry, but her ability also related to her training. She had studied with the celebrated Mlle. Prévost of the Opera. In a fit of jealousy over La Camargo's public acclamation, Prévost refused to teach her further, so La Camargo sought lessons with Dupré as well as Pécours and Blondy. These gentlemen perfected her penchant for brilliant footwork and soon she seriously rivaled the great male dancers of the age. She could manage with ease all the virtuoso jumps and beats usually performed by men only. Yet, history has recorded that she had many physical defects as a dancer. It is a tribute to her as an artist that she knew how to avert attention from her faults by emphasizing her vivacity, gaiety, and expressiveness. She became the rage of Paris and more so when she caused a scandal by shortening her skirts to the ankle in order to display consecutive *entrechat quatres*. Although moralists agonized over this impropriety of costume, the shorter skirts remained and opened up new possibilities for technical innovations. La Camargo's contemporary and popular rival was Marie Sallé. However, their styles and hallmarks were at opposite ends. When Voltaire commented on them, he diplomatically averted outcry from their respective fans and expressed the comparison in the following: "Ah! Camargo how brilliant you are! But, great gods, how ravishing is also Sallé''.

RETROSPECT

Before continuing the circuitous route of dance history toward the next great creative upsurge in classical ballet, it might prove helpful to review the ninety years of so-called decadence which dates from approximately 1670 to 1760. Ballet enjoyed a spectacular rush of development in the first 20 years (1643-1663) of Louis XIV's reign. Virtually within one generation, ballet soared to great heights in its development. But, by the time of Beauchamp's retirement and Lully's death in 1689, the creative period was over, although its grand patron Louis lived on to 1715. At the same time, however, it must be remembered that the *ballet d'entrée* and opera ballets still remained immensely popular at court and at the public theatres. What the ballet lacked in directorial and creative genius, it made up for in gorgeous display and pomp until at last the force of the original aesthetic ideas of Beauchamp and Lully totally dissipated. The nobles who still participated as dancers in the late 1660's did not seem to mind the lack of genuine artistic activity nor did the general public seem to notice its absence. Theatrical dancing in whatever form it took was still a major source of entertainment at Versailles and in Paris.

Yet, there were outspoken critics of the ballet throughout the long period. They were not the dancing masters but the aestheticians and

writers of the age who seized afresh on rediscovering the art of the an-
cients. They read and re-read Aristotle's emphasis on art as meaningful imitation of nature. For these scholars, this notion illuminated a
vast range of human experience which they felt was expressible in
movement. Art, according to Aristotle, is a distillation of life expressed
in a harmonious and unified manner. How then, these writers won-
dered, did the theatrical absurdities being presented at the time relate
to the meaning of art? In 1668, the Abbe de Pure wrote that the dancing masters were embarrassed by the stupidity of most of the nobles
and other persons of quality with whom they had to work. These people could not correctly execute the steps they had been taught and it
was, thus, impossible for the dancing masters to carry out their ideas.
In comparing new productions with those of Louis' earlier court ballets, the Abbe gives us a clear picture as to what state theatrical purpose and taste had assumed in 1668.

> . . .luxury having prevailed over intelligence, greater stress was laid on
> expense than on perfection, on showiness than on solidity and on ac-
> cessories than on the principal. Little regard now came to be had for the
> various talents of the dancers, the originality of the steps was despised,
> and, worst of all, it was desired to please the Court and the Ladies, who
> are the two rocks on which common sense is wrecked and are the evil
> destinies of fine works. The scene was packed with people of quality
> who were shamelessly sought out that a part of the expense might be
> unloaded on them and who accepted out of vanity. All that the intelli-
> gent professionals, who found themselves burdened not only with this
> large number of people of quality, but also with their clumsy, presump-
> tuous and, therefore, incorrigible efforts, were able to do was to compli-
> cate the *entrées* by a large number of figures and mask as best they
> could by these various changes the faults of these great nobles, who
> were either badly made or poor dancers.

By the turn of the century, this uncreative period was, on the other
hand, busily constructing theatres and supporting ballet schools and
companies to insure a constant flow of new dancers to participate in
opera and ballet production. Great public institutions copying the
Paris Opera (1669) were London's Haymarket (1705) and later Covent Garden (1732); the Royal Danish Opera (1726), the Vienna
Burgtheater (1748), the Royal Swedish Opera (1773); La Scala in
Milan (1778), and the Bolshoi in Moscow (1776). In addition, there
were countless other superb court theatres such as the Wurttemberg at
Stuttgart, the exquisite Curvilles theatre in Munich, and the

Drottingholm at the summer palace near Stockholm. The ballet schools and companies associated with these houses fortunately relied on the royal purse for subsidy thereby assuring high standards of training and performance.

As history looks back at this period, it is clear that there were talented individuals dancing as well as urging reforms in theatrical customs and costumes. Schools were opening which cried for dancer's services as teachers for the multitude of students flocking to their doors. There were additional theatres being built to house the paying public. All that seemed to be missing was artistic leadership to provide vision and consolidation.

In summary, the reign of Louis XIV witnessed the formal inception of what is known theatrically and pedagogically as the ballet. The dance moved from the domain of an elegant pastime, to that of serious profession upon the monarch's retirement from his own dancing career. Louis, characteristically, surrounded the development of the art of the dance with men of genius, Lully and Beauchamp being the most celebrated. Lully as composer, dancer, and visionary created ballets which were unified and interrelated wholes, supported on the plinth of their very own aesthetic. Beauchamp was most notably instrumental in devising the *danse d'école* in which ballet instruction was based on codified steps and formal positions of the arms and legs.

The early 18th century ballet was forged out of decades of high artistic creativity as well as years of sterility. When the French ballet receded into arid formalism, John Weaver in London experimented with the seeds of expressive *ballet d'action* as did Hilferding and Angiolini in the Viennese court. Two wonderful artists, Marie Sallé and La Camargo, contributed to the novel concept of the "ballerina" as being a genuine and sensitive interpreter of human feeling. Finally, the 18th century witnessed the profession of dance gain status and enjoy popularity in the construction of numerous public theatres throughout Europe.

REFERENCES

Brinson, P. *Background to European Ballet.* Leyden, Netherlands: A. W. Sijthoff Printing Division, 1966.

Christout, M. *Le Ballet de Cour de Louis XIV.* Paris: A. et. J. Picard, Cie, 1967.

Hilton, W. "May I have this dance, Mrs. Millament?". *Dance Magazine,* July, 1972.

Kirsten, L. Dance, A Short History to Classical Theatrical Dancing. Brooklyn: Dance Horizons, 1969.

Kirsten, L. *Movement and Metaphor.* New York: Praeger Publishers, 1970.

Lawson, J. *A History of Ballet and Its Makers.* London: Chameleon Press, Ltd., 1973.

Lynham, D. *The Chevalier Noverre.* London: Chameleon Press, Ltd., 1972.

MacGowan, M. *L'Art du ballet de Cour* (1581-1643). Paris: C.N.R.S., 1964.

Prunières, H. *Le Ballet de Cour en France avant Benserade et Lully.* Paris: H. Laurens, Cie, 1914.

Searle, H. *Ballet Music.* New York: Dover Publications, Inc., 1973.

Wolf, J. *Louis XIV.* New York: W. W. Norton & Co., Inc., 1968.

SUGGESTIONS FOR FURTHER READING

Cohen, S. *Dance as a Theatre Art.* New York: Dodd, Mead & Co., 1974.

Duchartre, P. *The Italian Comedy.* New York: Dover Publications, Inc., 1966.

Guest, I. *The Dancer's Heritage.* Baltimore: Penguin Books, 1960.

Tomlinson, K. *The Art of Dancing and Six Dances.* (First published, London, 1724) Brooklyn: Dance Horizons, 1970.

CHAPTER 5

The Growth and Refinement of European Ballet

Almost a hundred years after the Abbe de Pure's lament, the ballet remained stagnant as a form of artistic expression. In 1757, the Encyclopaedist Denis Diderot summed up this long and barren period by pleading with all artists to...

> forget the sensational; seek for picture; get close to real life and first of all leave room for the exercise of pantomime to the fullest extent...I really believe that neither the poets, musicians, decor artists, nor dancers, have as yet a true conception of their theatre. Is it prostituting philosophy, poetry, music, painting and dancing to busy them with an obscurity? Each of these arts in particular has for aim the imitation of nature...
>
> The dance awaits still a man of genius; it is everywhere bad because it is barely suspected that it is an imitative (expressive) art...

Diderot's statement, "The dance awaits still a man of genius" suggests what these years lacked. Granted history has acknowledged the advanced work of such talents as Sallé, Hilferding and Angiolini, and the earlier creative innovations of Prévost and Balon at Seaux, and of Weaver's experimental *ballet d'action*. But were these not lone voices crying in the night of a hundred years? These dance personalities who inhabited the early 18th century represented isolated moments in a period which was moving toward a very special reformation.

These dancers were responsible for singular instances where the evolution of ballet was slowly forged. For example, special dance music was appropriated for the movement at one time; mime and meaningful gesture replaced sung verse at another just as skirts were shortened and occasionally masks and wigs were put aside. But what was needed was a centralizing force that would emerge from a consistent and logical philosophy of art. The man of genius who was to reestablish the dance in its original purity and synthesize all the positive contributions that had gone before finally appeared. In the course of his visionary career, Jean Georges Noverre (1727-1810) would bring about the rise of the choreographer which was to effect the needed reformation and point the way for the future ballet.

JEAN GEORGES NOVERRE: FATHER OF MODERN BALLET (1727-1810)

When Noverre entered the Opera Comique as a professional dancer around 1743, the laws governing ballet were inviolate. The innovations of Lully, Beauchamp, and Berain were by this date formalized, devoid of inspiration, and slavishly followed. For example, all the leading dancers in every opera ballet performed their specialties with the most skilled virtuoso concluding the choreographic sequence, whether or not this format related to the thin thematic action of the piece. Dancers frequently made up for the appalling lack of artistic direction by exhibiting their spectacular technical abilities which, despite all the dramatic indications, should have led them to the contrary. In certain instances, superb dancers, such as the Vestris family, the Gardel brothers and the Daubervals were often kept from giving their best performances, so weighted down were they with the traditional helmets, plumes, and masks. In an atmosphere sadly lacking the Lullian genius for rich collaboration, the young Noverre witnessed composers, choreographers, and designers working independently of each other's ideas, indifferent to their common goal.

The dissatisfied Noverre left Paris for a position as a dancer at the court in Berlin but soon accepted another invitation to compose his first ballets in Marseilles. Next he moved to Lyon where, in addition to composing, he also partnered the famous Camargo. In 1755, Noverre contracted to create for David Garrick's theatre in London *Ballet Chinois* for which he had already received acclaim in France. His acquaintance with Garrick resulted in mutual respect and a lasting friendship but most of all, it had an indelible influence on Noverre's artistic formation. Unfortunately, his Chinese ballet fared less well. It opened on the eve of the Seven Years War. The public was vehement that a French ballet was playing in London. Garrick tried to assuage the matter by announcing that Noverre was actually Swiss and engaged many English dancers in the company, but it was to no avail. Riots broke out between the common people and the nobility within the theatre. Noverre's ballet was forcibly removed from the stage and Garrick paid him compensation for the time remaining in his contract.

NOVERRE'S INTERNATIONAL INFLUENCE

In 1760 Noverre moved to the Stuttgart court of the Duke of Wurttenburg, who was renowned as a patron of the theatre. Noverre was engaged as ballet master and the Duke made available to him every consideration conducive to a working atmosphere such as the services of the Neapolitan composer, Jomelli and the illustrious scenic designer, Servandoni. Most important, and because of the Duke's celebrated reputation for providing an artistic haven, Noverre enjoyed the cooperation of the famous dancers of the times. Gaëtan Vestris was a frequent guest artist; Dauberval danced under Noverre's direction for nearly two years; and Noverre discovered the great talent of le Picq at this time and elevated him from the *corps de ballet* for special training. Other dancers, many of them well known from Noverre's London days, were engaged and all-in-all formed a company of seven leading dancers and a *corps* of 23 men and 21 women. Both the ballet itself and Noverre prospered in this idyllic setting. Noverre's production of *Jason et Medea* was a great triumph, featuring Mlle. Nency, whom he had trained in London. Mlle. Nency represented a new trend in dancers which in certain ways recalled the earlier pioneerism of Sallé. Nency was said to have an amazing dance talent, but in addition, she demonstrated an acting ability which brought to mind the incomparable Garrick.

While in Stuttgart, Noverre profited from the court's artistic climate and produced many ballets including *Orpheus and Euridice*. So great was his reputation that he even earned the esteem of Voltaire, who, along with Garrick and a few others of like calibre, were perhaps the only people who fully appreciated the extent of Noverre's talents in his lifetime. Due to internal politics, Noverre's contract was terminated in 1767 although he retained the respect of the Duke and his court.

Noverre immediately journeyed to Vienna where his life would begin a series of events, all of which would further wet his ambition to be associated with the Paris Opera. In Vienna he was appointed ballet master at the Burgtheater and dancing master to the young princess Marie Antoinette. Ballet was by no means new to Vienna. Hilferding and Angiolini had both preceded Noverre at the Burgtheater before

Empress Marie Theresa had sent them each in turn to Czarina Catherine, the Empress of Russia. In addition, Noverre's reputation acclaimed him in Vienna by way of the dancers he had worked with in London and Stuttgart and by his famous student Vestris, who revised the master's ballets for the Viennese audience. At this time, Noverre worked with the composer Gluck on several productions to their mutual benefit and pleasure. According to a contemporary account, Noverre was able to solve a major staging problem of Gluck's unplastic chorus in *Orpheus* by placing the singers offstage and allowing the dancers to mime the choral work. In 1773 Angiolini returned from Russia to witness Noverre's work in Vienna. The two of them engaged in a bitter literary struggle when Angiolini claimed Noverre had usurped his teacher Hilferding's ideas on the inherent dramatic possibilities in ballet. Disheartened by the unpleasant atmosphere which his confrontation with Angiolini produced and needing a change of scene, Noverre left Vienna and arranged to work at the Royal Theatre in Milan which was, at the time, part of the Austrian Empire.

By 1776 Noverre's ideas and activity influenced ballet in most of the capitals in Europe, but he longed for the coveted appointment of ballet master at the Paris Opera. It had always been his greatest desire to work at the very heart of the ballet in the Academy itself. This ambition was finally realized through the intercession of his former pupil, Marie Antoinette, now Queen of France. His appointment at the Paris Opera was acclaimed by various literary publications as the arrival of a great composer of ballets, who "excelled in the art of speaking to the eyes with gesture and movements". However, Noverre's advanced ideas, published in his *Lettres sur la Danse* in 1760, soon threatened the reactionaries within the Opera. Furthermore, the Queen's intervention was viewed as more of her political meddling since Maximilian Gardel, by rights, should have had the post which went to Noverre. From the very start, Noverre's tenure at the Opera was frought with a network of enemies working to undermine his artistic conceptions. His colleagues at the Opera fostered bitter controversy over his appointment. From the hierarchical position of the reigning ballerina, Madeline Guimard, down to the least employee, Noverre was viewed as an upstart foreigner from the provinces. His wish to reform the dance shook those who clung to the lax traditions and the security provided by the reactionary establishment of the Opera. Intrigue from within the Opera piled upon intrigue. None of his ballets

Fig. 1. This etching of Auguste Vestris shows him in a particularly elegant pose and contradicts the many grotesque cartoons depicting his style. Courtesy of the New York Public Library for the Performing Arts.

satisfied the dancers or the management and they were subject to unceasing flow of petty criticisms, although more objective literary accounts attest to the excellent quality of the ballets and their composer. Noverre, for his part, attempted to compromise whenever he deemed it possible according to his artistic standards. But by 1780, the man was completely disillusioned and after three and a half years at the

Opera, he tendered his resignation, an action which also proved to be tainted with the unsavory machinations of his old enemy, Gardel.

Upon leaving the Paris Opera, Noverre contracted to work in London where his ballets were received in triumph during the 1781-82 season. He continued to work, alternating his time between London and Lyon. Soon after the King's Theatre in London burned down, he retired to his home outside Paris. But, probably due to the holocaust produced by the French Revolution, he again returned to London when the King's Theatre was reopened. Noverre's successes there continued and it was soon said that he displayed such powers of taste and imagination that he was considered to be a poet insofar as he could create poetical effects.

When Noverre returned to Paris toward 1795, he was ill and his savings, property and pension had been lost in the French Revolution. The last fifteen years of his life were devoted to revising the Lettres and writing about the theatre, a subject on which he displayed a very deep knowledge and insight into the technical as well as artistic problems. He attended performances and rehearsals at the Opera; he followed the careers of young dancers; and he deplored the fact that fewer male dancers were being formed. He was saddened to see pompous and dull spectacles presented at the Opera and especially the way the young Auguste Vestris was allowed to waste his enormous talent owing to his personal lack of taste and incompetent artistic direction. At the same time, Noverre's greatest ballets continued to be revived, even in far-off Russia by the young and talented Didelot. New editions and translations of the Lettres were continually spreading his messages so that after his death in 1810, his fame and influence were stronger than ever.

LETTRES SUR LA DANSE

The sources of information on Noverre's accomplishments in the development of ballet are chiefly his Lettres sur la Danse (1760), the professional activities of his students who personally spread his ideas over the face of Europe, and who saw to it that his ideas were handed down through generations of dancers. The ballet d'action, associated with Noverre's work, was a novel theatrical form for the time in that the dancing itself strove to develop and extend the dramatic action. Noverre did not single-handedly create the ballet d'action, but rather his work was the product of decades of evolving ideas and practices. Noverre's merit, in fact, reaches beyond the scope of the *ballet d'action* in that he receives the credit for gleaning, refining, and actualizing the most elite aesthetic ideas of his time. More often than not, he worked in unsympathetic circumstances, while producing over one hundred examples of *ballet d'action*.

According to his philosophy of art, Noverre strove to represent a more naturalistic style by making his ballets a creative synthesis of what was essential in nature as opposed to merely copying it along with its abundant details. To accomplish this, he dealt specifically with: (1) correctness in dance technique, as laid down by Beauchamp and others to be tethered with sensitivity to the individual's anatomy; (2) pedagogical consideration of the dancer's personality and style; (3) validity and sincerity of gestural expression within the dramatic context of the ballet; (4) logical development of plots which were thematically integrated while omitting all superfluous solos and irrelevant dance techniques; (5) use of music appropriately suited to the dramatic development of the plot; (6) costumes, decor, and lighting made compatible with the introduction, plot and climax of each act within a ballet; and, (7) advanced ideas on stage make-up for dancers.

His procedural methods for composing choreography were evolved from his many years of experience. First he sought a plot and worked out the moment-by-moment sequential action. He then created dance movement and gesture which would clearly express the plot. At this point he would engage a composer to write a score to fit the structure of the ballet as outlined.

Perhaps the most remarkable aspect of his writings is his extraordinary insights into the artistry which is necessary to the role of the teacher. His very advanced ideas of what enters into the education and nurturing of dance artists and choreographers are as true today as they were then. So enormous was Noverre's philosophical and practical impact on ballet, that his presence is ever with us. While his influence was great at the time of his death in 1810, it was not until another hundred years of incubation that his ideas were fully understood and implemented in the work of Isadora Duncan and Michael Fokine.

Although Noverre stands out as the visionary giant of his age, the times were blessed with other choreographers who were also wonderful dancers and, each in their own way, contributed to the development of art. Jean Dauberval (1742-1806) is remembered for his in-

Fig. 2. Artist's version of an early production of *La fille mal gardée* attests to the ballet's charm and hence its longevity. Courtesy of the Author.

74

vention of the comedy ballet. *La Fille mal gardée,* his most famous work, has been in the repertory of the Royal Ballet and American Ballet Theatre, although the original choreography has been lost. Like Angiolini, Dauberval also used scenes from everyday life as his inspiration and his emphasis on rustic and comic aspects added to the development of character dance.

Among those personalities remembered for their technical ability as dancers were Pierre and Maximilian Gardel, the latter being one of the first dancers in history to accomplish a triple pirouette. Anne Heinel was a German dancer, distinguished as the first woman to perform pirouettes *à la seconde,* a feat which was facilitated by her heelless shoes. The illustrious Vestris family were all dancers of the first order. Gaëtan Vestris, pupil of Dupré and the glory of the Paris Opera, displayed the grand and stately manner of his great teacher. Gaëtan married his talented pupil, Marie Allard, whose extremely feminine style earned her the most extensive praise from critics and public alike. Their celebrated son, Auguste Vestris inherited his father's popular title as "God of the Dance" and reigned supreme during his long career at the Opera. An amusing anecdote relates that the older Vestris publicly acknowledged that only his son Auguste was his superior as a dancer by stating that, "The explanation is simple. Gaëtan Vestris is his father, an advantage which Nature has denied me."

CHARLES DIDELOT AND THE BALLET IN RUSSIA

The theatrical dance had been slowly developing in Russia from the time of Peter the Great. In 1698, Peter had made the princely grand tour of Europe and had become enamoured of Western Culture. Wishing his own land to forsake its vast cloak of medievalism, Peter began the habit of importing numerous European artists and artisans to westernize Russia. He had grown particularly fond of French masquerades and, so, instituted them at his court. In keeping with the precedent for importing Western culture, Czarina Anna commissioned Jean Baptiste Landé in 1734 to teach French court dances to the cadets in an aristocratic military school. Delighted with the natural aptitude of his Russian pupils, Landé sought permission to teach them the steps of the *danse d'école.* Several years later, these same students appeared in the first professional ballet divertissement of an Italian

Opera. At the same time, Landé founded the St. Petersburg Ballet School. Hence, there was created an educational institution that was continuously filled with students to supply the Russian theatres with dancers. While a number of the dancing masters and the large *corps* of dancers were now Russian, the choreographers and stars were still imported from France or Italy.

From the early 1700's, rich landowners, emulating the Imperial support of the ballet, instituted satellite ballet schools in which they employed dancing masters to instruct their serfs to perform in the strict *danse d'école* as well as the brilliant native folk dances. These serf dancers were often wonderfully skilled artists whose lives centered around dancing class, rehearsals and working in the fields. They were bartered or sold into the public theatres or remained to dance in the provincial theatres of their owners. By the early 1800's, serf dancers ceased to exist due to the expense of their training, and the Imperial ballet schools could sufficiently supply the theatres with competent dancers. Today the distinctly Russian quality in the Bolshoi Ballet in Moscow can be traced back to an energetic style first developed by this sociological phenomena known as the serf dancers of Russia.

By the 1750's, many events conspired to provide Russian theatrical dance with a healthy atmosphere for growth and generation. Public theatres in St.Petersburg were not uncommon and admission to the opera-ballet could be gained by the nominal price of a ticket. Prior to this time, admission to theatres was only possible via one's aristocratic birth and as often as not admission depended on a royal invitation. Eventually Hilferding and his pupil, Angiolini, worked in St. Petersburg and Noverre's precepts on the *ballet d'action* were disseminated by his disciples and his well-read publication, *Lettres sur la Danse*. What's more, advanced balletic ideas were appreciated by the keen, theatre-going Russian audiences. Noverre's emphasis on the importance of expressiveness in dancing found fertile ground in the deeply sensitive slavic personality. In 1766 Catherine the Great founded the Directorate of the Imperial Theatre which gave further status and support to the development of ballet. Dancers continued to entertain the court, but they now enjoyed the introduction of certain advanced notions such as performing for a paying public and receiving state pensions for their services.

Ivan Valberg, a pupil of Angiolini in St. Petersburg, was the first native Russian teacher and choreographer of note. He was familiar with Noverre's precepts as well as the decadent style of the Paris Opera, this being information he gleaned from a brief visit to France in 1792. Valberg's own ballets sprang from Noverre's seminal ideas on mime and dance and he proceeded to create characters based on historical or literary personalities. In so doing, he inaugurated an aesthetic trend toward the sentimental in ballet. It is this tendency that marks Valberg as a forerunner of the Romantic era. In 1794, Valberg was appointed director and manager of the Imperial Ballet School in St. Petersburg and he was responsible for setting the school on a solid foundation. Throughout his career and until his death in 1819, Valberg continued to form many excellent Russian dance artists. As a consequence, when Didelot arrived in Russia in 1801, it was a fairly sophisticated dance atmosphere which the Frenchman entered.

Charles Didelot (1767-1837)

While the French Revolution of 1789 had disrupted the country's life, it was, oddly enough, beneficial to the growth of the ballet. Many French dancers at the Paris Opera left the country to find employment and opportunity in England and other parts of Europe. Thus was the composite of technical knowledge, and specifically the *ballet d'action* as developed by Noverre and his contemporaries, further extended. Due to the dispersal of dance artists throughout the continent, France temporarily relinquished its position as the mecca of ballet. Russia was the country which would assume responsibility for furthering the evolutionary process of ballet with a superabundance of artistic success. The individual most instrumental in this movement was Charles Didelot (1767-1837) who worked in Russia on two extended and highly productive occasions.

Didelot's father had been first dancer and choreographer at the Royal Swedish Theatre. Displaying considerable talent, the young Charles was sent by the Swedish King to Paris to study dance. As a student of Dauberval and the Vestris family, he had the best possible training in the tradition of the *danse d'école*. But he, too, suffered the same frustrations as Noverre in not being acceptable to the administration of the Paris Opera. Although his debut there as a dancer was a personal success, professional envy and the usual petty intrigues associated with the history of the Paris Opera kept him from realizing his enormous creative ambitions. Like Noverre before him, Didelot sought a better working atmosphere and soon enjoyed considerable professional experience and success in London. While there he was fortunate to dance in the ballets of Noverre and Gardel. He also staged a remarkable production of *Zéphyr and Flore* in which he deftly employed flying machines which emphasized his ballet's etherial thematic material. Hence, Didelot extended the path toward the Romantic ballet in that he presented a classical theme couched in fantasy and illusion which, in turn, was heightened by mechanical devices. Another novelty introduced in this London production was the ballerina occasionally rising on the points of her slippers. Lawson suggests that this novel effect initially resulted from the dancer momentarily holding her position as the flying machine took her weight in preparation for a suspended flight. That the dancer herself was standing on the point of her foot was, of course, illusory but the idea was born that such a desirable effect as the use of the *pointes* could be developed into a technical reality.

Due to the need for financial security which London could not offer and only a permanently state-supported ballet could, Didelot chose not to remain in England. Instead, he contracted to go to St. Petersburg as a dancer and ballet master because the new Russian culture was enjoying a period of unprecedented growth, thanks to Imperial as well as public support of the theatre. Didelot's first stay in Russia (1801-1811) centered on the development of dance training. As ballet master, he extended the period of dance schooling beyond the usual two or three years. He instituted the study of mime as well as music and, of course, he introduced the use of supported lifts to his students in St. Petersburg. In 1811 he left his Russian position and returned to spend a successful period of choreographing ballets in London. But, in 1813 he hastened to Paris to accept the coveted position of ballet master at the Paris Opera. Once again, the Opera responded to innovative ideas with hostility and sabotage. Didelot, however, had the last word regarding his professional worth when he produced a new and brilliant version of his *Zéphyr and Flore*. This was followed by enthusiastic offers from the die-hard directors mixed with more disillusionment. As a result of this trying situation, Didelot returned to Russia and produced many great pantomimic ballets which were presented as vehicles for the growing number of excellent Russian dancers. He also created new works which did not rely on mythology. In these new, realistic ballets such as *The Hungarian Horse* and *Prisoner of the Caucasus* he developed scenes which effectively mixed the comic and tragic styles of dancing.

Didelot's pedagogy and his choreography centered around a new synthesis toward artistic expressiveness in dance. His dancers were firmly grounded in mime and his ballets accomplished a new level of dramatic action. In addition to his use of such innovations as point work, expressive *pas de deux,* and simple lifts, he shaped a Russianized *danse d'école* with a brilliant understanding of the Russian body and its artistic potential.

Didelot's most significant legacy to the balletic corpus of knowledge was his development of the danced mime or mimed dance. In Noverre's *ballet d'action,* mime and dance had been separate entities, each of which were employed to enhance the dramatic line. Didelot merged these two facets of Noverre's dance so that the mimed part necessary to the drama took on the quality of dance movement and the dancing integrated significant gesture into its flow of movement. He furthered the development of the *pas de deux* by eliminating the man and woman's dual performance of the same steps and supplied, instead, varying steps denoting dramatic interaction for each dancer. He, thereby, created a conversation in movement previously hinted at in the isolated artistry of Sallé. The male-female relationship in the *pas de deux* was more distinctly contrasted in that Didelot devised simple lifts to express the dominant role of the male while emphasizing the submissive and womanly qualities of the female.

SALVATORE VIGNANO AND THE ITALIAN CHOREODRAME

Perhaps the only contemporary to rival Didelot's work in terms of innovative contributions was Salvatore Vignano (1769-1821). During the rampage of the French Revolution, while Didelot was doing his early work in London, Vignano was emerging as a unique, creative artist in his native Italy. His background could not have better prepared him for his career as a choreographer. He came from a family of dancers, musicians and intellectuals who provided him with the ideal professional education such as was set forth in Noverre's *Lettres.*

As a young man Vignano had impressed the celebrated Dauberval who saw to it that Vignano learned the whole inheritance of the *danse d'école* which at that time was tempered by the critical attitude of Noverre. As a young artist Vignano accepted engagements in Venice,

Vienna and Milan. During this period, he collaborated with his family friend, Beethoven, to create his fledgling work, *The Creatures of Prometheus.* With this experience, Vignano's artistic direction began to solidify. Leaving virtuosity and the mimed equivalent of spoken words behind, he directed his conception of dramatic dance toward expressive gesture which he envisioned would be rigorously set to music. This form of dance art he referred to as *choreodrame,* a heightened form of the musical drama which had employed both movement and music.

Vignano's *choreodrame* was characterized by its realistic settings, and genuine pantomime was used to supplant conventionalized gesture. The dance movement in the *choreodrame* was a combination of expressive, realistic gesture and traditional dance perfectly cadenced in its subordination to the music. Vignano dispensed with the large *corps de ballet* performing gestures in unison. Instead, each dancer retained his individuality within plastic groupings in which minutely specified movements were precisely set to the music. To emphasize the total expressive effect of the dancers, he often dressed them in tunic-styled costumes of softly draped fabric. Kirstein notes that Vignano was probably the first choreographer to achieve the ancient ideal of a perfect synthesis of music, dance and mime. He consumed vast amounts of time on developing and putting together his ballets which perhaps caused him to be less prolific than Noverre and Didelot. His special talent for creating this highly expressive use of dance lay in his predilection for painstaking detail. So ingenious in its precision was his coordination of dance, mime and music that he died without disciples or imitators to carry on the *choreodrame* for there was no one of his stature who could reproduce such complex dance innovations.

Although Vignano made an impact on the ballet of his time, his rhythmic pantomime perfectly subordinated to music would probably seem less like dancing to our modern mind just as it did to some of his critics. His work, while differing from that of Didelot in style, nevertheless emphasized the expressive possibilities inherent in dance movement. Both gentlemen were genuine precursors of the Romantic era. While Didelot's choreography and his pupils actually carried over into the early years of the Romantic period, Vignano, during his life, was able to show the art world a fresh, if not long-lasting, conception of the ballet.

Aside from the creative innovations of Noverre, Valberg, Dauberval, Didelot and Vignano, the early 1800's had its share of lesser talents who hacked out inferior copies according to formulas which resulted from the life work of first-rate artists. The ballets of such labors were staid conventionalities devoid of purpose or meaning, and so for a time, ballets once again became dull spectacles or vehicles for the dancer's technical display.

To sum up, the middle of the 18th century saw the ballet firmly established as a profession, but radically in need of artistic guidance. The giant of the age was Jean Georges Noverre, father of modern ballet. His life work centered around identifying all the most expressive elements of the art of dance as he knew them in his time, and casting them anew into his vital conception of the *ballet d'action*. Noverre dealt with the molding of the individual dancer as artist and technician. He also raised the art of choreography to new heights of expressive possibilities by examining the very nature of theatrical dance itself. Under the influence of Noverre, European and English dance experienced a forceful rebirth which, in many instances, is ongoing in 20th century ballet and modern dance.

Charles Didelot was Noverre's counterpart in Russia by way of his own innovative influence. He was familiar with Noverre's intent of furthering the development of the ballet as an expressive rather than a decorative art, so that his chief intent in creating a ballet was the "soulful expression of an idea." Aside from his productive teaching, wherein he expanded the Russian dancers' knowledge of ballet steps beyond the meager twenty-five or so in their repertoire, Didelot's most significant creative contribution was the development of the *pas de deux,* simple lifts and the techniques of flying dancers on wires for the rendering of illusory, artistic effect. Didelot also managed to forge a technique for the dancer's execution of more refined pirouettes and he developed the dancer's feet for the rudimentary moves of *pointe* work years before the blocked toe shoe came into being. So all-encompassing was his great life work that the Danish ballet master, August Bouronville, noted upon viewing the ballet of Didelot's later years in Russia, that it was superior in quality to that of Paris.

Salvatore Vignano, who lived somewhat later than Noverre, was only indirectly influenced by the ideas of the master. Yet, Vignano's artistic accomplishments centered around perfectly synchronized works of dance, mime, music, and meaning which he called *choreodrames.*

REFERENCES

Brinson, Peter. *Background to European Ballet.* Leyden; Netherlands: A.W. Sijthoff Printing Division, 1966.

Kirstein, L. *Dance, A Short History of Classic Theatrical Dancing.* Brooklyn:: Dance Horizons, 1969.

Lawson, J. *A History of Ballet and Its Makers.* London: Chameleon Press, Ltd., 1973.

Lynham, D. *The Chevalier Noverre.* London: Chameleon Press, Ltd., 1972.

Migel, P. *The Ballerinas, From the Court of Louis XIV to Pavlova.* New York: MacMillan Co., 1972.

Roslavleva, N. *Era of the Russian Ballet, 1770-1965.* New York: E.P. Dutton & Co., 1966.

Searle, H. *Ballet Music.* New York: Dover Publications, Inc., 1973.

Swift, M.G. *A Loftier Flight.* Middletown, Conn: Weslyan University Press, 1974.

SUGGESTIONS FOR FURTHER READING

Cohen, S. *Dance as a Theatre Art.* New York: Dodd, Mead & Co., 1974.

Kirstein, L. *Movement and Metaphor.* New York: Praeger Publishers, 1970.

Lynham, D. *The Chevalier Noverre.* London: Chameleon Press, Ltd., 1972

CHAPTER 6

The Romantic Ballet

The Romantic era refers to a period in 19th century Europe in which the Romantic style of theatrical dance was but one of a multitude of historical manifestations. Paramount among the artistic trends of the times were a return to nature, the exaltation of feeling and a desire to transcend the human condition. Like all advances in the aesthetic development of mankind, the Romantic era's art forms emerged from a violent reaction to a number of factors which were social, political, economic and philosophical in essence. For instance, the French Revolution had shown the European that he could, by force if necessary, determine his political fate. Along with this newly liberated mentality, went an equal amount of social responsibility which the newly altered class structure was not yet equipped to handle and this caused further political upheaval. Massive social change, coupled with the novel complexities of rapid economic growth such as the Industrial Revolution, blanketed continental Europe and England with an avalanche of evils that rivaled a decadent monarchy or the Napoleonic Wars. The Industrial Revolution with its large-scale manufacturing resulted in overcrowded cities, and a waning agrarian life also contributed to the overwhelming socio-economic problems affecting the greater part of society. Thus, the spirit of the times was one of striving to discover meaning in the nature of human events and this effort was uniquely reflected in its art and literature.

EXPRESSIVENESS IN THE BALLET

French and German artists and writers responded to the trying, post-Napoleonic years with aesthetic principles based on escapism. Because much of life was dismal and sordid, it seemed preferable that their artistic creations should aspire to represent expressions of an ideal world filled with poetic love, delicate feelings and exotic places peopled with poignant sylphs. In developing the emotional aspect of the Romantic style, therefore, the artists of the era were revolting against the previous age of reason when excessive attention was placed on the form of an art work as opposed to its content. As we have seen, prior to the 1830's, the ballet had so deteriorated that instead of being a vehicle for the expression of human experience, it comprised, at its worst, a showcase for ceaseless pirouetting and other acrobatic tricks devoid of meaning. The fresh ideas of Noverre's neo-classicism had become conventionalized and what had been so gloriously new in the structure of the works of Noverre, Dauberval, Didelot, and Angiolini developed into a frozen and formalized tradition. In the interim between the peak of neo-classicism and the advent of Romanticism, it was considered heretical to suggest change, especially in Paris where the aged Pierre Gardel still directed the Opera. Albeit, as time passed, the momentum for change built up until resistance was no longer possible. The artists and writers of the early Romantic age, therefore, sought to de-emphasize stylized form and accent the creation of content characterized by lyrical and dramatic narrative. Thus, the Romantic ballet was noted for its emphasis on an escape into a fantasy world where the growing working class audiences could empathize with the alternately intense and delicate emotions of human beings interacting with unworldly creatures.

The significance of the Romantic ballets was their appealing and often profound emotional content. In the two greatest ballets of the period, *La Sylphide* and *Giselle,* the librettos dealt with the realism of rustic settings juxtaposed to the ethereal world of fairy creatures. Not only did this dual aspect of contrasting worlds depicted in Romantic ballets provide the interest of contrasting styles, but it enriched the dance's store of thematic content as well as the choreographic mode and the dancer's technique. For example, the realistic or local color portion of *La Sylphide* and *Giselle* used the *terre à terre* steps of the *danse d'école* and the character and demi-character styles introduced by Dauberval. The unreal or fantasy parts of the ballets called for a greater development of the aerial aspects of the *danse d'école*. That is, *ballon* or the quality of lightness in a dancer's movement signified the epitome of her achievement as an interpreter of the ethereal. During this period, the use of point work became mandatory for all female dancers since it provided the ultimate suggestion of weightlessness proper to the nature of the unreal creatures depicted in the ballets of the period. The first point shoes were delicate, close-fitting, satin slippers which were part of the fashion of the times. They were reinforced around the leather sole and the toes with extra stitching and featured long ribbons which were wound about the ankle. Not until 1880 were the first blocked shoes introduced so that the Romantic dancer had to develop her foot and ankle strength without artificial aids.

Technical improvements in the theatre itself furthered the attainment of the ideal Romantic stage setting. The use of gas lighting increased the potential for atmospheric fantasy and designers were able to achieve effects of breath-taking illusion unheard of before this time. Rustic scenery strove to be realistic, while machines designed to fly or "magically" move dancers short distances heightened the fantasy of the ballet's unrealistic aspect. Peasant-style costumes were designed accordingly to contrast with the bell-shaped gossamer layers of the white "Romantic tutu" of sylphs and wilis. Maillot, designer at the Paris Opera, contrived the first tights, which became standard leg covering for all dancers on stage and in the classroom and to this day, French dancers commemorate his invention when donning their "maillots".

Music assumed a new importance in the Romantic ballet in that it was asked to evoke the contrasting atmospheres of the real and unreal aspects of the ballet. Before 1820, very few great composers had been seriously associated with ballet and then never for very long. An exception to this rule occurred in 19th Century Russia when Glinka introduced principles of symphonic development of the score so that the dance music in his operas grew out of an integral whole. These dance pieces remain fine examples of first-rate ballet music. In France, Adolphe Adam composed the score for *Giselle* which was so sensitively related to the scenario, choreography, and decor that ballet music attained a new level of development.

Due to the thematic material of the Romantic ballets, the female dancer reigned supreme. Although there were some very good male dancers, notably Jules Perrot, most were used merely to porter the idolized ballerina around the stage. Not only were male dancers ignored and even scorned by critics, but eventually they participated only as teachers and choreographers, their dancing roles often assumed by women en *travesti*. Comparatively few male dancers were enrolled in the professional ballet schools by mid-19th century. While the lack of significant participation of the male as dancer in the Romantic ballet was deplorable, the situation was not a totally negative factor in that the emphasis on the female dancer allowed for enormous strides in the development of the ballerina's technique. Let it not be forgotten that while the women were celebrated as dancers, it was the genius of a number of men who provided them with the pedagogical and choreographic advancements on which their individual fame rested. While the Romantic ballet's peak years were brief (1830–1845), they possessed a creative intensity which served to synthesize the cummulative results of well over one hundred years of dance experience and experiment into a veritable golden age.

Théophile Gautier

The Romantic ballet enjoyed a very great popularity and much of what we know of its dancing is due, in part, to the author, Théophile Gautier (1811–1872). Gautier was not only a prolific and articulate critic of dance who commanded a lucid literary style, but he was one of the brilliant poets of the age. His deep interest in the ballet led him to research and even create the scenarios for several ballets. That a literary artist could provide choreographers with first-rate thematic material for their ballets greatly added to the quality of the final product of many of the Romantic ballets. Furthermore, the association of an illustrious literary figure like Gautier with the ballet gave the art a unique status not previously enjoyed. Thus, the Romantic ballet was forged by the accumulation of decades of technical development, but triggered much of its own unique synthesis by being grounded in the stimulating literary and intellectual genius of the epoch. Gautier, himself, commented that the Romantic movement was. . .

> akin to the Renaissance. A sap of new life circulated impetuously. Everything sprouted, blossomed, burst out all at once. The air was intoxicating. We were mad with lyricism and art. It seemed as if the great lost secret had been discovered, and that was true: We had discovered the lost poetry.

Broadly speaking, the Romantic period emerged from a reaction to the late 18th century neo-classicism, which in turn revived certain aspects of the classicism of the Italian Renaissance. Gautier's use of the word "Renaissance" to describe the creative activity of the Romantics is somewhat misleading, therefore, in that he intended for the term to indicate the spirit of the times rather than any 15th century similarity to the tastes of antiquity. In retrospect, we are able to see that the Romantic period, in light of its own spiritualism, essentially picked up where the Middle Ages left off. It was the interest of many 19th century scholars to collect and preserve the heritage of those legendary deeds of the Crusades and the age of chivalry which gave rise to so much rich folkloric tradition still in evidence in the 19th century. Just as artists of the Renaissance had an insatiable curiousity in the archeological ruins of antiquity, so did the 19th century Romantics dreamily contemplate the disintegrating gothic cathedrals, long-ignored medieval manuscripts, folklore in legends of death dances and the theatrical imagery evoked by enamel and ivory artifacts which served as the font of their artistic conceptions.

While the genius of Gautier was felt both as a poetic story-weaver and dance critic during the Romantic age, his interests were shared by other literary contemporaries such as Scribe, Nourrit and Saint-Georges. Together these men and others of less historical significance produced ballet narratives which espoused both dream worlds and local color, set in the historical context of Gothic tales. Guided by the wealth of literary knowledge of scenarists, the ballet was able to stir emotions and ignite the imaginations of an audience as never before.

Carlo Blasis

Carlo Blasis (1797–1878) was not only an important figure in the development of the Romantic ballet, but our own era which is witness to the most incredulous technical feats, is indebted to his pedagogic theories more than any other individual up to his time. Born in Milan and educated in the classics, painting, sculpture and music as well as dance, he had the best possible background for a choreographer and teacher. He had studied in Bordeaux with Dauberval and was thereby instructed in the precepts of Noverre. He also attributed much of his development to Gardel and Vestris from whom he learned the pirouette and later analyzed it so significantly for his own students.

Blasis gave up performing at an early age due to a leg injury. In 1830 he published his *Code of Terpsichore*, subtitled *The Art of Dancing*, which became the standard European ballet instruction. The *Code of Terpsichore* not only gives the history and aesthetics of ballet, but its technical theory rooted in the *danse d'école* expounded many of the precise formulas in use today. Blasis methodically applied the physical laws of equilibrium to the human body and this approach in turn gave rise to contemporary notions of balance, placement, alignment, centeredness, and turnout. In addition, he was the first ballet master to consistently demand from his students the aplomb that is associated with the bearing of a dancer. His geometrical interpretation of the classical ballet positions developed in his students a sense of the same body placement and alignment which today's dancers strive to achieve.

The structure of the 20th century ballet class stems from Blasis's own class procedure in that the dancer begins with *pliés* followed by various forms of *petit* and *grand battement, terre à terre* steps, the *grand adagio, pirouettes* and *allégro.* Blasis made a point of analyzing the various body types and how certain physical characteristics of a dancer relate to his unique, natural style and movement qualities. Blasis' manual is illustrated with his own fluid drawings and while present tastes demand higher leg extensions, more fully stretched arms and thinner bodies, his drawings reflect the same consummate grace, perfectly balanced poses and solidly placed pelvises stipulated in current teaching methods.

In 1837, Blasis was installed as the Director of the Imperial Academy of Dancing and Pantomime in Milan. Due to the introduction of his stringent classical methods and ideals into the Academy, Italy recovered its reputation as an important dance center of Europe. From this citadel were developed dancers and teachers who spread his precepts over the Continent and in time, the world. Blasis, paralleling some of the pedagogical works of Filippo Taglioni, improved and enlarged the techniques of ballet. He devised long combinations of steps known as *enchaînements* to develop lung capacity, leg strength, and stability in the dancer so that the dancer could cope with the new complexities which choreographers were inventing. So swift was the technical development that only a generation before difficult *enchaînements, pirouettes* and a rich variety of steps were unheard of. Blasis prize pupil, Lepri, taught Cecchetti who became in turn, ballet master in 1911 to that amazing Russian exodus of Diaghiliev dancers. Through Cecchetti's influence on these dancers, his methods are inextricably mixed with the schools of today's dance centers in Continental Europe, England, the United States, Canada, South America, South Africa and Australia.

Taglioni: Symbol of Ballet's Golden Age

Marie Taglioni (1804–1884) was the earliest and the most renowned of the Romantic ballerinas. She had been trained by Jean Coulon and her father, Filippo Taglioni, a ballet master at the Paris Opera and eventually danced only in ballets he created for her. Taglioni's effect on dance technique was both revolutionary and extensive. After the extraordinary debut of her art, novel for its effortless perfection, all the dancers who saw her wished to "taglionize" their own technique. It was said that no language could describe her motion and that she "swims in your eye like a curl of smoke or a flake of down". While Marie did not originate dancing on point, she was the first ballerina to meaningfully incorporate this feat into her performances as the ultimate artistic expression of the unworldly aspects of Romantic ballets. Up to then, dancers were occasionally known to display their strength by rising on point, but this was generally viewed as a trick and no definite techniques had yet been devised to teach its accomplishment. Ivor Guest notes that when dancers prior to Taglioni were seen to rise on point, there were few exceptions that were not accompanied by bulging muscles and heaving shoulders, an effect which must have been vulgar indeed. Under the ceaselessly demanding eye of her father, Taglioni presented the dance world with not only an effortless quality in her dancing, but an artful use of the *pointes*. Thereafter, every female dancer was obliged to follow suit and once the artistic and technical potentiality of dancing on *pointe* was understood, the ballerina became supreme while the male was relegated to the demeaning role of her porter.

Certainly, Taglioni had a natural grace and a talent for movement, but her extraordinary lightness was something which had been envisioned by her father and taught to her by means of his genius as a teacher. Various accounts tell how she would religiously devote two of her six hours of daily practice to foot exercises which made her soundless landings the sensation of Paris, and how she worked at special exercises to maintain the pliability of her leg joints. In other words, Taglioni's very great art was as much the product of her talent as it was her own enormous effort and the visionary artistic and technical objectives set by her father. It is unfortunate that Filippo did not leave a permanent, written legacy for surely he was a most gifted teacher and could have had a more fully credited impact on posterity if we knew

Fig. 1. This portrait of Marie Taglioni in *La Sylphide* illustrates many of the contrasting elements found in ballets of the Romantic age. Courtesy of the New York Public Library for the Performing Arts.

him better. What we do know, however, is that behind every great dancer in history, there is at least one predominant personality responsible for shaping the dancer. In view of Marie's historic career,

Filippo himself was certainly one such inspired and outstanding artist-teacher.

Filippo Taglioni achieved his greatest creative work in devising ballets to display his daughter's unique qualities. His most famous ballet was *La Sylphide* (1832) and with an original score by Schneitzhoeffer, it skillfully combined a rustic Scottish setting and the presence of ghostlike sylphs. This production, besides providing Marie with a superlative vehicle for her talent, introduced to Europe an artistic use of point work, the famous billowing white costume called the Romantic tutu, and the perfect synthesis of a Romantic theme. A break-

Fig. 2. Eric Bruhn and Rudolph Nureyev in *La Sylphide*, National Ballet of Canada. Photo courtesy of Linda Vartoogian.

through was made, too, in the evolution of the *port de bras* in *La Sylphide*. Filippo wished to bring out the contrasting effect of the gossamer sylphs in the midst of Scottish highlanders and he did so by devising the sylph's arm movements in such a way that they appeared to be weightlessly responding to the pressure of the air. Likewise, the footwork reflected the differences of the real and unreal worlds. Exuberant folk dance steps of the highlanders were a marked contrast to the quality of the Sylph's ethereal point work and *ballon*.

The particular chemistry of Taglioni's talent and the scenario by Nourrit for *La Sylphide* enjoyed a triumph which established the archetype of form and taste which the Romantic ballets would follow. *La Sylphide* is the story of a sylph who falls in love with James, a Scotsman about to marry his childhood sweetheart. Torn between the real and the ideal woman, the young man chooses to leave his fiancée and pursue the air-like creature. He accepts an enchanted scarf from a witch he had insulted earlier in the ballet. When he innocently places the fabric around the sylph, her wings fall off, she dies and more sylphs appear to bear her aloft to a fairy heaven.

The introduction of gas light illumination in theatres made gradual variations in light intensity possible for this exciting new ballet. Moreover, house lights were now lowered during the performance, whereas in the previous century, the entire stage and house areas were lit by hundreds of candles. At this time, it became the custom to lower the house curtain between acts so that scenic surprises could be arranged. All in all, *La Sylphide* contained the right combination of reality and the supernatural which caught and held the imagination by means of ingenious new mechanical and lighting techniques.

Catering to the tastes of the time, *La Sylphide* was an enormous artistic revelation as well as a public success. It was often observed, however, that every ballet which Filippo created and Marie danced in thereafter was *La Sylphide* all over again. Be that as it may, their conception, production, and interpretation of *La Sylphide* represented the ballet's finest achievements up to that time.

THE CREATIVE HIGHPOINT: GISELLE

In 1835, the great German poet, Heinrich Heine published *De l'Allemagne,* a collection of ancient Slavic folktales. Upon reading Heine's book six years later, Théophile Gautier found the perfect inspiration for a new ballet. *Giselle,* a work which came to epitomize Romantic ballet, was to be the creative highpoint of the period with its remarkable synthesis of scenario, choreography, music, decor, and lighting. While this work was being created, *La Sylphide* was not yet ten years old, and in the evolutionary process of ballet, many of its innovations were borrowed and grew into traditions. For example, the concept of the heroine, who is a supernatural creature superior to the man she loves, was repeated in *Giselle,* as well as later ballets. The style of costuming was also borrowed from *La Sylphide.* Colorful peasant costumes in the first acts of both ballets contrast with the tight bodices, wings, and full white skirts of the fantasy creatures who appear in the second acts of each ballet.

Giselle, more than any other ballet of the era, was the milestone in establishing the choreography as the central means for communicating a narrative. In other words, the choreographic intent was primarily conceived to present dancing for its own sake in a perfectly contrived dramatic frame. Its story-line was not relayed by formal pantomime, nor was the story meant to moralize. Rather a compositional device, termed the *leitmotiv,* was introduced whereby various ballet steps and gestural motifs uniquely associated with each role corresponded to matching musical themes. As the ballet progressed, these movement motifs and musical themes accumulated and served to act as aural and visual reminders of the characters passing from one situation to the next. In this way, *Giselle* perfectly expressed a story through the dancing itself while its musical structure underscored and reflected the meaning inherent in the choreography. Due to the unity of conception on the part of its talented creators, *Giselle* proved to be an artistic work capable of penetrating the sensitivities of an audience to a profound degree.

The story of *Giselle* was rooted in Slavic legend but theatrically elaborated on by its authors, Gautier and Saint-Georges. Giselle, a peasant girl falls in love with a nobleman whose real identity is kept secret. When she discovers the truth, she succumbs to madness and kills herself with his sword. In the second act the remorseful prince carries lilies to Giselle's grave and is surrounded by the ghosts of other young women who died unrequited. Giselle has joined these will-o-the-wisps and is commanded by their queen to dance her beloved to death. As the night wears thin, however, Giselle's intense and pure love spares the young man as she vanishes into her tomb.

Fig. 3. Carlotta Grisi and Jules Perrot performing the *pas de deux* from *Giselle,* Act I. Courtesy of the New York Public Library for the Performing Arts.

Carlotta Grisi and Jules Perrot

Giselle was created in 1841 for Carlotta Grisi, a beautiful Italian-trained, Austrian dancer who was one of the age's five great ballerinas. Grisi (1819–1899) had become a pupil of Jules Perrot, himself one of the few remarkable male dancers of the age, having been taught by Auguste Vestris. By the time Grisi was 22 years old she was dancing at the Paris Opera and her special talent was noticed by press and public alike. Both Gautier and Perrot were interested in her ability and, as a consequence, the role of Giselle would be her triumphant vehicle for the next eight years. Jean Coralli of the Opera was the official choreographer for the ballet although it appears certain that Perrot created all of Grisi's dances. Since Perrot was not a member of the Opera, he could not collect royalties for his work nor could his name appear on the program. His satisfaction was obtained, no

Fig. 4. Mikail Baryshnikov and Natalia Makarova in American Ballet Theatre's *Giselle*, Act II. Photo courtesy of Linda Vartoogian.

doubt, from Carlotta's triumph in the role, for by this time, the two had long been lovers.

Throughout the Romantic period, its vibrantly forged creative intensity enlarged the scope and popularity of theatrical dance. Numerous ballets were created in Paris, all attempting to emulate the success of *Giselle* and to acclaim a new star to follow in the footsteps of Taglioni. A scurry of ballet masters, choreographers and dancers traveled back and forth between Paris and other European capitals, spreading their skills and sharing in the popularity that a new age brought to the theatre. Taglioni had danced in Russia in 1837 at the peak of her career where the public eulogized her as the "synonym of air." In 1842 *Giselle* was staged in St. Petersburg with Andreyanova who became the country's first native, Romantic-style ballerina.

In 1848 Perrot became ballet master in St. Petersburg where his talents were happily exploited. Thriving in the rich artistic atmosphere and the high quality of the disciplined dancers, he created numerous works where the dance was an integral part of the unfolding plot. Perrot spent many fruitful years choreographing and teaching in Russia and when Gautier visited the country around 1856 he was duly impressed with the quality of ballet at the Maryinsky Opera House. He admitted that Russian ballet, further refined by Perrot's presence, surpassed in development that of France, and commented that the Russian audiences were most discerning. He noted that these sophisticated balletomanes demanded ballets with several acts and involved dramatic plots which were handsomely conveyed by means of much dancing. To a large degree, it was the presence of audience expectation which ultimately shaped the ballet as a self-sufficient art in Russia. Gautier also commented on the excellent quality of both the soloists and *corps de ballet* trained by Perrot, remarking on their perfection, speed and line. He also admired the lack of coquettishness, giggling and amorous glances so prevalent in the later stages of Romantic ballet in Paris.

AUGUST BOURNONVILLE
AND THE ROMANTIC STYLE IN DENMARK

Until recent years, dance teachers and writers have had little awareness of the high level of development of the Romantic dance style in Denmark. It was August Bournonville (1805–1879) who was chiefly responsbile for an astonishing nucleus of dance activity. August had studied with his father Antoine, a French dancer and ballet master at the Royal Danish Opera, who had been a student of Noverre and thereby passed on the master's precepts to August. Later, the young Bournonville was sent to Paris to study with Coulon and the aged Vestris. During his youth, August studied and performed widely, becoming noted for his spirited, joyful, and elegant style which has become the hallmark of today's dancing Danes. He danced to great acclaim both in London and at the Paris Opera before accepting a contract in 1830 in his native land to dance, teach, and create at the Royal Danish Opera in Copenhagen.

Not long after Paris acclaimed Taglioni in the role of La Sylphide, Bournonville created his own choreography for the ballet as a vehicle for his promising student Lucile Grahn. In addition to different choreography, the Danish version of the ballet boasted a new musical score by Lovenskjold and the lead male role of James was considerably strengthened.

La Sylphide is still lovingly preserved by the Royal Danish Ballet and the numerous magical (mechanical) effects never cease to enchant the 20th century viewer just as they did well over one hundred years ago. For instance, the sylph disappears in a wink up a chimney, she gently alights the six feet from window ledge to floor without moving her legs, she vanishes from an armchair when the Scotsman wishes to conceal her presence and when she dies, she is carried off diagonally upward through the stage space by as many as ten beautifully grouped sylphs.

As Bournonville's own performing days drew to a close, his creative forces produced a number of ballets in addition to his version of La Sylphide, many of which are still in the repertory. In 1840 he composed Napoli which was inspired by a brief visit to Italy. As in most of his ballets, the Danish master interjected local color and the atmosphere of foreign lands, an exotic element which particularly pleased his audiences. In 1849 Bournonville created Konservatoriet, an enchanting recollection of his student days in Paris in the classes of Vestris. Years later he again drew on inspiration from his trip to Italy and composed Flower Festival in Genzano from which the pas de deux is frequently performed today. Bournonville ballets are unusual for the Romantic period in that they featured choreographically developed male roles. Having been a brilliant dancer himself, he geared his teaching efforts toward the preparation of technically strong male dancers who could fulfill his choreographic aspirations. At the height of his creative powers, Bournonville spent a season working at the Vienna Opera and at the Opera House in Stockholm before returning to Copenhagen. Thus, his personal influence in Europe was extensive while his ideas would also be promulgated by his more celebrated students, in particular Christian Johansson, who emigrated to Russia and would someday contribute to the artistic formation of Pavlova and Nijinsky.

In the course of Bournonville's career he absorbed and combined the most important discoveries of earlier masters in a manual written for the edification of his students. Entitled *Études Chorégraphiques*, the booklet presented his theories, many of which were rooted in ideas of Noverre and Angiolini. The technical and artistic topics under discussion reflect Bournonville's sensitivity and wisdom as an artist-teacher. From the *Études* we know his classes contained a rich variety of exercises and dance steps although he put very little emphasis on the barre work, considering it merely as a brief warm-up period. His classes demanded the acquisition of *ballon* and brilliant beats for the women as well as men. Different approaches to elevation underlined the contrast between the masculine and feminine qualities of dancing. Where the men were noted for the strength and breadth of elevated movement, the women's *ballon* was characterized by lightness and delicateness crowned with lovely arm carriage. One of the most interesting things to be found in Bournonville's writings is a list of five major qualities and their comprehensive sub-divisions which he drew up for his students in order that they could check their own progress and hopes against his expectations. It would behoove career-minded student dancers even now to consider this list.

Under the general headings of the various qualities that a dancer must have he includes the following:

Physical Qualities

1. beauty
2. vigor
3. suppleness
4. vivacity
5. musical ear

Intellectual Qualities

1. taste
2. energy

3. perseverance
4. imagination
5. harmony (i.e., emotional maturity)

Artistic Qualities

1. grace
2. lightness
3. aplomb
4. mellowness (i.e., a qualitative manner of attacking movement)
5. precision

Dramatic Qualities

1. stature (i.e., dynamic presence)
2. facial reflection of inner character
3. dynamic manner of walking
4. carriage
5. ability to communicate through gesture

Technical Qualities

1. good placement
2. turnout
3. well-shaped feet and developed arches
4. elevation
5. quickness

CULT OF THE BALLERINA

There is no question that one of the most memorable aspects of the Romantic ballet was its cultivation of the individual, female dance personality and hand-in-hand with this phenomena came the rapid growth of pedagogical innovations in classroom instruction. The new-styled, dazzling ballerina inspired a large number of dramatic ballets built around a central female character. The negative aspect of this tendency to concentrate on training female artists resulted in so few male dancers being formed that, in time, there were women taking male roles *en travesti*. Although the male was scorned as a dancer except for his respected position in Denmark and Russia, he did fill the vital roles of teacher and choreographer. Significantly, male dancers during the Romantic period served as the creators of these exquisite new ballerinas. We have already seen how Filippo Taglioni developed the genius of his daughter Marie, making her a legend in her own time while Jules Perrot immortalized Carlotta Grisi in *Giselle*.

Fanny Elssler

Shortly after Marie Taglioni's historic appearance, an Austrian dancer named Fanny Elssler (1810–1884) embarked on an equally distinguished career. A child prodigy, Elssler possessed extraordinary dance qualities which were opposite those of the ethereal Marie. Fanny was an exuberant dancer blessed with enormous powers of strength and endurance, brilliant pointwork, personal magnetism, and an instinctive theatrical flair, all of which was capped by her enchanting personal beauty. She had learned the folk dances of Spain and incorporated their lively spirit and rhythms into her own staccato style of precise, quick steps called *taqueté*. From the time of her debut at the Paris Opera, a spirited rivalry between Fanny and Marie was instituted by the Opera's director as part of a publicity campaign, and the interested public was stimulated by actual performances as well as literary commentary to join forces with the Taglionists or the Elsslerites. Before long, the balletomanes were ardently supporting either the ravishingly sensuous dancing of Elssler or the angelic floating of Taglioni.

Elssler had been born into a family of musicians, her father and grandfather having worked in the service of Joseph Hayden. In quite humble circumstances, she and her older sister, Therese, began their dance training with Jean Aumer and Filippo Taglioni in Vienna. From the start. Fanny was noticeably prettier and more talented, and Therese, who grew to be extremely tall, often partnered her in the earlier years of her sister's career. Later Therese was to choreograph dances for Fanny and even re-set ballets before she retired and subsequently married into the Prussian aristocracy.

Fanny's career was to take her to the capitals of Europe, the United States, and Cuba which, incidentally, made her a very rich woman. So great was her success in attracting audiences in America that Congress adjourned for lack of a quorum on the day she performed in Washington, D.C. She danced roles in numerous good and bad ballets of the Romantic period while she excelled in certain masterpieces such as *La Fille mal gardée* and *Esmeralda,* wherein her flair for character dancing was shown to advantage. Fanny insisted on dancing *La Sylphide* in her competition with Taglioni, but it was ill-advised in that her sensuous style was not appropriate for the role of the sylph. She mastered individual dances such as her renowned "Cachucha" which she choreographed and performed as a solo and on occasion

Fanny Elssler
in the Character of

LA CACHUCHA

ATWILL Publisher 201 Broadway NEW-YORK.

Fig. 5. Fanny Elssler exhibiting her flair for dances of Spanish origin. Courtesy of the New York Public Library for the Performing Arts.

inserted into a full-length ballet. She was praised for her superb acting as well as her brilliant style of movement, a unique combination at that time. Fanny also enjoyed considerable notoriety for her many love affairs with aristocracy and wealthy bourgeoisie. In her private life she remained mild-mannered and serene in spite of her enormous successes. Toward the end of her long career, Fanny accepted engagements to dance in Russia where she was partnered by Bournonville's student, the young Johansson. She also collaborated with Perrot on several ballets. While her physical powers were less, her supreme artistry as an actress made a lasting impression on the Russian public. In 1850 she retired and lived in Vienna until her demise in 1884. While Taglioni died forgotten and a pauper, Fanny aged in comfort and the good company of family and friends she had made over many years.

Lucile Grahn

Lucile Grahn (1819–1907) was Bournonville's most celebrated student. Known as the "Taglioni of the North", her dancing was described by Gautier as conveying "melancholy grace, dreamy abandon, nonchalant lightness, a Valkyrie walking on the snow". Having begun dancing at the age when most children learn to walk, she was an accomplished dancer at sixteen. She had worked with the despotic and possessive Bournonville from the age of ten in what was not always a calm, professional relationship. Ambitious and restless, she insisted on going to Paris in 1837 to study with Barrez, the renowned director of the Opera's ballet school. This move eventually estranged Grahn from Bournonville, as well as Denmark, and from then on she conquered the hearts of balletomanes from Paris to St. Petersburg, enjoying special successes in Germany.

Elssler, who reigned at the Opera after Taglioni had left, assumed the leading role in *La Sylphide* for herself. Due to illness one day, Elssler was not able to appear, so the director of the Opera chose to substitute Grahn in the role of the sylph. Grahn thus became recognized as a rival to Elssler at the Paris Opera during the latter's sojourn in the United States. Grahn's particular quality proved her to be more suitable for the part than Elssler and thereafter the role remained, in addition to that of Giselle, her most celebrated part.

Grahn's career was apparently not enlivened with the notoriety and emotional entanglements associated with the lives of other Romantic ballerinas. In 1856 she married an opera singer, settled in Germany, and in 1863 she retired from dancing. At first she taught privately but later became a dancing teacher at the Hoftheatre in Munich where she also choreographed for ballet and opera productions.

Fanny Cerrito

Fanny Cerrito (1817–1909) was one of the youngest of the cluster of five extraordinary Romantic ballerinas to grace the stages of Europe. While she introduced no innovative techniques as did Taglioni and Elssler, she enjoyed a spectacular career as a dancer. Born and trained in Naples, Cerrito became the darling of that city's San Carlo Opera. After conquering the dance audiences in many Italian cities, she was well received in Vienna which in turn obtained for her the position of prima ballerina at La Scala when she was only 21. Fortunately for her, Carlo Blasis had become the director of the Imperial Academy of Dancing at La Scala in 1837 and so she was able to profit from his wonderful pedagogic methods.

Cerrito's vivacious charm and stage presence tended to enhance her public image in many of the now-forgotten ballets in which she danced. While we might consider her pleasingly plump as a dancer, we know that *ballon* was one of her strongest dance qualities. Eventually she collaborated as dancer and choreographer in several interesting productions which were artistically successful and suggest that she was a dancer of considerable intelligence. In London Fanny worked with Perrot and dazzled the English public in *Alma* and *Ondine* and in the latter ballet, she herself devised some of the loveliest choreography in the work. During this period, Fanny met and later married Saint-Léon, a remarkable dancer, second only to Perrot in an age bereft of male dancers. The couple's partnership produced some unusual ballets as well as considerable professional rivalry between them. The newly wed Fanny continued to be pursued by the young gallants of the theatre, as were all the Romantic ballerinas. Jealous of his adored wife and aware of his need to create, Saint-Léon chose to accept work in Russia while Fanny pursued her separate career.

Within a few years, Cerrito and Gautier collaborated on *Gemma,* the first ballet to have hypnotism as its theme. The ballerina not only choreographed the piece, but danced the leading role as well. By the time Cerrito appeared in Russia she was past her prime. Moreover, Russia was beginning to recognize and appreciate its native ballerinas so that her success there was limited. Cerrito retired in 1856 and devoted herself to bringing up her daughter, born from one of her liaisons. Financially comfortable, she did not teach although her keen interest in young dancers caused her to keep in touch with the dance world for many years to come.

The era of the Romantic ballet was peopled with a host of many more good female dancers from Europe and England. While these dancers did not measure up to the genius of a handful of exceptional ladies, they did their share in furthering the popularity and practice of theatrical dance. Many of them would be all-but-forgotten except through the tireless efforts of dance historians by whose research they live again for us in the flowery language and the faded prints of their era.

Pas de Quatre: A Choreographic Turning Point

In any discussion of the Romantic ballet, comment on Perrot's ballet *Pas de Quatre* is essential for several reasons. First, *Pas de Quatre* was a turning point in the development of choreography in that it is generally considered to be the first abstract ballet. At a time when narrative ballets were the rage, a composition without story was inconceivable, but through the theatrical acumen of the famous London impressario, Benjamin Lumley, *Pas de Quatre* was created and remains a favorite vignette of balletic art.

Lumley had conceived the exciting possibility of presenting together several great ballerinas after Elssler and Cerrito had enjoyed a huge success appearing in a duet in 1843. While glittering solos by famous personalities were common, Lumley reasoned that a ballet with four of the greatest ballerinas, each exhibiting her particular qualities in the context of the superior choreographic ability of Jules Perrot, was bound to please and to succeed. Working directly for the impressario, Perrot arranged a group of variations presenting Taglioni, Grisi, Cerrito and Grahn. To minimize squabbling between the spoiled Grisi and the spirited Cerrito as to who would have the honor of dancing immediately before Taglioni, Perrot decreed that the more senior of them would take the enviable place. Such subtle diplomacy saved the day and aided in producing an extraordinary theatrical coup. An eye-witness description of Perrot's work is mentioned in Kirstein's *Movement and Metaphor* and is quoted here as follows:

Fig. 6. *Pas de Quatre* with Alicia Alonso in the role of "Taglioni," second from left. Ballet Nacional de Cuba. Photo courtesy of Linda Vartoogian.

The quartet commenced with an equally-balanced ensemble for the four, who had entered together simply, hand-in-hand. They then assumed posed groupings with Taglioni centered, as if paid homage by her juniors. 'A quick traverse movement' led to a brisk solo by Grahn, followed by a *pas de deux* for Cerrito and Grisi, then a series of broad leaps all across the stage by Taglioni (her specialty). Each tour de force was greeted by rising applause, acknowledged by the individual dancer's curtsy. Grahn, in a brief allegro, turned on point 'with dainty semi-circular hops'. An andante for Grisi was all coquetry and spice. This contrasted with the ensuing andantine for Taglioni and Grahn in a slower, more Romantic vein, which was interrupted by a brilliant series of turns, bounds, and balances by Cerrito. Taglioni followed in an allegro. The coda was a four-cornered contest. At the curtain call, Cerrito crowned Taglioni with a wreath of white roses while the public deluged the stage with bouquets.

Pas de Quatre served in the long run to glorify the dance rather than individual personality of the dancer. Its highly refined choreography geared to bring out the truest artistic and technical aspects of each of the brilliant, individual dancers created a new and exciting dance form complete in and of itself. As a result of this innovative ballet, theatrical dance advanced in that it demonstrated how the most exciting characteristics of each dancer could be blended with well thought out and tasteful choreographic design to form an extremely high level of dance presented in an abstract manner.

The set for *Pas de Quatre* was simply a garden landscape while the bell-shaped Romantic-style costumes were done in pale pink. Gone were the little wings of the willis and sylphs and instead the ballerinas were simply adorned with roses about their hair and on their dresses. Although Pugni's music was not distinguished, it has survived to our day intact. The original cast of *Pas de Quatre* gave only a handful of performances, although the piece itself continued to be performed for some years. Unfortunately, Perrot's choreography has been lost, but the English dancer, Anton Dolin, revived the ballet in 1941 supplying his own lovely rendition of steps and .poses.

Summary

It was during the Romantic period's soul-searching for meaning that the ballet started to catch up to the infinitely greater development of the other arts and literature. By the early 19th century, music as an example, had long reached its highest level of organization and efficiency. Music contained the capacity to express an enormous range of human aspirations and feelings while the dance remained comparatively immature as an expressive medium. Ballet's inferior existence was to be altered in the France of the 1830's when numerous choreographic advances and the improvement of production techniques in the theatre rectified the dance's imbalance in its degree of artistic attainment as compared to the other arts.

A galaxy of individuals contributed to what is commonly known as the golden age of ballet. Not only did a good number of dancers, teachers and choreographers shape the emerging dance-art, but competent poets and composers also left their respective artistic imprints. Once the artists involved in theatrical productions fully realized the possibilities open to their artistic efforts, a whirlwind of creative activity enveloped them. At the same time, and for a number of reasons, the ballet ignited the public's imagination. For the first time in dance history, performers, notably the ballerina, became idolized by the masses. Often her outrageous temperament matched her uniquely superb artistry so that her notoriety as well as her talent served to make her the first superstar. The ballet itself arrived at a turning point when the cult of the individual ballerina gave way to the emergence of the very essence of dance, i.e., choreographic structure as utilized in the creation of *Pas de Quatre*. This storyless ballet achieved for the first time the perfect blend of personality, technique and choreographic intention which exemplified the Romantic aesthetic, ''art for art's sake''. By 1850 the golden age of the Romantic ballet had all but disappeared in Western Europe. The unique enthusiasm and vision upon which it was founded faded as its brilliant creators slipped into retirement. Just as had happened in Paris a half-century earlier, Russia now became the center of ballet. As in the days of Didelot, this country would once again nurture the ballet's most significant advances for the next fifty years.

REFERENCES

Blasis, C. Translated by Mary Stewart Evans. *An Elementary Treatise Upon the Theory and Practice of the Art of Dancing.* New York: Dover Publications, Inc., 1968.
Brinson, P. *Background to European Ballet,* Leyden, Netherlands: A. W. Sijthoff Printing Division, 1966.

Bruhn, E., & Moore, L. Bournonville and Ballet Technique. New York: *Dance Horizons,* 1961.
Guest, I. *The Romantic Ballet in Paris.* London: Sir Issac Pitman and Sons, Ltd., 1966.
Guest, I. *Fanny Elssler.* London: A. C. Black, Ltd., 1970.
Guest, I. *Fanny Cerrito, The Life of a Romantic Ballerina.* London: Dance Books, Ltd., 1974.
Lawson, J. *A History of Ballet and Its Makers.* London: Chameleon Press, Ltd., 1973.
Levinson, André. *Marie Taglioni.* London: Dance Books, Ltd., 1977.
Roslavleva, N. *Era of the Russian Ballet, 1770–1965.* New York: E. P. Dutton & Co., 1966.

SUGGESTIONS FOR FURTHER READING

Guest, I. *A Gallery of Romantic Ballet.* London: New Mercury, Ltd., 1965.
Migel, P. *The Ballerinas.* New York: MacMillan Co., 1972.

CHAPTER 7
The Post-Romantic Ballet

Shortly after the star-studded presentation of *Pas de Quatre* in London, the Romantic ballet style began to show evidence of an imminent decline. The debut of the tantalizing singer, Jenny Lind, is often cited as the immediate reason. More realistically, the Romantic concept of ballet had run its creative course and the falling off was marked by a variety of reasons, including the crucial if prosaic one of dwindling box office receipts. Valiant attempts on the part of the established ballet masters and choreographers failed to come up with compositions to equal those created between 1830 and 1845. Perrot continued to compose dances often to mediocre musical scores while Joseph Mazilier made numerous choreographic efforts to revive the glory of the ballet at the Paris Opera. But their works and that of others tended to repeat what had already been done in previous years. The fatal lack of fresh creative talent was evidenced by the fact that no new ballets were produced which even approached the quality of the poetry-filled *La Sylphide* or *Giselle*. Important too in understanding the post-Romantic period is the fact that aesthetic tastes have always been altered by changing times and so what satisfied the sensibilities of one age, failed to do so in the next.

A major characteristic of the Romantic style was exhausted in that the ballerina cult was no longer successfully used as the central element in the creation of a ballet in spite of Gautier *et al.*, who continued to devise such scenarios. The artistry of Taglioni, Elssler, Cerrito, Grisi, and Grahn had been responsible for raising interest in the Romantic ballet to a fever pitch and in their startling uniqueness, each of these ladies had added vastly to the technical and interpretative horizons of the corpus of ballet knowledge. The young dancers who followed these great ballerinas, however, had not sufficient talent or did not live long enough to arrive at equal distinction. Sad circumstances too often played a part in the paucity of stellar talent. The extraordinarily gifted Emma Livry, protégé of Marie Taglioni, died of

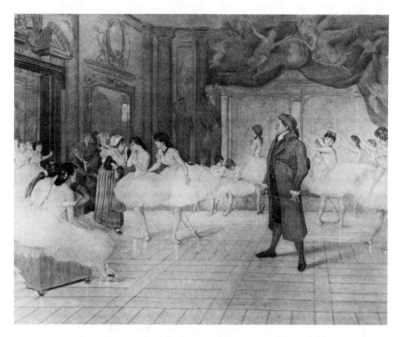

Fig. 1. Class at the Paris Opera. The decline following the golden age of Romantic ballet was characterized by a lack of creative energy and perceptive artistic direction. Courtesy of the Author.

burns as did the promising Clara Webster when their tarletan costumes caught fire from stage lighting and so their dancing was lost when the ballet needed it the most. In addition, war, malnutrition and the various 19th century diseases took their toll of many aspiring young dancers.

The deplorable lack of the use of the male in any significant sense was the Romantic age's greatest artistic flaw and this fact well contributed to the decline. In overlooking the male dancer, the Romantic ballet ignored the possibilities for developing and expanding the technical and creative range of the dance. The Romantic age of ballet in the major European dance centers, thus, spent itself. Without emerging choreographic talent and stellar dancers to forge new ideas for the next decades, the flame that was the golden age simply flickered out.

PERIOD OF DECLINE IN EUROPE

The post-Romantic period in France (1845–1870) is also known as the ballet of the Second Empire, referring as it does to the return of the Bonaparte dynasty to the throne of France. While the ballet of this period never succeeded in reviving the glory of the previous age, it did boast some achievements. Except for a few singular choreographic ideas, no artistic innovation occurred in France from the mid-1840's onward, but one exception was Mazilier's ballet *Le diable à quatre* with music by Adam. Created around a popular idea, the ballet succeeded in amusing the audience with its moralizing tone of illustrating a proverb and it started a new, if minor, vogue in ballet. With the creation of ballets like *Paquita,* more and more themes tended to be melodramatic in nature. What kept French ballet alive, if not healthy, was the institutionalization of its company and school within the structure of the Paris Opera.

Another exception is accredited to Saint-Léon who returned from Russia to produce *Coppélia* in 1870. This ballet had the advantage of his distillation of certain elements of Hungarian and Polish national dances blended with the *danse d'école,* a superior score by Léo Delibes, and a charming use of novelty. The little ballerina who created the first Coppélia, Giuseppina Bozzacchi, had only danced the role eighteen times when Paris came under siege and all theatrical activity was suspended. Due to the hardships of war and smallpox, she died on her 17th birthday and another promising talent was lost to the dance world.

By the time the Second Empire fell in 1870, those who had ushered in and sustained the Romantic ballet, were living in retirement, past their creative prime, or dead. From that time to the present, French ballet has never regained its prestige as a national artistic force, although there have been a number of individuals achieving international acclaim as dancers, choreographers, composers and scenarists.

Italy's post-Romantic years are memorable for a singular production entitled *Excelsior,* produced at La Scala and choreographed by Luigi Manzotti. *Excelsior* was an amazing mixture of theatrical show and as an extravaganza, it achieved a great success in Milan, as well as several other countries where it toured. It used a cast of five hundred people moving in precision formations and was intended to celebrate the invention of the telegraph, the construction of the Suez Canal, the

Costume for the dancers of the Csárdás in "Coppélia" Ballet with choreography by A. Saint-Léon. Presented at Théâtre Impérial de l'Opéra, Paris, 1870.

Bibho. de l'Opéra, Paris

Costume for the women dancers of the Csárdás in " Coppélia."

Costume for Dawn in " Coppélia."

Costume for Farfalla in " Le Papillon," Act I, Scene 1. Ballet with choreography by Marie Taglioni. Pres.: Théâtre Impérial de l'Opéra, Paris, 1861.

Fig. 2. 19th century costume designs emphasized the dancer's apparel rather than the lines of the body. Courtesy of the New York Public Library for the Performing Arts.

112

digging of a tunnel through the Alps, *etc*. Unusual for the time was the presence of some very good male dancers in *Excelsior*. They not only took substantial dancing roles but they were cited for their masterly partnering as well. Manzotti, however, failed to achieve an equal success in his later attempts. Such ballets became tedious repetitions of grandious but empty presentations. The public responded with indifference to these costly reviews and critics rightly declared that such dance was not worth serious attention. While Blasis' sound teaching methods kept the Milanese school turning out some extraordinarily accomplished technicians such as Legnani, Sangalli and Zambelli, these dancers were to achieve their renown outside of Italy. Without a richness of choreographic talent, the art of ballet stagnated in the very country of its birth.

In England, the post-Romantic ballet, now referred to by historians as Empire Ballet since it concurred with the British territorial amassment, became relegated to the music halls. Katty Lanner, choreographer, dancer and daughter of the renowned Viennese waltz king, emigrated to London and for many years produced frothy ballets for the Empire Theatre. Lanner's contribution to this era peaked when in 1897 the Danish ballerina, Adeline Genée, was engaged as part of the national festivities to celebrate Victoria's fifty years as reigning Queen. So popular was Genée's engagement, that she remained ten years to enchant the adoring English public. As a very old lady, Genée had the distinction of serving as the first President of the British Royal Academy of Dance when it was founded in 1954.

The Alhambra was another large London music hall that also produced Empire-style ballet. Due to size, this theatre specialized in ballets displaying spectacular effects, up-to-date topics and celebration themes. For its star material, ballerinas were generally engaged from Milan. The most famous was the pyrotechnical Pierina Legnani who will forever be remembered by ballet students as the first dancer to perform thirty-two consecutive *fouettés* in public.

The post-Romantic ballet met a stranger fate in Denmark, but lucky for us, an artistic void in Danish ballet at that time provides present dance enthusiasts with what is perhaps the clearest picture of the lyrical quality of the Romantic dance. After Bournonville's death, his disciples regarded his teaching so sacred, that nothing of his pedogogy or choreography was allowed to change. The Bournonville ballets and their special style of movement were, therefore, frozen in time and in that state of fortuitous preservation they are performed today in the same manner as over a century ago.

BALLET IN THE UNITED STATES

Ballet in the United States during the 19th century took a different shape from that of its extravagantly gilded European counterpart. While there had been a modicum of theatrical dance activity in the country from 1700 onwards, various reasons dating from the earliest settlements existed for its less than steady growth. To more fully understand this void in early American dance history, we must consider some of the contributing factors.

From the very start, theatrical dance in North America had no breeding ground. Nor did a tradition evolve for three centuries that would establish the presence of dance as meaningful in the cultural life of the country. In the 1600's, the early settlers exerted all their energies merely to sustain life in a rough new land. Starvation, disease, Indian attacks and harsh weather were only a few of the perils which the early Americans faced daily. Dance as a performing art is a product of leisure in the noblest sense of the word so it is apparent that not until a man could meet the basic needs of life, was he able to revel in artistic creative expression. When the effort to survive became less arduous and the American gained time to turn his efforts toward his aesthetic development, he had long been cut off from his ancestral cultural heritage. Certainly the American merchant and the farmer could not be expected to adopt a vigorous interest in ballet, a form of European court entertainment, since it was not available to him in any case. When the native American interest in dance did emerge around 1790, it began with performances which included a variety of movement idioms ranging from acrobatic tricks, folk dances, and questionable fragments of ballet technique.

Alien also to the early development of theatrical dance were religious reforms originating in the thought of Calvin and Huss. So far-reaching was their influence in dictating moral conduct that public merry-making and entertainment on any scale were considered degenerate and not tolerated as a part of the proscribed pattern for Christian living. The pilgrims and puritans represented the largest of the religious sects affected by the thinking of Calvin and Huss in the New World. These groups chose to profess a severe faith rooted in a firm adherence to sobriety and simplicity which were intrinsic values in the Reformation movement. The Protestant work ethic breed by the religious reformation prevailed, meaning that each man was required to fulfill his "calling," a duty inseparable from the salvation of his soul. Any activity beyond his life sustaining daily labor was frowned upon and, therefore, all forms of theatrical amusements were strictly banned by law.

By the early 1700's, cities began to grow and their internal security and prosperity helped to raise the expectation and standard of life. For some time, recreational dance had been considered an appropriate part of education so that a number of dancing masters imparted their knowledge of gigues, gavottes and minuets to the more prosperous colonists. As the quality of colonial life improved, bans against public amusement were relaxed. It is known that amateur groups were on occasion organized by an ambitious dancing master and would present entertainments wherein dancing was featured as a form of spectator amusement. A number of visiting theatrical troupes from abroad also appeared, mediocre though they were, with repertories of tight rope dancing, mime, hornpipes, tumbling, prestidigitation, and specialty acts which were often advertised as "moral lectures" to quiet the zealots of persistently staunch ethical standards. Contributing to the lack of quality in these productions was the fact that there was little money to be earned by artists when public entertainment was still looked down upon. Also, no real theatres existed in which to perform so that the better performers remained in Europe and only third-raters plied their trade on our shores.

No lasting imprint of the value of dance was felt in the next century because in 18th century America almost nothing of worth was to be seen. Consequently, at the framing of the Constitution in 1789, its authors were not pressured by the states they represented to provide for the performing arts. No stipulation calling for a Secretary of the Arts was designated by the Constitution. In defense of history, however, it is important to understand that at the time the document was written, the country was straddling the fence of a fledgling nation on one hand and possible renewed oppression from England on the other should ratification of the Constitution not occur. The authors of the Constitution had as their task to achieve a working instrument whereby the new country could operate in an effective manner. Practically speaking, the document needed to be succinct as possible and, at the same time, as open to interpretation as it could be in regard to the future.

The performing arts, particularly ballet and opera, were traditionally associated with the European royalty and being indicative of a distant aristocratic culture, they were not perceived in 1780 as a welcome or natural part of the new country. Therefore, the arts were not reckoned with in the creation of the government, in part because they really had no previous existence here, and in part because they were considered to be off-spring of a despised political heritage.

Despite the lack of ideal conditions for the early growth of a native American dance art, there were several foreign touring companies and individuals mentioned in late 18th century newspapers and pamphlets which establish the occasional presence of bona fide dance performances on our shores. Prior to the American Revolution, Lewis Hallam introduced his English troupe of entertainers on a tour of various colonial cities. In 1785, a young Philadelphian, John Durang, debuted with Hallam's company and was destined to be remembered as the first significant American professional dancer. In 1791, Alexander Placide and a number of his French compatriots immigrated to the United States in flight from the holocaust produced by the French Revolution. Besides operettas and pantomimes, the Placide repertory included French ballets which were shown in cities as far north as Hartford and as far south as Charleston. Young John Durang associated with these well-schooled stage veterans, profiting greatly from their instruction and example. By 1795, Durang had learned enough to partner the elegant Anna Gardie, a dancer from Placide's original company. Both dancers enjoyed considerable acclaim, according to the Boston press, in what could be regarded as the first full-fledged ballet in the United States. This ballet drama, called La Forêt Noire (Maternal Affection) followed a complex plot employing all sorts of daring-do and was well-received during a number of performances.

Following the American Revolutionary War, theatres were constructed at an increasing rate to meet the financial challenge represented by a successful season and in conjunction with the necessity of housing the visiting opera, mime, and ballet troupes from abroad Conversely, the presence of the theatrical houses served to whet the public's appetite for more entertainments and enterprising theatre managements did this by presenting the most popular, amusing or amazing acts that could be found.

The majority of the foreign performers were French and often had been schooled by that powerfully organized and developed body, the

Paris Opera. As theatres appeared, better artists were attracted and the form and content of dance improved until the classical ballet became a recognized, if elite, entertainment among the *cognoscenti* of the seaboard cities. To some degree, ballet's popularity was due to the exotic note lent by its very Frenchness. Even before the Revolution, things French, thanks to the uniquely dynamic flowering of French Renaissance civilization, had been considered the ultimate in taste and fashion. And now, in the United States, there were Americans informed enough to appreciate and, indeed, demand it.

Some years later, when the United States had achieved its national identity and the energy and wealth of the Industrial Revolution altered men's thinking and life-styles, theatrical entertainment came to be in demand. By the mid-1800's, theatrical enterprises from Europe could be lucrative ventures and the healthy curiosity of Americans, fed by a booming economy, were demanding the excitement and luxury of amusements which only theatrical productions could provide.

New York, Philadelphia, Boston, Richmond, and Charleston were the foremost theatrical cities and continuous invitations were extended to European troupes and individual artists to visit. A number of dancers displaced by the aftermath of the Napoleonic fray found their way to American shores and began, on a very small scale, to teach their craft. As a consequence, by the dawn of the Romantic era in Europe, some talented Americans had been developed. Among them was Mary Ann Lee who traveled to Europe and back again, to produce from memory a version of *Giselle* for the American audience. Julia Turnbull and George Washington Smith were two more American dancers who performed on programs which resembled variety shows since there were no official ballet companies. According to some critics of the time, one American was a match for the superb Romantic ballerinas. She was the remarkable Augusta Maywood and the lady had such success dancing in Europe, she never returned home.

Augusta Maywood received her early training in Philadelphia at one of America's first ballet schools run by Paul Hazard and his wife. The Hazards were products of several European opera houses and seem to have been excellent teachers, forming a number of aspiring American dancers. After only two years of classes, twelve year old Augusta made a sensational debut which led her to try her wings abroad. When the Paris Opera engaged her after she had studied with Mazilier and Coralli, the critics marveled at the unique flexibility, bouyancy and grace in the dancing style of the ballerina from the "land of savages."

Likewise, visiting European dancers had considerable impact in America, if not always personal success. Jules Perrot had danced in New York as did Paul Taglioni, Jean Petipa and his son Marius. The *danse d'école,* as absorbed into the Romantic era, was introduced to America via these dancers. Prior to their presence, few in American audiences had seen anything beyond Irish reels and Negro minstrel clogs.

When Fanny Elssler arrived in 1840, a large number of Americans were at least ready for her glamour even if they were unschooled in her art. Although the general quality of the ballets in which she appeared was far from that of the Paris Opera productions, Elssler's personal genius could not fail to penetrate the sensitivities of an essentially unsophisticated ballet audience. Within two years of her arrival, Elssler returned to Europe after countless American engagements had enriched her pocketbook. While many Americans treasured the sweet memories of Fanny's visit, her presence had been essentially the personal success of a famous and exciting foreigner. In the long run, Elssler's American tours did not generate a significant desire for the development of ballet sufficient to overcome a situation where there were almost no ballet schools and no companies to nurture it.

Both Julia Turnbull and George Washington Smith had joined Elssler's troupe in America and learned immeasurably from the experience, but lack of opportunity unfortunately kept the profession of dance a precarious and impoverished one. Although ballet had received its most significant initial airing in the United States during the Romantic epoch, it would not begin to develop as a flourishing American art until the times provided the right circumstances. Throughout the 19th century, the American interest in ballet would be confined to

As we will see in Chapter 8, the New York appearance of Diaghilev's Ballet Russes in 1916, and the later efforts of the indefatigable Anna Pavlova, planted the seeds for the 20th century American ballet which is more completely characteristic of our artistic ex-devoted presence of a fleet of teachers, schools and performing opportunities to create the foundations for a dance-aware public.

As we will see in Chapter 8, the New York appearance of Diaghilev's Ballet Russes in 1916, and the later efforts of the indefatigable Anna Pavlova, planted the seeds for the 20th century American ballet which is more completely characteristic of our artistic expressiveness than any other performing art. That the arts were not specifically provided for in 1789 was not necessarily the tragedy that it is often made out to be. Let it suffice to say that things happen in their own time as is witnessed by the immense popularity of American professional, regional, and campus ballet.

MARIUS PETIPA AND THE ASCENDANCY
OF THE RUSSIAN BALLET

Looking back on the Romantic ballet, it seems peculiar that Western Europe's glorious dance art did not metamorphize into a new and even more splendid age of kinetic expression. In France where the ballet was protected and housed by the Paris Opera, a lack of significant talent and public understanding of art contributed to its decline. In Italy, the music-loving populous was beginning to prefer the melodic operas of Rossini and Verdi to the repetitious ballet extravaganzas produced at La Scala. In London, site of many of the finest Romantic creations, the public sought to be amused rather than elevated by art and within several years of the triumph of *Pas de Quatre,* the ballet had descended to the English music halls.

While the ballet receded in the European public's eye, it was enjoying a healthy development in far-off Russia. Since 1738, ballet had received Imperial protection and support because it initially existed as a court entertainment. The talents of Valberg, Didelot and Blasis had steadily combined to develop Russia's own Romantic age which boasted intense activity. Although there were some excellent Russian dancers in St. Petersburg, foreign artists from the great dance centers of Europe were usually engaged as were foreign choreographers. We saw in Chapter 6 that the most celebrated of the Romantic ballerinas counted the adulation of Russian audiences in their lists of successes while Perrot, and later Saint-Léon, were also appreciated for their choreographic talents.

A new age dawned when a Frenchman, Marius Petipa arrived in St. Petersburg in 1847 as *premier danseur.* He eventually initiated a fresh thrust in the development of ballet which would synthesize the most significant technical advancements achieved in the Russian and European Romantic era. Born in Marseilles, France, Petipa studied with his father, Jean Petipa and with Auguste Vestris in Paris. As a very young man he partnered Carlotta Grisi and Fanny Elssler. In his youth he

Fig. 3. A modern version of Petipa's *Swan Lake*, Act III with Rudolph Nureyev, Cynthia Gregory, and Lucia Chase, American Ballet Theatre. Photo courtesy of Jack Vartoogian.

120

also traveled to the United States with his father for an engagement, but after some unfortunate financial dealings on the part of the theatre's management, they returned to Europe to seek more fruitful employment. Within a short time, the opportunity to dance in St. Petersburg presented itself and the ambitious young Frenchman embarked on the path of his destiny.

With the presence and eventual leadership of Petipa, the Maryinsky Theatre in St. Petersburg became a vital dance center while the rest of Europe witnessed a decline in the ballet. For nearly forty of the sixty years that he was in Russia, Petipa's concepts of training, choreography, and production dominated the dance at the Imperial School of Ballet and the Maryinsky, and, to a lesser extent, that of the Bolshoi Theatre in Moscow. His long tenure is attributed to his genius as well as his prodigious choreographic output. It is noteworthy that the young Petipa had spent twenty years prior to his becoming principal ballet master observing first-hand and then distilling into his own creative style the compositional approaches of Perrot and Saint-Léon. He also learned from these two highly-skilled professionals how to deal with the bureaucratic administration, how to soothe ruffled feelings and the fiery temperaments of his dancers, and especially how to please an audience. Without compromising his artistic vision, he created ballets which fit the general theatrical taste of the times and still met the hearty approval of the keenest balletomanes. From Saint-Léon he learned in these early years to tailor a ballet to the particular talent of a ballerina, and from Perrot he acquired the finer points of crafting brilliant combinations of steps. Petipa's cultivated tact and diplomatic manner dignified his work and this was, indeed, significant to the growth of the ballet in that it gave him political power in the Theatre's administration. He was thereby able to create a working mechanism for the ballet to prosper in and, at the same time, produce a viable repertory at the Maryinsky, although his singular domination at the Theatre was decried by the following generation. However, in Petipa's heyday of the 1880's and 1890's, his control contributed much to his own volume of work and to the general healthy state of the dance. On the other hand, his domination over dance at the Maryinsky was no doubt a detriment to the creative potential of his colleague, Lev Ivanov, a choreographer whose career was, for the most part, overshadowed by the master.

Early on Petipa had been responsible for the training of young dancers at the Maryinsky and the investment of those years paid off in the development of such native talents of ballerina stature as Vazem, Geltzer, Sokolova, Kschessinska and Preobrajenska. Even so, the energetic Italians continued to be imported for their verve and dazzling tricks since their glamour alone could insure sustained audience interest. The Milanese dancer, Virginia Zucchi, danced for Petipa in Russia and achieved such success that she personally inspired a number of creative people, who in the years to come, would be instrumental in reviving the popularity of ballet in Western Europe and in America. Pierina Legnani achieved immortality when Petipa utilized her special aptitudes by inserting the famous thirty-two *fouettés* into her solo in *Swan Lake,* Act III. Another Italian who danced under Petipa was Enrico Cecchetti, esteemed for his staggering endurance and technique. At the request of Petipa, Cecchetti stayed on in St. Petersburg to teach at the Imperial School where his own dance heritage, rooted in the pedagogy of Blasis, would reinforce and enrich the classroom practice of countless Russian dancers.

Among the characteristic elements in Petipa's choreography were successions of exquisite symmetric patterns for the *corps de ballet.* The master placed great emphasis on divertissementation which gave soloists the opportunity to perform choreography designed to highlight their particular qualities. For the richly designed sections of his ballets, he arranged combinations of steps which were often executed three times and then concluded with a variant step. So impressive was the final result of his compositional approach that Petipa's intricately crafted use of spectacle and spectacular dancing replaced the poetic expressionism of the previous age.

In establishing his choreographic method, Petipa analyzed the classical steps of the *danse d'école* and then categorized them according to quality and importance. He listed seven divisions which comprised the classical vocabulary from which he created his ballets:

1. Auxiliary steps (such as *failli, tombé,* and *pas de bourrée*) link one step or movement phrase with the next.
2. Large and small elevation steps (such as *pas de chat, ballonné* and *grand jeté en tournant*) contribute to the lightness and breadth of ballet movement.
3. *Batterie* or beaten steps (such as *brisé* and *entrechat quatre*) lend brilliance to the compositional structure.
4. *Port de bras* or arm movements provide the completion of the dancer's body line as well as to the design of the choreographic pattern.

5. *Pirouettes* (turning steps executed on one leg in a variety of body positions) add speed and excitement.
6. The classical poses (such as *arabesques* and *attitudes*) are effective in creating lyrical and elegant highpoints within a phrase of movement.
7. The tasteful use of *pointe* work is the finishing touch to the total compositional picture created by the first six categories.

Among Petipa's masterpieces which continue to be performed, the most popular are *Raymonda, The Bayadère, Don Quixote, Swan Lake, Sleeping Beauty* and *The Nutcracker*. The last three ballets are especially noteworthy in that they are compositions with outstanding musical scores. In these works, the revered Tchaikovsky joined Petipa in a collaboration that would, over the years, bear stunning results. Petipa, who wrote his own ballet scenarios, enjoined the great composer to coordinate precisely designated measures and counts with the moment-by-moment choreographic action. On occasion, Petipa even specified the musical instruments for a given passage of music. The choreographer was more interested in creating dances for the ballerina and often relegated large production numbers, character dances, and male variations to his assistants, Ivanov, Johansson and Legat. We can still observe an example of the product of Petipa's choreographic assignments to his subordinates in Act II and Act IV of *Swan Lake*, which were the work of the talented Lev Ivanov.

Petipa's penchant for composing *divertissements* (special dances for one or more performers) for his ballerinas was essentially a return to the classical style of the French court's *ballet d'entrèe*. It was from this approach that he created *Sleeping Beauty* in 1890. The choreographic structure of *Sleeping Beauty* employed a relatively thin plot which served to string together, in the eighteenth century manner, richly composed *divertissements*. While the technical vocabulary he used had made enormous strides since the time of Lully and Beauchamp, great elegance and dignity remained hallmarks of Petipa's work, just as they had been in the ballets produced for the Sun King.

Petipa's longevity allowed him to contribute a wealth of ballets to the dance profession and his best efforts remain a significant part of the dancer's heritage. He personally succeeded in accomplishing an about-face to the richly narrative and emotional Romantic style of ballet, thus renewing the early eighteenth century emphasis on form. Hand-in-hand with his choreographic output, he built on all the peda-

Fig. 4. *La Bayadére* choreographed by Marius Petipa in 1877. Natalia Makarova and Mikail Baryshnikov with American Ballet Theatre. Photo courtesy of Jack Vartoogian.

124

gogical advancements engineered by the improved techniques of the Romantic ballerina to evolve a classical dance infinitely more complex than the one which Feuillet had codified. Too close to his own life's work to view it as it would be reflected in historical perspective, Petipa died deposed and embittered by the younger generation at the Maryinsky. How pleased he would have been to see a number of his ballets still beloved while many of his choreographic concepts enjoy expansion a century later in the United States through the genius of George Balanchine.

Lev Ivanov (1834–1901)

Petipa's assistant, Lev Ivanov, deserves mention in a brief look at the development of Russian ballet. If Petipa's position at the Maryinsky had not been so omnipotent, there is no question that Ivanov would have achieved more opportunities, recognition and personal fulfill- ment in his work. As it was, the work Ivanov did accomplish was often circumstantial as exemplified by the time when Petipa had become ill and Ivanov assumed choreographic responsibilities for *The Nut- cracker*. Unfortunately, in this ballet Ivanov worked under handicaps in that others had already laid the groundwork for this production. Moreover, the lack of close collaboration with Petipa and Tchaikov- sky, whom he considered his betters, impaired his having a free artis- tic hand. In spite of such professional difficulties, he did manage to craft a small body of extremely refined choreography.

Ivanov's aesthetic method was to interpret the sonorous essence of the music and then transmit the idea into movement. A perfect exam- ple of this creative process is the "Dance of the Sugar Plum Fairy" from *The Nutcracker* in which the traditional steps illustrate the sound so perfectly that the dance seems to blossom from the music. The most exquisitely poetic sample of his work is preserved in his choreo- graphy for *Swan Lake* (Acts II and IV) which firmly establishes his abil- ity to weld musical phrases to expressively inventive movement. Whereas Petipa's compositional approach often made working with Tchaikovsky's symphonic-styled music a difficult task, symphonic continuity was the precise musical element that inspired Ivanov to cre- ate his expressive movement wherein the device of the *leitmotivs* heightened the emotional impact of his choreographic design. While Ivanov did not duplicate Perrot's formula for using movement motifs as he did in *Giselle*, he managed to contrive expressive poses and movements to suggest swans in flight, in fear, alighting onto water, soothing feathers and so on. Actually, Ivanov superceded the music-movement breakthrough which was manifested in the *leitmotivs* of *Giselle*. Adam's music was composed in sections to accomodate the story as unfolded by dances and mime scenes and these melodies, in turn, were reflected in the movement motifs of the characters in the ballet. Tchaikovsky's unbroken streams of sound were, however, of a musically superior nature and Ivanov's handling of his music vastly enlarged the expressive scope of the *danse d'école*. Ivanov was responsible for a closer unification of music and movement than had been known up to that time and, no doubt, his innovations influenced the future choreographic advances of Gorsky and Fokine. While often a silent victim of Petipa's personal domination, Ivanov's artful handling of music and movement would serve to effect important choreographic developments in the 20th century.

Alexander Gorsky (1871–1924)

Since the 1959 appearance of Moscow's Bolshoi Ballet in the United States, Soviet ballet has been of great interest to American dance enthusiasts. At the turn of the century, Alexander Gorsky introduced certain reforms that lead to the present style of the Bolshoi Ballet. Gorsky had trained in cosmopolitan St. Petersburg where he profited from the expert teaching of its many superb instructors, including Petipa, and obtained a deep knowledge and love of character dancing as well as the classical dance of the old French school. He was interested in choreographic experimentation from the start and admired the artistic ideals of Isadora Duncan who was performing in Russia at the time. Influenced by the views of Lev Ivanov, he analyzed the softer approach to classical dance as it was utilized by the Romantic choreographers and strove to give movement even greater expressiveness by increasing its relationship to the music.

In 1898 Gorsky traveled to Moscow to set Petipa's *Sleeping Beauty* for the Bolshoi Ballet. His fresh approach did not go unnoticed and he was eventually invited to stay on as ballet master. What Gorsky inherited when he assumed his post at the Bolshoi was a company which traced its existence back to 1776. For some years a large segment of the personnel had been serf dancers. Besides a healthy tendency toward slavic character dancing inherent in its style, the Bolshoi also had

had European influences such as Perrot and Saint-Léon who staged choreography using Western ballerinas.

While never a match for the Maryinsky, the Bolshoi Ballet, prior to Gorsky's arrival, had experienced a decline owing to a wholesale lack of artistic leadership. Roslavleva's description of the Bolshoi at this time suggests a style of ballet reminiscent of the music hall variety. While gifted dancers waited to have their talents tapped, machines, masks and multi-colored costumes dominated the production and would invariably distract the viewer from questioning the lack of "proper choreography." In spite of the mediocre situation, Gorsky was fortunate in that Moscow was far removed from the bureaucratic influences in the Imperial Theatres of the Capitol. The Bolshoi Ballet was far more democratic in its administration than was the Maryinsky. It permitted artistic experimentation on the part of the staff unlike the tradition-bound Imperial Theatres in St. Petersburg. While never losing sight of his revered classical legacy, Gorsky shaped the Bolshoi Ballet into a mature artistic ensemble based on aesthetically sound innovations. Moreover, during Gorsky's time, Moscow was caught up in the excitement of a movement to develop Russian drama, opera, painting and literature. He knew and admired the work of such artists as Stanislavsky in theatre, Rimsky-Korsakov in music, Repin, Serov and Golovine in painting, and Chekov in literature. The general trend of the entire Russian art movement was away from artifice and toward realism and it was to this challenge that Gorsky addressed his choreographic efforts. Gorsky himself was perfectly in tune by bringing his own aesthetic conceptions to bear on the overhauling of Russian ballet. For example, when he began re-staging or creating new ballets, he used the coaching techniques of the Stanislavsky method so that his dancers would "live" their parts as did the actors of the Moscow Art Theatre. Furthermore, he gave each dancer individualized movement sequences so that crowd scenes established a realistic atmosphere. Unlike Petipa, Gorsky subordinated his choreography and his ego to the creation of the whole. He felt the dance, drama, design, musical score and their creators in his ballets should serve each other toward the common aim of an artful production. In keeping with the development of Russian art, Gorsky strove to make the final outcome more distinctly Russian by employing a great deal of charater dancing and by using only Russian composers and designers to collaborate in the balletic rendering of Russian stories and fairy tales.

Gorsky's experimentation led him to construct symphonic ballets which were, in essence, the forerunners of the so-called abstract ballets produced years later by Massine, Lifar, and Balanchine. These ballets were without any dramatic content whatsoever and their sole purppose was to kinetically interpret the conorous content of the music.

Gorsky's efforts toward achieving a more national spirit in Russian ballet were possible precisely because he worked in Moscow during a propitious time and in an auspicious atmosphere. Whereas St. Petersburg had been influenced by all styles and vogues of Western Europe, Moscow in its comparative geographic isolation, was the scene of the awakening Russian artistic consciousness. In time, this nationalistic identity manifested itself in all the arts, and in the ballet it produced works rich in exotic folklore, interpreted with dramatic imagination, and performed with tartar energies. These essentially Russian characteristics were evident in the ballets engineered by Diaghilev for Paris audiences some years later and so overwhelming was the effect on the public, that a brilliant new age in Western ballet commenced. Furthermore these particular elements are still visible in much of what is unique in current Bolshoi productions.

Summary

Petipa's domination over the ballet in Russia in the latter part of the 19th century is immensely significant in the history of ballet. Not only did his genius advance the art from a technical and compositional point of view, but his unswerving devotion to traditional principles preserved the previous link between the ancient *danse d'école* of Vestris and the Romantic heritage at the Maryinsky. While this link was broken and forgotten in France during the post-Romantic decline in Western Europe, it remained intact in far-off Russia. Petipa founded his choreographic aesthetic and his pedagogic theories on these ancient principles, thereby generating around him remarkable dancers and teachers sympathetic to the realization of their master's artistic vision. In time the circle completed itself and younger men like Lev Ivanov and Alexander Gorsky, while adhering to the very same ancient rules passed onto them by Petipa's generation, brought fresh interpretation to this balletic life-line. Although the next step forward in the development of ballet was masterminded by Russians, it did not take place on Russian soil. Indeed, the dance of the brilliant Imperial

Ballet was eons away from the extraordinary artistic event that would rocket the Paris of 1909 into a dance renaissance.

REFERENCES

Bonnat, Y. *Ballets de Moscow.* Paris: Editions Cercle D'Art, 1956.

Cohen, S. The Fourth of July, or, the Independence of American Dance. New York: *Dance Magazine,* July, 1976.

Fanger, I. Boston Goes to the Ballet, 1792–1797. New York: *Dance Magazine,* July, 1976.

Guest, I. *The Ballet of the Second Empire, 1847–1858.* London: Adam and Charles Black, 1958.

Guest, I. *The Ballet of the Second Empire, 1858–1870.* London: Adam and Charles Black, 1953.

Lieven, P. *The Birth of the Ballets-Russes.* New York: Dover Publications, 1973.

Miguel, P. *The Ballerinas.* New York: The Macmillan Co., 1972.

Moore, L. *New York's First Ballet Season, 1792.* New York: The New York Public Library, 1961.

Petipa, M. Edited by L. Moore. *The Memoirs of Marius Petipa.* London: The Chameleon Press, Ltd., 1958.

Roslavleva, N. *Era of the Russian Ballet, 1770–1965.* New York: E.P. Dutton & Co., 1966.

Searle, H. *Ballet Music.* New York: Dover Publications, Inc., 1973.

SUGGESTIONS FOR FURTHER READING

Anderson, J. *Dance.* New York: Newsweek Books, 1974.

Guest, I. *The Empire Ballet.* London: Headley Brothers Ltd., 1962.

CHAPTER 8

The New Dance

In May, 1909, Fanny Cerrito, the last vestige of the great Romantic ballerinas was all but forgotten as she lay dying in her Paris home at the age of 92. In another part of the city, feverish activity consumed a troupe of Russian artists who prepared to open a season at the Chatelet Theatre. The history of this theatrical event is not only a fascinating story in itself, but for us it is still so close to our own times that we come to recognize ourselves among the multitude of forces which are still rounding out this most tangential of all periods in the evolution of the art.

The Ballets Russes, as this ballet company would eventually be known, was the result of a complex process whereby a variety of creative urges manifested themselves through the ballet medium as the new dance. Master-minding this amazing effort was Serge Diaghilev whose veritable genius for organizing, talent scouting and accomplishing the impossible earned him immortality in the history of Western theatre art. The Ballets Russes was inseparably bound up with his personality and due to this factor his leadership accomplished a fresh revival of ballet everywhere save his native land. Under the aegis of Diaghilev, the ballet finally reached the point where it became a full-fledged art form equal to music, drama, and painting. In various ways the seminal ideas of almost two centuries of dance-making were realized in the highest fashion by Diaghilev's company. His conception, realized by his collaborators that the ballet ought to represent a perfectly balanced and unified style of movement, music, and painting was actually and perfectly achieved for the first time in dance history.

For years the Imperial Russian Ballet, primed with Czarist subsidy, had produced sumptuous three and four act ballets which mounted its brilliant dancing in every facet of spectacle. The grand manner of the Petipa choreographic style served to reflect the glittering life of aristocracy in Russia much in the way that the baroque ballets of Lully and Beauchamp mirrored the elegant artifice that was the way of life at

Versailles. It was never Diaghilev's intention to wholely transport the Imperial Ballet to Western Europe, for such an ambition would have been managerial and probable, artistic folly. Instead, Diaghilev's particular genius caused him to extract the Russian technical advancements in the dance and its production and enjoin them to the modern ideas of the talented young Russian artists he personally selected to create for him. The ballets which they evolved in their collaborations were an entirely new form of dance theatre. The ballets resulting from his unique approach were a number of masterworks of relatively short duration, where scenario, music, color, and the dancing itself were immeshed in an astonishing new format, perfectly in tune with the advent of "modern times" of the early 20th century.

SERGE DIAGHILEV, CATALYST OF GENIUS (1872–1929)

Born into a family of minor nobility, Diaghilev grew up in a provincial but gentile atmosphere which encouraged a love of the arts. At eighteen he arrived in St. Petersburg to enter the university as a student of law which was considered to be a proper line of study for a gentleman. Diaghilev stayed in the city with a cousin and through him was introduced into a circle of brilliant young artists and intellectuals, all of whom shared intense ambitions in the arts. At first the group viewed Diaghilev as a "country boy," coming from the provinces as he did. In time, however, life in the cultural capital of Russia polished his manner and opinions sufficiently so that he became readily accepted by the group. The circle's unofficial leader was Alexander Benois, a young painter of noble family who counted several fine architects among his distinguished and cultured ancestors. Two other members of the group who, along with Benois, were to figure in the later work of Diaghilev, were the painter Leon Bakst and Walter Nouvel, an intellectually inclined young musician. The group met often and their avid conversations stimulated discussions on a variety of artistic topics.

Diaghilev added music to his law studies, thinking he would pursue a career in composing. Discouraged by a genuine lack of musical talent, he soon developed into a rabid connoisseur of painting and began his own collection of pictures with a small inheritance. During these formative years several trips to western Europe served to shape his tastes in painting as well as his native instinct for recognizing creative talent in others. In addition, he began to show a flair for attracting important personages and enlisting their interest in his projects by means of his personal charm and well thought out aesthetic convictions.

In 1897 he had organized a successful watercolor exhibition in St. Petersburg. The following year, Diaghilev persuaded a Russian princess to back the publication of a new art magazine to be prepared by the circle of friends which he now led. With Diaghilev as editor, the *World of Art* was a beautifully designed review of painting, drama, and music devoted to encouraging modern art and revealing to Russians their own rich slavic heritage. Of course, the group also used the *World of Art* as a platform for its own passionate views which often led it to be outspoken in its criticism of the artistic establishment. Within the first year the magazine became the most advanced and vital force in Russian art and at the same time promoted the careers of its staff until it ceased publication in 1904.

That year Diaghilev was engaged in the preparation of an exhibition of historical portraits which he personally gleaned from all over Russia. So successful was this venture that the Imperial government agreed to back him and his associates in presenting an exhibition of Russian art in Paris. This exportation of Russian painting came at a politically favorable time in that the Franco-Russian alliance had just been signed. The exhibition proved to be fascinating indeed for the cultured French elite and as a result it was decided that the following year the energetic Diaghilev would export Russian music to Paris.

The Paris music concerts of 1905, like the art exhibition, were well received and lucrative. With the practical help of his close circle of Russian friends and important new French ones, he undertook the preparation of a season of Russian opera in the French capital. Seemingly, no expense was spared to achieve an artistic success for the production of Moussorgsky's *Boris Godunov* which also served as the European debut of the magnificent basso, Feodor Chaliapine. Neither a composer or designer himself, Diaghilev was already intricately involving himself in the total effect of theatrical production. During the rehearsals for the opera he offered advice on all artistic matters and his keen aesthetic judgment was matched only by his amazing skill in managing the business aspects of the venture.

Living at peak excitement from the success of *Boris,* another Paris season was inevitable and Alexander Benois suggested they include ballet on the program. As a youth, Benois had been overwhelmed by the dancing of Virginia Zucchi when the famous Italian ballerina guested in St. Petersburg. So profound was her effect on Benois that from that time on he was a devoted balletomane. Since the art of ballet in Paris in its current trivial form was all but forgotten, Benois reasoned that the showing of a sample of the magnificent Imperial Ballet would be a welcome change for the novelty-loving French. A number of exceptional young dancers willing to join the venture during their vacation time were available. Benois had also previously worked with the promising young choreographer, Michael Fokine, on the Maryinsky production of *The Pavilion of Armide* and suggested that this ballet be taken to Paris in addition to several other works by Fokine.

As it turned out, the Russian financial backing for the 1909 season was withdrawn at the last minute so Diaghilev relied on his newly cultivated French associates to supply funds for the undertaking. He economized by presenting only one full opera, *Ivan the Terrible,* in its entirety and combining acts from other Russian operas with two ballets on each program. As for dance, this production decision necessitated the modification of existing ballets and the development of fresh ideas in planning new ballets to fit the needs of an evening's program. Instead of the traditional full-evening ballets which were presented in two, three or four acts, a program of three or four one-act ballets, often differing in style, was devised. Thus, almost accidentally, was created the balletic format of the new dance that would become the unique contribution of the Ballets Russses. That opera was a part of the Paris 1909 season is now but a footnote in the history of the Ballets Russes.

BALLETS RUSSES (1909–1915)

Diaghilev's Ballets Russes took its original formation in 1909 in providing a temporary organization to present Russian ballet abroad. His professional life in Russia to this point had been fruitful but by no means free of aggravation. His forceful convictions on artistic matters had made him many enemies at court and, due to one scandalous altercation in St. Petersburg, he was banned from further association with the Imperial Theatres. Diaghilev understood he would have to make his mark outside Russia and this fact, no doubt, weighed heavily

when he created a permanent dance company in 1911. He kept this
company in almost continuous operation until his death in 1929.
These 20 years are commonly viewed in three distinct phases during
which the Ballets Russes reflected its maker's ever-changing tastes, his
unerring aesthetic judgment in assembling the right combination of
artists to bring about the creation of new ballets and his showmanship
instincts which attracted, stimulated and educated the public.

The first phase which began in Paris (1909–1915) lasted until the
outbreak of World War I when travel and engagements were interrupted. In many ways these years were the most brilliant period.
Dance, music, and decor were equally presented in a perfectly
blended product developed according to the joint dictum of Diaghilev
and Benois. While the dancers had come from the Imperial Theatre,
the ballets they danced in no way resembled those at the Maryinsky.
Brief, compact, dramatic, and chic are all adjectives which describe
the style of the new form of ballet evolved by Diaghilev's choreographer, Michael Fokine. At first Benois was responsible for the artistic
direction while Diaghilev shouldered that of organization and management. However, Diaghilev's artistic conceptions were already fully
formed and it only remained for him to take the reins in guiding his
collaborators toward the actualization of the artistic ends he forsaw.
He was closely advised by Benois and Bakst who created the sets and
costumes and continuously exerted their long-standing knowledge of
ballet. True to form, he redecorated the Chatelet Theatre to enhance
the sumptuousness of what was presented on stage. A new stage floor
was laid and the best stage machinery and lighting equipment to be
had was installed in the old house.

The Choreographic Contribution of Michael Fokine

The choreography shown the first season, except for divertissements
from Le Festin and Petipa's Raymonda, was that of Michael Fokine
whose masterful ideas only needed an appropriate showcase such as
the Ballets Russes offered. Four complete one-act ballets were given,
all of which Diaghilev had modified to suit the particular event. The
Pavilion of Armide opened the season and its exquisitely detailed
18th century French style was duly appreciated by the Paris cognoscenti. Benois had previously lived in the town of Versailles and had
spent countless hours researching the art and architecture of its great
palace, which, in turn, provided him a scholarly command and inspi-

ration for the design of *Pavillion*. Its choreographic style was suggestive of Petipa's work and indicates that Fokine was still under the early influences of his school days during the ballet's inception in 1907.

Fokine's *Chopiniana*, renamed *Les Sylphides*, made its first appearance under the new title devised by Diaghilev to recall for the Parisians the legendary figure of Taglioni. Indeed, Diaghilev even supplied the reincarnation of Taglioni by presenting Anna Pavlova in the ballet. *Les Sylphides'* artful music enchanted the audiences and time has proven it to be Fokine's hardiest masterpiece. The season's greatest successes were *Cleopatra* and *Prince Igor*, two exotic ballets whose colorful and barbaric-styled productions caught the public's imagination. The soaring leaps and unbounded energy of the Russian male dancer in these works stunned the refined French audience. Since Gautier's caustic writings had all but banished male dancing during the Romantic age as something ugly and unfit to be seen, masculine participation in dance performances outside Russia and Denmark had been neglected. In 1909 no one in the audience of the Chatelet Theatre had ever seen the likes of the aerial grace of Vaslav Nijinsky or the barbaric bounding of Adolph Bolm. In a different vein, one more aspect of Diaghilev's theatrical flair for presenting the unexpected showed itself when he successfully presented the beautiful mime, Ida Rubenstein, in the leading, non-dancing role of *Cleopatra*, supported by a cast of outstanding classical dancers.

With the exception of *Les Sylphides*, the music used for the 1909 season was Russian and was eminently suited to the choreography, but it was the painter's contribution to the productions that made the stronger artistic impression with its marriage of color to choreography. Benois and Bakst were first-rate artists, no mean theatrical hacks they, and Benois' decor for *Pavilion*, with its real water-jetting fountains, was as exquisitely conceived as many a painting in the Hermitage. The scenery for *Les Sylphides* painstakingly received a delicate, lilting treatment reminiscent of the Romantic epoch. Bakst's rendering of sets and costumes for *Cleopatra* happily suggested a strikingly exotic atmosphere, and the Russian artist, Roerich, designed a stunning backdrop for *Prince Igor* which effectively called to mind the vast scope of the Russian plains.

Disregarding the past conventions of choreography, Fokine created original and exuberant movement which his dancers performed to perfection. The extraordinary dancing of these Russian artists proved to be the sensation of the season for the press and public alike. Interestingly enough, in Paris the ballet was such a forgotten medium of expression that the press failed to appreciate the specific contribution of Fokine as choreographer in its reviews, lumping Fokine's choreographic concept and the dancers' performance of his spacial design together in their comments.

Fokine's Imperial training and his genius were indispensible to the outcome of the first phase of the Ballets Russes. Like Diaghilev, he was appreciative of many of the ideas of Isadora Duncan who also wished to create a dance form which reflected the meaning and the emotional content of music. Diaghilev was quick to appreciate Fokine's fresh choreographic approach rooted in the classical principles as well as his inventiveness which sprang from his broad artistic education. Fokine's most significant accomplishment was to fully achieve the epitome of human expressiveness in his ballets. In this context, he managed to perfect the search for expressiveness begun by Sallé which was to be continued down the years through Noverre, Dauberval, Didelot, Perrot, and Ivanov. Fokine firmly believed ballet's purpose was to extol beauty through the portrayal of man and his feelings. The dancer needed to be an expressive instrument from head to foot — an idea considered revolutionary in Petipa's Russia. By aligning himself with the first Paris season, Fokine was able to realize his burning ambition to reform the ballet in a setting where prominent artists and musicians joined him in the creation of his choreographic works which were performed by excellent dancers, many of whom he himself had trained in Russia. Eventually, Fokine formulated his five-point choreographic aesthetic which elaborated the following maxims:

1. Each ballet should have a style of movement created especially for it according to the demands of the subject matter and the musical scores. The classical steps should also be modified or restyled according to the dictates of the thematic material.
2. The dance movement itself should convey the unfolding of the dramatic action, thus eliminating the inclusion of mime.
3. The formalized pantomimic gesture of the previous ages should be replaced by an expressiveness created from total body movement which would, in turn, meaningfully communicate ideas and feelings.

4. All dancers in a work, including the corps de ballet, should be an intricate part of the whole and not serve to decorate the stage at various interludes.
5. All aspects of the ballet should be on an equal footing. Namely, the dancing, the music, sets, and costumes should reflect a collaborative effort toward the total creative product.

In reading Fokine's list of major principles, it is amazing that his comprehensive choreographic method seemed so novel at the time. It is even more astonishing when one notes that much of what Fokine advocated had been seminal in Noverre's thought concerning the *ballet d'action* but not accomplished prior to the ballets of this young Russian.

At the close of the first season, Benois enthusiastically wrote that everyone connected with the company felt that he was bringing to the artistic capital of the world all that was best in Russian art. Benois went on to prophesize that the event would begin a new European theatrical art. While it certainly achieved a renaissance for the European ballet and theatre arts in general, the presence of the Russian ballet in Paris would even influence fashion design and interior decoration. Benois summed up the first season by concluding that the greatest triumph did not belong to anyone in particular but to Russian culture itself, with its uniquely Russian characteristics, its great sense of conviction, its freshness and spontaneity, its wild force and, at the same time, its Russian spirituality that overshadowed the sophistication of Paris.

Second Paris Season

So successful was the first season of Russian ballet in Paris that a return engagement for 1910 was inevitable. The Russians had demonstrated in their productions that the ballet was capable of being an autonomous art and, happily, the lofty Paris Opera was offered as a proper setting for the forthcoming season. Returning to Russia, Diaghilev set plans in motion to prepare for the following year, knowing he would have to match the success of 1909. As it turned out, the second visit of the Ballets Russes to Paris surpassed the first. Four ballets were added to the original repertoire. Three of them were works by Fokine while Benois persuaded Diaghilev to produce a revival of *Giselle*. The cherished old Gautier-Perrot ballet had been lovingly

Fig. 1. A recent production of Fokine's *Scheherazade* performed by Dance Theatre of Harlem with Frederic Franklin as the chief Eunuch. Photo courtesy of Jack Vartoogian.

preserved in Russia although the time was not yet right for the French public to accept its revival. Next to the flamboyant Russian works, its story and musical score seemed quaint despite its exquisite interpretation by Nijinsky and Karsavina. Fokine's works, however, were another matter. In creating *Firebird, Scheherazade,* and *Carnaval,* he wrought three distinct ballets which added to the already splendid material in the repertoire.

Firebird was by far the most significant artistic offering of 1910. Both Diaghilev and Fokine had wanted to do something based on genuine Russian folklore and seized upon a theme developed from several old fairy tales. Diaghilev had heard a composition by a rising young composer, Igor Stravinsky, and felt he could provide the right score for *Firebird.* During its preparation in St. Petersburg, Stravinsky and Fokine worked closely and the final result was a musical event of the first order. Stravinsky's inventive tones and complex rhythms enormously advanced the level of ballet music and they provided an unexpected challenge for the dancers. Furthermore, Stravinsky's fresh musical style seemed to stimulate the musically trained Fokine to create many exciting choreographic moments. Pavlova apparently disliked the music, so Karsavina replaced her in creating the role of the Firebird and she proved to be incomparable in the part. Fokine, himself, danced the prince who pursues the dazzling Firebird. For the final touch, Diaghilev engaged the established Russian artist Golovin to create the decor for the enchanted atmosphere.

Scheherazade was the second ballet to be created for the 1910 Paris season. It was conceived by Benois who had enthusiastically researched Persian miniatures. *Scheherazade* proved to be one of the most stunning successes of the entire Diaghilev era. Fokine was at the height of his inventiveness during its creation and after the difficulty of acclimating the dancers to the perplexing music of Stravinsky's *Firebird,* the melodic Rimsky-Korsakov score, rearranged for *Scheherazade,* was a relief for the dancers and the work progressed swiftly. Grigoriev, the company's stage manager, relates the dancers' amazement when Fokine actually started the *Scheherazade* rehearsals with the corps de ballet and soloists sitting on the floor moving arms, head and upper torso only. Apparently, it was necessary to assure them that they would eventually be allowed to rise and move in a more conventional manner. Bakst's riot of colors and fabrics lent to the production the most startlingly exotic texture imaginable. A harem atmosphere was achieved with the juxtaposition of such colors as reds and fuschias on billowing silken tent hangings, glittering metal mosque lamps, and dancers costumed as voluptuous odalisques. The leading female part was designed for the mime, Ida Rubenstein, and Nijinsky interpreted the golden slave whom she seduces. At the ballet's end, Nijinsky's acrobatic death spasms electrified the audience. According to accounts of the opening night, the reception of this ballet was over-whelmingly enthusiastic. Indeed, *Scheherazade* was such exciting theatre that the public's reaction caused the management some effort in restoring order in the theatre before the next ballet could be pres-ented. Grigoriev recounts that with *Scheherazade,* Diaghilev achieved an aim once dreamt of by Noverre when the old master wishfully complained that if only a painter, composer, and choreo-grapher could work harmoniously, what wonders they could show the public. The third ballet slated for the 1910 season was *Carnaval,* a delightful work Fokine had previously done for a charity benefit in St. Petersburg. Based on the Italian *Commedia dell'Arte* characters of Harlequin, Colombina and Pierrot, with music by Schumann and new costumes by Bakst, it provided the repertoire with a humorous satire.

In reviewing the Ballets Russes' second Paris season, the compa-ny's tendency toward constant personnel change became apparent. While Diaghilev achieved a great coup in discovering Stravinsky for his company, he lost Pavlova who disapproved of his modern tenden-cies and also resented the public's acclaim of Nijinsky and Karsavina. An exquisite young dancer, Lydia Lopokova was added to the com-pany's roster when she temporarily replaced Karsavina in *Firebird.* By season's close, Benois had also left the company over an uproar con-cerning the authorship of *Scheherazade.* He had provided the ballet's scenario but Diaghilev gave Bakst the program credit, saying that Benois already had *Pavilion* on his list of accomplishments and Bakst needed the authorship as well as the design credit for a ballet, too.

The sensational repetition of the Ballets Russes season in Paris se-cured the company's position as a major event in the artistic life of Paris. The soloists were treated as heros even though Fokine's chore-ography had deprived the ballerina of her exclusive importance as es-tablished during the Romantic era. The ensemble dancing was a reve-lation as to what lengths the corps de ballet could be used as an expressive instrument and the almost superhuman quality of the male dancing remained for Paris a great joy to behold.

The Ballets Russes is Permanently Established: 1911

Diaghilev received enough offers after the 1910 successes to establish a permanent company. Prior to the next season in Paris the company was contracted to appear in Monte Carlo, Rome, Paris, and London. Again, Diaghilev rallied round himself a sufficient number of devoted artists eager to participate in the now famous Diaghilev venture. With the company on a permanent basis, Fokine was hired as choreographic director to continue his innovative work, an opportunity for him which was possible only outside the tradition-laden Russia. Karsavina was engaged as the company's prima ballerina since she was senior enough at the Maryinsky that she was only bound there by a limited number of months. The company's acquisition of Nijinsky was finally made but only after considerable scandal, probably induced by Diaghilev himself. In St. Petersburg, Nijinsky had altered his costume for *Giselle* so that it failed to meet the Imperial Theatre's regulation which required a male dancer to wear trunks over his tights. Nijinsky's insubordination to authority caused him to be expelled from the Maryinsky and Diaghilev was only too pleased to engage him on a permanent basis. Aldolph Bolm, who had previously distinguished himself as a character dancer, also agreed to join the company, as did the famous Maryinsky ballerina, Olga Preobrajenska.

Recruiting minor soloists and an adequate corps de ballet for the company was Diaghilev's most pressing problem since they had to be found outside of Russia and there were few sufficiently capable dancers in Europe who could meet the challenge of dancing with the Russians. After considerable search, the necessary dancers for the corps de ballet were found. Fortunately, Diaghilev understood his dancers' essential needs and was able to attract the services of the great Italian maestro, Enrico Cecchetti who had been most recently working for the Maryinsky. His formidable teaching methods were directly rooted in the pedagogy of Carlo Blasis. As ballet master, Cecchetti was not only able to pull together the technically uneven group of dancers gathered for the corps, but was able to homogenize their efforts into a single style. The company's soloists were also overjoyed to have the opportunity to benefit from the classes of the renowned Cecchetti and morale as well as technique remained on a high level.

Four new Fokine ballets were added to the repertoire for the third season. The pieces were, for the most part, planned before the company assembled for rehearsals and their opening in Monte Carlo. Fokine and Stravinsky repeated their exceptional collaboration in realizing *Petrushka,* the theme of which Diaghilev had fervently wished to see materialize into a ballet. After lengthy negotiations couched in the enmeshing Diaghilev charm, Benois agreed to create the sets. *Petrushka* centered on the touching theme of a puppet with the heart of a human being. This ballet was set in a Russian carnival where the chief characters are puppets who act out the poignant story. The ballet remains perhaps at the pinnacle of all the masterpieces produced under the aegis of the Diaghilev collaborations precisely due to the perfection of each creative component, as well as the interpretation of the leading roles which were created by Nijinsky, Karsavina, and Orlov. Once again Diaghilev's timely theatrical instincts for joining the particular talents which forged the creation of *Petrushka* confirms what a catalyst of genius he was.

The second great achievement of this season was *Le Spectre de la Rose* inspired by a Vaudoyer poem and set to music of von Weber. The haunting theme is founded on a young girl returning home after her first ball. She is visited in a dream by the spirit of the rose still in her hand and they dance, recreating the pleasures of the waltz. At the end of the dance, the spirit disappears as fleetingly as he came, leaving the girl to dream on. Bakst provided the delicate decor of the girl's room and the romantic costumes for the two characters danced by Karsavina and Nijinsky. This exquisite *pas de deux* met with immense success for both dancers while Nijinsky outdid himself in the eyes of the public. Fokine choreographed the spirit of the rose leaving by one of the large windows in Bakst's set. Due to Nijinsky's extraordinary elevation, the dancer was able to accomplish a leap so amazing that an illusion was created in that the spirit seemed to soar beyond the window clearing. The other ballets, *Narcisse* and *Sadko,* completed the bill but met with only minor success.

The 1911 season was once again received by an ecstatic public and the company returned to London for a fall season that year. While French tastes had preferred the more exotic works in the repertory, the English favored the romantic ones. The *prima ballerina assoluta* of the Maryinsky, Mathilde Kchessinka, was delighted to be associated with the successful company and agreed to dance a modified version of *Swan Lake* in London. According to Grigoriev, for the first performance Diaghilev engaged the virtuoso Mischa Elman to play the violin solos in the Tchaikovsky score. Again, Diaghilev's supreme

Fig. 2. Tamara Kasavina and Vaslav Nijinsky in one of Fokine's most popular ballets, *Le Spectre de la Rose*. Courtesy of the New York Public Library for the Performing Arts.

touch provided unforgettable moments in the history of ballet. The year was to end with a special season in St. Petersburg where Diaghilev proudly planned to present his company, but fate decreed otherwise. The Russian theatre burnt to the ground dashing his hopes for a triumphant homecoming.

Nijinsky's Choreographic Debut: 1912

Some marked changes occurred in the Ballets Russes during the 1912 season which reflect the artistic quest of Diaghilev himself. Fokine was already creating *Daphnis and Chloë, Le Dieu Bleu,* and *Thamar* when it became apparent that Diaghilev was grooming Nijinsky to choreograph for the company despite Fokine's proven excellence. Nijinsky's experiments with a new style of movement, rooted in Dalcroze's doctrines on eurhythmics, resulted in his first choreographic work, *Afternoon of a Faun.* This work went into a series of over one hundred rehearsals, lengthy and agonizing for everyone involved. The ballet, which was probably conceptually devised by Diaghilev, attempted to suggest the figures on Greek vases and the dancers were expected to dance without turnout and to move their bodies in profile to the audience. Through Nijinsky, Diaghilev achieved his aim to present something new to his audiences while it unexpectedly evoked a scandal in the press and a riot in the theatre. Nijinsky, who took the part of the faun, ended the ballet with what was considered at the time an indecent gesture. Chaos broke in the theatre and the press followed the next day by censuring Diaghilev for allowing such allusion to immorality. *Afternoon of a Faun,* however, weathered the storm and actually enjoyed a certain success due to its genuine beauty and originality.

Fokine was deeply hurt that his choreographic competence had been devalued in deference to Nijinsky's novice attempts at dancemaking. With little regret Diaghilev allowed the disgruntled Fokine to leave the company when his contract expired even though his creative capacity was far from exhausted. This left the Ballets Russes without a proven choreographer, but Diaghilev evidently felt Nijinsky could create more important works given the opportunity.

During the 1913 season the company continued its successful tours to major European cities with Nijinsky as the leading male dancer and choreographer. At this time Nijinsky was working on a new ballet to Stravinsky's *Rite of Spring.* This ballet had no plot but was a collection of dances representing primitive rites performed by ensembles of dancers. As in *Afternoon of a Faun,* Nijinsky employed turned-in legs and unclassical movements. The dancers heartily disliked the unmelodic music and the stomping steps they were made to perform. Grigoriev wrote years later that occasionally he resorted to calling rehearsals of the eminently danceable Fokine ballets simply to restore the dancers' morale. When Diaghilev heard of the unpopularity of *Rite of Spring* with the dancers, he merely noted that their irritation augured well in that it proved the originality of Nijinsky's composition.

The complexities of the music combined with Nijinsky's inexperience and uncommanding personality suggested that the projected ballet was almost impossible to finish. Countless hours of rehearsals had been called and still the ballet remained incomplete. Following the advice of Dalcroze, Diaghilev engaged a young English woman, Marie Rambert, who was able to disentangle the rhythmic complexities for Nijinsky and the dancers so he could proceed with his choreographic intentions.

The 1913 season in Paris opened at the distinguished new Théâtre de Champs Élysées. A third Nijinsky ballet *Jeux* was on the first program. Set to music of Debussy, its theme evolved around a tennis game which provided the enigmatic basis for the movement of its trio cast of Karsavina, Schollar, and Nijinsky. The ballet's strangeness and immaturity as a choreographic work puzzled the audience and it was not a success. However, the standard Ballets Russes fare, created mostly by Fokine, a new work by Boris Romanov, and the presentation of Russian operas gave the company its usual successful season. When the avant garde *Rite of Spring* was finally presented during the season, it was intentionally included amidst the standard ballets. Even then, the hostile indignation of a section of the audience was so pronounced that it became all but impossible for the orchestra and the dancers to continue. Stravinsky's music shocked to such an extent that fighting broke out in the theatre. No sooner were the offenders ejected by police and the lights turned back down, then the commotion again erupted and continued to the end of the ballet. Stravinsky later recalled how his life was endangered that night after the première when his carriage was mobbed by members of the irate audience. Nijinsky in his peculiar way was hurt by the ballet's lack of acceptance while the experience deterred Stravinsky from composing another ballet score for some years. However, the aftermath of the public's uproar over *Rite* proved that Diaghilev had succeeded again in forging ahead in the production of a new and significant artistic creation. Many of the dancers recognized that they had participated in an epoch-making event. In their own way, after overcoming the trials of so many difficult rehearsals, they grew to appreciate this work, born as a precursor of its time.

The Ballets Russes Visits the New World

The company sailed for engagements in South America toward the end of the summer of 1913. Diaghilev, fearing the sea, stayed behind. The most noteworthy occurrence of the South American tour was that Nijinsky met and married a young Hungarian dancer who had just joined the company. When the tour was over, Diaghilev responded to Nijinsky's marriage by dismissing him from the company. It seemed that the docile Nijinsky, under the influence of his wife, refused to dance one night, reasons for which are contradictory. Diaghilev used this incident to claim Nijinsky had broken his contract and summarily fired him.

Diaghilev began plans for the 1914 season by coaxing Fokine back to the company not only to resume his choreographic responsibilities but also to substitute for Nijinsky as the leading male dancer. The replacement of Nijinsky did not seem to affect the brilliant successes of the Ballets Russes and Fokine enjoyed the distinction of having fifteen of his works in the repertoire at the time. That year the company added Pierre Vladimirov and the novice, Leonide Massine, to their roster. Diaghilev had Massine exposed to the elements of composition, sensing in him rich possibilities as a choreographer. In addition, Massine, who had trained as both an actor and dancer at the Bolshoi, was put to further hard study with Maestro Cecchetti.

Of five new ballets produced that season, only Fokine's Le Coq d'Or was an unqualified success. This ballet was set to Rimsky-Korsakov's opera and incorporated both singers and dancers on stage. Goncharova's vibrant decor produced a sensation of glowing color and primitive fantasy which admirably added to the impression made by Karsavina, who danced the lead, the orchestra, and the magnificent Russian singers and chorus under the baton of Monteaux. Le Coq d'Or was an experiment in the best Ballets Russes tradition and with its success, Diaghilev was exonerated by the public for the weaker creations of the previous two years.

THE BALLETS RUSSES (1916-1921)

The outbreak of World War I marked the beginning of the second phase of the Ballets Russes. When engagements in Germany and England had to be cancelled, Diaghilev spent the following year in preparation for a tour to the United States. A new generation of leading dancers had to be engaged to replace the absence of Karsavina, who was in Russia having a baby, Fokine, who had again parted ways with Diaghilev, and Nijinsky, who was incarcerated in a Hungarian concentration camp. Leading the list of new stars were Lopokova, Tchernicheva, Sokolova, Nemchinova, Massine, Idzikowsky, and Woidzikowsky. The end of the year also marked Massine's debut as a choreographer with *Soleil de Nuit* and Diaghilev felt he had discovered someone who could readily respond to and interpret the fruits of his own rich imagination.

The company opened its North American season in New York in January, 1916. The public showed great interest in what for them was a novel form of theatrical entertainment and the press issued exceedingly favorable notices. After departing the city for an arduous sixteen week tour of the United States which included many one-night stands, the Ballets Russes returned to New York to dance at the Met-

Fig. 3. Autographed photo of Maestro Cecchetti and his wife teaching company class for Diaghilev's Ballets Russes de Monte Carlo. Courtesy of the New York Public Library for the Performing Arts.

ropolitan Opera House. By April, Nijinsky had been released from prison and had arrived to fulfill a contractual stipulation that he dance with the company when he was freed. In his chronicle of the Ballets Russes, Serge Grigoriev suggests that the first signs of the dancer's madness began to show itself in his antagonistic and unfriendly behavior during rehearsals. Diaghilev and the company departed for Spain without Nijinsky to perform and to plan new works for the coming year. In the fall, the Ballets Russes returned to New York, this time without Diaghilev. In spite of the problems Nijinsky had caused and due to various circumstances, he was asked to direct the second American tour. At this time, Nijinsky premiered *Tyl Eulenspielgel,* his fourth and last ballet. The ballet's choreographic conception represented more of Nijinsky's unorthodox choreographic approach to dance. Still ineffectual in communicating his intentions to his dancers, the ballet failed to achieve a general success. It was seriously apparent that Nijinsky was incapable by nature or training to handle the managerial responsibility that goes with running a company. Consequently, the Ballets Russes under Nijinsky's direction ended its American season by incurring heavy debts and at the same time damaging the company's artistic reputation.

It has often been said that under different circumstances, Nijinsky would have been an excellent choreographer. Indeed, what we can glean from his own and others' interpretations of his choreographic aesthetic and intentions, old photographs and first-hand memories, it would appear that he was, in fact, compositionally very much a harbinger in his time, but lacked the ability to transmit his ideas to those who could have helped him the most, namely, the dancers.

Massine as Choreographer

By 1917, Massine had developed into a promising choreographer and Diaghilev leaned upon the young dancer's creative output to supply the company with such new works as *Parade,* a collaborative effort which included the composer, Satie, the French poet, Cocteau, and the painter, Picasso. For *Parade,* Diaghilev commissioned Picasso to create a special act curtain which was used as an integral part of the production. This scenic innovation was to be repeated for a number of successive ballet decors. Following a brief season in Spain, a country less affected by the war, the company returned to South America, minus Diaghilev and Massine. It was in Buenos Aires that

Nijinsky performed for the last time. His meteoric career terminated as his schizophrenic behavior erupted in a series of incidents making the continuation of his professional career impossible.

The Ballets Russes ended its tenth year with a season in wartime London where they shared a music-hall bill at the Coliseum, performing one of several ballets twelve times a week. Two new Massine ballets were added to the repertoire, *La Boutique Fantasque* and *Three Cornered Hat,* the latter being the first of several Spanish-styled ballets which Massine would prove to be so skilled in creating.

THE BALLETS RUSSES (1922–1929)

At the halfway mark of the Ballets Russes twenty years of existence, not only had the various European cities become accustomed and educated to its fresh style of theatrical dance, but to some extent so had cities in North and South America. The company's regisseur, Serge Grigoriev, has suggested in his journal that a greater effect could have been had in the United States had not Nijinsky's failure to competently lead the company led to a loss of further bookings. Be that as it may, after ten years of touring, wherever the Ballets Russes appeared, dance was applauded and appreciated by an ever-eager following.

The third phase of the Ballet Russes was marked by an increasing taste for novelty on the part of the great entrepreneur. Diaghilev's oft-quoted command to Cocteau *"étonné-moi, Jean"* summed up his changing aesthetic in regard to new productions. Genuine artistic quest seemed to be replaced by novelty and gimmickry for its own sake. In 1921, Massine left the company once more after having contributed twelve ballets to the repertory. Lacking a choreographer, Diaghilev imported four flamenco dancers from Spain and successfully produced their music and dances under the title *Cuadro* while Picasso designed the sets for this prefabricated ballet. Without a choreographer at work developing collaborative ideas into fresh pieces, however, Diaghilev realized that the Ballets Russes would soon be at a loss for new material to present to its public. In the same breadth, he decided to depart from the usual program offering of three ballets in one evening and to attempt a full-length work which he hoped would run for six months. Sergeyev, a former regisseur at the Maryinsky, was therefore engaged to stage Petipa's *Sleeping Princess* in an effort to show London audiences a sample of the Imperial Russian Ballet style. Diaghilev made suggestions for rearranging the Tchaikovsky score, Bakst outdid himself in what was to be his last work, and a stellar array of new Russian dancers were engaged to perform the leading roles. Recently emigrated from Russia were the ballerinas, Trefilova, Egorova, Spessitseva, and Anatole Vilzak. Vladimirov, who had already been with the company, danced the role of the prince and the role of the princess was shared by the various ballerinas in addition to Lopokova and Nemchinova. In the course of rehearsals, Diaghilev encouraged Bronislava Nijinska, who had left the company when her brother departed, to return and arrange some new choreography where certain changes had been made in the old Petipa classic. She did her work well and Diaghilev was duly impressed.

The Sleeping Princess was an artistic success, delighting the London public as it did, but it proved to be a financial fiasco. After 105 consecutive performances it was forced to close two months early. Enchanted though many Londoners were with the Petipa fantasy, there simply was not a large enough dance following to support a half year run of one ballet. Although grossly disappointed, Diaghilev arranged to present in Paris excerpts from The Sleeping Princess and renamed the ballet Aurora's Wedding.

Choreographic Contribution of Bronislava Nijinska

The spring season of 1922 began at the Paris Opera and marked Nijinska's first complete work for the Ballets Russes. Her conception of Le Renard was similar to Le Coq d'Or in that its sixteen minute duration included singers whose words were interpreted by a cast of four dancers. Toward the end of the run, an all-Stravinsky program was presented which included a revival of Petrushka and Massine's 1920 version of Rite of Spring. The year ended with the company finding a permanent home at the Garnier Theatre in the principality of Monaco on the French Riviera. For six months out of every year Diaghilev contracted for the renamed Ballets Russes de Monte Carlo to have its own season, perform the ballets in operas during the opera season and also to rehearse and create new works.

The only new piece slated for the 1923 season was Les Noces, choreographed by Nijinska in collaboration with Stravinsky, Larionov and Goncharova. Nijinska's distinctly personal style served to create an intensely moving and austerely beautiful ballet which gained immediate success in its eight Paris performances. The première firmly established Nijinska as a creative talent of the first order and *Les Noces* remains her greatest contribution to the choreographic evolution of the ballet.

Diaghilev had also commissioned works from two young French composers, Poulenc and Auris, and with the new scores, Nijinska began composing *Les Biches* and *Les Facheaux,* respectively. *Les Biches* was a plotless ballet consisting of a number of charming dances performed to Poulenc's light-hearted music. Marie Laurencin provided decor and costumes of fashionable streetwear, completing the totally chic composition. After two hundred years, Molière's play, *Les Facheaux,* was once again modeled as a ballet. Contemporary in every sense of the word, however, its scenario was adapted by Boris Kochno and the artist, Georges Braque, supplied appropriate scenery for the French classic. Nijinska created an additional ballet toward the season's end entitled, *Le Train Bleu.* This work utilized a scenario by Jean Cocteau, music by another young French composer, Darius Milhaud, and costumes by Coco Chanel which consisted of bathing suits and sport clothes. It was during this period that Anton Dolin, Ninette de Valois, and Alicia Markova joined the company. During their careers, these dancers took a great part in the establishment of British ballet.

Before long, Diaghilev was secretly attempting to develop the choreographic talents of Serge Lifar, one of Nijinska's students who had previously joined the company. Diaghilev had grown tired of Nijinska's work and was searching for new directions and people who would realize his visions. This tendency to discover and then discard his artists was perhaps Diaghilev's greatest failing. Although Nijinska, like Fokine and Massine before, had hardly exhausted her creative energies, leaving the Ballets Russes deprived her work of its most likely setting.

For the 1925 tours Massine returned to the company to create *Les Matelots* and a new version of Didelot's *Zěphyr et Flore.* These were to be followed by *Ode* and *Le Pas d'Acier. Les Matelots* enjoyed considerable success while *Pas d'Acier* also held special interest in that its set was designed by Pevsner and Gabo and was in the constructionist style currently popular in Soviet Russia. While this ballet met with only relative success, it was kept in the repertoire because it afforded audiences the opportunity to hear the Prokofiev score.

Balanchine as Choreographer

Of all the new young dancers in the company, George Balanchine appeared the most promising choreographically. Basically, his ideas were already formed so Diaghilev could not use him as a personal medium of creation in the manner he had developed Nijinsky and Massine. Already, Balanchine's talent stood on its own merits and his version of *Le Chante de Rossingnol* and *Barabau* both proved excellent ballets. In the last four years of the company's existence, Balanchine was to choreograph nine more ballets for Diaghilev of which the most memorable were *The Triumph of Neptune, La Chatte, Apollo Musagate, The Gods Go A' Begging, La Bal,* and *The Prodigal Son.*

The dancers who performed in these works were now a mixture of émigré Russians, English, and some Slavs. Of Diaghilev's original organization, only his advisor and friend, Walter Nouvel, and Serge Grigoriev, the regisseur, remained with the company at the twenty

Fig. 4. George Balanchine costumed for a major role in one of his ballets created for Diaghilev. Courtesy of the New York Public Library for the Performing Arts.

year mark. The dancing style, however, fared more permanent. After Diaghilev hired Cecchetti in 1911, the Maestro stayed with the Ballets Russes for 15 years, imposing his own Italian tradition of the Blasis pedagogy on his Russian dancers. After Cecchetti's retirement and subsequent appointment to the great school of Milan's La Scala Opera House, Nicholas Legat was engaged to assume the teaching position. Trained at the Maryinsky, Legat followed the French pedagogical methods in force from the time of Petipa. This different approach met with severe criticism from the nomadic Diaghilev dancers, many of whom now had never been trained in Russia at all. As a result, Legat was presently replaced by Lubov Tchernicheva, who was not only one of the company's leading soloists, but had already developed into a fine teacher, having absorbed much of her knowledge from Cecchetti himself and had integrated it into her Maryinsky training.

Diaghilev in Retrospect

By the end of the spring season in 1929, Diaghilev was showing signs of ill health. Not heeding his doctor's warnings, he died on August 19 in Venice, leaving the company, who was dispersed and on holidays, without future prospects. Thus came to an abrupt end the saga of the fabulous Ballets Russes of Serge Diaghilev.

Diaghilev's legacy to our time is inestimatable. His activities inaugurated a major cultural interchange between East and West with artists from every country lending their ideas to a common cause. During the years from 1909 to 1929, Paris again resumed its position as the world's most important artistic center, only relinquishing it due to the effects of World War II. Never before had an artistic event such as the Ballets Russes continuously intrigued the many capitals of Europe for such a lengthy period of time. Diaghilev's destiny was to found an enterprise that lasted twenty years, to be instrumental in creating a huge repertoire, to bring up several generations of wonderful dancers, to raise ballet to new heights and diffuse it over Europe and the Americas. The ballets he produced represented a new approach in dance-making. Relatively short and dramatically compact, they often boasted a perfect integration of choreography, music, and painting. During two decades, Diaghilev employed the distinctively varied talent of five major choreographers, numerous contemporary composers and first-rate painters, not to mention a staggering list of several generations of extraordinary dancers.

Upon his death, the company scattered across the face of Europe with some dancers returning to Russia and a number of the finest venturing to the New World. It was precisely the disruption of the Ballets Russes which jettisoned a number of dance talents onto soil already made fertile by Diaghilev's incessant touring. Tragic on the surface in that the company died with its director, it was in the long run a fortunate turning point in that these dancers, in seeking a livelihood, caused the ballet to begin its enormous international growth. Whereas before this migration of dancers the ballet was known only to relatively small and select groups, within 50 years their work has made ballet touch the lives of millions.

ANNA PAVLOVA (1881–1931)
DANCE PIONEER TO THE WORLD

An equal if different force, as compared to Diaghilev's, in the rapid growth of ballet during the early 20th century, was that exerted by Anna Pavlova. A student at the Maryinsky, Pavlova's talent was evident long before graduation. Frail and slim with exquisitely formed legs and feet, she embodied the antithesis of the muscularly powerful, turn-of-the-century Russian ballerina. Her teachers, principally Gerdt, Johansson, Vazem, and Cecchetti, recognized her unique gifts and were jointly instrumental in developing her artistry. Instead of allowing her to compete with the athletic feats of her contemporaries, they encouraged her delicacy, lightness, and natural grace. Pavlova's highly personal style marked a revival of the appreciation of qualities made so famous by Taglioni, whose artistic heir she came to be.

From an early age Pavlova aspired to travel, following the example of the Romantic ballerinas and so she never lost an opportunity to venture on foreign tours during her vacation periods at the Maryinsky. She was the first Russian ballerina ever to dance outside of Czarist Russia when, in 1905, she and Adolph Bolm toured Scandanavia. By the time Diaghilev invited her to participate in the Paris season of 1909, she was an established star in St. Petersburg. Eager to be part of Diaghilev's maverick successes and to have the opportunity to work with Fokine again, she readily accepted. The choreographer had pre-

ANNA PAVLOWA.

Fig. 5. Anna Pavlova became a symbol for the ballet when Fokine created "The Dying Swan" for her. Courtesy of the New York Public Library for the Performing Arts.

156

viously created *The Dying Swan* for her, an exquisite solo which will forever be synonymous with her name, her life, and her style of dancing. During the first Paris season, Pavlova danced with the young Nijinsky in *The Pavilion of Armide,* the premiere of *Les Sylphides,* and *Cleopatra.* While her success was highly acclaimed in Paris, she chose to leave Diaghilev's organization the next year and found her own company.

By many accounts, Pavlova's own troupe seemingly lacked all nature of artistic direction. Rather, it served to provide the ballerina with a showcase for her own marvelous dancing which was enhanced by such superb partners as Bolm, Mordkin, Volonine, Vladimirov, and Novikov. Eye witnesses agree that so great was her artistry, the trite choreography and even worse music which she employed were completely transformed into beauty when she interpreted them. The company was also Pavlova's vehicle for realizing an ambition to take her art to the ends of the earth. Indefatigable, the ballerina toured every part of the world where travel was feasible. In Java she danced before loin cloth covered natives on a make-shift stage while in New York she performed at the Hippodrome on the same bill with magicians and elephants. Her effect on audiences was prodigious, owing to an almost hypnotic power she exerted in each of her roles. Some said her bow-taking was an art in itself and that the applause grew rather than diminished as her artful acknowledgements enraptured the audience.

Trained to perform for Russian aristocracy, Pavlova delighted in dancing before the most common laborer in cities and towns across the United States. In the last twenty years of her life, Pavlova toured constantly, traveling over half a million miles which was an incredible feat in those days. Far from an audience of cultural elitists, vast crowds of Americans from various backgrounds came to high school auditoriums, convention halls and movie houses out of curiosity while her beauty, talent and devotion to her art sent them away deeply touched. A man might not have read Shakespeare, but he could easily have heard of Pavlova. Not since the advent of Fanny Elssler to these shores had Americans been so excited by the dance and, due to improved transportation, many more people had the opportunity to witness Pavlova's performances.

Pavlova had inspired a desire to dance in countless young people long before there was a supply of properly trained teachers in this country. It was not until the dissolution of Diaghilev's company that a number of his dancers migrated to the United States in the early

1930's and helped institute a teaching force which ultimately created the American ballet. While the accomplishment of Diaghilev's enterprise was in terms of the total development of the balletic art form and its production, Pavlova succeeded in being the initial, personal inspiration for an entire generation of dancers. Pavlova was indeed a dance pioneer to the world but her work has a very special significance in this country.

REFERENCES

Alexander, A. *The Decorative Art of Leon Bakst*. New York: Dover Publications, 1972.
Balanchine, G. Edited by Mason, F. *Great Ballets*. New York: Doubleday & Co., 1954.
Buckle, R. *Nijinsky*. New York: Avon Books, 1971.
Cohen, S.J. *Dance as a Theatre Art*. New York: Dodd, Meade & Co., 1974.
Grigoriev, S. *The Diaghilev Ballet 1909-1929*. Baltimore, Md.: Penguin Books Ltd., 1960.
Haskell, A. *Ballets Russes*. London: Trinity Press, 1968.
Kochno, B. *Diaghilev and the Ballets Russes*. New York: Harper & Row, 1971.
Percival, J. *The World of Diaghilev*. New York: E.P. Dutton & Co., 1971.
Searle, H. *Ballet Music*. New York: Dover Publications, 1973.
Svetloff, V. *Anna Pavlova*. New York: Dover Publications, 1974.

SUGGESTIONS FOR FURTHER READING

Fokine, M. *Fokine: Memoirs of a Ballet Master*. Boston: Little, Brown, 1961.
Karsavina, T. *Theatre Street*. Brooklyn, N.Y.: Dance Horizons, 1931.
Macdonald, N. *Diaghilev Observed*. New York: Dance Horizons, 1975.
Massine, L. *My Life in Ballet*. New York: St. Martins Press, 1968.
Nijinsky, R. *Nijinsky*. New York: Simon and Schuster, 1935.
Sokolova, L. *Dancing for Diaghilev*. New York: Macmillan, 1960.

CHAPTER 9

Twentieth Century Ballet in the Western World

At Diaghilev's death the future directions of ballet were already determined largely by his all-consuming efforts to produce brilliant dance art throughout Europe. Diaghilev had been the inspiration and driving force for the creation of a number of the most perfect ballets ever conceived, thereby creating a new audience for dance. In keeping with the art nouveau spirit of his times, he facilitated the injection of avant-garde attitudes into the tradition-bound classical dance, thus freeing the ever-present choreographic challenge in order to open the way for a full-blown dance theatre. Especially significant during Diaghilev's last years was the fact that his organization provided fertile ground for several young artists whose life work would spring from an effort to nurture the new dance evolving from their mentor's immense contribution. A young Balanchine would be central in the growth of ballet in America; a young Lifar would reëstablish the ballet in Paris; two ambitious young women, Marie Rambert and Ninette de Valois, would establish a national ballet in England that would be the pride of this most civilized of countries.

THE LEGACY OF DIAGHILEV IN EUROPE

England: Marie Rambert (b. 1888)

In 1920, Rambert opened a ballet school in London after a career which included an unorthodox beginning in the dance world. Early on she had been influenced by the ideas of Isadora Duncan and later by Emile Dalcroze whose unique studies in movement provided her with invaluable training as a dance innovator in England. Through Dalcroze, Rambert was employed by Diaghilev to assist Nijinsky in his choreographic efforts. She continued with the company as a dancer where she was able to observe first-hand the making of brilliant theatre, partake in the joys and pitfalls of choreographic experimentation, and benefit from the technique classes of Maestro Cecchetti. Upon the advice of Nijinsky, she eventually left the Ballet Russes and returned to England where the great dancer suggested to her that her future lay. Armed with nothing but her experience and youthful ambition, she began training young dancers with an eye to presenting them in performances. Within the decade it was evident to her dancers and the small number of ballet lovers who supported their performing efforts that here was the making of an English national ballet. Rambert proceeded to form the Ballet Club later to become Ballet Rambert and offered regular performances, some with famous guest artists, in a theater where her dancers could also make their fledgling choreographic attempts. Among these protégés were Frederick Ashton and Antony Tudor whose brilliant works continue to give important original dimensions to contemporary ballet on both sides of the Atlantic.

Frederick Ashton (b. 1906)

Since 1930, Ashton has created ballets remarkable for their variety of style, subject matter and danceability. Essentially all his works are rooted in the technique of the *danse d'école* which he has skillfully adapted to the stylistic requirements of each ballet. Over the years, Sir Frederick's choreographic output has exerted the greatest influence in creating what might be called the English style of ballet, stately and elegant, yet witty and colorful, in a word, well-bred. Ashton may be credited with introducing back into European ballet the popularity of the full-evening spectacle ballet. Among these are his restagings of *Sleeping Beauty, Swan Lake, Giselle,* and *Coppélia* and his original versions of *Cinderella, Sylvia,* and *Ondine* for the Royal Ballet. Numerous shorter ballets such as *Facade, Les Patineurs, Enigma Variation,* and *Jazz Calendar* are kept in the company's repertory. Ashton's immense influence on all facets of ballet in his country is confirmed by Brinson's comment:

> To write about Sir Frederick Ashton is to write about the history of the Royal Ballet; in Ashton's ballets lie a portrait of the company; their range reflects the range of its dancers, their demands have enriched and ennobled its dancers' style and abilities. As Ashton's genius has de-

veloped, so has the Royal Ballet; the mutual stimulus existing between a choreographer and his company, between creator and instrument—and notably with Ashton, between him and Margot Fonteyn (their association having lasted longer and more fruitfully than any other in the history of ballet)—has made for great ballets and a great company.

Ninette de Valois (b. 1898)

Dame Ninette de Valois has the unique distinction in dance history of almost single-handedly founding a national ballet school and company for England. Such a feat is all the more remarkable when one considers that such an accomplishment has traditionally taken the resources of a monarch and an incubation period of a century or two. While still in her teens, de Valois had participated in lesser forms of theatrical dance such as was presented in the London musical halls. Her early performing centered around frail remnants of the post-Romantic style popularized at the Empire and Alhambra Theatres. Quality ballet training was not available to her until Cecchetti opened a studio in London when he arrived during the war years with Diaghilev's Ballets Russes. It was during this time that she received her topmost form of technical study and shortly thereafter was invited to join the Ballets Russes. Several highly charged and colorful years with the renowned Russians proved invaluable to the destiny that awaited her.

In 1926 de Valois left Diaghilev to found her own school which would be the feeding source for a native English ballet. Fortified with pedagogic knowledge derived from intensive classes with Cecchetti and later with Legat and Espinosa, she established the school. Being gifted with administrative and organizational talents, and no doubt sharpened by close association with the Ballets Russes, she eventually set about founding the Sadler's Wells Ballet at the request of the theatre's director, Lillian Baylis. Supportive of de Valois' efforts and generously contributive with their own talent in these first years were former Diaghilev ballerina, Lydia Lopokova, and her husband, the famed economist, Lord Maynard Keynes. Other personnel from Diaghilev days who lent assistance were Serge Grigoriev and his wife, Lubov Tchernicheva; Nicholas Sergeyev, who assisted in restaging the classics and setting the old Ballets Russes' repertory for the company; Tamara Karsavina, who coached the young Margot Fonteyn in *Fire-*

Fig. 1. The youthful Margot Fonteyn as the Sleeping Beauty in Sir Frederic Ashton's recreation of the Petipa ballet. Courtesy of the New York Public Library for the Performing Arts.

162

bird. Constant Lambert, who became the architect of English ballet music, was nigh indispensable to the cause.

During World War II the British company requested the Sadler's Wells Ballet to tour the continent with the intention of restoring morale amidst the enlisted troops and allied countries. Withstanding the enormous difficulties of wartime touring inadvertently seasoned the company to sufficiently attract the help of the British government. The company moved from its inadequate quarters to Covent Garden Opera House where the company continued to develop, opening opportunities for its up-and-coming choreographic talents, namely John Cranko and Kenneth MacMillan. Having steadily grown despite the war and its accompanying assimilation of male dancers, the company began its great international tours. In 1949 its appearance in New York dazzled the public with a sumptuous version of *Sleeping Beauty.* A bevy of superb dancers, led by Margot Fonteyn, helped inaugurate what was to be the American ballet boom of the 1950's. By 1954 the company had become sufficiently distinguished as to be honored by the Crown with a new charter and its present title, the Royal Ballet. When the first of the Russian dance defectors, Rudolf Nureyev, accepted an invitation to partner the company's prima ballerina, Dame Margot, an incomparable ballet team emerged to touch the hearts of audiences all over the world.

The solid foundation of the company accrues from the fact that the entire ballet operation is rooted in the unique system of early training offered to the dancers. Based on the model of the Imperial Russian Ballet Schools, carefully selected ten-year-old children are boarded at White Lodge where they receive academic schooling and an uninterrupted eight year period of carefully developed technical work in the Royal Academy of Dancing method. This particular ballet pedagogy, which is now considered distinctively English, derives from a variety of sources which in the end is traceable back to the work of Noverre and Blasis. Direct influences stem from Cecchetti, Legat, and later Volkova from the Kirov in Leningrad. The backgrounds of these teachers represent the combined influences of Lepri via Blasis on the Italian side; Legat, representing the pre-revolutionary Russian-French influences of Petipa via Noverre; and Volkova, introducing the more recent Soviet approach developed by Vaganova.

A number of other companies have existed in England, producing their own ballets and dancers. The Festival Ballet, founded in 1950 by Dolin and Markova, has provided a special dimension to England's

Fig. 2. Kenneth Macmillan created *Gloria* for the Royal Ballet to commemorate those lost in World War I. Jennifer Penney and Wayne Eagling dance the *pas de deux*. Photo courtesy of Jack Vartoogian.

164

dance scene in that foreign artists as well as English have traditionally staffed the company. A junior company to the Royal Ballet, called the Sadler's Wells Theatre Ballet, has provided more performances for the growing appetite for dance in England since the 1950's. Currently a number of larger English cities also support companies and Scotland boasts of its own Ballet Theatre.

Extending to the dominions, the British ballet establishment has had a profound influence on the organization of ballet schools and companies in Canada where activity peaks with Toronto's National Ballet of Canada and the Winnipeg Royal Ballet. Australia's ballet has emerged under the leadership of Robert Helpmann, and a number of fine dancers and choreographers, notably John Cranko, have emerged from the thriving ballet activity in Johannesburg, South Africa.

France

The feverish excitement generated by Diaghilev's first seasons in Paris affected to some extent the ballet at the Paris Opera, suggesting new approaches to an art that had been steadily on the downgrade since the waning of the golden age of the Romantic ballet some fifty years before. The fact, too, that during the Opera's off-seasons, the Ballets Russes had occasion to perform in the great house also stimulated French interest in dance. Likewise, stellar guest artists such as Pavlova, Spessivtzeva, and Nijinska with her own company did much to sustain public interest in dance performance as well as increase interest in the Opera's excellent ballerina, Carlotta Zambelli.

Following Diaghilev's death, Serge Lifar, who had been the impresario's last protégé, created an original version of *Prometheus* at the Paris Opera. Its success led to his appointment as choreographer and for the next quarter of a century Lifar served as dancer and choreographer. Two of his most notable roles were Albrecht in *Giselle* and the spirit in *Spectre de la Rose.* Lifar also distinguished himself as a choreographer during these years creating over sixty works of which *Icare, Le Chevalier et la Damoiselle* and *Suite en Blanc* are most often cited as his masterpieces. Although the Second World War interfered greatly with the workings of the Paris Opera, a number of superb dancers emerged from the School. The fabled Yvette Chauviré crowned a list of artists including Ludmilla Tcherina, Solange Schwartz, Lycette Darsonval, Serge Peretti, and Michel Renault.

In many ways Lifar has been the spiritual father of the 20th century French ballet. His presence at the Opera provided a link for a new generation to the traditional past which had been lost at the close of the Romantic age. His own training reflected the Imperial School of old Russia while his Diaghilev association provided him with first hand experiences in new directions for the classical dance. Lifar's influence directly extends today to such dancers as Roland Petit who displayed early on in his career a solid choreographic talent. After leaving the Opera, Petit created for *Les Ballet des Champs-Élysées,* and his own companies, the *Ballets de Paris* and the *Ballets de Marseilles.* Other French choreographers of Petit's generation who have greatly contributed to French ballet by creating for their own companies are Janine Charrat, Jean Babilée and Maurice Béjart. Since 1960, Béjart has dominated the dance scene in Belgium where he directs *Les Ballet de XX siècle.* He has become Europe's most controversial avant-garde choreographer having created or staged numerous unconventional works for the company.

In keeping with its long history, French dance, unlike that of other European countries, still beckons the work of artists regardless of their national origins. To name a few, Harald Lander, Flemming Flindt, Margot Fonteyn, and Marjorie Tallchief have enjoyed the privilege of participating in French ballet. Likewise many French dancers, especially Nina Vyroubova and Violette Verdy have been happily received outside of their own country.

While some of the best remembered French dancers and choreographers in recent times have emerged from the state-supported ballet school of the Paris Opera at one point or another, Paris has abounded with great teachers since the fateful presence of Diaghilev's Ballets Russes. For many years Olga Preobranjenska, *prima ballerina assoluta* of the Imperial Russian Ballet, taught privately as did her fellow *émigreé,* Lubov Egorova. Dancers from all over the world still desire to study in Paris, benefiting from the classes of Mme. Nora, Raymond Franchetti, and Yves Casati. Numerous ballet companies, large and small and often short-lived, have employed their students and using Paris as their home-base, have in recent decades, provided dance of uneven quality in this nostalgia-filled dance center.

Hoping to achieve acclaim similar to Diaghilev's Ballets Russes, several smaller dance companies were founded in France and enjoyed varying degrees of success and longevity. The most notable were organized by Ida Rubinstein shortly after the First World War and continued until 1935. Staffed with many Ballets Russes dancers such as Nijinska, Massine, and Schollar, it also included such artists as Jooss, Lichine, Dolin and Ashton. In keeping with the style of ballets introduced by Diaghilev, Rubinstein presented their works in collaboration with first-rate composers and scenarists. The company gave performances in Paris and subsequently performed around the world. Four other companies enjoying brief successes in France were the Ballet Suedois, the Soirreés de Paris, Nijinska's own collection of dancers who performed in Paris as well as on various tours, and Balanchine's Les Ballets 1933.

The death of Diaghilev unleashed an entire company of dancers in Europe, many of whom were unwilling to retire, teach or go abroad in search of work. Thus, when René Blum and Vassili de Basil established the Ballet Russe de Monte Carlo in 1932, a number of these artists were brought back into close association. Massine created a considerable number of works, notably *Le Beau Danube, Les Présages* and *Symphonie Fantastique*. Balanchine also contributed to the repertory, setting *Concurrence, Cotillon,* and *Le Bourgeois Gentilhomme*. These ballets had the good fortune to be interpreted by such undisputed artists as Danilova, Lichine and the "baby ballerinas," Toumanova, Baronova, and Riabouchinska. It was at this point in history that the company visited the United States, reintroducing the glamorous Russian ballet to audiences who remembered or had heard of the fabled visits of Pavlova and the Diaghilev Ballets Russes.

In 1936, de Basil broke with the Ballet Russe de Monte Carlo and formed another company bearing his own name. Later renamed the Original Ballets Russes, de Basil's company toured the world presenting much of Massine's creative output. Their extended stay in the Western Hemisphere was particularly important to the establishment and continuing growth of the classical ballet in South America.

Revitalizing his organization the same year, René Blum created anew the Ballets Russes de Monte Carlo. Securing the choreographic services of Fokine, the company was able to present new works which displayed the fresh talents of Markova, Youskevich, Franklin, and Skibine in addition to the indomitable Alexandra Danilova.

Denmark

Denmark holds a unique position in the 20th century ballet. The pedagogic contribution of Auguste Bournonville has been handed down by generations in unbroken succession at the Royal Danish Ballet School in Copenhagen. Unlike the disintegration of the French ballet of the Romantic period, the Danish ballet has managed to keep intact all the detailed and precise aspects of training which gave it the unprecedented ballet style originally shaped by Bournonville. Moreover, the Danes continue to perform the master's ballets as they were intended, without revision or restaging, so that one can presently observe Danish ballet as it appeared over one hundred years ago.

Although theatrical dance in other parts of Europe declined artistically after the golden age of the Romantic ballet, certain technical advances were achieved in the further development of point work, height of extension, *pirouettes* on point and complexities of partnering. With this growth of greater technical facility, many of the old approaches to ballet dancing, including certain steps and styles of executing a number of other steps were completely forgotten. In Denmark, however, the Bournonville approach to ballet with all its 19th century exercises, steps and style has been continuously kept in the technical training at the school and in the Bournonville ballets presented at the Royal Theatre. After Bournonville's death, technical innovations and creative trends occurring elsewhere, such as those introduced by Diaghilev's choreographers, never fully penetrated the Danish Ballet, leaving its lively art uniquely archaic. Fokine worked briefly with the Danish Ballet in 1925 setting a number of his works for the Royal Theatre but his presence seemed not to affect the honored Danish traditions. From 1932 to 1951 the Danish balletmaster, Harald Lander, created a number of works for the company, most notably *Qarrtsiluni* and *Études* so that while fresh works were added to the repertory the Bournonville foundations were not altered.

In 1951 Vera Volkova, a dancer trained in post-revolutionary Russia was invited to Denmark to reorganize and update the Royal Danish Ballet School. In the course of her tenure, Volkova succeeded in eliciting a greater technical range from the dancers. She presented along side of the peerless Bournonville tradition the pedagogic method of Imperial Russia as reinterpreted by her own teacher, Agrippina Vaganova. As a result, the Danes have for some time been remarkably equipped to perform with authority the contemporary works of Balanchine, Ashton, Petit, and Culberg among others while maintaining the ability to recreate their precious heritage.

The Royal Danish Ballet is recognized throughout the dance world for the splendid training given at its school, the women being noted for their femininity, *ballon* and *batterie* and the men for their elegance and prodigious elevation. Edel Pederson has been the leading expert on the Bournonville style in Copenhagen having been trained by one of the master's own students. Directly handed down to her are the six codified ballet classes and three ballet barres which comprise the Bournonville syllabus composed after his death. While the syllabus as such is not currently taught, the classes at the school are strictly based on the Bournonville principles of *épaulement, port de bras,* and musicality.

The variety of works represented by the Royal Danish repertory have had the good fortune of being interpreted by numerous superb dancers. Following the example of their first great native ballerina, Lucile Grahn, the school has produced such artists as Juliette Price, Margrethe Schanne, Flemming Flindt, Kirsten Simone, Eric Bruhn, Toni Lander, Niels Kehlet, and Peter Martins.

Scandinavia

The Scandinavian countries have been considerably affected by the proximity of Danish ballet. Sweden is the most advanced of these small northern lands having been the earliest to adapt the artistic trappings of 18th century French court life. The Opera in Stockholm also houses the major ballet company which performs works ranging from the classics to those of the widely recognized Swedish choreographer Brigit Culberg. Norway and Finland likewise enjoy a growing interest in ballet. While Norway has reached out to western Europe in its developmental stage, Finland has been considerably influenced by its Russian neighbor, particularly in its training methods.

Germany

Since the early 18th century the ballet has always had an unofficial home in Germany. The wealthy nobility of the country's various city-states required theatrical entertainments in their magnificent baroque palaces. Not only were theatres built to house such amusements but dancers, actors, and singers were retained for participation in performances designed for the inhabitants and guests of a particular estate. We have seen, for example, that Noverre was patronized by the Duke of Wurttemberg for some years, to create lavish ballets for his private theatre and during this time there was considerable trafficking of foreign dancers engaged by similar private theatres. Due to the historical fact that the German states were not unified into a nation until 1870,

Fig. 3. Marcia Haydée and Richard Craggun are seen here rehearsing Cranko's ballet, *Eugene Onegin* for the Stuttgart Ballet. Photo courtesy of Jack Vartoogian.

the concept of a central national ballet never emerged. Likewise the number of ballet schools was minimal compared to other European countries and, accordingly, did not produce a comparatively large number of native dancers and choreographers. Yet public theatres and opera houses suitable for ballet productions have been abundant since the 19th century so that the rarely seen full ballet evenings in Germany were limited to visiting companies for many decades.

The devastation of the country in the World Wars I and II added to the lack of serious development of ballet although one would be hard put to place all the blame on the Wars. The Germans are music lovers of the first order. Indeed, Germany has been the birthplace of many of the world's greatest composers, singers, and musicians, and the study of music has always been a strong part of German education. It would seem that they do not possess such a profound love of ballet as they do for the musical arts. This assumption has been considerably altered in recent years due to fresh importation of foreign choreographers and dancers.

Following the energetic reconstruction of Germany after the Second World War, the growing economy produced great wealth which in turn encouraged the enhancement of the quality of human life. New theatres replaced the war-wasted ones in the larger cities and the small cities and resort towns polished up their often rustic-styled little opera houses. The city of Stuttgart is currently reliving the brilliant years of ballet brought to it by Noverre two centuries ago. A part of a large cultural complex called the Wurttemberg State Theatre, the Stuttgart Ballet under the guiding hand of South African John Cranko, rose to become a first rate company. Among the many fine German and foreign dancers, its Brazilian ballerina, Marcia Haydeé, has been recognized as being in the highest echelon. The Stuttgart Ballet has to some degree served as a model for other developing companies such as those in Frankfurt, Hanover, Hamburg, and Munich. Not to be outdone, many smaller cities likewise have ballet companies which supply the dance segments in the opera productions and produce occasional ballet evenings for German audiences.

Italy

Once the cradle of the ballet, Italy has lost its reputation as a dance center. While the Italian contribution to the art in the 19th century played an integral part in the development of the present form of the classical dance, it has not maintained its importance outside the country. The systemization of the technique class by Carlo Blasis produced generations of stellar dancers and teachers in Milan but a strong national awareness of ballet has not emerged in present times. Throughout Italy the municipal opera houses maintain ballet groups to serve as part of the opera productions and these frequently provide a number of ballet performances.

The best dance to be seen in post-war Italy has been at the summer festivals such as those held in Spoleto and Nervi. Here international companies as well as guest appearances of the world's finest artists perform for large audiences of Italians and the vibrant tourist trade. Unfortunately, such top flight dance does not sufficiently penetrate the Italian dance world to invigorate its dormant creative spirit. Strict labor laws generally forbid the permanent hiring of non-Italian dance personnel which is always a potent source of fresh ideas. At the same time the overwhelming governmental bureaucracy would seem to stifle the nurturing of the creative spirit in the totally subsidized Italian ballet. As a result, there are no internationally recognized choreographers. On the other hand, Italian ballet masters have always excelled in turning out remarkable dancers since the inception of the ballet art itself. In the last century, the names of Cerrito, Rosati, Legnani and Zambelli attest to superlative training. The masterful teacher Cecchetti chose to end his lengthy career refining the teaching methods at the Imperial Academy in Milan which produced such dancers as Luciana Navaro and Mario Pistoni. Today the profound artistry of Carla Fracci and a host of other accomplished dancers not readily known outside Italy give evidence that there is still quality teaching in the country.

Holland

The popularity of dance in Holland stems from the post-World War II years when Holland was engaged in its massive reconstruction program. The country's great collective courage seems to have been reflected in the birth of a vibrant interest in dance. Two government subsidized companies dominate the Dutch cultural scene, the Dutch National Ballet in Amsterdam and the Netherlands Dance Theatre in The Hague. The Dutch National Ballet, formed by Sonia Gaskell in 1961, boasts a large repertory and an equally large company. It performs the ballets of Perrot, St. Léon, Petipa, and Fokine as well as works by contemporary choreographers. In the vanguard of current Dutch creators at the National Ballet are Rudi van Dantzig and Hans van Manen who have long produced works for the company.

Since the Netherlands Dance Theatre was formed in 1960, it has excelled in producing contemporary ballets rooted in the technique of the *danse d'ecole* as well as works based on the technical system of Martha Graham. From the beginning, the company profited from numerous creative efforts of Hans van Manen, and two Americans namely, Glen Tetley and Benjamin Harkarvy. Possesssing remarkable talents as a teacher and artistic coach, Harkarvy has also contributed greatly to the formation of a number of fine Dutch dancers. In 1975 Jiri Kylian became the artistic director of NDT. He has created a repertory of startingly moving ballets which include *Sinfonietta,*

Fig. 4. Arlette van Boven and Eric Newton perform in Jiri Kylian's *Sinfonietta* for the Netherlands Dance Theatre. Photo courtesy of Jack Vartoogian.

Psalmensymfonie and *Soldatenmis*. His choreography is uniquely characterized by a subtle pervasion of deeply felt patriotism for his Czech homeland, rendering his ballets a particularly poignant tone.

As the first generation of Dutch choreographers and dancers have matured sufficiently to absorb the early international influences instrumental in the birth of Dutch ballet, they have established a healthy identity with modern dance idioms. Synthesizing the best of American influences, and current avant-garde Continental trends in theatrical dance style, the Dutch choreographers produce both dramatic and exquisitely lyrical dance works which appear to fuse much of the two hundred years of classical heritage into their distinctively Dutch dance theatre.

SOVIET RUSSIA: 1918 TO PRESENT

Before the Revolution of 1917, the Russian ballet, which had achieved the greatest aesthetic and technical heights the art had yet attained, was concentrated in the Imperial Theatres of St. Petersburg and Moscow. Due to the radical changes in thinking and living that the political upheaval brought on, the ballet, as all other facets of life, underwent drastic reforms. During the 1920's, the Soviet struggles to stabilize and extend the services of government coincided with the reformation and further development of the ballet. Today all fifteen Republics of the Soviet Union enjoy the benefits of ballet companies and their adjoining schools which number thirty-four major performing organizations. These are government owned and operated as are all schools, factories, hospitals, and businesses in the Soviet Union. The very highest standards are maintained from the thoroughness of the Soviet ballet's training syllabus to the most minute details of the complexities of multi-faceted ballet productions.

From the outset Soviet dancers receive the fullest possible preparation for careers in ballet which not only deal with physical and material aspects of the work, but provide an enlightened mental attitude toward it as well. As future dancers they are taught that they are individually responsible to the State and therefore to all Soviet people to achieve maximum goals for themselves. As future artists of the USSR they will have a predetermined place in the scheme of Soviet life and a duty to fulfill it. Hence, this politically derived philosophy influences the total development of Russian dancers, making them as a whole the best equipped, best prepared, most capable, healthiest, devoted, and secure in the world. On the other hand, periodic defections by a number of Soviet dancers focus attention on the growing demand for uncensored artistic experimentation, a central element of creativity which is unfortunately contrary to the dictates of any totalitarian government.

We have seen that prior to the Revolution of 1917 there had been considerable advanced thinking in the art circles of Moscow. In the dance field, it was clear that the long years of Petipa's influence had run their course. Choreographers such as Alexander Gorsky in Moscow were not only questioning tradition but were breaking with it. Voices calling for balletic reforms were particularly articulate in St. Petersburg at the turn of the century. Very young dancers such as the Legat brothers, Pavlova, and Fokine were speaking out, clamoring for changes in the entire structure of the Imperial Theatre. One of their strongest artistic criticisms was that the emphasis on spectacle should be redirected toward expressiveness. Fate and youthful impatience allowed Pavlova and Fokine to realize their destinies in Western Europe while for those who stayed in Russia, reforms did not occur until after the Revolution had suceeded in annihilating the old order.

Under the auspices of the fledgling Soviet government the very purpose of dance art underwent radical change. No longer was ballet for the privileged few but the art was to be committed to ennobling the feelings of the vast Soviet audiences. Ballet was to reflect meaning, having man and his emotions at the thematic center of choreographic works. Due to the nature of dance, according to the official Soviet aesthetic, the thematic material should reflect the positive aspects of man's life. Emphasis on tragic, sordid, or grotesque subject matter must be minimal to blend with the essentially joyful nature of dance. In our time, Soviet ballet prides itself in having retained selected aspects of this national treasure which have stood the test of time while harmonizing them with new technical discoveries, novel theatrical ideas, fresh artistic concepts, and socio-political needs.

Agrippina Vaganova (1879–1951)

Most responsible for the intensive and swift advancement of technical reforms in the Soviet ballet was the ballerina, Agrippina Vaganova. As a pupil of Gerdt, Vazem, and Legat, her early training had reflected the highest attainments of the Imperial School and in time she also absorbed the influences of Cecchetti and Fokine. Acknowledged for her outstanding *batterie* and *ballon,* Vaganova was known as the "Queen of Variations" during her dancing career. Today her contribution to Soviet dance reaches beyond this historical footnote which attests to her performing years. Rather, Vaganova was personally responsible for rennovating the entire pedagogic system which trained Russian dancers. Her methods synthesized and expanded the entire body of technical knowledge in such a comprehensive manner that it continues to be the basis of all ballet training in the USSR.

After the Revolution, which to some extent precipitated her premature retirement from the stage, Vaganova was invited to teach at the Maryinsky, renamed the Leningrad Choreographic Technikum. At once she began to blend the vast knowledge of her personal training and experience with her own ideas on ballet instruction. As the

Fig. 5.   The Bolshoi Ballet's production of Fokine's "The Dying Swan" is interpreted here by Maya Plisetskaya. Photo courtesy of Jack Vartoogian.

176

Technikum's leading teacher, Vaganova was soon turning out a bevy of ballerinas, unique in their ability to conquer space. Among her many renowned pupils were Semenova, Dudkinskaya, Lepeshinskaya and Galina Ulanova, the latter being the only one seen by western audiences when she appeared in Europe and in the United States toward the end of her career. Never before had *pirouettes* and *grand jetés* been so dazzling yet pure in their classical line as when performed by these dancers. The expressive capacities of the elegantly poised head, back and arms had never reached such degrees of subtlety. For sheer amplitude, these Soviet ballerinas outsoared the leaps of any dancer in living memory. Likewise, Vaganova's teaching methods influenced the entire training system at the school so that her ideas further expanded the technical horizons of male dancing. Carefully following the choreographic trends of her times, Vaganova was able to break down numerous daring innovations in partnering which were being attempted in the contemporary choreography of her colleagues. Once these novel movement ideas received a systematic approach, they were absorbed into the syllabus, thus extending the male's technical expectation in *pas de deux* work. Often acrobatic in essence, the complex and demanding lifts achieved by the Soviet male dancer went through considerable artistic refinement in the hands of Vaganova to become genuine amplifications of the *danse d'école*. Roslavleva best sums up the impact of Vaganova-trained dancers in words which still apply to the generations that have followed her personal influence.

"Everything was subordinated to the main goal of bringing the human body into a state of complete and harmonious co-ordination of all its parts. However, the "Vaganova back" was the first thing that struck the eye in Vaganova-trained dancers. This was due to the exceptional placing of the *trunk* that, according to the professor's maxim, should be the "master of the body". She taught the pupil to "dance out of the body," so that the muscles of the trunk governed the movement of the limbs. This could be reached only after a prolonged education of muscular sensations on the part of the dancer, learning how to bring into action any part of her body and any muscles without applying unnecessary energy to its other parts. Vaganova pupils were famed for their *equilibre*. At the same time, while being firmly placed on the ground, the strength of their backs enabled them to "take off" at any given moment and soar in the air, continuing to move and to maneuver their body *during* the flight."

Since 1956 the West has been able to observe Soviet dancers on a number of occasions when the Kirov Ballet of Leningrad and the Bolshoi Ballet of Moscow have visited the capitals of Europe and North America. Both companies had tremendous impact on their audiences from the standpoint of their individual styles and the superlative qualities of their dancers. While the Kirov Ballet astounded the western public with the exquisite lyricism of its dancers, the Bolshoi won the day for sheer exuberance of its dramatic performers. These central characteristics in each company are traced back many decades, being essentially present prior to the artistic reforms instituted by the Soviets.

Soviet choreography has gone its own direction in the past fifty years, not being influenced by western trends until recently. This is in part due to the overriding Marxist political thought that all activity is subservient to the needs of the State and artistic work is subsequently guided by these official needs to provide a kind of ballet for vast audiences which is easily understood and appreciated. As a result, the compositional output of Soviet choreographers often appears uneven in quality and unfamiliar or dated according to western tastes. Be that as it may, any westerner observing the Soviet dancing as such never fails to be astounded by its sheer level of human attainment.

THE UNITED STATES: 1933 TO PRESENT

The recent growth of ballet in the United States has been unparalleled in the entire history of the art. From its modest American beginnings in 1933, native participation and interest in classical dance has steadily expanded to a point where the United States stands alongside England and Russia. Based on sheer numbers alone, the incalculable list of ballet students in the United States, the staggering number of performances ranging from professional to amateur, the wealth of creative and technological talent, and the enormous audiences all combine to outshine any other country past or present.

While never of wide interest in the country's earliest cultural life, Europen ballet had been enthusiastically received on intermittent occasions in the 18th and 19th centuries. A handful of American ballet dancers even emerged from their native soil as we have seen in Chapter 7, but with no large organized companies or schools for them to expand their potential and hand down their spottily begotten knowledge, the classical dance had no means to thrive. In the beginning of the present century the art was presented to American audiences with the visits of Diaghilev's Ballets Russes and Anna Pavlova's extensive tours. Following them were the performances in Chicago staged by the former Diaghilev star Adolph Bolm. In addition several performances prepared by Bolm's compatriot, Mikhail Mordkin and his Russian Ballet Company were given in New York. Between 1928 and 1931 Massine staged *Scheherazade* at the Roxy Theatre, giving four performances daily. Later he recreated *The Rite of Spring* for performances in Philadelphia and the Metropolitan Opera House in New York.

The Ballets Russes in America

In 1933 the American impresario, Sol Hurok, negotiated with Colonel de Basil to bring his Ballets Russes to the United States. The presentation of the company at this time is usually cited as the major occurrence which permanently established an American interest in dance that would accelerate uninterruptedly into the present time.

For the historic visit of the Ballets Russes, Massine was appointed artistic director and the heavily dominated Massine-Balanchine repertory, based on an extension of Diaghilev's artistic policies, was danced by the veteran Russian ballerinas Tchernicheva and Danilova. The three "baby ballerinas," Baronova, Toumanova, and Riabouchinska, proved to be a great box office draw, cathing the American imagination for the novelty as well as the young girls' genuine talents. The superb character dancer, Leon Woizokowski, represented the male contingent along with David Lichine, André Eglevsky, Roman Jasinsky, and Paul Petroff. Before long, a number of American dancers would be swelling the ranks of this Russian-dominated company, demonstrating that nationality had no special claim on sheer dance ability.

Paradoxically, the 1933–34 season was a time of incredible glamour for the ballet even though there was virtually no sophisticated ballet audience in America. The press made the most of the exotic and temperamental dancers and the intrigued Americans flocked to the theatre in the larger cities where the Ballets Russes played. During the following seasons ballet was fast becoming engrained in American cultural life. And when Hurok's business acumen helped the company gross over a million dollars yearly, it demonstrated that this extravagant form of entertainment was for once in its history a financial success.

The annals of the Ballets Russes between 1933 and 1940 is one of considerable administrative entanglement. It included a number of name changes for the company, rival companies being set up by Blum and de Basil or taken over by Serge Denham, and attempts to merge these rival Ballets Russes by Hurok. On the artistic side, the situation was equally fraught with turmoil what with dancers shifting their allegiances from one company to the other. Most devastating perhaps was Massine's legal battle over his choreographic rights arising from the fact that the rival companies were both claiming his ballets as their exclusive property. While artistic deterioration took its toll, the magic name of Ballets Russes still managed to retain its fascination for the American audience in general. Unfortunately for the profession, the Ballet Russe de Monte Carlo rang down its final curtain in 1962 due to an overwhelming array of administrative and financial problems.

What is historically significant is that the Russian ballet as managed by Hurok and directed by Blum, de Basil and eventually Denham, provided the American public with the opportunity to cut its eye teeth. What audiences in major cities across the country saw was a comparatively substantial amount of classical ballet during these years. Furthermore, the Ballets Russes companies were the gateway for countless dancers who would set up ballet schools all over the nation, create a climate for performing wherever they eventually settled and contribute vastly to the evolution of the classical dance in the New World.

To a large extent, the burgeoning interest in ballet generated by the Ballet Russe de Monte Carlo brought about the successful inauguration of two native American companies, the New York City Ballet and the Amerian Ballet Theatre. While the inspiration for and establishment of these organizations was independent of the Ballet Russe, much of their initial strength derived from individual dancers and choreographers who at one time or another had had affiliation with the Diaghilev organization. Thus, the honored and proven traditions which are the dancer's heritage passed naturally from this old-world reservoir into the mainstream of American dance.

New York City Ballet

A central figure in the development of American ballet is Lincoln Kirstein. Both scholar and patron of the art, Kirstein has been the visionary behind the long and painstaking fostering of one of the country's brightest assets, the New York City Ballet. As a result of his extensive and published research on dance in the early thirties, Kirstein formulated the core of a long range plan which would establish the timeless *danse d'école* on American soil with American trained dancers preparing for American audiences.

Like Diaghilev, Kirstein has not revealed any artistic ambitions of his own in the many ballet companies he has founded. Yet his immense erudition, his sense of history and his unerring aesthetic judgments have caused him to be the creative spirit behind a life-time of forming artistic organizations. Through Kirstein's conceptual centrality on the American dance scene, George Balanchine was offered the field to create a new classicism which is essentially an amplification of a century-old theatrical instrument capable of infinite manipulation and growth. In emphasizing the importance of the motivation toward a new classicism, Kirstein has pointed out that not only must those who create ballets understand its ancient language, but in a more profound sense, they must comprehend the emotional and moral spirit of their times. In other words, the richer a choreographer's contemporary experience, the greater impact the choreographer's art can have on the quality of a society's cultural life.

The first major undertaking in Kirstein's grand design was the foundation of the School of American Ballet in 1934. Dedicated to the preservation and further growth of the classical dance, the school aimed to train the best dancers possible to provide the essential human material for a new national art. At the helm of such a school, Kirstein understood there would have to be a central figure steeped in ballet's great tradition while at the same time open to contemporary trends and have an artistic and productive potential extensive enough to move into the future. He had found such a man in Balanchine whom he considered an exponent of the purest contemporary rendering of classical theatrical dance. After considerable persuasion, Balanchine came to New York and commenced putting the school in operation in studios that once served Isadora Duncan. Begotten as a means toward an end, the school prepared dancers for performing. In a little over a year the company, named the American Ballet, gave a New York season. Although Balanchine's choreography and the technical competence and vitality of the young Americans was lauded, some critics lamented that the style of the company did not exhibit a true American *genre*. The short season, however, clearly indicated that their systematic approach to training young people for the ranks of the company was on solid ground. In November, 1935, the Metropolitan Opera engaged the American Ballet to create opera ballets and further develop its own repertory. While this affiliation with the prestigious opera was a great boon for the fledgling company, it was short-lived. Balanchine set an imposing number of opera ballets on the young company but it became clear that the Metropolitan's administration was not serious about the development of the ballet as an autonomous art in their precincts. In 1938 this opera-ballet relationship was dissolved, the American Ballet disbanded, and Balanchine turned to choreographing Broadway musicals.

Determined not to forsake his vision, Kirstein opened a second company in 1939 which was called Ballet Caravan. The dancers were former members of the previous company and additional recruits from the school. This time Kirstein engaged only American choreographers, namely Lew Christensen, Eugene Loring and William Dollar, in an effort to underscore the presence of homegrown talent. A number of ballets with indigenous themes were created in a short time. *Filling Station* and *City Portrait* were two ballets conceived by Kirstein himself and choreographed respectively by Christensen and Loring. These works and a number of others in the growing repertory, employed colloquial gesture in conjunction with the classical technique to achieve an atmosphere of Americana. Dollar began his substantial choreographic output with Ballet Caravan creating two works in the classical vein, *Promenade* and *Air and Variation*. Loring's *Billy the Kid* has passed the test of time with flying colors and is today lovingly preserved in the repertory of American Ballet Theatre. Ballet Caravan disbanded at the outset of World War II but temporarily reorganized in 1941 for a Latin American tour. Balanchine returned with the company and added *Serenade, Apollon Musagète, Ballet Imperial* and *Concerto Barocco* to the earlier repertory. Except for the continued operation of the school, the war interrupted Kirstein's activities and the company ceased to exist.

Then, in 1946, Kirstein announced plans for another company called Ballet Society which would present all new works prepared in the Diaghilevian manner, employing first-rate collaboration among progressive choreographers, composers and designers. No longer was the self-conscious American idiom originally favored by Kirstein emphasized but a broader more encompassing artistic vision emerged. Avoiding the pitfall of Diaghilev's Ballets Russes, Kirstein again established his organization on the solid foundation provided by

Fig. 6. The New York City Ballet's production of Balachine's *Stars and Stripes* is danced by principals, Merrill Ashley and Peter Martins. Photo courtesy of Linda Vartoogian.

183

the excellent school so that a continuous flow of highly proficient talent was available to staff the company. Additional objectives associated with the formation of Ballet Society were the provision for scholarships to talented young students and choreographers, the publication of books and periodicals and the promotion of records and films to advance the interest in ballet.

In 1948 Ballet Society became affiliated with the New York City Center of Music and Drama and was renamed the New York City Ballet. From that time on the company, under the artistic leadership of Balanchine, has achieved international recognition taking its unique place among the world's five or six major companies.

George Balanchine (b.1904)

Balanchine left Russia during the transition years between the end of the Imperial era and the firm establishment of the new Soviet style of ballet. After a highly productive period with Diaghilev, which lasted from 1925 until the Impresario's death in 1929, he managed to engage himself in several choreographic assignments which led to his own company in Paris, *Les Ballets 1933*. It was at this point that Kirstein, with the cooperation of another American, Edward Warburg, invited Balanchine to America with the systematically designed intention of implanting the great heritage of classical ballet in relatively virgin soil.

During his lengthy career, Balanchine has created a wealth of ballets. The majority of his works are unchallenged for their intimate relationship with the musical score and the sheer beauty of their choreographic invention. In his development of neo-classicism he has emphasized the dominance of the choreography over the component dancers so that they are as instruments of an orchestra. He requires his dancers to submerge their individuality for the sake of the greater whole, absorbing themselves in the perfection of the classical purity of the ancient technique. Thus, Balanchine, a man who has lived very much in his time, is able to employ the *danse d'école* through his living instruments to create works which bespeak the essence of "nowness." The movement his dancers generate is brilliant, infused with speed and clarity, reflecting the kinetic spirit of the modern world. In precisely this way Balanchine has amplified the classical purist style of Petipa, renewing the aesthetic validity of "dance for the sake of dance."

American Ballet Theatre

In the late thirties the former Diaghilev soloist Mikhail Mordkin formed a small performing company in order to provide the students of his New York school with dancing experience. Taking the leading roles in a limited traditional repertory were an American heiress named Lucia Chase and an exuberant young man from New Jersey, namely Leon Danielian. After several brief but encouraging seasons it was decided by the general manager, Richard Pleasant, to expand the company into a major effort. Hence, Ballet Theatre came into being in 1939.

While the magnanimous patronage of Lucia Chase made the project feasible, its ambitious aesthetic foundations provided an idealistic plan of action. The emerging company was to harbor vital traditions and preserve choreographic masterpieces of every style and period. At the same time it planned that contemporary trends in dance should be encouraged and that a healthy organization should by its very nature offer provocative works created by contemporary artists. Pleasant seems to have believed, and rightly so, that there was an enormous audience in the United States waiting to be molded and shaped into ardent lovers of this lively art. As a result, when Ballet Theatre debuted in 1940 it boasted the largest artistic collaboration in dance history, comprising eleven choreographers, fifty-six classical dancers of whom fifteen were soloists, nineteen Spanish dancers, fourteen Black dancers, eleven designers and three conductors preparing the music of numerous composers. Having eighteen ballets in its repertory, Ballet Theatre opened with a brilliant success, offering a varied program comprised of ballets by Fokine, Loring and Mordkin. A large adoring New York audience, already initiated by the mercurial Ballets Russes seasons, was ready to follow the proverbial piper. While the nationalities represented in the company were heavily Russian and Western European, Americans such as Agnes de Mille and Eugene Loring would choreograph their fresh visions which in time would become American classics. While the company was definitely not one made of native-born artists, it was a representative American company for American audiences and has ever since maintained this honor.

In 1941 Sol Hurok assumed responsibility for booking Ballet Theatre on international tours which presented the company throughout the world. Ballet Theatre showed itself to be a virtual melting pot of American ballet what with the additional works of Antony Tudor, Michael Kidd, Frederick Ashton, Jerome Robbins and George Balan-

Fig. 7. A modern version of St. Léon's *Coppélia* is danced by Natalia Makarova and Mikail Baryshnikov, American Ballet Theatre. Photo courtesy of Linda Vartoogian.

186

chine. Of its many leading dancers over the years, only the brightest few are cited here to include Alicia Markova, Alicia Alonso, Nora Kaye, Melissa Hayden, Cynthia Gregory, Robert Joffrey, Igor Youskevitch, Eric Bruhn, and the Russian defectors, Natalia Makarova and Mikail Baryshnikov.

Among Ballet Theatre's enormous contributions to ballet's evolution are two outstanding achievements in the creative output of Agnes de Mille and Antony Tudor. As a native of this country, de Mille has been most sucessful in creating ballets which use American themes such as *Rodeo* (originally done for Ballets Russes de Monte Carlo) and the harrowing *Fall River Legend*. Of special importance was Antony Tudor's influence on contemporary ballet. As a former student of Rambert he shared in all the formative excellence of his British counterparts but proceeded to develop creatively on American soil. Just as Noverre, Didelot, and Fokine opened up new frontiers in the choreographic conceptualization of ballets, Tudor has managed to bring a new and heightened form of genuine expressiveness to his works. Often referred to by critics as psychological ballets, he employed the classical technique with sublime sensitivity, insight and economy of movement to mount his incomparable *Pillar of Fire, Lilac Garden, Undertow, Romeo and Juliet, Dark Elegies* and *Dim Lustre*.

During the years that the Mordkin Ballet and the American Ballet were forging themselves into the major organizations they would eventually become, other forces and dreams outside of New York City were at work. Inspired to some degree by the infrequent and scattered dance events, a number of young Americans pioneered the permanent establishment of ballet in their home states. Catherine Littlefield formed the Littlefield Ballet in 1935 in Philadelphia. She had received her training from her mother and with Albertieri in New York. Later she studied in Paris with the former Diaghilev ballerina, Lubov Egorova. Littlefield's contribution to the early American dance scene as a choreographer, teacher and artistic director of her own company was considerable for her time. She created a number of ballets and is most remembered for *Barn Dance*. Deftly synthesizing her own eclectic style ballet training, Littlefield produced several fine American dancers as well. Her tenure as director of the Philadelphia Ballet provided lengthy tours of the United States and a successful European tour in 1937.

Ruth Page was another determined woman, central to the growth of ballet outside of New York City. Page's earliest dance experience reached back to the heyday of the Pavlova and Diaghilev companies. During these years she studied the Russian and Italian techniques presented by her teachers, Bolm and Cecchetti. In 1933 she danced for Bolm who was then choreographing for the Chicago Opera. Shortly thereafter she decided to anchor her career in Chicago and in conjunction with a colleague, Bentley Stone, she formed a new company in 1938. Within a decade Page had blossomed as a choreographer, producing fresh ballets which exhibited her own brand of American dance style. Among a number of works, the sordid tale of *Frankie and Johnny* was perhaps most inventive.

By the 1950's her company, renamed the Chicago Opera Ballet, was firmly established and represented the only major ballet force in the midwest. During these years Page began demonstrating a penchant for converting operatic scenarios into the balletic medium. These musical masterpieces turned unique dance works were substantial box office successes, attracting a wider audience to the ballet seasons. Included in a number of such ballets was the chilling *Revenge* converted from *Il Travatore, The Merry Widow,* and *Carmen.*

The development of ballet on the West Coast has been on-going since 1933 when Adolph Bolm founded the San Francisco Ballet as an affiliate of the Opera. However, the brothers William, Lew and Harold Christensen were among those largely responsible for the current expanse of ballet in the western United States. After the war, Lew followed William as the director of the San Francisco Ballet while Harold ran the company's school. William subsequently distinguished himself by forming the ballet department at the University of Utah.

As has been mentioned earlier, Lew Christensen was among the budding American choreographers encouraged by Lincoln Kirstein in the days of the American Ballet. Not only had he composed novel and brilliantly fresh works, but had enjoyed numerable successes as a dancer and was especially applauded for his creation of "Pat Garrett" in Loring's *Billy the Kid.*

To date Lew Christensen has crafted almost one hundred ballets, most of them being in the San Francisco Ballet's repertory at one time or another. His works continue to evince a native American style of dancing suited to the American temperament and physical characteristics. His lengthy career has inspired several generations so that a plethora of remarkable dancers continue to emerge from the school and into the ranks of the company. Due to his leadership, the enthusiasm caused by the company's national and international tours has sparked municipal pride and support for the organization.

Since the 1950's a number of ballet companies have emerged to enhance the status of American ballet. In 1956 an ambitious young dancer, Robert Joffrey, formed a tiny touring company of six artists and proceeded to concertize in hundreds of theatres throughout the country. Following the tried and true formula, Joffrey established his own school in New York City to produce a steady flow of dancers for his company. Besides being a superb teacher and artistic director, Joffrey has choreographed a number of works ranging from the rock *Astarte* to the romantic *Remembrances*. An impressive array of adjunct choreographers have set their works on the company but Gerald Arpino remains the predominant creative personality, showing himself to be both prolific and a master craftsman with such ballets as *Viva Vivaldi, Trinity,* and *Kettentanz.* When the New York City Ballet vacated its home for new quarters in the Lincoln Center complex in 1966, the Joffrey company filled the gap and was renamed the Joffrey City Center Ballet.

The Harkness Ballet formed in 1964 added another dimension to the country's growing dance awareness. Formed in New York with a number of Joffrey's dancers and his repertory, the company was largely subsidized by the Harkness Foundation. During its eleven year existence the company gained wide acclaim for stirring productions of contemporary choreographers.

For several years Washington, D.C. also enjoyed the prestige of its own professional ballet. Under the artistic direction of Frederic Franklin, the National Ballet performed the standard ballet repertory as well as the works of Balanchine, Skibine, and Franklin himself. Although excellently received, the National Ballet met an early demise owing to financial problems.

On better organizational grounds are the emminently popular Pennsylvania Ballet directed by Barbara Weisberger and the Boston Ballet forged by E. Virginia Williams. Just a few of the many American cities boasting professional ballet companies are Houston, Akron, Los Angeles, Pittsburg, Milwaukee, and Atlanta. All these companies have substantial home seasons as well as tours so that the dancers perform much of the year and are able to derive their livelihood from the profession. The Pennsylvania and Boston companies have been awarded several Ford Foundation Grants in recent years, which gives them a certain amount of freedom from financial woes and the liberty to further develop themselves and their regional public.

Even the briefest survey of the classical ballet from the post-Diaghilev era to the present serves to underscore the phenomenal amplification of the art. The most advanced developments in this cultural explosion have occurred largely in the United States where dance has become the country's number one artistic industry. Calling to its support thousands of new adherents yearly, the American ballet style in general has not only become renowned but New York City has emerged as the dance capital of the world in just a few decades.

The American ballet style, rich in the entire spectrum of the art's tradition, fortunate in its heritage of numerous European step-parents, enervated and rendered enormously creative by its indigenous idiom, i.e. the modern dance, extended to millions through its vast television audiences, is a flowering unique in the history of any art form in any era. The initial thrust which catapulted American dance into first place originated in the Old World but along the line it merged and synthesized with the American experience into a fresh vision of movement expression. By contrast such was not the case in England and the continental dance centers. England and Soviet Russia are the principal leaders in European classical ballet, each with their distinctive aesthetic, suited to national tastes and trends. Both countries have given the world exquisite dance artists. England to be certain, has enriched the art with the compositions of a handful of brilliant choreographers. And, just as England has presented today's dance student with the marvelous pedagogy developed by the Royal Academy of Dance, so is Russian ballet particularly distinguished by way of the superb Vaganova-inspired method of imparting the classical technique.

To a much lesser extent other European countries have also contributed to the present state of ballet. But in none of them has there been such an all-encompassing artistic achievement as that in the United States. In spite of a general lack of support in the early years, American ballet appears to be an on-going, upward-moving spiral into the future as is witnessed by the mushrooming of sizable ballet companies all over the country.

REFERENCES

Amberg, George. *Ballet in America*. New York: Duell, Sloan & Pearce, 1949.
Bellew, Helene. *Ballet in Moscow Today*. Greenwich, Conn.: New York Graphic Society.

Brinson, Peter & Crisp, Clement. *Ballet for All*. London: Pan Books, Ltd., 1970.

Chujoy, Anatole. *The New York City Ballet*. New York: Alfred A. Knopf, Inc., 1953.

Hurok, Sol. *S. Hurok Presents*. New York: Hermitage House, 1953.

Sutton, Valerie. Edel Pedersen: Denmark's High Priestess of the Bournonville School. *Dance Magazine*, May, 1976.

SUGGESTIONS FOR FURTHER READING

Clarke, Mary & Vaughan, David. *The Encyclopedia of Dance and Ballet*. New York: G.P. Putnam's Sons, 1977.

Kraus, Richard. *History of the Dance*. Englewood Cliffs, N.J.: Prentice Hall, Inc., 1969.

Kirstein, Lincoln. *Dance, A Short History*. Brooklyn, N.Y.: Dance Horizons, 1969.

Roslavleva, Natalia. *Era of the Russian Ballet, 1770-1965*. New York: E.P. Dutton & Co., 1966.

Taper, Bernard. *Balanchine*. New York: Harper & Row, 1963.

Vaughn, David. *Frederick Ashton and His Ballets*. New York: Alfred A. Knopf, Inc., 1977.

CHAPTER 10

New Directions

The history of the classical ballet has been one of an ever-expanding art form. The gradual emergence of its techniques, firmly based on the classical tenets of unity, harmony, and economy provides the ballet with infinite aesthetic possibilities only restrained in the end by the limitation of the dancer's body. Several centuries of human intelligence, accompanied by refined sensitivity and a profuse amount of collective energy have molded an ingeniously contrived form of artistic expression whose end product is both magical and rarefied. Even the perfection of the theory underlying the ballet's pedagogical systems startles the thoughtful practitioner. For example, the numerous fundamental barre and center exercises which contribute to the proper execution of a simple *pirouette* are not only meaningfully ordered in the students' classroom work, but they represent an enlightened synthesis of decades of lengthy experimentation in the evolution of the multiple *pirouette*. The precise manner in which these exercises deal with the "pirouetting" dancer's relationship to gravity, balance, and strength is no less than admirable. But, the way in which these very exercises simultaneously serve to arrange the body during the *pirouette* into the most eye-pleasing shapes and lines is no less than amazing. From another viewpoint there would seem to be no limit in the application of ballet's technical percepts to the kinetic innovations of the most avant-garde styles of modern dance. Clearly, what modern dancers in performing their novel works would deny the physiological requisites for correctly executed extensions and jumps, the techniques of which are ultimately rooted in the classical system? Indeed, the ballet barre is often the modern dancer's physical preparation for performance, so wonderfully complete is its warming and coaxing of the body preparing to dance.

Classical ballet's inherently elegant character is ancient, co-originating with the very first expression of the nobility of the prehistoric's human spirit, but its energy is derived from living forces of the present world. That the heritage of the classical ballet's theory and style is useful as an extraordinarily successful means for expressing contemporary experience is witnessed by the fact that the ballet endures and yet continues to develop on the strength of its growing universal appeal.

At present, two major thrusts outside of the incomparably strong impact of the American professional ballet world are evident in the growth of the country's dance consciousness. They are the activities of the regional ballet movement present throughout the United States and the promising contributions put forth by the college-university setting.

Regional ballet companies are nonprofit organizations established throughout the country by dedicated teachers who wish to provide a professional environment in which dancers and choreographers can gain experience and develop performing skills. The presence of a regional ballet company enhances the entire art form by promoting community interest in ballet and in time creating larger and more dance-educated audiences on the local level.

The regional ballet movement was born in 1929 with the foundation of the Atlanta Civic Ballet. Its guiding light, Dorothy Alexander, who taught and choreographed for her young company, is credited with inspiring similar companies all over the country. At present five general geographic areas in the United States represent the participation of numerous companies, both amateur and semi-professional. They are the Southeastern Regional Ballet Association, Northeastern Regional Ballet Association, Mid-States Regional Ballet Association, Southwestern Regional Ballet Association, and the Pacific Regional Ballet Association; all are affiliated with the National Association of Regional Ballet.

Following the example of Alexander's initial blueprints, the regional ballet companies are composed of dancers from area schools who audition for apprentice or senior dancer status. The dancers then receive special training in addition to classes at their home studios from the company's staff, many of whom have had substantial experience with professional companies. The dancers are rehearsed in ballets created for them and occasionally they also have the opportunity to learn the traditional classical ballets, depending on the company's level of advancement. The principal activity of regional ballet is to present its companies in public performances, lectures, and demonstrations which in turn increase local awareness and appreciation of ballet. Every effort is made to prepare programs of the highest quality and this is reinforced by yearly regional ballet festivals. At such times, local choreographic works are adjudicated by well-known professionals whose task it is to select the most representative ballets of a particular company to be shown at festival concerts. In addition to the participation in performances, series of classes taught by experts in ballet, modern, jazz, and ethnic dance are featured at the regional festivals. Participants also benefit from workshops in choreography, lighting, and scenic design, lectures geared to the rhythmic and musical needs of dancers and choreographers, and seminars in the care and prevention of dancer's injuries.

While the regional ballet movement has proved itself to be a magnificent undertaking in the interest of the development of ballet, the individual companies who make up its ranks are still plagued by the perennial problem of financial support. While some companies receive ample support from the local business communities, others must rely solely on the director's personal funds and the small yearly dues collected from the individual dancers. Being non-profit groups, all box office receipts and private donations are turned back to the company to pay operating costs. Fortunately, many companies in recent years are benefiting from small grants awarded by state and city arts councils.

Of special concern in regional ballet companies is the yearly loss of the upcoming talent which the companies through their striving for high quality training and performing experiences have developed. Young dancers of considerable merit are understandably led by their ambitions to greener pastures where they might have the possibility to become fully paid professionals. Consequently, the regional movement which was designed to decentralize ballet by encouraging the art outside of New York City and one or two other dance centers in the country finds its best dancers embarking for careers in companies housed in New York and a number of other companies which were formed in the last decade in our larger cities. A viable solution to the problem of regional companies being denuded of their brightest talent is to elicit financial support not only great enough to sustain the company's existence but substantial enough to retain its native dancers.

A tremendous force in the growth of this country's ballet consciousness is due to the dance activity generated on the American campus. Since the 1930's the recognition of the educational values of dance rapidly expanded in academic circles. The presence of the early forms of what is now termed modern dance found support in the arguments of its exponents who noted that dance contributed to the physical and mental well-being of the student, strengthening those aspects of personality development which contribute to the whole person. As a result, a number of colleges and universities instituted programs in dance education which were usually housed in physical education departments. From the beginning, collegiate programs were enriched with the occasional presence of professional dancers such as Martha Graham, Doris Humphrey, and Hanya Holm. These artists influenced the thinking and goals of academic dance educators during periods when they accepted invitations to teach and speak at professional meetings and workshops, and in time dance on campus came into focus as an autonomous art form. Added to the early emphasis on individual creativity and freedom of expression in college dance, was the professional dancer's accent on the technical discipline which underlies dance art. Hence, it was at this time that classes in ballet were occasionally introduced with the intention of augmenting the college dance student's level of endurance and general skills. While classes in ballet were also meant to broaden the scope of dance programs and the range of the dance student's knowledge, their real value often lay in their unique service to the modern dance idiom. To a large extent this remains true today in that modern dancers whether in the professional or collegiate world, actively seek the merits of studying ballet techniques for its results in producing greater stretch, strength, and speed in the body.

In 1947 dance critic Walter Terry surveyed a number of college dance programs in the interest of investigating the current and future trend of nationwide dance. Out of 105 colleges who reported they offered dance courses, only 15 included ballet classes. Terry's conclusion, however, was that dance in general was on an upward swing, and by the late 1960's the ballet boom America experienced in the 1950's infiltrated the campuses. While ballet courses which serve the general college student are ever popular, ballet major programs or those which emphasize ballet are also enjoying healthy expansion. From hundreds of small colleges to the major universities, ballet is establishing itself with an intensity not previously known to campus arts. Its locale varies, sometimes housed in physical education, music or theatre programs, but in a number of institutions ballet enjoys autonomy within a dance department.

Because of the inherent difficulty in the study of ballet, the level of achievement for the college student is not always high. It is well-known that it takes eight to ten years to become a fully developed ballet dancer, twice the time the majority of students spend on campus. Confounding the time problem, it is physiologically too late to begin to study for a professional ballet career in the freshman year. On the other hand, American campuses are peppered with very good ballet dancers who arrive at college with years of previous training under their belts. Often these students have had the privilege of dancing with regional ballet companies in their hometowns. Bringing their achievements with them, their abilities are absorbed into ballet programs, collegiate dance clubs and campus performances and serve to enhance the country's total dance picture. Many of these ballet students, while having already become excellent dancers, chose to attend college to prepare for other careers rather than pursue the life of a professional. It is a credit to higher education in this great country that such students can attend college and still experience the joy of performing during that time of life which are dancer's peak years.

Dance historians in future years will surely look upon campus ballet as a major American contribution toward the evolution of the art. The long range significance of its presence in colleges and universities will undoubtedly be the building of a vast and enlightened new audience which will in turn generate an even stronger nationwide awareness that we are currently witnessing.

II.   BALLET TECHNIQUES

CHAPTER 11

Introduction to
Ballet Technique

There is certainly room for a teacher's personal approach to the beginning level of ballet instruction, but most experienced teachers adhere to a traditional format that is historically traced to the writings of Carlo Blasis (1797-1878), an Italian who first constructed the ballet lesson as we know it. The class format presented here is based predominantly on Italian, Russian, and French methods of instruction. In the United States, the dancer's training will generally stem from the Italian or Russian method or a combination of these. Although there are variations in approaches to teaching these two methods, the content of the contemporary ballet class still consists of barre exercises, traditional arm and head movements, movements that emphasize turns, steps danced close to the floor, or steps that propel the body off the floor.

THE BALLET CLASS BASED ON TRADITION

The Italian method of teaching ballet technique consists of a series of formalized and pre-designed classes that are based on many of the ideas and preferences of Maestro Cecchetti (1850-1928). According to the manner in which this great Italian teacher developed his classes, each day of the week had its own special barre and specific center work which never varied. Within the scope of a week of classes in his method, all the essentials of balletic technique were practiced. This method is still employed today. In the United States, an organization called the Cecchetti Council of America has codified and preserved the teaching of the master as much as possible. The Cecchetti method was for many years the standard technique taught at the Metropolitan Opera Ballet School in New York City. In recent years, master teachers such as Margaret Craske and Vincenzo Celli have been recognized as leading exponents of Cecchetti's work.

The Cecchetti method is characterized by a greater emphasis on the absolute correctness of line and execution of the classroom exercises, rather than the kinetic involvement of the student. Teachers adhering to the Cecchetti method as it is presented today, also emphasize the importance of a more complex rendering of the standard French terminology. The Cecchetti method is especially recommended for the very serious student's earliest training. One problem inherent in this method is that its pre-set barre work and center movement tend to deprive the student of the inspiring elements of surprise and curiosity in coping with new exercises and novel combinations of steps. On the other hand, the student has the opportunity to more completely fulfill movement in exercises where the sequence of arm movements or steps are familiar and previously learned.

The Russian method of instruction involves the same developmental format within its barre and center movement as does the Italian method. When compared to the Cecchetti method, there is some difference in execution of steps and style of body lines. The Russian method, as it is used today in Western Europe and in North and South America, dates back to the 19th Century teachers who trained the young students at the Imperial Ballet Schools of Czarist Russia. Many of these students (Karsavina, Fokine, Preobrajenska, Mordkin, Pereyaslavec, Doubrovska, Oboukoff, Bolm, and Balanchine) became the incomparable Russian dancers who emigrated to Europe and the United States as a result of the 1917 Russian Revolution. They brought with them the methods of teaching they themselves were to employ as teachers in the Western world.

The Russian method of teaching class calls for the student to be especially alert to the "class in progress". It insists that each student develop his visual memory by constantly coping with new combinations of familiar component exercises, and combinations accompanied by varying and subtle approaches to the dynamics of execution.

The total commitment to either the Italian or Russian method generally leads to extremes that may ultimately be undesirable in the interest of the student's development. For instance, experience demonstrates that the set class, as done in the Italian method, often results in the drudgery of going through one's well-known and precisely unvarying paces just to give the body its accustomed workout. The outcome of such a lack of intelligent effort produces rigidity in the dancer's movements and inhibits appropriate personality projection, thus hindering artistic growth and technical gain. On the other hand, a class excessively fraught with innovation, such as the most complex form of Russian classes, can often raise the anxiety level of the student so that mental barriers are transformed into inappropriate muscular restraints. Unrelenting and excessive mental taxation in the effort to remember complex or novel sequences of steps serves to cut efficient motor activity rather than to provide the student with a challenge. This results in an "unkinetic" experience, the antithesis of the dance experience.

In summary, while the Italian and Russian methods each have their respective positive and negative facets, a most satisfactory approach in ballet training is a careful composite of the most artistically effective features of both methods so that the resulting skill of the dancer is both *correct* and *kinetic*. It should be noted that both schools of training contribute to the student's entire dance experience. The combination and juxtaposition of both methods in the student's overall training can contribute to greater technical knowledge and to the uniquely personal touches that ultimately separate the artist from technician. Indeed, in the American professional schools of today, one observes the veritable "melting pot" of many methods, and it is even possible to see the occasional influence of the French, Bournonville (Danish), and the Vaganova (Soviet) methods.

The notion of the American "melting pot" of balletic technique is incomplete without mention of the contribution of Agrippina Vaganova (1879-1951). This great Soviet teacher has influenced American Ballet since the 1946 English translation of her technical manual *Basic Principles of Classical Ballet*. Although her personal work was carried on entirely within Stalinist Russia, the clarity of her writings on technique have served to better dance in this country. It was her purpose to consolidate the best features of the Cecchetti approach, as he himself taught his method in Russia, with the most Russian characteristics of the French and Russian methods surviving in early 20th century Russia. The outcome of her amalgamation of these ideas is the official Soviet or Vaganova method, which is the balletic foundation in Russia today. The quality of this method speaks for itself through such stellar exponents as Ulanova, Plisetskaya, Nureyev, Makarova, and Baryshnikov.

Much of the current prestige of the American dancer is founded on the European assumption that they are so well trained. And, indeed, they are, due to the accumulation and continuous evolution by Americans of technical and pedagogic knowledge. Ballet has become a science as well as an art.

THE STRUCTURE OF THE BALLET CLASS

The structure of the ballet class, according to any of the widely-practiced methods, whether Italian, Russian, French, or Danish, can be viewed as occurring in three distinct phases. These phases are the exercises at the barre, the dance movement studies done in the center of the room, and the movement executed as the dancer moves from place to place within a given spatial context. These three parts consist of interrelated material: the barre work evolves into the center exercises, which in turn prepare the student for the full-out demands of the movements that are the essence of ballet, i.e., dancing per se. The internal order of these three parts should not be altered, nor should the second or third part be attempted without the all-important barre, whether it is in a beginning or an advanced class.

The student will find it most helpful to arrive at the dance studio 20 to 25 minutes before the class is to begin. This allows 10 to 15 minutes to don tights, leotards and shoes, and to tightly secure the hair for class. This will also leave a few minutes for some preliminary stretching as well as quickly pulling together one's concentration. Considering the physical and emotional output that a ballet class can demand, the "calm before the storm" is necessary.

Prior to the start of the class, various small movements such as reaching upwards, stretching through the arms and the spine, rolling the head in circles, and flexing the hip and knee joints are desirable. This gentle, pre-class activity not only physically and mentally reminds the muscles and joints to prepare for class, but such movements feel good to the body. Caution must be exercised, however. The student who habitually employs violent movements or extreme stretching, such as with the leg extended on the barre above hip-high level, invites chronic injury to the legs. Such premature exercising is dangerous before the body has been gradually warmed through the carefully developed and time-honored process of barre work.

BASIC CONCEPTS USED IN THE BALLET CLASS

Before an analysis of the execution of the various barre exercises takes place, it would be helpful to consider certain fundamental and related concepts of ballet technique. These concepts deal with the balletic notions of stance at the barre, posture, spinal alignment, pelvic and shoulder placement, balance, turnout and body directions. Also included here is a listing of the classical positions and basic poses in the context of their spatial relationships. While not all of the classical positions and poses are used early in ballet training, they are mentioned here more for the sake of completeness than for practice.

THE SUPPORTING LEG AND THE WORKING LEG

The terms "supporting leg" and "working leg" are used throughout any technical discussion of ballet. Attention to their precise meaning will facilitate the student's understanding from the start. Both legs, whether at the barre or in center work, are totally active according to their function at a given moment. The leg that bears the weight of the body, whether it is standing, jumping, or turning, is termed the "supporting leg" for the duration of the "supporting activity." The opposite leg, which is freed from supporting the body, is termed the "free" or "working leg." Its activity is always that of the completion of the formation of a classical body design or movement.

It is important to understand from the beginning that in ballet the entire body is never completely relaxed as it might be in normal, everyday life. Whether in class exercises or in performance dancing, it is always at work even if it is posed in non-movement. This is not to suggest that the body is rigidly tense, however. Instead, the head, the arms, the torso, the supporting leg, and the working leg are vitally involved and energized in every movement or pose. The posed ballet body presents a picture of supreme aplomb, elegance, and superb vitality, ready to take flight in an instant.

POSTURE

The students in a beginning class will begin barre work by standing in profile (sideways) to the barre and about eighteen inches out from it with the left hand resting on the barre. Since the profile position of the body is used during the entire barre, the left hand will hold the barre at a point about ten inches in front of the body. Care must be taken that the angle of the elbow in no way affects the normal placement of the left shoulder and its proper relation to the spine. If the line of the shoulder girdle is out of its normal position, the spine, and thus the entire body, will be incorrectly held. Each barre exercise is repeated so that the student turns around and holds the barre with the right hand. The movement of this exercise is then converted so that the supporting leg performs the movement of the working leg.

The basic posture demands are the same throughout all barre exercises. Good posture can be thought of as beginning with the spine stretching upwards and downwards. The feeling in the thoracic area is one of lifting upward although it is not rigidly held in an upward and vertical pull. The rib cage is depressed rather than expanded. Although the latter may "feel" better, it is not correct. The slight natural give, due to the spine's flexibility, as well as the natural curve of the upper area of the spine must be maintained or else the hard lines of tension will show themselves around the throat area. The tension that accompanies a rigidly held spine will more quickly bring about fatigue. Sensitization of the student to the continuation of the spine right up into the back of the head is important because it determines how stylishly, in the balletic sense, the student uses the neck and carries the head. At the same time, the head should not be allowed to fall back, but rather the chin should feel as if it were parallel with the floor. As pliés are done at the barre, the student must be helped to discourage the natural tendency to cast the head and eyes downward to see if the feet and knees are working correctly. Correctness in ballet is kinetically sensed and reinforced by being reflected back to the visual perception from the mirror. The gaze is always projected outward with intelligence and natural charm, just as if one were before an audience. The frozen, bored, strained or fierce looks unintentionally projected by the student dancer are due to the tremendous effort and concentration going on within the body. The careful teacher will constantly cajole the student out of this tendency. The frozen gaze is a perennial problem, and is solved by substituting a bad habit with awareness of the problem and acquired, learned counter-action. Poetically speaking, the student should strive for the feelng of "having one's head in the clouds" as well as be able to impart this impression to others whether they be teacher or audience. This usage of the head is automatically part of the physical poise of polished dancers whether it is conscious or not. The proudly held head is simply a result brought about by practicing with these specific performance values in mind. Such use of the head is an essential part of the proper carriage of the ballet dancer.

ALIGNMENT

The term alignment is used to denote the precise vertical positioning of all the sections of the torso in relation to all parts of the legs as it is seen in profile. The spinal extension from the center of the spine downward begins with the proper alignment of the pelvis. Although there is always a variety of postures found in the beginning ballet class that need re-alignment for good health as well as for the needs of ballet technique, the area most in need of correction is generally the lower spine and pelvis. So often the sway back of the tilting pelvis is the root of technical difficulties on any level of advancement.

The new student is instructed for the very first time to stand in first position with the weight on both feet, the legs turned outward from the hip joints, and the backs of the knees pressed together. However, placing the legs in this position will cause the lower spine to increase its

Body Alignment

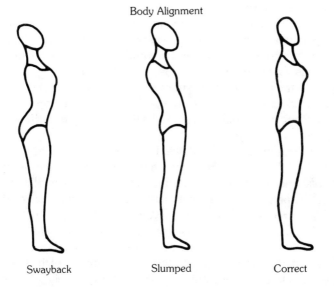

Swayback   Slumped   Correct

Fig. 1. The first two drawings represent extreme examples of bad alignment which can be corrected by proper exercise at the barre.

natural curve, and the pelvis will tip forward drastically. By thinking such a verbal cue as "roll the buttocks under" or "drop the seat," the spinal curve is reduced and the pelvis more or less correctly held depending on the individual's ability to meet the ideal of perfect turnout and a properly aligned pelvis.

The inspirational teacher, Muriel Stuart, is very clear both in her classes and in her book on this particular matter of pelvis alignment. She readily points out that the pelvic area and its relation with the thighs are the. . .

> dancer's center of muscular energy and control. The muscles in the thighs are pulled upward, causing a slight tension in the buttocks and abdomen; this frees the torso above the waist from strain and eliminates tension from the neck, shoulders, and arms. The pupil must be made aware of the importance of this control before making the first movement in classical dance, the *demi-plié* in five positions. It will then be possible for her to execute this movement with the slight counter-pull upward in the muscles of the thighs, abdomen and buttocks. . .

Most students will instinctively question such discomfort being imposed on their bodies because this new positioning of the body produces extraordinarily uncomfortable sensations. It must be pointed out, however, that the alignment of the pelvis over the turned out legs is an extremely artificial way of holding the body. Excessive effort in "dropping the seat" and in turning out the legs will produce dangerous knee strain as well as the lancination of overworked muscles in the pelvic area. Therefore, gentle insistence with regard to "rolling under the buttocks" over a period of time will reduce the artificial feelings in the pelvic area and safely allow the desired pelvic alignment to occur gradually in the student.

Merely learning to hold the lower back correctly in a stationary context is difficult enough. However, after numerous practices of the *demi-plié* and barre work in general, the muscles eventually "learn" to hold the pelvis in proper alignment without constant conscious effort. The correct lower spine and pelvis position becomes "natural" or at least less artificial in feeling. Learning to move and to dance with the correct lower spine position seems impossible at first, but eventually the training of the muscles to react properly by means of the barre exercises, facilitates and accomplishes the feat. Eventually, even in the daring of a *pirouette,* the hips will habitually stay in the proper position. Likewise, in coming out of a *grand jeté,* the hips will automatically return to the correct position.

It is significant to note that in the act of dancing, the lower spine constantly moves in and out of the so-called correct alignment we are describing when we suggest "rolling the buttocks under." For example, the ability to return to center from a back attitude position, where the spine is held contrary to the prescribed "correct" vertical position, is merely another way of indicating a strong technique in a dancer. No matter what degree of angle the classical steps or poses (or for that matter, the inventive machinations of modern dance) cause the lower spine to assume, the muscles of the correctly aligned pelvis will move the pelvis back to its correctly aligned position.

PLACEMENT

The term "placement" in ballet refers to the precise horizontal positioning of the shoulder and pelvis areas as viewed from the front or back planes of the body. That is, the horizontal lines of the shoulder joints and crests of the pelvis are parallel to each other and to the floor when the body is supported by both legs. Correct placement in ballet technique hinges on two rules of thumb.

Placement

Fig. 2. Correct placement of the pelvis. Muscles on both sides of the body maintain the horizontal line.

The lifted hip on the working side is a common fault of the adult beginner in ballet.

First, when the body weight is momentarily transferred to one leg, as is inevitable in most exercises and steps, the horizontal and/or parallel lines of pelvis and shoulder in relation to the parallel floor line, must not be upset.

Second, in large movements using extensions and leaps, the shoulder and pelvis lines will loose a degree of their parallel relationship with the floor. However, the balletic concept of placement insists that the horizontal and parallel lines must be regained as soon as the body weight changes to one or both legs.

CENTEREDNESS

The combination of proper alignment and correct placement is often described by the common dance phrase "to be centered." "Centeredness" results from the conscious control over the vertical stance of the body as it moves horizontally through space. The strength derived from the proper spinal alignment reinforces the body's horizontal relationship with the floor on and from which it moves vertically. A dancer who is "centered" is technically stable and in control of the execution of ballet steps relative to his or her level of development. The continuous shifts of weight from one leg to the other, which stems from jumps and turns, in no way affects the concentration and distribution of energy radiating from its origin in the pelvis. Should the torso be momentarily out of alignment, the kinetic habit of returning to "center" will rectify the loss almost immediately.

TURNOUT

It must be remembered that the characteristic torso-centered posture of ballet technique taken even in the very first exercises is unnatural for the body. This is due to the "turnout" of the legs in the hip joints. Turnout is immediately encountered in the five classical positions at the barre and is the root of a technique which demands the body learn a modified way of holding itself erect.

Turnout originates in the hip joint and is characterized by the ball and socket (*enarthrosis*) type articulation of its components in which the head of the thigh bone (*femur*) fits into the concavity of the lower part of the pelvis bone (*ilium*). Anatomically, turnout is defined as the

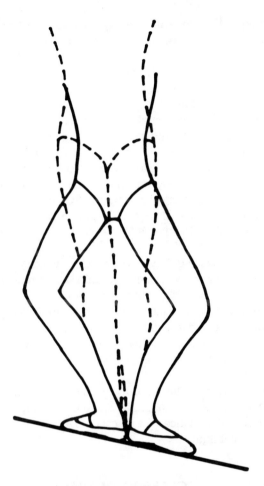

Fig. 3. Turnout. The *demi-plié* in first position aids in acquiring turnout and the control over it. Maximum outward rotation of the legs in the hip sockets provides the dancer with freedom to move quickly in all directions.

outward rotation of the entire leg, beginning at the large rounded head of the *femur* within the *acetabulum* cavity of the *ilium*. The head of the *femur* (ball) rests in the *acetabulum* (socket) and is enclosed in tissue where its activity is membraneously lubricated.

In ballet, there are essentially two reasons for the turnout; one is functional and the other is aesthetic. From a functional point of view, full command of the turnout allows greater balance and speed and, therefore, the greatest possible freedom in the execution of any movement. For example, when quickly moving sideways, such as in a *glissade*, it is almost impossible to keep from tripping oneself if turnout of the legs is absent. This gives rise to the pithy axiom that states, "perfect technique is total freedom." Of course, the steps of ballet have evolved out of the choreographic needs of the times as well as the material that was devised for the barre work. But due to the presence of turnout, the range of invention of steps was and is enormous. All virtuoso steps were made possible for the body to learn to do because the barre's developmental body-training aspects were based on turnout as well as the inventive usage of it by creative teachers and performers. To execute the classical steps as they are handed down from generation to generation, is impossible without the body's acquired use of turnout.

Aesthetically speaking, these classical steps which employ turned-out legs in body design and in movement execution were devised as such because they were thought to be beautiful in the context of the aesthetic of the time. We still favorably react to the elegance of the turned-out fourth position stance of Louis XIV as he is depicted in Riguad's court portrait, just as the same elegant aplomb of the contemporary silhouette of a fencer or a bullfighter strikes a note of visual pleasure in us.

Indeed, because the turned-out classical ballet and poses so enhance the natural movement facility and aesthetic lines of the human body, a 16th century dance style is accepted as part of our contemporary American culture.

CLASSROOM SPACE

The space in which the dancer works has special indications in the study of ballet. In the classroom setting, the four walls and four corners are considered fixed points and are numbered accordingly. As the student learns to respond to movement directions and body positions as they relate to walls or corners, he develops a special sense of direction which will eventually become second nature.

In the Italian method, the corners are first numbered counterclockwise and are then followed by the counterclockwise numbering of the walls. The dancer faces the front of the room (which would be the au-

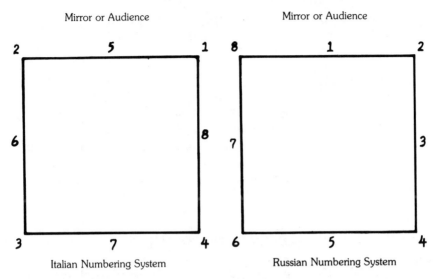

Fig. 4. The Classroom Space

dience in a theatre). This is called "wall five," the wall immediately to the dancer's left becomes "wall six," etc.

Vaganova, following the Russian-French tradition, stipulates that the dancer facing the front of the room or the audience, is facing "wall one" and that the adjacent corner, moving clockwise, is "corner two," etc.

The Vaganova numbering system would appear to be the more commonly used in the United States.

DIRECTIONS OF THE BODY

The term "directions" refers to the body as it relates to the space surrounding it. In general, we think of this space as encased by the walls of the classroom or the perimeter of the stage. Basically, the directions in which the body faces in this encased space are front, side, back, and diagonal. These spatial concepts are among the very first objectives to be learned by the dance student. Without a keenly developed sensitivity to the directional relationships of the body to the classroom or stage space, the classical steps performed by the dancer will not be assured of expressing the precise balletic lines to the viewer's perception.

An important result of correctly practiced barre exercises is the seminal development of the student's kinesthetic awareness of the spatial concepts of front, side, back, and diagonal directions. At the barre, the student's point of reference is the barre to which he stands sideways. However, he becomes aware of his relationship to space as the working leg constantly moves toward the front, side or back directions. As the barre work increases in difficulty, the body also learns to work the diagonal directions of *effacé* and *croisé*. This kinesthetic awareness of relating to space in a balletic context is further strengthened in the *petit adage* section of the class where the student's primary spatial relationship is to the front of the room as he executes movements derived from barre work.

ELEVEN BODY POSITIONS

Together, the Italian and Russian methods of classical ballet comprise eleven positions of the body. That is to say, the torso, head, arms, and legs are compositely and uniquely arranged in eleven distinct body designs. These are:

1. *croisé devant* or *croisé* front
2. *à la quatrième devant* or fourth position front
3. *effacé devant* or *effacé* front
4. *écarté devant* or *écarté* front
5. *à la seconde* or to the second position
6. *écarté derrière* or *écarté* back
7. *effacé derrière* or *effacé* back
8. *épaulé devant* shoulder to the front
9. *épaulé derrière* shoulder to back direction
10. *à la quatrième derrière* or fourth position back
11. *croisé derrière* or *croisé* back

All eleven of these positions are recognized and can be found in American pedagogy.

These various body positions with their, head, arm and leg designs are learned in reference to the front of the classroom, but they are employed choreographically to face the side, back and diagonal directions as well.

Not only must these body positions be learned in terms of their respective design, but eventually they must become motor memorized. In other words, there are specific kinetic sensations associated with each position. Hours upon hours of repetition will develop the keenness and preciseness of the kinesthetic sensation. Just as the vocalist "goes for" the particular sensation of the desired sound, so too does the dancer "go for" the particular muscular sensation registered by

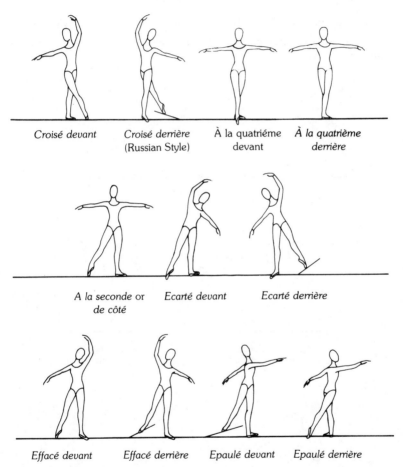

| *Croisé devant* | *Croisé derrière* (Russian Style) | À la quatriéme devant | *À la quatrième derrière* |

| *A la seconde* or *de côté* | *Ecarté devant* | *Ecarté derrière* |

| *Effacé devant* | *Effacé derrière* | *Epaulé devant* | *Epaulé derrière* |

Fig. 5. Eleven Body Positions shown *à terre* (on the floor). They may also be done *demi-hauteur* (45° off the floor) or *en l'air* (90° or more off the floor)

the perfect *croisé devant, à la seconde,* etc. Only after a thorough grounding in the body's directions and positions as they relate to the various spatial areas of the classroom, will the dancer be confident and comfortable in this directional and positional aspect of ballet training.

TWO CLASSICAL POSES

In addition to the eleven classical body positions, there are two traditional poses and their respective variations. These are the *arabesque* and the *attitude.*

First Arabesque   Second Arabesque   Third Arabesque
                                           Russian Style

Fourth Arabesque   Arabesque penché
(Russian Style)

Arabesque allongeé à terre   Arabesque fondue   Arabesque à terre

Fig. 6. Eight commonly used forms of ARABESQUE.

The *arabesque* is distinguished as a pose by the linear extension of one leg behind the body. The several forms of *arabesque* accrue to the variation of arm positions and head inclination. The Italian method discerns five forms of *arabesque* while the Russian school teaches four *arabesques*.

The *attitude* is essentially distinguishable by the extended leg being flexed at the knee joint. The leg may be extended to the front (front *attitude*) or to the back. In certain contemporary ballets, an unorthodox side *attitude* has been created, a technical enrichment in ballet resulting from the powerful presence of the modern dance idiom. The directions of front and back *attitudes* are *de face, croisé,* or *effacé. (The* terms *croisé* and *effacé* refer to classical body positions as well as the two variations of the diagonal directions.) That is, the *attitude* pose is assumed squarely facing the front or it is done on the diagonal. The Italian and Russian forms of the *attitude* are again created and distinguished by the subtly varying designs of the arm, head, and torso lines.

Vaganova lists the *écarté* as a third pose in ballet. Since *écarté* is essentially a stylized *à la seconde* position with the leg extending

Attitude croisée
devant

Attitude effacée
devant

Attitude croisée
derrière
(Russian Style)

Attitude effacée
derrière
(Russian Style)

Fig. 7. Four Attitudes. *Attitude croisée devant. Attitude effacée devant. Attitude croisée derrière* (Russian style) *Attitude effacée derrière* (Russian style).

above the waist, it is often taught as a body position instead of one of the poses.

As early as 1820, Carlo Blasis discussed the particular merits and beauty of the *arabesque* and the *attitude*. Referring to the *arabesques*, he notes that those "charming positions. . .have been inspired by the bas-reliefs of antiquity and fragments of Greek painting as well as by the delightful frescoes from Raphael's drawings. . .Dancers should learn to portray these spirited and lovely effects of sculpture and painting in their own art." Continuing his loving but instructive directives to students, Blasis goes on to say. . . "infuse your *attitudes* and *arabesques* with feeling and expression. The position which dancers specifically refer to as the *attitude* is the loveliest and most difficult of execution in dancing. In my opinion, it is an adaptation of the much admired pose of the celebrated Mercury of Bologna."

CHAPTER 12

Introduction to
the Barre Work

The barre work consists of approximately ten exercises ingeniously devised over the past three centuries by the great ballet masters.

The chief purpose of these exercises is twofold. The long-term purpose of barre work is designed to train the muscles and joints to form the required positions and movements characterized by the art of ballet. The immediate purpose of barre exercises provides a precise activity whereby the body is conditioned or "warmed up" prior to dancing.

Barre exercises are structurally based on the five classical positions of the legs which were stipulated by Beauchamp around 1670 for the newly and royally established profession of ballet dancing. All balletic movements are rooted in the basic stances these positions demand from the body. Indeed, all the movements that are part of the classical ballet steps pass through these five positions and their elaborate derivations. These five classic positions are usually demonstrated individually by the teacher in the first few classes, but are thereafter always employed in barre exercises and dance steps.

The ten barre exercises concentrate on the development of the legs and may be viewed in three categories. These categories consist of: (1) bending (*demi* and *grand pliés*); (2) extending the legs (all forms of *petits battements, grands battements,* and *développés*); and, (3) rotating (*ronds de jambe à terre* and *ronds de jambe en l'air*). Included in these three categories of exercises are arm movements, called *port de bras*, which develop the carriage of the arms according to the maxims of the ballet aesthetic. Specified head and shoulder movements, called *épaulement,* provide subtle variations of body line and lend the visual effect of shading to the mass of the body's form. The fundamental use of *épaulement* insures even the beginning dancer a measure of elegance and style.

The barre work also includes bending movements called *cambré* which develop the flexibility and use of the spine. The barre exercises

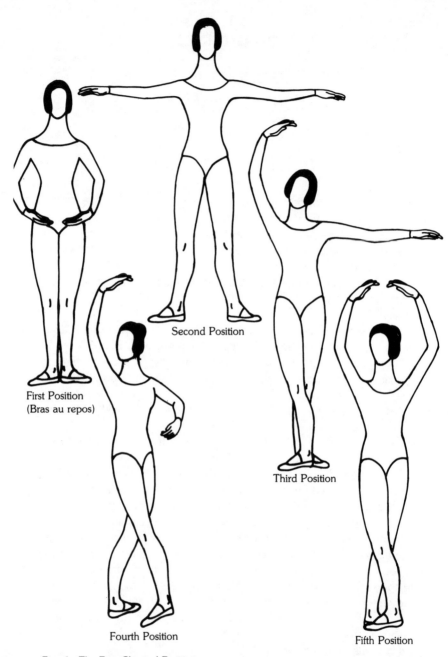

First Position
(Bras au repos)

Second Position

Third Position

Fourth Position

Fifth Position

Fig. 1. The Five Classical Positions
All ballet steps are based on at least one of the classical positions of the legs. The arm
positions shown here represent the French School.

are listed here according to name and are placed in the commonly-followed order for classroom instruction.

1. *Demi-pliés* and *grands pliés*, bending movements in first, second, and fifth position.

   Third position is archaic and of historical interest only. Its similarity to the fifth position has generally precluded it from the vocabulary of ballet positions and steps.

   Fourth position is extremely demanding, in that it puts excessive strain on the knees and feet. For this reason it is temporarily omitted, especially in the *grand plié* exercise, until the legs are strengthened and the student fully understands the correct approach to execution of the fourth position *grand plié*

2. *Battement tendu, Battement dégagé, Battement jeté,* and *Battement relevé,* small extending movements of the legs which vary in design, rhythm, quality, and quantity.

3. *Rond de jambe à terre,* emphasizes the rotation movement of the legs within the hip joint.

4. *Battement Frappé,* percussive flexion and extention of the knee and ankle joints.

5. *Battement fondu,* the flowing and sustained flexion and extention of the knees and ankles of both legs.

6. *Battement retiré,* the vigorous flexion of hip, knee, and ankle joints.

7. *Développé,* the slow and sustained unfolding extension of the leg.

8. *Rond de jambe en l'air,* emphasizes rotation of the lower leg within the knee joint. Introduced later on during beginning ballet in a simplified and introductory manner.

9. *Grand Battement,* large extending movements of the legs done with precision and vigor. Demands considerable strength.

10. *Cambré and stretches,* flexion of the vertabrae; elongation of the torso and leg muscles.

While the barre work comprises the same ten exercises for the beginner as for the most advanced dancer, the movement content of the exercise will vary in complexity of design, rhythm, and quantity. It will take the beginner several classes to learn enough of the barre exercises before the body begins to feel and show results in the acquisition of these new movement skills.

In this chapter, only the basic forms of the exercises employing the simplest rhythms will be discussed in terms of instruction and execution.

PLIÉS

The word *plié* comes from the French verb *plier,* which means "to bend." In ballet terminology, *plié* refers primarily to the first exercise at the barre. *Plié* involves standing in the turned-out stance of the classical position during which the body is lowered and raised as the legs bend and straighten at the knees.

The purpose of the plié is to elongate the achilles tendon and strengthen the muscles of the legs.

The class traditionally begins with a combination of two forms of the *plié,* the *demi-plié,* and the *grand plié.* They are practiced in the classical positions, and are done in numerical order but with the following exceptions. The third position has become archaic in ballet training and is generally omitted since it is so similar in design to the fifth position. The *grand plié* in fourth position is usually omitted in the first weeks of beginning ballet classes because it imposes exceedingly strenuous demands on untrained legs.

Since *pliés* are of two kinds, *demi* (half) *pliés* and *grands* (full) *pliés,* they each have specifically different approaches to their execution. Physiologically, both *demi-plié* and *grand plié* exercises must be done with a "straight" spine. That is to say, the spine with its natural amount of curvature is perpendicular to the floor during the *plié* and does not lean, however, slightly, forward or backward. The legs are turned out to the individual's capacity from the hip socket. The feet are properly placed on the floor so that body weight is equally distributed on each leg. The weight falls on three points of the foot, the heel and both sides of the ball of the foot. At all times, the knees are held precisely in line with the toes so that an imaginary line downward from the center of the knee is aligned with the middle toe. This position protects the knee joint by allowing the joint to function without internal friction. The balls of the feet are always solidly on the floor. All ten toes are relaxed and unclenched. The arches are upheld in their natural degree of arch by consciously placing a certain amount of pressure along the outsides of the turned-out feet.

DEMI-PLIÉ

The central purpose of the *demi-plié* is to elongate the achilles tendon. The more pliable this tendon becomes, the greater the total movement potential of the entire body. Specifically, the development of the *plié* is the basis for all jumping movement. Broadly speaking, without a pliable achilles tendon, no lyrical quality of movement is possible.

The depth range of the *demi-plié* is gauged by the amount of *plié* (flexion in the knee) obtained while the weight of the body holds the heels securely to the floor. It is this firm adhesion of the heels to the floor at the moment of maximum *plié* which stretches the achilles tendon. At the moment the point is reached when further bending of the knees would demand a release of the heels from the floor, the knees begin to straighten out of the *demi-plié* and return to their initial taut position. That is, as the legs straighten, the inside of the knees press together in first and fifth position, and toward each other in second and fourth position. The muscles above the knees and at the front of the thigh become contracted. During the entire *demi-plié,* the spine maintains its precise verticality and its natural curvature while it resists a tendency to lean forward or backward.

The frequently used *port de bras* for *demi-plié* is the slight opening and closing movement of the free arm. This movement is produced during the *plié* as the arm opens from the low preparatory position to the *demi-seconde* position and then back to the preparatory position.

The head positions during the *demi-pliés* may be practiced early in beginning ballet training. Its basic principles carry through all of the barre work. In first and second position, the head faces straight ahead. The head inclines slightly to the side, depending on which leg is forward in the fourth and fifth position. That is, if the right leg is forward in fourth or fifth position, the head will incline very slightly to the right. If the right leg is back, the head will incline toward the left.

GRAND PLIÉ

The chief purpose of the *grand plié* is to develop enormous strength in the legs since they must support and guide the body through its balletic designs which involve balancing, turning, leaping, etc. *Grands pliés* are practiced in first, second, fourth, and fifth position.

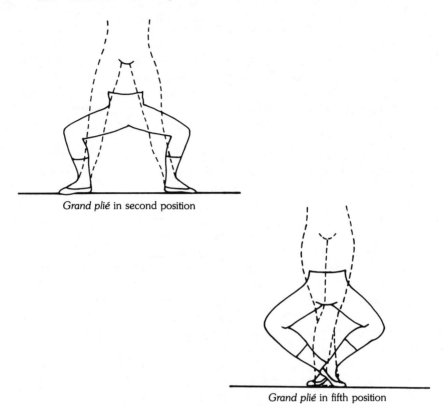

Grand plié in second position

Grand plié in fifth position

Fig. 2. Grand Plié

The *grand plié* is achieved by going first to the limit of the *demi-plié*. The student then allows both heels to release gradually and at equal distances from the floor as the body descends to the *grand plié*. The depth of the *grand plié* is gauged by going as low as possible without allowing the turnout (which begins in the hip joint) to change its initial and perfect position. The moment the *plié* reaches its greatest depth, the legs immediately propel the body upward with the slightest burst of energy so that the body is not allowed to sink and relax into the lower legs. To be precise, if the spine is correctly aligned, the control of the leg muscles is secure so that the faulty relaxing or "sitting" in the depth of the *grand plié* position is avoided. It is most important to press the balls of the feet and then the heels into the floor during ascent. This provides a greater muscular contraction and awareness of the inside thigh muscles as the legs return to their fully straightened stance. Incidentally, the second position *grand-plié* is one of the few ways to "tone up" and reduce the mass of the inner thigh area.

Qualitatively speaking, the flow of movement of the *grand plié* is continuous and ongoing. The body must be free from halting movements and minute attempts to adjust the position or to self-correct along the way. Although the slight impetus of energy guiding the body into its upward movement is present exactly between the last moment of descent and the first moment of ascent, it does not break the *legato* (smooth) flow of the exercise.

The commonly used *port de bras* which accompanies *grand plié* is the free arm moving from second position to the preparatory position as the body reaches the depth of the *grand plié*. The arm then moves up to the first position and out to the second as the *grand plié* is concluded. The eyes follow the moving hand, thus providing subtle head movement.

In *grands pliés*, there is a very special exception in the execution of the second position *plié*. Here, the heels do not lift off the floor as the body lowers in the descent of the *plié*. There is no need for them to do so. In fact, throughout this *plié*, the student feels the heels pressing into the floor. To get the optimum benefit from *grand plié* in second position, it is necessary that each dancer learn the most suitable spacing of the feet in accordance with one's body proportions and leg length. Too narrow a second position does not allow for the adequate range of *plié* which is necessary for a maximum amount of stretch at the achilles tendon. Too wide a second position will not develop jumping power in the legs. Furthermore, when the second position *grand plié* is transferred into various dancing movements, too wide a second position will minimize the body's control, stability, and available strength. Too wide a second position used while dancing, recklessly overtaxes the muscular structure of the inner thighs. Therefore, it is essential that the span of the second position be proportionate to the dancer. Depending on individual height and leg length, the distance between the heels in second position ranges from twelve to eighteen inches.

Special attention must be focused on the spinal profile (alignment) in the second position *grand plié*. The destructive habit of letting the lower back loose its ramrod straightness (verticality) as the body descends, is a constant and recurring fault. It requires persistent vigilance and effort on the part of the student and teacher. If the lower spine is allowed to move backward, even slightly, the arches, knees, and head loose their correct positioning and invite the possibility of injury as well as technical impropriety.

The fourth position *grand plié* is not recommended for beginners of any age since it is beyond the new student's ability to correctly execute. When, however, the student is ready to include the fourth position *grand plié* in the barre work, it is important that care be given to the shoulder lines and hip lines so that they remain perpendicular to the barre. Since it is most difficult to sustain an equal amount of *plié* and an equal and maximum angle of turnout in each leg during the *grand plié* in fourth position, constant self-reminding must accompany the execution of the exercise.

SIGNIFICANCE OF PLIÉS

The correct acquisition and use of both *demi-plié* and *grand plié* is so intrinsically a part of ballet technique that without continuous practice of it, there can be no dancing of quality. Specifically, the *demi-plié* grants the achilles tendon pliability which is half of the mechanism of the jump. The ability to jump with *ballon* and land quietly and fully in control, is based on the fluid, automatic and full use of this pliable and elastic-like facility of the tendons in the ankle area. Hence, the quality of all *allégro* movement is directly related to the quality of the *demi-plié*.

While pliability is one-half of the mechanism of the jump, sufficient strength is the other half. The *grand plié* uses all the muscles of the legs, and, thereby develops the supporting strength necessary to carry the body through space in all ballet movements. Furthermore, the perpendicular maintenance of the spine during the *grand plié* is directly related to the control and use of balance in *adage* and *legato* exercises.

Both the *demi-plié* and *grand plié* aid in the development of the kinesthetic awareness of one's center. In analyzing the path of a particular segment of movement, the spinal verticality is constantly lost and regained as weight is alternately shifted from one foot to the other. While ballet dancing is most often a subtle loss of center, moving off center may be more obviously visible in large *legato* combinations or in the work of the more rigorous styles of modern dance. Both excellent ballet and modern dancers fully utilize this natural occurrence of the continuous loss and return to center. In other words, they are using the pull of gravity on their body to make the movement of the dance flowing and kinetic instead of allowing the body to rigidly resist gravity. The accomplished dancer has the necessary strength to pull the body back and forth through its center so that the movement has a wider range in space. In modern dance training, these concepts are dealt with extensively and often give the modern dancer the artistic edge over the ballet dancer when called upon to produce the total kinetic involvement of the body in dance movement. In other words, dancing in both ballet as well as modern techniques ought to display the qualities of fullness and daring which are empathically transmitted to the audience as exciting theatre.

Ballet dancers who naturally possess and utilize a correct and deep *demi-plié* move in a kinetically pleasing way. The controlled and refined quality of their movements as they spatially flow from one classical position to another is the essence of good ballet movement. The underlying cause for this happy state is the perfected use of the *demi-plié*. Without adequate *demi-plié,* ballet dancing is reduced to rigidly assuming one classical position after another. With adequate *demi-plié,* the unfettered flow of the movement pattern through space is embellished and formed by the classical shapes of ballet design. Through careful movement analysis and long practice, it is possible to acquire this capacity for good *demi-plié.* Unless the achilles tendon is abnormally short, it can be gradually lengthened over a period of several years by daily stretching its associated ligaments.

It should be remembered that one learns to dance beautifully not by merely following the rules of technique. Rather, the lengthy process of learning to dance beautifully is rooted in intensive and precise movement analysis, observation, and emulation of those dancers who already possess the ability naturally or who, through enormous effort and discipline, have become excellent dancers. The good teacher will intersperse much of the technical teaching with such additional knowledge, while the student must actively seek to self-improve by learning from living, dancing examples.

Movement analysis on the part of the student essentially involves close examination of movement in a "model" dancer as it emanates from the spinal area. Careful and habitual movement analysis by the student also reveals how the *demi-plié* expresses the presence of the spinal center as the core of all ballet movement.

The *plié* exercise as performed at the barre may consist of the following:

The student begins the *pliés* while holding the barre with the left hand. Two cords of music provided for the preparatory *port de bras* precede the slow 4/4 tempo.

1. First position: Two *demi-pliés* to the first measure of music.
2. One *grand plié* to the second measure of movement.
3. *Relevé* and balance on *demi-pointe* during the third measure.
4. Resume the first position, heels down and execute a simple *porte de bras* with the free arm on the fourth measure. Change to second position.

Repeat this movement pattern in the second and fifth position. Eventually include the fourth position but omit the *grand plié*. It may be replaced by additional *demi-pliés*.

The entire exercise repeats facing the opposite direction so that the right hand now holds the barre.

PETIT BATTEMENT

Pliés are followed by a group of exercises which come under the generic title of *petit battement* or "small opening and closing of the legs." The term *"battement"* (literally, beating or clapping) has no adequate one-word translation into balletic English so the awkward, but accurate, phrase "opening and closing of the legs" is used to best express its meaning.

The various kinds of *battement* exercises are distinguished by their tempo or their spatial movement design. These *battement* exercises are directly related to the physical development of the legs and to the various qualities of movement which dance employs in its unique poetic expression. Each form of *battement* was evolved to develop a specific part of the legs for specific movements. For example, the *battement jeté* aids the execution of the *glissade; battement retiré* aids the performance of the *pirouette,* etc. Furthermore, the specific construction of each exercise elicits a particular quality of movement from the body which directly relates to the ballet steps themselves. That is, if the *battement retiré* is not performed with *brio*, the *pirouette* will be sluggish in quality as well as faulty in technical execution.

The following exercises come under the heading of *petit battement.* In their classroom practice order, they are: *battement tendu, battement tendu dégagé, battement tendu jeté* or *glissé, battement tendu relevé, battement fondu, battement frappé,* and *battement retiré* or *raccourci.*

DEFINITION AND PURPOSE OF BATTEMENT TENDU

The *battement tendu* is very different in design and purpose from the preceding *plié* exercise. The term, *battement tendu,* means the opening and closing of stretched legs.

Battement tendu is primarily designed to give the body stability by teaching it to continuously shift the burden of weight from two legs to one leg without letting the forces of gravity intervene. The dancer learning the *battement tendu* at the barre is learning in a new way to resist the pull of gravity. Just as the toddler, while attempting his first steps, learns to resist gravity while shifting from the right to the left leg, the student ballet dancer is confronted with this same difficulty rendered even more complex by the imposition of the unnatural turnout and the precise rhythmical structure of *battement tendu.*

A second purpose of *battement tendu* is the acquisition of the "straight leg." With this exercise the student begins to learn to straighten the leg so that it can assume the special demands and beauties which ballet technique will impose on the body. The use of the "straight leg" throughout the past several centuries has come to

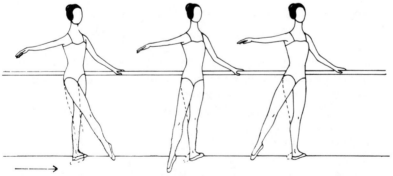

Battement tendu devant *Battement tendu de côté* *Battement tendu derrière*
from fifth position   from fifth position   from fifth position

Fig. 3. Battement tendu

develop an aesthetic of body line and movement quality of its own. In the various forms of *petit battement*, the knee, ankle and metatarsal joints are trained out of their natural inclination to flex or relax. The straight line of the leg from hip to toe results in the functional and aesthetic elements necessary to classical ballet. The knee and ankle joint must learn to become fully extended to form the taut leg in order to meet the physiological demands that all the classical steps will impose on the leg.

In summary, the *petit battement* exercises have been evolving for several hundred years and are rooted in the physiological necessities demanded by the classical steps of which the shift of weight from one leg to the other and the straight leg are integral components.

PROCEDURE

The student stands sideways to the barre just as he has done for the *plié* exercise. The left hand is slightly in front of the body as it gently rests on the barre. The weight is held high off the legs. Care must be taken not to expand the rib cage. The right arm does the traditional preparatory *port de bras* by moving from its low preparatory position to first position of the arm on the first musical cord and continues to second position of the arms on the second cord. The legs begin in fifth position with the right leg (working leg) in front. From this position at the barre, the directions to which the *battement tendu* will be performed by the working leg are as follows: (1) front (*devant*) meaning the working leg will *"tendu"* directly in front of the center of the body; (2) side (*de côté*), meaning the working leg will *"tendu"* at a right angle from the front, or side as in second position or side, meaning the working leg will *"tendu"* in line with the side of the body; (3) back (*derrière*) meaning the working leg will *"tendu"* directly behind the hipsocket or at a right angle from the side position.

Some specific points related to the execution of *battement tendu* are discussed as follows:

1. *Devant.* The working leg disengages or "opens" from the fifth position and moves to the front direction. As this "opening" part of the *battement tendu devant* occurs, the weight is shifted from both feet to the supporting leg even though the working foot retains contact with the floor. The working leg extends to the front direction as far as possible without pulling the weight or pelvis forward. That is, the

movement of the leg is perfectly isolated at its origin in the hip joint. The student's perfected and subtle transfer of weight in the *battement tendu* onto one leg will provide the psychological assurance necessary to the acquisition of balance.

The "opening" *battement tendu* movement requires the foot to brush itself frontward with the heel in advance while keeping the entire sole of the foot on the floor as long as possible. When half-way forward, the heel will begin to release from the floor, and then the ball of the foot will release until only the tip of the shoe remains touching the floor. The entire leg for one instant is totally extended from the hip joint downward and it is in the state of intense muscular contraction and concentrated energy. The path of the leg and foot to this front direction is neither a diagonal one or a self-adjusting path, but is directly front and accomplished with assurance. Likewise, the working leg must not "overcross", a term which refers to the tendency of the leg to veer to the opposite side, crossing the imaginary center line of the body.

As the working leg returns to its fifth position, still maintaining the turnout from the hip, the outside of the lower foot aims to move slightly in advance of the heel section in closing to the fifth position. The practice of this highly artificial way of manipulating the foot is what lends the beautiful upward curve to the foot as it is extended in an *arabesque*. It also serves to develop muscles to counteract the unaesthetic "sickle foot" which turns inward at the ankle joint. Correctly practiced, the *battement tendu* also alleviates the tendency of the protruding heel which mars the leg's classical line.

It is difficult to be more precise in the verbal directions as to the path of movement in *battement tendu* since the numerous and diverse shapes of human legs account for subtle adjustments within the context of the more general directions. Only the personal touch and taste of the teacher can make the instruction more individual.

2. *De côté* or *à la seconde*. As the leg disengages from the fifth position to the *battement tendu* side (*à la seconde*), it follows precisely the rules set for the *battement tendu devant*. The sole of the foot brushes out to the side direction in a line perpendicular to the barre and alternatively closes in fifth position in front or in back of the supporting leg depending on the particular design pattern of the given exercise.

In beginning ballet classes, the strain of disengaging the working leg to the exact side direction is often detrimental or seems impossible to correctly accomplish. Therefore, the entire leg, while maintaining its maximum turnout within the hip socket, is allowed to "cheat" forward one to two inches. The turnout of the hip joint maintains its maximum outward rotation. However, the advanced dancer must strive to achieve the ideal position without allowing the supporting leg to turn in, which would cause injury to the supporting knee and arch.

When the working leg closes to fifth position back from the open position, it is invariably confronted with the presence of the convex calf muscle of the supporting leg. Ideally, the knees remain straight. However, the presence of hyper-extended knee joints in many dancers calls for some alteration of this taut knee position. The rule of thumb is that the knees must at least give the visual impression of remaining straight. The knees do not give in by bending to the pressure of the legs pressing together, although the knee joints definitely release some of their tension (which was created in the open position of the *battement tendu*) when returning to the fifth position. At the same time, effort is made to pull up even more of the mass of the thigh muscles toward the torso. This effort is commonly referred to as "pulling up".

3. *Derrière. Battement tendu derrière* involves the opening and closing of the legs in the back direction of the body. As the leg disengages in the *battement* movement, care must be taken to keep the hip on the working side of the body pressed down in its placement. The brushing action of the foot aids in preventing the inordinate lift of the hip. The leg, turned out to the maximum, extends backward into an as elongated extension as possible, but the crest of both hip bones remain absolutely perpendicular to the barre. To help insure this correctness of procedure, the reverse process of thinking that the heel leads as the leg extends frontward in the *battement tendu devant*, is applicable. That is, as the leg disengages from the fifth position on its way to the back position, the reverse foot movement applies. The heel stays engaged as long as possible while the ball of the foot leads the projection of the movement into the back direction.

In *battement tendu derriére*, the torso must remain perfectly placed. That is, the shoulder and hip line remain solidly unaffected by the isolated excursions of the working leg as it disengages from the fifth position.

At the start of the exercise, the turned-out legs forming the fifth position set the turnout which is rigidly maintained during the exercise. In other words, whether the weight is on both legs or on one leg during the exercise, the maximum turnout is constantly maintained in both. For example, the turnout must be "locked" in the hip area in *battement tendu derriére* so that the leg will not travel a diagonal path but will move directly backward to the *battement tendu derriére*.

This common misplacement of the leg to the back direction is partly due to the physical construction of the body, but mostly it is because the dancer does not visually see the space behind him. Our knowledge of moving the leg within that area is always less secure. Therefore, dancers must rely on the "mind's eye" so to speak. This calls for kinetically memorizing the feeling of the leg working behind the body and constantly checking its accuracy by means of the mirror and corrective instruction.

In the beginning classes, the basic *battement tendu* with and without the addition of *demi-plié* is practiced slowly *en croix*, (i.e., to the front, side, and back directions). This usually employs a 2/4 musical structure for the minimum duration of 32 measures. The exercise is repeated with the other leg so that when the exercise is finished on the first side, the dancer turns and faces the opposite direction to assume the fifth position in preparation to repeat the identical movements with the alternate leg.

Over years of study, countless variations in spacial and rhythmic design for *battement tendu* are introduced to challenge the dancer with different movement possibilities. The variations of *battement tendu* also serve to break the tedium of an exercise which requires thousands of repetitions. Further benefits accrue as these variations of *battement tendu* provide the mind with a situation that demands it quickly learn to cope with and absorb novel movement and rhythmic designs.

Several additional forms of *petit battement* are eventually added to this point in the barre work. They are *battement tendu dégagé,battement tendu jeté, battement tendu relevé, battement fondu, battement frappé* and *battement retiré*. Each of these forms of *battement* also have countless variations of spatial and rhythmic design. They differ essentially in that each provides the practice of a different design and quality of movement. They are also practiced *en croix* except for *battement retiré*. They are always done first on one leg, followed by the other.

Significantly, the major directives previously mentioned for the proper execution of *battement tendu* are also the technical basis of the *battement dégagé* and the *battement jeté*.

BATTEMENT TENDU DÉGAGÉ

Battement tendu dégagé is a variation of the *battement tendu*. The term, *dégagé* refers to an additional stipulation in the opening and closing of the legs. That is, the working foot disengages approximately two to four inches from the floor when the leg arrives in its *pointe tendue* or "open" position. The outward thrust of the leg into the disengaged (*dégagé*) position accompanied by the foot's brushing movement off the floor greatly aids in developing the instep and the well-stretched ankle joint.

The tempo for the *battement tendu dégagé* is somewhat accelerated compared to that of the *battement tendu*.

BATTEMENT TENDU JETÉ

The term *battement tendu jeté* translates as "thrown" *battement*. It logically progresses from the *battement tendu* and the *battement tendu dégagé* in that its tempo is so lively that it suggests a glistening and brilliant effect in the working leg as it rapidly opens and closes the fifth position. It is generally done *en croix* but when maximum speed is called for it is practiced to the side direction only, closing in the first or fifth position. The successful accomplishment of the *battement tendu jeté* exercise assumes that the *battement tendu* and *battement tendu dégagé* are competently mastered and muscularly "memorized" so that an increase in speed in no way causes the *battement* to be less precisely done.

BATTEMENT TENDU RELEVÉ

Battement tendu relevé is essentially the *battement tendu* exercise with the addition of a movement provided by ankle articulation. The primary purpose of the exercise is to further aid in the development of the instep of the dancer. While it is practiced *en croix*, it is more commonly done to the side direction (*de côté*). When the working leg arrives in its open position, called *pointe tendue*, the heel lowers to the floor and then raises back to the *pointe tendue* position. This "up and down" action is what is referred to as *relevé* in the name of the exercise. As the *relevé* occurs, half the body weight may be allowed to shift onto the working leg as the heel lowers or the weight may be retained on the supporting leg as much as is possible. The first way practices the weight shift while the second way develops holding power in the supporting hip. Both manners of execution have their respective merits.

A fundamental kinetic concept common to the *battement tendu*, *battement tendu dégagé*, and *battement tendu jeté* is that they inculcate a combination of movements which elongate and tense the legs as they extend from the hip joint and the fifth position. At the same time, they slightly relax from this extension as they close back together in fifth. While the visual effect of the leg as it disengages from the fifth position is an elongated leg and is, therefore, often said to be a "stretching of the leg forward," it is more accurately a gradual contraction of the leg muscles as the leg achieves its lengthened position. The larger leg muscles are energized rather than stretched. There is, however, a genuine sensation of stretch that is actually experienced in the knee and ankle joints. As the leg retraces its path back to the fifth position, the muscular tension gradually decreases so that there is some muscular relaxation in the fifth. Ideally, the knee joint stays straight unless *plié* is added to the exercise. In the case of the hyper-extended leg, it is impossible to keep the knee from bending a small amount and still attain a properly tight fifth position.

Finally, when closing the leg into fifth position in the various *petit battement* exercises, it is necessary to emphasize that the weight is fully distributed through both feet. The weight of the body on both feet serves to relax them so that, while the foot muscles still hold the foot in its proper arch-pulled-up position, pinching or cramping of the metatarsal area and toes is avoided.

HYPER-EXTENSION

In first learning and practicing the *battement tendu* exercise, some students will encounter the perplexing matter of their hyper-extended legs. Hyper-extension is a term commonly used to describe a physical condition which is characterized by the degrees of the curvature of the fully extended leg. In other words, the knee joint, when extended goes beyond rendering a straight leg line of 180°to perhaps 210°.

A slight curvature of the legs produced by hyper-extension of the knee joint is always beautiful and is technically desirable for such feats as balance and point work. Hyper-extension is generally accompanied by finely arched feet and flexible body joints. If the curvature of the hyper-extended legs is extreme, the development of the student will be fraught with difficulties both technical and aesthetic.

Due to the various degrees of hyper-extension in students, the problem must be dealt with on an individual basis according to one of the several solutions provided by correct training. It is important to keep the legs visually straight and free from any giving-way or wobbling movements in the *battement tendu,* while striving to internally keep the knee joint as extended as possible. At the same time, effort and care must be taken to maintain the control and placement of the pelvis. In *battement tendu* and all other barre exercises beginning or ending in fifth position, a muscular effort is always made in pressing or squeezing the legs against one another in the fifth prior to the first movement or at the finish of the last movement of the exercise.

As the leg moves outward to its point of extremity in the side direction, the cue word "brush" is again used precisely to suggest the brushing of the sole of the shoe of the working leg against the floor. This verbal imagery, i.e., "brush", insures not only a foot on its way to becoming fully stretched, but it requires the knee also to become taut. This tensed condition of the leg is crucial since it allows the dancer to experience the feeling of the totally straight leg. This sensation, in turn, is utterly necessary in the supporting leg for any step which requires full body support on one leg at a given moment.

As the leg closes to the fifth position, the knee joint is both straight and slightly relaxed. When returning from the side direction, the heel of the working leg aims directly at the heel of the supporting leg and moves slightly behind the supporting heel on its path to closing in the fifth position. This small adjustment often solves the difficulty brought about by not being able to close in a tight fifth position due to hyper-extended legs.

If hyper-extension is present in the student's legs, it will have to be dealt with as a permanent condition in the barre work. The individual's ballet technique will have to be adjusted to the curvature of the leg at the knees. However, the fact remains. The fifth position must look correct even if the knees are not straight. The dancer must learn to use the legs fully pulled and straight as possible in the presence of considerable hyper-extension.

DYNAMICS IN BALLET
QUALITATIVE AND QUANTITATIVE

Dynamics is a term used here to refer to the continuous changes which the body experiences as it is involved in ballet movement. These changes are essentially two, qualitative and quantitative. Qualitative dynamics pertain to the muscular changes within the body (internal) while quantitative dynamics deal with the many variations of extensions of the body into space (external).

Ballet consists of an uninterrupted and interrelated combination of qualitative and quantitative dynamics. These are specifically expressed in the duo kinecepts of contraction and release; extension and retraction. The dancing body is continuously involved to some degree in the physical expression of these kinecepts. That is, it is constantly contracting and releasing muscles at the same time that it is extending or retracting its skeletal frame in space. It is helpful for the student who must constantly struggle with the difficult body of kinesthetics and physiological material of which ballet consists, to understand it in terms of its qualitative and quantitative dynamics.

In the following, the *battement tendu plié* will be used as the model exercise since the beginning student is most familiar with its execution. However, the discussion on dynamics applies to all of the *petit battement* exercises and, consequently, to the dynamics of all ballet movement.

When the *demi-plié* is added to the *battement tendu* exercise, the stretching movement of the calf muscles and achilles tendon result from the *plié*. This adds up to four movement ideas. The legs *tense* and *stretch* at the same time that they *extend* from and *return* to fifth position. These four movement ideas can be viewed as two fundamental and interrelated kinecepts (movement concepts) which underly all of classical ballet. They are the kinecepts of the qualitative dynamics expressed by tension and relaxation and the quantitative dynamics of spatial range as expressed by the combination of extending and retracting the limbs or entire body in space.

1. The qualitative dynamics of dance movement as expressed by the kinecept of tension-relaxation is similar in function to the movement ideas incorporated in the technique evolved by Martha Graham. The Graham technique in modern dance supports the principle

that the dual actions of muscular contraction and release form the physiological basis of dance movement.

The muscular contraction and release, as taught in the Graham technique, is generally visible because it involves the emphatic flexion of the spine and/or arm and leg joints. This flexion is expressed in the angular body designs which, in turn, powerfully convey specific emotional content to the observer. In classical ballet, however, the physiological presence of contraction and release refers to the *general* rather than isolated *concentration of strength and then the release of it*. Ballet does not aesthetically and, therefore, intentionally involve the spine in design-forming contraction and release. Instead, it purposely weaves its classical designs with the limbs although the spine remains the center of strength for accomplishing these designs. For instance, *battement frappé, battement retiré, flic-flac* and the *fouetté* are all examples of hip, knee, and ankle flexion accompanied by muscular contraction. Here, the *varying amounts of strength are concentrated and are immediately followed by an equal degree of relaxation.*

It must be remembered that in all of natural human movement, there is continuous tension and the release from it. Likewise, in *battement tendu plié* as in all ballet movement, the body is constantly contracting the muscles and releasing the contraction. A series of *piqué* turns is an example of a steady flow of contract-release or tension-relaxation. A simple *pirouette*, a *relevé en arabesque*, or a *changement de pieds* are all based on the qualitative dynamics of tension and release. Without the natural use of this continuous flow of tension followed by relaxation, dance movement is inorganic, awkward and uncontrolled.

2. The quantitative dynamics of dance movement refer to the physical range of the body in space, whether it is in one place or is traversing space from one point to another. For instance, the *battement tendu plié* is an example of this range of the body in a barre exercise. In the *battement tendu plié*, the quantitative range of the opening of straight legs and closing into the *plié* in fifth position is minimal. The mechanism of this very same movement, the *battement tendu plié* is quantitatively extended when transferred to *grand battement* with *demi-plié*. This latter exercise is quantitatively further extended when it traverses through space in a series of *grands jetés* (large leaps). As movement changes quantitatively, it requires a commensurate amount of modulated force or energy. The *battement tendu plié* requires minimal energy while maximum energy is concentrated and channeled into the *grand jeté*.

The enormous importance of mastering the *battement tendu* with its related movements of the *demi-plié* and eventually the *relevé*, is evidenced in that this barre exercise houses, in miniature form, the nucleus of the entire qualitative and quantitative dynamics of classical ballet. Insofar as all leg movement in ballet technique can be reduced to the continuous flow of *plié* to the straightening or extension of the leg joints, the significance of the *battement tendu* cannot be underestimated. The more perfectly practiced the *battement tendu* is, the greater the potential technical development in the student. The leg extension coupled with the *demi-plié* and the *relevé*, are fundamental movements whereby the body supported by the legs, is able to extend its range of movement in its own immediate space. Furthermore, as the body's spatial range traverses from one point in space to another, the continuous shifts of body weight onto one leg and then the other are rooted in the *battement tendu* exercise. This is clearly seen in observing the leg movements in slow-motion filming of ballet. The legs, from hip to toe, are seen to continually flex and elongate in the knee, ankle, and metatarsal joints. Body weight is also seen to continuously shift from one leg to the other no matter what directions are taken, or what movement designs are formed, or what rhythms are created.

ROTARY MOVEMENT

At this point in the class, the *pliés* and the *battement tendu, dégagé,* and *jeté* have sufficiently begun to warm the feet, knee and hip joints. The next exercise at the barre consists of rotary movements which introduce an additional aspect of the movement possibilities of the legs. Rotation of the leg within the hip socket is designed to loosen the hip joint so that it can initiate a considerable range of movement without altering the stability of the torso.

ROND DE JAMBE À TERRE

Rond de jambe à terre translates freely as the rotation of the working leg while it maintains contact with the floor. The exercise itself is essentially the hip rotation of the working leg in a D-shaped spatial design while the other leg firmly sustains its turnout. The *rond de jambe* is traditionally done to 3/4 time and its movement is thus rendered

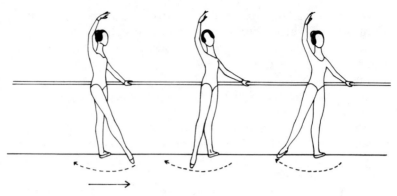

Fig. 4. Rond de jambe à terre
The working leg inscribes a semi-circle as it moves through the front (*devant*), side (*de côté*), and back (*derrière*) directions.

more lyrical in quality than the previous exercises. Although there are countless variations of the *rond de jambe à terre* exercise, especially as it is often combined with the beautiful *port de bras* and *adage* movements, only the fundamental technical procedure will be discussed here.

The dancer stands at the barre in fifth position with the right leg in front. A special preparation unique to the *rond de jambe à terre* is explained as follows: The arm is low in the preparatory position. On the first musical chord of the preparation, the right arm extends forward to first position, as the working leg brushes its foot forward (*à la quatrième devant*). The supporting leg simultaneously lowers in a well-turned out *demi-plié*. Next, the arm and leg move to their respective positions *à la seconde* or *de côté*, and the supporting knee straightens from its *demi-plié*. The exercise is as follows: By the first beat of the first measure, the working leg has swiftly moved from its preparatory second position, through the *rond de jambe* and into the first position to begin a series of eight *ronds de jambe à terre*. It goes by way of the following path: The working leg with a very well-stretched foot and extended ankle joint (*pointe tendue* position) moves from the side direction (*pointe tendue à la seconde*) to the back direction (*pointe tendue à la quatrième derrière*). The working leg moves directly forward through the first position with the working heel dropping and brushing the floor as it passes through the first position and on to the front direction (*à la quatrième devant*). When the working leg arrives in front, the actual exercise begins so that one *rond de jambe* is executed to each three beat measure of music.

At first, the beginner best learns the correct approach by taking one musical measure for each leg extension to the front, side, and back direction, but soon the entire *rond de jambe* movement can be accomplished to one moderately timed measure of music. Advanced students should occasionally be given the opportunity to test their uppermost limit of speed with a very quick tempo for *rond de jambe à terre*.

The *rond de jambe* rotates in two directions. The term *en dehors* indicates that the rotation is "outward" or in a clockwise direction when the right leg inscribes the semi-circle. *En dedans* refers to the "inward" or counter-clockwise rotation when the right leg works. Eight *ronds de jambe à terre en dehors* are usually suggested before the exercise reverses its direction *en dedans*. The reverse occurs at the end of the eighth musical measure as the working leg arrives front. On the first beat of the next measure it brushes backward through the first position and arrives at the back direction on the first beat of the ninth measure. The leg proceeds to move on its semi-circular or D-shaped path forward through the second, front and back direction. At the end of the sixteenth measure, the leg comes to stop in fifth position front. The addition of *port de bras* movement is optional. In intermediate and advanced ballet, the length of the exercise is doubled, varied and embellished by the addition of an infinite number of combinations of *port de bras* and *développé* movements.

In beginning ballet, the addition of 16 or 32 measures of simple *port de bras* is generally incorporated into the second half of the *rond de jambe* exercise. Its duration and complexity is dependent on the technical level of the class. *Port de bras* is discussed separately in Chapter 14.

Musicality requires that the working leg in *rond de jambe* always arrives in the front direction (*pointe tendue à la quatrième devant*) on the first beat of the *rond de jambe à terre en dehors* or in the back direction (*pointe tendue à la quatrième derrière*) if the movement is *en dedans*. Occasionally, it is taught that the accented first beat of the measure occurs when the working leg comes to the first position whether the working leg is moving *en dehor* or *en dedans,* but this is less common.

Points of difficulty are numerous in the *rond de jambe à terre* exercise and need constant scrutiny on part of both teacher and student. During the exercise, it is imperative that the supporting side of the body remains stable. The supporting side of the torso around the hip area has a tendency to swivel inward to the center of the room because of pressure and movement caused by the working leg. The supporting hip must stay firmly held and supportive of the turnout demanded in the leg. The taut knee is evidenced by the contraction of the small muscle immediately above the knee cap as well as the contracted thigh muscle. The supporting foot, by maintaining its correct position supports the weight without cramping the toes, and indicates the hip is carrying the full responsibility in maintaining the turnout. The full body weight on the supporting leg is only lessened for a brief moment when the working leg passes through the first position and assumes a very small amount of weight. At this point, the crucial presence of tension and release is apparent in the dancer's body. The working leg experiences a slight release of tension. Although the working leg does not stop in the first position, the extraordinary hold on the working leg is lessened for an instant as some of the body weight subtly shifts onto it in the first position.

The common faults pertaining to the working leg are basically four and they involve hip placement, rotation, the working knee and ankle joints, and "overcrossing."

1. *Hip Placement.* The hip line in *rond de jambe à terre* must stay absolutely perpendicular to the line of the barre and absolutely parallel to the floor line. In other words, as the leg rotates backward in *rond de jambe à terre en dehors* or forward *en dedans,* its force can easily pull the outside hip backward, sideways or forward with it, thus losing the hip line perpendicular to the barre. Further difficulty arises in that the rotation *en dehors* or *en dedans* can minimize the torso's control over the placement. This allows the hip to lift on each rotation or permanently rise and sustain the lifted hip in faulty placement.

2. *Rotation.* The working knee must be utterly straight throughout the exercise unless *demi-plié* is included in one of the many design variations of *rond de jambe à terre.* For most students, however, the working knee tends to buckle or relax in the first position and as the leg approaches the back direction whether proceeding *en dehors* or *en dedans.* This is the same problem mentioned previously in the *battement tendu* exercise. Due to the body's construction and the dancer's inability to see behind, the activity of the leg when moving behind the body is more difficult to perfect. Providing the *rond de jambe à terre* is done carefully and slowly at the beginning of ballet study, this ever-

recurring problem can be controlled and quickly corrected when it inevitably shows up.

3. *Knee and Ankle Joints.* Similar to the preceding fault, the ankle joint also tends to give way, especially as it moves to the back position *en dehors* where it is not directly visible to the dancer. This "giving way" naturally cuts the semi-circular or D-shaped line. This serious minimization of the back extension of the foot eventually carries over to a lack of leg range, beautiful line, and the all-important sensory identification of the leg placement in the back direction. This fault occurs even though the full potential of leg range is present in the dancer with average flexibility. If the range and extension of the leg in the back direction is never totally identified (kinetically sensed) and used, this flexibility will, in time, dissipate. Therefore, it behooves the student dancer to pay special attention to the perfection of the semi-circular path of movement in the *rond de jambe à terre* exercise.

4. *Overcrossing.* This term describes a common fault in the execution of *rond de jambe à terre.* It refers to the working leg crossing inward or beyond the precise position of the front direction (*à la quatrième devant*) or the back direction (*à la quatrième derrière*). In other words, instead of the leg inscribing a semi-circle of 180°, overcrossing causes the movement to cover perhaps 220°. The technical danger that ensues with a 220° *rond de jambe* movement is the loss of the pelvic placement. This fault is apparent in the swivel of the hips which accompanies each *rond de jambe à terre.*

ROND DE JAMBE EN L'AIR

A far more complex and difficult rotary movement is the *rond de jambe en l'air.* In this exercise, the working leg is raised in second position while the lower leg inscribes circular movements in the air by rotating within the knee joint. Due to the muscular subtlety of *rond de jambe en l'air,* many months of fairly intense training should precede its introduction into the barre work. The proper place for *rond de jambe en l'aire* is toward the end of the barre exercises when the body is warmed and stretched. At this time the legs are ready for high extensions and since *rond de jambe en l'air* is generally done with the working leg at a 90° angle, it is usually practiced just before or after the *grand battement*. Therefore, a more specific discussion on the basic execution of the *rond de jambe en l'air* is included in Chapter 13.

CHAPTER 13

Flexion Exercises

EXERCISES FOR THE ANKLE, KNEE AND HIP

BATTEMENT FRAPPÉ

A contrast of movement quality is provided by the next exercise at the barre, the *battement frappé*. As its translation indicates, *frappé* is a striking, sharp and percussive movement. The basic action during the *battement frappé* is the rhythmic opening and closing of the working leg to the open *pointe tendue* position from a special closed position at the ankle called *sur le cou-de-pied*.

The *sur le cou-de-pied* position, which literally translates as "on the collar of the foot," is based on the working leg's maximum correct turnout with the knee and ankle joints flexed. The working foot is placed slightly above the ankle bone of the supporting foot when in the front position. With the *cou-de-pied* in the back position, the working foot is flexed and placed well behind, but touching the supporting ankle. Depending on the particular school of technique or on the particular exercise, the foot is variously styled with the ankle joint completely flexed, fully extended, or in the wrapped position.

All three foot positions *sur le cou-de-pied* will be used in the course of lengthy study since each has its particular advantages. *Frappé* incorporating the flexed position at the ankle, whether in front or back, emphasizes the fullness of ankle articulation when combined with the speed-giving capacity of the *frappé*. *Frappé* practiced with a pointed foot develops the muscular "feeling" of straightness in the ankle joint and doubly functions as an anti-sickling device. *Frappé*, executed with the foot "wrapped" *sur le cou-de-pied* indicates that the heel of the working leg is pressed forward and placed over the ankle bone of the supporting foot while the arch and metatarsal areas wrap themselves convexly around the supporting ankle. The foot position when behind the supporting leg is identical except that it has nothing to "wrap"itself around. This foot style is essentially an aesthetic position and therefore visually more desirable. However, it is also valuable in necessarily disguising the absence of beautifully arched feet.

Because it is physiologically more complex in that it utilizes certain twisting procedures at the ankle and knee joints, the "wrapped" *sur le cou-de-pied* position should not be immediately taught to children or adult beginners. The reason for avoiding the "wrapped" position is that this demands extra muscular effort and mental concentration. When new students attend to the "wrapped" position, they inadvertently allow the working thigh to swing forward while the foot is still attached to the ankle of the supporting leg. This occurs because the strength and correct motor habits holding the turnout have not yet had time to develop.

The same unfortunate result is demonstrated in the insufficiently strong student when the wrapped foot is in the back position, *sur le cou-de-pied derrière*. The knee swings forward, allowing the turned out position to disintegrate, the abdomen to sag, and the shoulders and chin to drop forward because sustaining strength is lacking. The immediate method for dealing with this problem is verbal correction, and, the acquisition of strength will, in time, support and sustain the verbal correction. If this problem is not dealt with, and less than adequate execution is allowed, wrong motor habits will become ingrained. For this reason, *frappé* practiced solely to the side direction is recommended in early training. *Frappé* is described here to include the use of the flexed foot in the *cou-de-pied* position.

Battement frappé begins in fifth position and on the two chord introduction as the arm executes its standard preparation to the side direction, the working leg brushes in a single *battement tendu* to the second position *pointe tendue*; the foot then retracts to the *cou-de-pied* position as its unique starting point. (1) The *frappé* exercise commences with the working foot moving by means of a striking action from the *cou-de-pied* to the side direction within the duration of this first count. As the leg is in the process of extending outward, the ball of the working foot "strikes" the floor suggesting the percussive quality which exemplifies the *frappé* exercise. (2) The leg retracts from this *battement dégagé* following the same path in reverse except that the "strike" does not reoccur nor does the ball of the working foot have any contact with the floor. Hence, the muscles of the working leg have run the gamut from being in a slightly relaxed position to the ex-

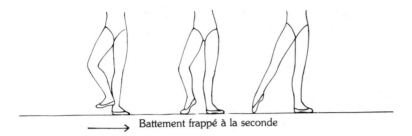

Battement frappé à la seconde

Fig. 1. Battement Frappé

tremely taut and open position in the *pointe tendue*. The leg joints have gone from their flexed position to the elongated tautness of the straight leg and back to the flexed position *sur le cou-de-pied*.

Rhythmically, there is a subtle asymmetry which the beginner is soon capable of accomplishing. Although the *frappé* is done to a symmetrical "1 and 2" tempo, the speed-giving purpose of the exercise is maximized as the retraction of the leg on the "and" count is swifter than its extension into the open position. The minute amount of time left over from the retraction is applied to the outward striking on the musical accents as opposed to the "ands" in the 2/4 meter common to all *battement* exercises. The "strike" outward is the emphasized moment of what is essentially another contract-release exercise.

The resultant effect of *frappé* done with rhythmic asymmetry supplies the vitality of leg movement necessary to *allégro* dancing. The brilliant *frappé* and its application to *allégro* steps as such is aesthetically more desirable in that it has an element of kinetic surprise in place of the sluggishness that symmetrical rhythms and movements together inevitably produce. Equally important, the asymmetrical strike and retraction provided by the *frappé* develops "attack" which is the very seed of the ability to channel energy. And dancing (i.e. designed movement) is channeled energy! Indeed, a central objective for the student is that sufficient strength be developed so that energy can be efficiently and precisely harnessed to form various spacial arrangements of the body in relation to certain given moments in time.

The *frappé* executed *en croix* is technically complicated by the fact that the striking action of the leg to the front and back directions pulls the body off the solidity of its correct placement unless consciously counteracted. The shoulder and hip lines must stay perpendicular to the barre and the body's imaginary center line paralleling the spine must remain perpendicular to the floor regardless of the leg's percussive striking outward and away from center. Traditionally, the verbal cue has been to "prevent the working thigh from moving" as the leg performs the *frappé* so that the turnout is not lost. This is to say that while the thigh does not move by altering its spatial position during the *frappé,* the muscles within the thigh are actively involved in the *frappé* and can be seen to work. If the thigh does change its spatial position, the turnout is lost in which case the correctness of the entire exercise is foregone.

An appropriate *battement frappé* exercise for the beginner consists of sixteen *frappés à la secondes* (side direction only) and utilizes 32 counts of 2/4 meter. Eventually the beginner will attempt a series of four *frappés* done to each direction or one *frappé* done *en croix* and repeated three additional times. These latter two variations of *battement frappé* also use 32 counts of 2/4 meter.

FRAPPÉ EN RELEVÉ

Eventually the progressing student who has become familiar with the concept and practice of *relevé* will perform the *frappé* exercise in the *relevé* position. This exercise is eventually made more complex by an increase in tempo, with the inclusion of beats for the working leg and with *demi-plié* and *relevés* for the supporting leg. Variations of the *frappé* exercise which include *relevé* demand correct placement and strength acquired especially for this task.

DOUBLE FRAPPÉ

After some time, the double *frappé* done quite slowly is introduced to the class of adult beginners. A double *frappé* consists of simple *frappés* practiced *en croix* or *à la seconde* with the addition of a beating action by the working leg. The fully turned-out working leg maintains its *cou-de-pied* position as the lower part of the leg (the ankle area) alternates its relationship to the supporting leg by percussively moving from front to back or vice versa. The muscles of the thigh bear much of the responsibility for the movement although the thigh maintains its stationary spatial placement. The knee joint provides the point of leverage for the movement while the entire body is alert and the torso placement is impeccably held.

The double *frappé en croix* as it begins from the preparatory *pointe tendue à la seconde* is as follows: beat back, beat front, simple *frappé* to the front direction, beat front, beat back, simple *frappé* to the side direction; beat front beat back, simple *frappé* to the back direction, beat back, beat front, simple *frappé* to the side direction. A series of double *frappés à la seconde* requires the same rhythm and is also performed beginning from the preparatory second. The working foot *sur le cou-de-pied* moves as follows: beat back, beat front and simple *frappé* to the side direction; beat front, beat back and simple *frappé* to the side direction, etc.

Double *frappé* is done with the pointed foot style as well as the wrapped foot style utilizing the same pattern of movement. It is important to remember here that when the pointed foot style or wrapped foot style is used, the ball of the foot does not brush the floor as it moves outward from the ankle position to execute the double *frappé*. Also the tip of the big toe may or may not touch the floor when it attains the point of extremity with the pointed or wrapped position. When the flexed foot style *sur le cou-de-pied* is used with double *frappés,* however, there is the outward brush of the ball of the foot and the tip of the big toe does touch the floor (pointe tendue) immediately before it swiftly retracts to its home position.

FLEXION: TWO ASPECTS

Frappé exercises done with the flexed foot position provide necessary practice for the flexion of the leg joints which in turn produce balletic speed, precision and attack. In *frappé* the working foot rhythmically strikes back and forth from its flexed position to the limit of its elongated and extended position without having to support weight. This kind of articulation develops speed since it has little if any resistance to gravity to contend with. The facile manipulation of the knee and ankle joints as the legs move in the spatial design of *frappé* provides the desired brilliant flashes of movement. However, in *pas battu* (beaten steps) and *pas sauté* (jumping steps) such as *entrechat quatre* and *jeté sauté* where the steps are essentially jumping movements, there is a different aspect to flexion of ankle and knee. Before the body is freed in space to accomplish this movement, it must first escape from its gravity weighted condition. The action of the leg joints which makes the "escape" possible is that of the *sauté* movement which is rooted in *plié-relevé*. While *frappé* provides the knee and ankle joint articulation necessary to speed, precision, and attack, the *relevé* develops enormous leg strength resulting from knee and ankle articulation as it occurs under the weight of the body.

Joint articulation is practiced under two conditions. In the first condition as demonstrated by *frappé,* the leg moves freely in space from its ultimate spinal control point. Its purpose is swift and accurately placed movement, unfettered by the weight of the body. The second condition in which joint articulation is practiced is in relation to gravity and the resistance to it. In other words, to jump off the floor and to land from the jump is a combination of denying and giving in to gravity. The only way the jump is possible in the first place is through joint articulation which combines special strength to jump as well as precise spatial control as to where and with what body design the movement trajects and returns to the floor. These two aspects of joint articulation where the leg articulates freely in space on an oblique or horizontal plane, and where it meets with the resistance of the floor in its vertical use, are more or less obvious to anyone studying the technique of ballet. However, it is profitable to have them broken down into their two distinct areas for several reasons. While the essential practice of oblique or horizontal joint articulation such as *frappé, développé, fondu, retiré* and *ronde de jamb en l'air* aids the joint articulation in jumping steps by nature of their various commonalities, it cannot supplant the joint articulation which derives from the practice of jumping. The feeling of resisting gravity, giving into the pull of gravity and the need to pleasurably become accustomed to this condition simply results from familiarity, i.e., thousands of jumps of all movement qualities and shapes. Strength and endurance derive from jumping movements which are based on the correct *plié-relevé.* Strength and endurance only result from the actuality of using the legs in gravity-resistant joint articulations such as *changement, échappé, jeté, assemblé, sissonne,* etc. While classic techniques of modern dance supplied by the genius of Graham and Humphrey are responsible for having improved ballet study in countless ways, their special development of and commitment to floor movement leaves less time to developing the jump and its affiliated strength and endurance necessary to the ballet. For ballet students fortunate enough to acquire the movement versatility provided by modern dance study, a word of warning. While floor work offers one a great sense of body alignment, while it offers movement without having to fight gravity, while it offers safe and profitable stretching exercises and experiences of new dance qualities, especially with regard to the spinal area, it does not normally contribute to strength and endurance needs which the ballet commands. Ultimately only brutally rigorous and regular amounts of jumping done throughout the last third of the ballet class develop the jump. And those dancers who have already done six years or so of serious study will not deny the association of the word "brutal" with much of their experience.

Excessive joint articulation of both types can result in inflammation of the achilles tendons, bursitus, and metatarsal strain resulting from a separation of the web-like bone structure in the metatarsal area. Shin splints are the most common leg ailment produced by excessive jumping. Essentially, "shin splints" is a painful condition where the muscles in front of the lower leg pull away from the bone due to the shock of the jump. This temporary pain can be avoided or at least headed off in most cases by daily sitting on the heels for 60 seconds as the body rests in a kneeling position. This allows the "shin" muscles a reasonable stretch so that when the calf muscles are being vigorously worked, their comparatively enormous power does not overly strain their disproportionate abductors. Another preventative measure for "shin splints" where circumstances require extensive repetitions of jumps, is the use of an elastic bandage lightly wrapped around the lower leg. This gently aids the front of the lower leg muscles in their natural proclivity to adhere to the leg bone. Metatarsal aches are also relieved by lightly wrapping the area in adhesive tape. While only medical doctors may deal with bursitis by means of injection, it is usually cured by total rest of the legs.

BATTEMENT FONDU

The movement of *fondu* describes the descent of the body into *demi-plié* through the controlled use of the instep wherein its activity is coordinated by the knee. As the French term *fondu* implies, it is a melting or folding movement whereby the legs render an extremely pliant quality of design and motion to the body. One of the more complex barre exercises which will confront the adult beginner is the *battement fondu.* This exercise, like all forms of *petit battement,* is referred to as *battement fondu* because it involves an opening and closing of the legs.

In the *fondu* exercise both legs perform *demi-plié.* One leg supports the body weight while the working leg is free to flex and straighten itself toward the front, side, and back directions. A tango rhythm is often used to accompany this exercise. The inherent rolling sound of the tango qualitatively resembles and, hence, aids the movement of folding into and emerging from the *plié.*

The *fondu* exercise commences with the usual two chord preparation, i.e., the arm moves to second position at the same time as the leg brushes the floor to the second, keeping the foot pointed as it arrives. *Battement fondu* is comprised of two movements in that the working foot moves toward and then away from the supporting leg. It is described as follows: (1) on the count of one the supporting leg descends into a *plié* while the working leg, maintaining its pointed foot, moves directly *sur le cou-de-pied* in front. (2) On the count of two, the supporting leg straightens from its *plié* and the working leg unfolds directly to the front position *pointe tendue* (i.e., the tip of the foot is in contact with the floor). The exercise repeats the *fondu* movement to the side, back, and side directions so that it has been performed *en croix.*

Like *frappé,* the *fondu* can also be done to the second position only, either 8 or 16 times.

Once the basic *fondu* exercise is mastered, *port de bras* (arm movements) may be added. For each *fondu,* the arm has a complementary movement from second position through the preparatory position up through first and out again to second. The arm and leg movements are coordinated so that when the supporting leg *plié* occurs, the arm simultaneously moves downward. As the sinking *fondu* movement is reversed upward, the arm moves upward through the first to the second position.

In work at the intermediate level, the *relevé* may be added to the movement of the supporting leg. When this is done, the *fondu* unfolds on the *demi-pointe* (half toe) immediately before it folds into another *demi-plié.* In a more advanced variation, the *grand développé* is added to the efforts of the working leg, and this is known as *grand fondu.* The working leg must aim for a height at hip level or above. It is done both with and without *relevé,* and is enormously important in building strength and control in adagio movement. For advanced stu-

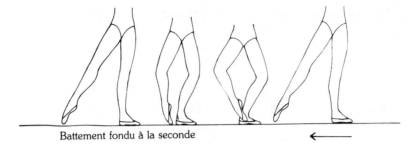

Battement fondu à la seconde   ⟵

Fig. 2. Battement Fondu

dents, *grand fondu* should be done very slowly while achieving as much *plié* and contrasting extention movement as possible. Done as such it is extremely demanding but highly rewarding. To do the *grand fondu* once or twice *en croix* in daily practice is generally sufficient for optimal benefit.

For beginners, the *demi-plié,* turnout, correct posture and straight knee sensation must all be separately mastered to the degree which *fondu* utilizes them before the exercise is attempted. While a clear conceptualization of the elements that combine to produce the *fondu* exercise is essential, the difficult muscular coordination must be aided by previously established correct motor habits. This will require, for example, that the supporting leg execute a *demi-plié* as the working leg simultaneously executes the *battement fondue.*

If the tempo or movement impulse of one leg is at variance with the other, the fondu is not coordinated. Lack of coordination in the elements of *fondu* produces design tensions which are ultimately reflected in awkward and clumsy movement quality. For example, the turning in of the knee of the supporting leg as it moves into the *plié* may be followed by the unfortunate release of the lower back which, in turn, produces a jutting chin and drooped shoulders. Thus, correct spinal alignment and the rudiments of an elegant stage presence are progressively lost. Each time the *fondu* is wrongly repeated with these faults, the faults are strengthened. Consequently, strength building which the *fondu* is designed to contribute to the whole body does not take place.

When *fondu* is attempted too soon, the beginning dancer runs the risk of forming incorrect motor habits. Therefore, it is desirable to work on the three exercises which provide the fundamental elements of the *fondu:* the *demi-plié, battement tendu,* and *frappé.* Ideally, the *plié,* with the weight on both feet and the legs well turned-out, should be thoroughly mastered before the *fondu* can be reasonably executed. The *fondu* employs the *demi-plié* with both legs, but with only one leg supporting the weight. The ability to straighten both the supporting leg and the working leg as they emerge from the *fondu* depends on how sensitive the dancer is to the leg-stretching sensation in the open position of *battement tendu.* While the rhythmic element and energy flow of the *frappé* differs from *fondu,* the flexion of the joints in the working hip, knee, ankle, and metatarsal are very similar in their movements. Full comprehension and correct execution of *demi-plié, battement tendu,* and *frappé* as individual exercises, will make the first attempts with *fondu* more satisfying and will speed mastery of this exercise.

The multi-faceted nature of *fondu* is a strong reminder that the more complex the balletic exercise, the greater the possibility for forming incorrect habits which impede progress. The acquisition of bad motor habits is time consuming for both student and teacher because it is difficult to extinguish incorrect habits and establish the rightful ones in their place. For this reason, a clear conception of the ideal *plié, battement tendu* and *frappé* is essential not only for the *fondu* exercises but is a technical prerequisite for the entire body of ballet movement.

BATTEMENT RETIRÉ

Battement retiré is the name given to one of the simpler elementary exercises. The name refers to a *battement* movement where the working leg retracts (retiré) from the fifth position upward as the knee flexes. The general purpose of *battement retiré* is to loosen the hip joints and teach controlled sharpness of leg movements. It also develops holding power in its retracted position. The dancer begins the exercise standing in the fifth position with the working leg in front as the usual two count preparatory arm movement is performed. For variation, the arm can move from the preparatory position to the first and then to the fifth position of the arms. (1) The exercise itself commences when the lower part of the working leg retracts upward with a snapping-like quality so that the thigh arrives well turned-out in its side or second position. The size of the movement is gauged so that the

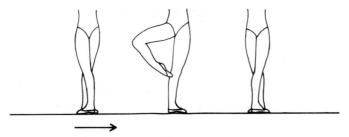

Fig. 3. Battement Retiré

thigh moves high enough to be almost parallel to the floor. The foot of the working leg follows suite by also snapping upward from the fifth position so that it arrives already fully pointed opposite the knee of the supporting leg. (2) The *retiré* movement resolves itself as the working leg returns to the fifth position, its foot being placed in fifth position behind the supporting foot. Eight to sixteen *battements retirés* are generally executed with the working leg alternately closing the fifth position in front and behind. Incidentally, this "passing" of the working foot from front to back in fifth position has led to the casual American usage of the French work *passé* to replace the more accurate and descriptive term, *battement retiré. Battement raccourci* is less commonly heard but is also correct terminology.

The simplest version of *battement retiré* takes form when the retracting leg starts and finishes its movement from the first position. This elementary approach is often used to introduce the exercise to the beginner although it is not necessarily practiced as such after the first few classes. The *battement retiré* is often done in beginning ballet as a separate exercise toward the end of the barre work. Not since the *grand plié* at the very beginning of the class has the hip joint been so involved in flexion movements. While the *rond de jambe* teaches the dancer to rotate the thigh in its hip socket, the *retiré* demands leg leverage power as well as flexibility in the hip area. Likewise, the central area of the body, i.e., waist muscles, hip joints and pelvic area is more visibly involved in the large and forceful *retiré* movement. This procedure is part of the logical and purposeful design of the traditional barre. Starting with practice of *pliés* and series of *petits battements,* the barre work develops in a gradual progression to the conditioning of muscles and joints of the pelvic area as demonstrated by *battement retiré.*

Battement retiré as an exercise is particularly important in that it teaches the dancer to correctly lift the thigh. Accuracy of turnout and precision-demanding strength which accompany thigh movement in *battement retiré* are the root of all large leg movements whether they be in *grand adage* or great leaping movements. Furthermore, the *battement retiré* aids in the limbering up of the hip joints and hence the lower torso. The hip joint is articulated by the rhythmic upward and downward movement of the working thigh bone. The muscles around the hip are trained to "hold the hip down." In other words, the upward moving thigh will displace the hip line in an upward tilt unless the muscles are trained and sensitized to press downward as the thigh lifts. This action ensures that the hip bones remain parallel to the floor line, maintaining one aspect of placement.

Just as it is important not to allow the hip line to tilt upward in *battement retiré,* so is it imperative that the hips do not swivel forward or backward. As the working leg alternately closes in fifth position front and then to the fifth position back, the hip bones which create the imaginary perpendicular line to the barre must be restrained by their encasing muscles to avoid the imminent swivel of the hip section.

In terms of placement, *battement retiré* is a particularly fortuitous exercise in that it teaches the body (specifically the lower spine) how to deal with the constant and legitimate "displacement of placement" which occurs in more advanced ballet movements. The placement provided by the barre exercises is a kind of neutral home base to which the body always returns no matter what extreme movements are demanded from it. Much of the kinetic experience that classical ballet is, physically displaces the pristine body positions on which its visual aesthetic is founded. A dancer having a strong technique is capable of unconsciously righting the pelvis displacement in a shoulder high leg extention because of ingrained good motor habits.

In beginning ballet, *battement retiré* is necessarily a separate exercise performed as previously explained. After *relevé* has been introduced, practiced, and clearly understood, the *battement retiré* can be combined with the *relevé*. This is significant in that it is generally one of the first times the student has the experience of going onto *demi-pointe* on one leg while the body maintains the complex balletic comportment. The peak of the *battement retiré* with *relevé* comprises a modicum of balance, involves placement of hips and the turnout of both legs, one being flexed and the other tautly stretched and supporting all the weight.

The obviously strong movement of the thigh of the working leg during *battement retiré* demands a great firmness in the supporting side of the body lest it become intimidated and waver from its turnout and stability. A conscious effort must be made to disallow the supporting side of the body to swivel inward. As in *battement tendu*, the *battement retiré* consists of a constant but subtle shift of body weight from both legs in fifth position to the supporting leg. To an extent the pull of gravity contributes to the solidity and stability of the supporting side since the weight is sustained there.

The word "snapping" is often used to describe the ideal quality of the thigh movement in *battement retiré*. The term serves as a verbal cue to deter the leg from moving in a "sluggish" manner. Anyone who has ever tried this exercise understands that much effort is required to do it. Yet, the balletic precept of effortlessness dictates that this arduous physical demand must be disguised so that the *battlement retiré* appears to be without effort. The "snapping" upward of the thigh therefore renders a special movement quality of elasticity.

This special quality of elasticity is best achieved by starting the upward movement of *retiré* on the "and" count so that the working leg actually completes the first *retiré* on the first count of the measure of 2/4 time. To vary the musical format of the barre work, 3/4 time is often used for *battement retiré*. In this case an excellent way to achieve a brilliant *retiré* is to use the first beat of the measure for the upward movement and the second and third for the descent. This is effective in that it gives speed to the upward flashing movement of the thigh which is necessary, for example, in the execution of a *pas de chat*. Equally important to the *pirouette* is the swift upward thrust of the thigh in the instant attainment of the *retiré relevé* position of the turn. Conversely, the second and third count which is used for lowering the leg into position demands a certain amount of control for "braking" the movement. Thus, the swift flash of movement upward on one count, contrasted with a more sustained two count descent incorporates two different flows of energy emitted by the body, both of which the beginner is capable of producing and experiencing. Not ony does such movement have visual interest but it is kinetically exciting to the one accomplishing it.

PETITS BATTEMENTS SUR LE COU-DE-PIED

Petits battements sur le cou-de-pied consist of small beating movements which result from the working leg continuously moving in the *cou-de-pied* position *devant* and *derrière*. The movement originates in the hip joint but must be only visible below the knee. The foot may be held in any one of four positions developed by the great pedagogic schools.

1. In the Russian style the foot is wrapped around the ankle bone of the supporting leg.*
2. In the Italian or Cecchetti style the foot is held so that the ball of the foot and all five toes are on the floor. This method helps maintain the precise angle created at the knee joint.
3. The French style calls for the foot to be held fully pointed.
4. The Danish school places much emphasis upon using the flexed foot postion.
5. In the United States all four styles are used and tend to enrich the fabric of American dance training.

Petits battements sur le cou-de-pied are designed to develop the facility for beating the legs in *petit allégro* work so they are always done rapidly. Vaganova states that the working leg should move front and back at an even tempo in beginning work. Only later should the rhythm become accented so that a greater stress is made on the beat front or on the beat back, as the case may be. The initial *port de bras* for the exercise is the arm held in the low or preparatory position.

Petits battements sur le cou-de-pied are not given until the student is well into ballet study. Of necessity the body must have already achieved the ballet stance and the muscles must be able to respond to the demand of holding the body while the working leg rapidly moves in isolation.

BATTEMENT BATTU

Battement battu, also called *battu serré*, is the sole vibratory movement in classical ballet. Its use in the classroom work is universal and its most often seen choreographic use is in *Swan Lake*, Act II.

*It is of historical interest that the wrapped foot position seems to have originated in the Romantic period with Bournonville.

The *battement battu* exercise generally becomes part of the regular barre work once it is introduced to the student. It is done *sur le cou-de-pied* on the *demi-pointe* using the French style of foot placement, i.e., the working foot is fully stretched. At very close range the tip of the dancer's foot beats against the heel of the supporting leg.

Since this exercise is really the fare of the intermediate dancer, the *port de bras* often begins *à la seconde,* moves down to the preparatory position and finishes a musical phrase as it moves up to the high fifth position. It then reverses the exact path of movement. The head and eye focus follows the hand of the moving arm as it moves in each *port de bras* movement.

RELEVÉ

The *relevé* movement in ballet terminology is defined as a raising of the body onto half toe where the weight is born by the *demi-pointe*.

The *relevé* movement is initiated from first, second, fourth or fifth position of the legs. In intermediate work the *relevé* is done from one leg as well as in such movements as *arabesque en relevé* and *retiré en relevé*.

Although the fundamentals of *relevé* are introduced in the very first lessons, it often appears as a special exercise in the progression of class work. It is occasionally introduced during *pliés* as a contrasting movement to *demi-plié* and one that offers the first experience of balancing the body in what seems to the beginner rather precarious positions. *Relevé* is occasionally combined with *battement tendu* and done from fifth position in a variation of one of the *petit battement* exercises. In this instance, the *relevé* functions primarily as a strength

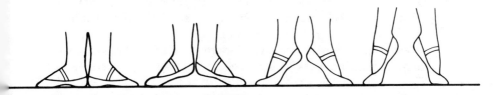

Fig. 4. Relevé
Relevé in first position. The feet move from first position through quarter point, through half point to three-quarter point or *demi-pointe*.

builder for the legs and as an instrument for flexing leg joints as the legs labor under the weight of the body. Most teachers concur that a moderately timed 16 count *relevé* exercise from first and/or second position early in the barre work is valuable for beginners. It is advisable to repeat the exercise after a slight pause.

This *relevé* exercise can be done facing the barre in a posture-perfect first position. The body rises onto the platform-like balls of the feet without allowing the knees or body in general to add movement by giving way. Often the beginning adult is extremely tight in the metatarsal joints of the feet and finds it difficult to rise up high enough. It must be pointed out that it is crucial to achieve the maximum *relevé* so that the entire tops of the feet feel the whole stretch. At the moment of rising, *en relevé*, the knees become taut but not jammed as the front of the thigh muscles contract. This condition of the legs is commonly referred to as "pulled up," meaning the muscles are in use, alert and ready to move. Conversely, the leg muscles are not "locked" or rigidly tense. If excessive tension is present, unnecessary fatigue results. Such tension, if not counteracted, will be responsible for unavoidable strain showing up elsewhere in the body, i..e., chronically clutched fingers and clenched teeth. The high point of the *relevé* is released as the ankle joints gradually flex and the heels lower to the floor. Again, the knees do not give in during the descent from the *relevé* nor does the body placement alter in any way. Particular attention must be paid to the lower part of the back as a tendency to sway is common. The *relevé* should be subsequently combined with *demi-plié* so that in four counts the spatial design of the exercise would read as follows: (1) from first or second position facing the barre, *demi-plié*, (2) straighten the knees, (3) *relevé*, (4) lower from the *relevé*. Because of the tightness in the big toe joint, a helpful variation of the *relevé* is the following eight count exercise. (1) *Demi-plié*, (2) straighten the knees, (3) *relevé*, (4) *demi-plié en relevé*, (5) straighten from the *plié* while still *en relevé*, (6) repeat the *demi-plié en relevé*, (7) straighten from the *plié* while still *en relevé*, (8) lower from the *relevé*. All the while turnout must be maintained and care must be taken during the *plié* and the *relevé* not to sickle the ankle area or allow the back to sway. These exercises can profitably be done in first, second, and even fifth position and by all means should be systematically practiced outside of class work.

CHANNELING ENERGY

Relevé takes on further significance in the beginner's repertory of exercises in that it teaches a simplistic command and control of movement. The burst of energy upward and its controlled modulation downward demands that effort be utilized wisely. The expension of energy must be economic and purposeful if movement is to be artfully expressive of human feeling by means of ballet technique. The concept dealing with the expansion of energy is commonly referred to as "channeling energy." Although human energy is inextricably interwoven with the balletically styled movement design, the duo concepts of energy and design may be considered separately for the sake of study. For example, physical energy can be abundantly produced by a dancer when initiating random movements. But energy is also produced when the demands of a predetermined balletic exercise are met by the dancer. The central point is that the energy be precisely adequate for the predetermined design. Channeling energy, therefore, suggests that only an amount of energy, force or effort, commensurate with the need of a specific movement is required. Any superfluous energy results in excessive movements such as "jarring" caused from too strong a *relevé développé,* "jerking" caused from too much energy in a series of jumping steps, or "bucking" when the lower spine is allowed to enter into the effort of jumping and causes excess movement in the upper spine. Endeavors to compensate for these situations are attempts to stifle the energy or to make constant kinetic and physiological adjustments with regard to the desired objective of performing the movement. All dancers pass through this stage of kinetic trial and error but the constant repetition built into ballet by its pedagogy eventually produces the beautiful flow of channeled energy as the body actualizes the classical design. Ballet technique is multifaceted. In dance the possession of technique bespeaks a combination of control, strength, and attack in various kinds of movements such as jumps, turns, and extensions, as they are architecturally formed within the context of the ballet aesthetic. The appropriate flow of movement when energy is released, is only one element of muscular control contributing to technical correctness. The greater the total technical correctness, the greater the freedom in movement. In a certain sense, technique is freedom, freedom to modulate at will the energy within the flow of movement of a given step. This subtle capacity is the physiological element which contributes to the entity that a great interpretative dance artist is.

HIGH EXTENSIONS OF THE LEG

Grand battement is the generic term for several forms of barre exercises which involve large spatial movements made by "the large opening and closing" of the legs. *Grand battement* is also the specific name of the last basic exercise absolutely necessary to the beginner's barre work. Other exercises such as *grand battement en rond, grand battement en cloche, grand battement en balançoire,* and *grand battement raccourci* are all complex variations of the basic *grand battement* exercise done *en croix.*

Grand Battement

The overall purpose of *grand battement* is to impart to the legs the facility to lift with ease, quickness and lightness. This three-fold ability provided by *grand battement* is absolutely essential to the large jumping steps practiced in intermediate work. The perfection of the *grand battement* directly relates to the successful execution of such steps as *grand jeté, fouetté sauté, grand jeté en tournant,* and *saut de basque.* As Karsavina readily suggested, the effect of the musical form of the march, a moderately slow 4/4 tempo, is most desirable for accompaniment to *grand battement* in the beginners class.

The correct approach to the *grand battement* exercise begins with the usual two chord preparation whereupon the outside arm moves to its second position. (1) The working leg initiates the *grand battement devant* as it brushes forward from its fifth via the action of *battement tendu.* The particular quality of the movement is typified by the thrusting or bursting-like manner with which the working leg lifts forward. The leg accomplishes this thrust in two counts as it arrives at a position parallel to the floor or at a 90° angle to the spinal line. The leg then closes the *grand battement* with a change of quality as it returns to the fifth position. This reference to "quality" means that the leg is actually using the relevant torso muscles in a controlled approach so that the leg resists the pull of gravity during its two count descent to fifth position. That is, this thrusting or bursting movement flow of the ascend-

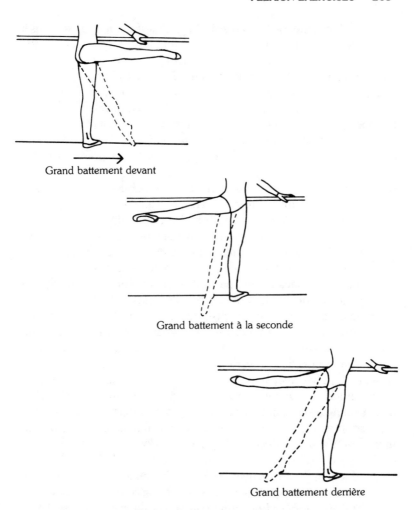

Grand battement devant

Grand battement à la seconde

Grand battement derrière

Fig. 5. Grand Battement

ing leg in *grand battement* is followed by a contrasting muscular restraint which allows the leg to descend to the fifth fully controlled.

(2) The leg proceeds to execute the *grand battement à la seconde* following the same method used as it moved to the front direction. It is important that the working leg, whether in ascent or descent, employs the use of the foot precisely as detailed in the execution of *battement tendu*. *Grand battement* constantly uses the brushing of the sole of

the foot so that the foot achieves its full pointed capacity as soon as it can do so by means of the "brushing" technique. Conversely, as the *grand battement* closes to the fifth position, the pointed foot is maintained until flexion in the ankle is caused by the leg closing into fifth. This brushing back to fifth position forces the pointed foot to give in to the inevitable flex. Resistance here is the key motor response in that the pointed foot is trained to resist the flexion to the last moment. This is most important because only in this way is the foot fully worked and developed. The brushing technique also is a fair assurance that the knee will maintain its tautness throughout the movement. The effort of the "brushing" foot from and into the fifth position acts as a motor reminder for the student to maintain a straight knee.

(3) As the leg initiates the *grand battement derrière*, the construction of the body interferes with the leg attaining the 90° angle or hip-high level. Consequently, there are two alternatives. For the beginner it is desirable to allow the leg to lift only as high as it can correctly do so while the upper back is held perfectly straight. For greater height of the leg, the beginner will learn in succeeding classes that it is permissible to adjust the upper torso slightly but squarely forward (both shoulders maintain a line perpendicular to the barre). As the leg returns to the fifth, however, the follow-up readjustment demands that the initial position be perfectly recovered. Special attention must be made to realign the pelvis over both legs as they establish their fifth position.

The *grand battement* exercise for beginners is generally practiced by executing a series of four consecutive *grands battements en croix*.

As soon as the leg work is fairly well mastered, variations of arm movements are introduced. They are as follows:

1. When the leg executes the *grand battement devant*, the arm moves to fifth position *en haut* on the first count of the measure.
2. The arms moves from fifth to second position on the first beat of the measure when the leg executes the *grand battement à la seconde*.
3. The arm moves to its first position with palm facing downward when the leg does the *grand battement derrière*.
4. The arm moves from the preceeding position to the second position again on the first beat of the measure as the leg executes the *grand battement à la seconde*.

GENERAL NOTIONS AND REMINDERS
FOR GRAND BATTEMENT

The hand which aides in stabilizing the body by gently holding the barre must be kept relaxed. A "gripping" hand indicates a concentration in the hand of excessive body tension. Tension in the hand quickly carries to the throat area where it is made further visible in protruding neck tendons.

The tremendous physical effort needed to perform a reasonable number of *grands battements* obviously causes strain relative to any developmental level of strength the student may possess. The ability to perform the *grand battement* without an excessive show of strain is partially psychological. When the correct technical method of performing the exercise is understood, the proper amount of energy required will soon be known from experience. Hence, the exercise can be paced by the student so that there is an adequate and equal amount of effort for each *grand battement* in the exercise.

Again, because of the great energy output necessary for the *grand battement,* the body alignment and upward spinal stretch need a bit extra physical reinforcement and considerably more psychological reinforcement. The large leg movements must not be reflected in the wavering of the body as a whole. The leg must appear to work in an independent and isolated manner although the real muscular "lifters" are working deep within the pelvis. In various *grand allégro* steps which incorporate the movement of *grand battement* such as *fouetté sauté, grand jeté en tournant* and *saut de basque,* the visual effect of the body's elevation is increased providing the *grand battement* is correct and high. For example, when the body springs into the air from the right leg into a *saut de basque,* the elevation (distance from the tip of the toe to the floor) appears to be greater if the left leg executes a full 90° *grand battement.*

The supporting side of the body is especially vulnerable to the strong movements of the working leg. The hip area on the supporting side will tend to swivel forward if not consciously kept in alignment. The supporting leg must maintain its full turnout from hip to foot. The knee must be kept taut and the foot must not be allowed to roll forward onto the arch or clench its toes within the shoe. Without constant vigilance by even the most competent dancers, the powerful thrust of the working leg in the *grand battement* can easily pull the weight, which is centralized in the hip area, off the supporting leg causing the spine to give into the pull and incorrectly move out of alignment in the front, side or back direction. This fault is particularly unfortunate in the *grand battement* because the whole body is allowed to move away from its axis. As the lifting leg returns to its fifth position, the whole body will likewise respond by returning more or less to its original placement. This slight extra movement is repeated with each *grand battement*. This in turn sets up a visual static. If this subtle but serious error of misplaced alignment and excess movement is not dealt with immediately, it will result in a reinforced, incorrect motor habit.

The hip area on the working side of the body can easily be lifted out of its balletic placement by the working leg as it lifts. Therefore, in beginners class, the leg must not be allowed to achieve a greater height than the 90° angle. Special concentration on hip placement must be constant.

In advanced work the hip does lift out of place when thrust *à la seconde,* but readjustment habits are so engrained, that the dancer automatically lowers the hip back to its proper placement as the leg closes to fifth position. It must be pointed out here that although the hip legitimately performs a very high *grand battement* in advanced work, the whole body does not reflect this irregularity by wavering or giving in to the lifting hip. Indeed, the extremely high *grand battement à la seconde* tips the pelvis upward with the accompanying upward thrust of the leg. At the same time the supporting leg and spinal line above the waist shows no involvement. When it is correctly high the weight is not pulled off the supporting hip. There is a definite "break" visible between the working hip and thigh which indicates the exact point of flexion within the hip joint.

The shoulder on the supporting side tends to lift if the barre is held too tightly or if the leg is actually lifting higher than it has developed strength to do correctly. The free arm when extended in the second position tends to drop the elbow causing an undesirable angular line. Slight rotation inward of the entire arm at the shoulder joint usually counteracts this bad habit.

The upper back and shoulder area on the working side of the body will often have a tendency to drop as the leg reaches its height unless effort to dispel this extra and unnecessary movement is made. A slight more effort in stretching the spine upward as the leg reaches its ascending climax usually counteracts the caving in or dropping of the upper back.

Grand battement involves a constant but subtle and careful shift of weight as the legs open and close from fifth. It is necessary to see that this habit is sustained so that the *grand battement* exercise is a persistent flow of tension-relaxation for the legs. As the weight is continuously shared by the working foot, it is kept relaxed. This is substantiated by the fact that a foot with weight squarely placed on it cannot remain tense.

The *développé*, like the *rond de jambe en l'air*, is not approached until the previously discussed barre exercises have been reasonably mastered. That is to say, the beginner can eventually "master" the *développé* and the *rond de jambe en l'air* according to his beginning capacities while the advanced dancer will "master" the same exercise with greater degree of technical and artistic perfection.

PREPARATORY DÉVELOPPÉ

Développé is a term used to express the movement made by the unfolding of the leg into any of the classical body positions such as *devant, à la seconde arabesque, croisé, effacé,* and *écarté.* The practice at the barre of the *développé* exercise is initiated only when the student is fairly skilled with the basic barre work. However, a simplified or preparatory version of *développé* which emphasizes body position and placement rather than its qualitative essence is usually introduced once the *battement retiré* and *grand battement* are reasonably well mastered. The *développé* as practiced in the traditional sequence of the barre work is done after *battement retiré* but usually before the *grand battement.*

The inclusion of the slow tempoed *développé* with barre work provides a needed contrast to much of the previously faster tempoed *petit battement* exercises. It also serves to introduce new design and movement quality in the barre work thus extending the range of movement possibility while still in the "warming up stages" of the class. The preparatory *développé* is introduced to the beginner not accompanied by its final *adagio* tempo, but one that approximates the tempo used for *grands pliés.* The slowness of the *développé* movement is too difficult for the beginner to sustain without appropriate strength and accumulated understanding of the complexity of the movement. Therefore, the capacity to create very slow *développé* movement is only gradually acquired through great effort and repetition so that a preparatory version is most desirable.

Movement analysis of all *développé* movement will demonstrate that its design is comprised of previously learned elements, the *cou-de-pied* position, the leg extension of *grand battement* and *battement retiré*. After the two chord preparation of the arm, the preparatory version of *développé* commences with a slow 4/4 tempo as follows: (1) On the count of one, the working foot releases from the fifth and snaps to a fully pointed position, moving through the *cou-de-pied* to the retracted and flexed knee position attained in the *battement retiré* exercise. (2) On the second count the leg must then extend to the front direction (devant) without allowing the hip line to lift upward or forward. In the *développé devant* this is more easily achieved if the student remembers to extend the leg from the *retiré* position by leading outward with the heel of the working leg as the knee is held back and slightly downward in relation to the heel. Furthermore, the area between the working thigh and hip joint is at an acute angle. The thigh is lifted against the depressed hip. This greatly aids in maintaining the turnout of the working leg. The leg upon its arrival in this extended position is said to be at "hip-height" or parallel to the floor or at 90°. As the leg extends outward, the thigh must never be allowed to lower from the height it achieved while in the *retiré* position although it may attain a higher position in more advanced work. (3) On count three the straightened leg is lowered in a controlled fashion so that the tip of the foot alights on the floor. (4) On count four the working foot brushes inward to close in the fifth position with the same toe-leading technique employed in closing the *battement tendu*. During these entire four counts the supporting leg maintains its maximum turnout. The hip and shoulder line stay impeccably correct, i.e., perpendicular to the barre. Both the arm on the barre and the extended one stay fixed but relaxed with fingers unclutched. Since the exercise is generally done *en croix*, the repeat of the preparatory form of the *développé à la seconde* and *derrière* directions follow. To secure the turnout of the leg as it extends to the side, the student must concentrate on the outward rotation of the thigh in the hip socket. This feeling of outward rotation must continue throughout the exercise. When the leg executes the *développé* to the back, the initial way of practicing it means the leg will be lower than "hip-height" as the body's construction will not allow the leg to achieve a height parallel to the floor. Eventually the technique of shifting the upper torso slightly forward will allow for a higher extended leg in the back direction. However, because this adjusting movement of the upper torso displaces the way in which the pelvis and leg lines relate during the adjustment, the torso displacement necessary to a higher back extention should not be attempted until the most basic motor habits are securely implanted.

Apart from the movement quality of *développé* (as opposed to the preparatory version of *développé* just discussed), the comparatively slow tempo and the difficulty associated with learning it, the *développé* is one of the most spectacular and memorable challenges presented to the beginner. Because it is one of the barre exercises which is recognizably incorporated into actual dance movement, it excites the student into wanting to practice the *développé* in its final qualitative form which is that of a sinuous, unfolding and sustained movement. However, while this advanced approach to working on the movement quality should be introduced conceptually, it should not be attempted by the student too soon. To avoid the first stage of "bad habit formation" to which the *développé* is open, the preliminary exercise should be practiced for correctness of torso placement and perfection of leg position. Once the prerequisites of placement and position are physically and mentally clear, the all-important aspect of movement quality should be practiced and refined without allowing the prerequisites of correctness to slip away. This suggests then that the four count preparatory *développé* movement be practiced so that each of the four positions softly "hit" the count as follows: count one, *cou-de-pied* and *battement retiré;* on count two, the full extension; on count three, the *point tendu* to the floor; on count four, then closing to the fifth.

The basic *port de bras* for the preparatory *développé* is added once the leg movement is established. Attention must be paid to the preciseness of the arm movements as they pass through the positions since their coordination with the leg movement and positions present a novel motor skill challenge. The *port de bras* begins with the arm in second position. (1) On count one the arm moves to the first position; (2) on count two it moves to second position; (3) on count three and four the arm lowers to the *en bas* position ready to repeat the *port de bras* as the leg works *en croix.*

When the preparatory *développé* is position and placement perfect, the student is ready to work on the essence of *développé* which suggests the quality of a sinuous unfolding of the leg. This gradual unfolding of the leg into the proper turned-out extension requires that the leg moves through the *cou-de-pied,* the *retiré,* the extension, the *pointe tendue* to the fifth while not stopping in any one position. At the same time the movement flow of the arm and leg is regulated by the relationship of the musical count and the body position so that it is a gradual and pleasing development and resolution of a movement pattern on four counts. It is extremely important to remember when the leg passes through the extension that while it does not stop in the position, the full extending process must be given enough time to register visually in the onlooker. This is precisely where the ability to control and sustain movement is crucial.

The next step in studying the *développé* occurs when it is combined with the *relevé.* This can be achieved in two ways. The first manner in which it can be done is entirely from the fifth position *en relevé* or *demi-pointe* position. The *développé* unfolds and closes to the fifth position on half toe without lowering the heels during the entire *en croix* exercise. The second approach which demands greater strength, starts with the fifth position *à terre.* On the first count the supporting foot executes a *relevé* at the same moment the working foot arrives in the *retiré* position. During the second and third count the leg carefully unfolds into the full extension of the leg. The heel of the supporting foot descends on count four while the working leg meets it as it closes to the fifth position. The same foot action required for the *relevé* repeats in this form of *développé* as it continues *en croix.*

PREPARATORY ROND DE JAMBE EN L'AIR

The *rond de jambe en l'air,* like the *développé,* is not approached until all the previously discussed barre exercies have been mastered. That is to say, the beginner can eventually "master" the *rond de jambe en l'air* according to his beginning capacities while the advanced dancer will "master" the same exercise with greater degrees of technical and artistic perfection. The *rond de jambe en l'air* is the name of an exercise in which the working leg describes an oval movement that ranges between the open *à la seconde* to the *retiré* or *raccourci* position. The lower leg describes oval circles either *en dehors* or *en dedans* while the thigh appears to be uninvolved in the movement. When included in the barre work, this exercise is practiced before the *grand battement*. Its introduction to the class is based on the correctness of *battement retiré*, the *grand battement*, the well-pointed foot and excellent placement in general. Only the discretion of the teacher can decide when the student is ready to attempt this complex exercise. Hence, certain preparatory exercises are included here along with theoretical discussion.

The study of *rond de jambe en l'air* recalls to mind one of the first exercises learned by the beginning student, which was the *rond de jambe à terre*. This was introduced as an exercise designed to use and increase the rotation capacity of the hip joint. The student learned to rotate the right working leg in the hip joint clockwise (*en dehors*) and counterclockwise (*en dedans*) as it described half circles on the floor. Similarly, rotation is the essence of the *rond de jambe en l'air*. However, it is a more subtle and complex form in that it deals with the rotation potential of the lower leg which takes place in the knee joint. Its mastery is the technical basis for *rond de jambe en l'air* done with *sauté, relevé* or *piqué*.

The adult beginner should not approach the *rond de jambe en l'air* until the entire body of elementary ballet is fairly well mastered. However, after the basic barre exercises have been learned, a preparatory version of *rond de jambe en l'air* may be introduced. Considering the difficulty of the *rond de jambe en l'air* and the fact that each aspect of it depends on previously learned elements, the clearest preparatory form possible is desirable. It is suggested that the student face the barre holding onto it with both hands. The visual aid of facing the mirror, if possible, while in this position is also extremely helpful.

The torso placement and fifth position, right foot front, should be impeccable. To reinforce the correctness of the working leg movement, it is helpful to remember that the shoulder and pelvis lines must remain absolutely parallel to the line of the barre which the student faces. Because most dancers are not blessed with a perfect (180°) turnout, the working leg will work in a plane of space slightly forward of the 180° ideal while still maintaining a safely and correctly placed supporting foot, knee, pelvis area and shoulder. Since the *rond de jambe en l'air* is usually done to 3/4 meter, it is well to use the same meter for the preparatory version.

1. On the first beat of the measure, the working leg lifts to hip level in second position, its foot having brushed from the fifth position through the *battement tendu* and on up to the climatic high

point of a 90° angle *grand battement*. If the student has been able to accomplish this "burst" of movement on the first count of the measure, the leg will have the opportunity to hold the second position to the end of the first measure. This gives adequate time to anticipate the next movement and to "set" the correct motor habits relating to this particular position.

2. On the first beat of the second measure the working leg retracts from the side extension into the *battement retiré* position. On the remaining two counts of the measure, the leg will simply hold the *retiré* position. Again this slight movement pause helps "set" the correct leg position. It is most important that the thigh has not been allowed to "drop." Rather, the thigh remains at hip-height in the *battlement retiré* just as it was at hip-height in the preceding second position.

3. Again the leg opens out to the second position on the first beat of the third measure. The knee regains its complete stretch and the foot retains its elegantly pointed position. This extension is held through the second and third count.

4. On the first beat of the measure, the leg lowers to a pointed position on the floor as in the open *battement tendu*. On the last two counts, the working leg closes to fifth position back.

The exercise is repeated exactly except that after the repeat the working leg will then close fifth position front.

Special care must be taken to maintain the proper placement of the hip on the working side. The hip must press down against the upward pressure caused by the thigh as the leg lifts to second. The thigh is immobile from the time it arrives in the second position, through the *battement retiré* position and back to the second. Great strength and tension is concentrated in the extended thigh and if this strength and tension is not properly harnessed, it will tend to interfere with the solidity demanded in the pelvis area. On one hand, the student has been instructed not to drop the thigh but to retain it at hip level. This effort, of course, keeps it in this contracted and tense state. By the same token, the thigh in following this command, over-energizes itself in this lifted position and shoves the hip area upward. It is important in the preparatory stages that the student understand the presence of these opposing forces. The hip area and thigh are two different entities meeting at the sharp angle provided by the hip joint where their independent functions in the *rond de jambe en l'air* are initiated.

First, correct hip placement is the most basic and crucial aspect of the *rond de jambe en l'air* exercise since it establishes stability in the power center of the body. For example, if the hip were allowed to lift and lower on any and every extension, there would be no firm foundation for any jumping, turning, or balancing movement which was based on the leg in an extension in second position.

Secondly, the level of the thigh establishes the spatial size of the total movement comprised by *rond de jambe en l'air.* It should be generous in height so that a hip-level extension is an acquired habit from the beginning. Both hip and thigh must maintain their own functions while not interfering with each other.

While this aspect of the preparatory versions of the *rond de jambe en l'air* teaches the general spatial design, there is another aspect which concentrates on the rotation movement and quality thereof. As has been pointed out, it is too difficult for the beginner to initially attempt the *rond de jambe en l'air* with both aspects of spatial design and rotation combined. Consequently, a separate exercise to practice only the rotary movement is desirable as well.

ROTATION EXERCISE

The student may stand facing the barre so as to better observe how his leg will operate in the exercise in its completed form. The right knee lifts waist-high to the side direction as the supporting pelvis and leg maintain their correct stance. The right hand clasps the knee cap of the right leg. The student consciously exerts downward pressure in the right hip as it works against the upward angle of the held thigh. Effort is made to hold the thigh and knee area immobile as the fully pointed foot of the lower leg describes small clockwise (*en dehors*) circles. Eight circles on eight counts of moderate 4/4 time are adequate. The reverse of the movement to form counterclockwise circles (*en dedans*) immediately follows to eight more counts of music, ending with the right leg closing in fifth position front.

Contrary to the flat plane of space in which the leg works as discussed in the preceding preparatory exercise, the rotation exercises involve spatial volume due to the circular movements described by the foot. The skillful combination of the flat plane leg movement with that of the voluminous circular movement is the essence as well as the major challenge presented by *rond de jambe en l'air.*

When each aspect of *rond de jambe en l'air* has been clearly understood and practiced, it is time to combine them into the basic *rond de jambe en l'air* exercise. If the spatial and rotary elements are not individually mastered, their combination can only be the source of incorrect motor habits. The more complex an exercise, the more difficult it is for student and teacher alike to correct the faults. Depending on the rate of advancement, number of weekly classes and age group, the student may be ready for *rond de jambe en l'air* by the end of a term's work. Only the teacher's discretion can decide when to introduce the exercise to a particular situation. Therefore, its basic explanation is included in this chapter.

ROND DE JAMBE EN L'AIR

Standing at the barre and holding it with the left hand, the right arm makes the usual two measure introductory movement to a moderate 3/4 tempo.

1. On the first beat of the measure, the working leg arrives at hip-level in second position. Its foot brushes with a "burst" of movement from the fifth through the *battement tendu* and on up to the climatic high point of a 90° angle *grand battement.*
2. On the first beat of the third measure the working foot continues the circular line by moving from the *battlement retiré* position going behind the imaginary line of the side direction.
3. On the first beat of the third measure the foot continues the circular line by moving from the *battlement retiré* back into the extension *à la seconde* by curing slightly forward of the imaginary line of the side direction.
4. On the first beat of the fourth measure the leg closes to the fifth position back in the same manner with which a *grand battement* would close. This completes one *rond de jambe en l'air en dehors.* The movement is then done *en dedans.*

Upon mastery of this exercise, the student progresses to a more sophisticated form of the *rond de jambe en l'air* where the the challenge is to execute it in a rhythmically more interesting manner. Here the complete circular movement is accomplished on one measure of music. The musical accent (first beat of 3/4 measure) during the rotation comes when the leg is at its extension point.

1. On the two introductory measures when the arm moves to second, the leg also prepares by brushing into the second position.
2. By the first measure the leg has completed the first *rond de jambe en l'air.*
3. It continues to complete two more rotary movements on the second and third measure.
4. On the fourth measure the extended leg closes fifth position back.

The entire four measures are repeated with the same process in the reverse direction.

In more advanced work the *rond de jambe en l'air* is done *en relevé.* Double and triple *ronds de jambe en l'air* are also part of the advanced technique. The "double" and "triple" indicates that either two or three rotary movements are executed to one measure of music. Because of the considerable speed involved, the circular design tends to be smaller although no less controlled and perfect in shape.

CAMBRÉ AND OTHER STRETCHING MOVEMENTS

The blanket term "stretching" is often used to refer to exercises which elongate any part of the body. Therefore, stretching is another one of the ways of moving incorporated into ballet technique. However, in ballet terminology there has existed for generations the term *cambré* which specifically refers to the stretching of the spine sideways and backwards. When the spine bends forward, there is a pronounced stretch along the back of the legs which particularly involves the outer hamstrings. Done from fifth position the exercise takes on the addition of a *port de bras* movement. The body has many balletically formed positions in which it stretches forward, from fifth position, from fourth position *pointe tendue,* or fourth position with *plié* on the front or back leg (*allongé*). While the legs are stretched in many ways, the arms are also moving so that the term *port de bras,* while literally meaning arm movement, also refers to the stretching in the upper body. Consequently, there are three terms: stretching, *cambré* and *port de bras* which are used interchangeably to mean movements which elongate and elasticize the body. Only the terms *cambré* and stretching will be used to describe the movements within the context of the following exercises.

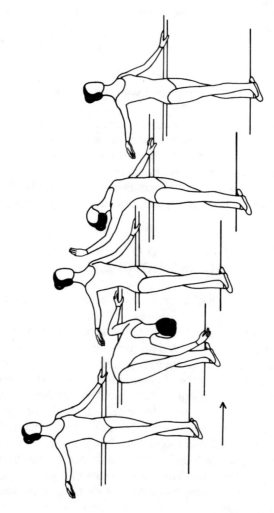

Fig. 6. A stretching and *cambré* exercise commonly referred to as *port de bras*.

276

Cambré and other stretching movements as specific exercises are systematically part of the ballet class although it is not harmful to periodically omit them from class since they are also done in varied and partial ways at the barre during *pliés* and *rond de jambe à terre*. *Cambré* and other stretching exercises are most safely and profitably done at the end of the barre and immediately before the center work.

Cambré, or "arched" as the term translates, primarily refers to exercises whereby the spine is arched backward or sideways from the waist up through the neck and head. *Cambré* also refers to the manipulation of the spinal column into oppositional rotation whereby the upper spine twists sideways away from the positioning of the pelvis. The movement quality of the *cambré* exercise is always fluid, elongating, and lyrical. Accompanying the *cambré* exercise are various other movements which involve the stretching of the hip area and the legs, namely the *gluteus maximus* and the *quadriceps femoris*. *Cambré* and other stretching movements ought never precede the barre since they demand muscular elasticity not yet functioning in the adult beginner (or for that matter, most dancers in any level of development) until the warming and conditioning function of the barre has occurred.

While there are many variations, a typical combination of *cambré* with other stretching movement is described as follows:

1. The student faces the barre and stands approximately ten inches from it. Taking care that the hip and shoulder lines are precisely parallel to the barre, the right leg is turned-out at the hip and placed on the barre, anchored there by the heel. The body is directly supported over the correctly turned-out and well pulled-up left leg. The right hand holds the barre at a position directly in front of the torso. The left arm arcs upward and over passing through second and fifth positions as the spine arches over the tautly extended leg placed on the barre. The objective is to cause the spine to arch sideways as much as possible without lifting the shoulder girdle, without altering the position of the pelvis and without allowing the knees and legs to release their tautness and turnout. Hence, the *cambré* and stretching movements increase the flexibility and elasticity of both spine and legs. The body resumes its verticality with the same emphasis on controlled lyricism and performs the same sideway *cambré* to

the left without changing the hip or shoulder position. The left hand replaces the right on the barre, the right arm aids in stretching the torso sideways to the left.

2. The *cambré* and stretch is next done with the leg in front of the body and this occurs by allowing the torso and supporting leg to move from facing the barre to directly facing the leg. In other words, the right leg rotates its turnout on the barre as the torso and supporting leg move as a unit slightly clockwise away from the barre. The left hand now holds the barre as the right arm moves from second to fifth. The spine follows the arm's vertical pull, upward and over the right leg. Ideally, the line from the base of the spine through the arm is parallel to the leg on the barre at the moment of greatest stretch. The spine and right arm then lift back as a unit to their vertical position and begin to move in to the *cambré* or backward arching of the spine from the waist upward. It is particularly important to begin the *cambré* by lifting upward in the general area of the sternum, pressing the shoulders downward as the arching becomes deeper. The spine returns to the vertical position by reversing the process. The upper spine arrives back in position and then the shoulders, neck, and head follow.

For beginning adults, this basic *cambré* and stretch exercise is liberally interlaced with careful *demi-pliés* and *relevés*. Often at the end of the *cambré* bending sideways and the stretch and *cambré* forward and back, the student is asked to lift the leg up from the barre and hold it several seconds before continuing or repeating the exercise with the other leg.

Later the same exercise is done with the leg anchored to the barre while in the back direction. This is more technically complex, however, and only more intermediate students derive benefit from practice of it. When the time comes for the student to attempt the *cambré* while in *arabesque,* the chief difficulty will be maintaining the torso squareness over the supporting leg. The greatest benefits in this exercise are the inner thigh stretch for *arabesque penceé,* and the *cambré* of the spine backward over the leg in *arabesque,* and at the same time the considerable stretch of the front of the suupporting hip as the spine goes into its backward *cambré.* The habit of holding this pronounced *cambré* and the *arabesque* as it is lifted from the barre, supplies extraordinary strength to the back and is one habit consistently worked on by Soviet dancers, vastly contributing to their exceptional spinal control and line.

CHAPTER 14
Introduction to the Center Work

EXERCISES PERFORMED IN PLACE

Following the completion of the barre work, the student commences the second phase of the lesson, the center work, which is executed in a confined space. Away from the support of the barre, the dancer is called upon to demonstrate variations of the barre exercises termed *petit* and *grand adage* movements. Center work, which assumes the reliability of a solid balance, emphasizes different aspects of movement which are studied singularly at first but are soon incorporated into the exercises making up the *petit* and *grand adage*. For example, the fastidious practice of the carriage of the arms, called the *port de bras*, is practiced while the legs maintain first or fifth position. The precise angling of the shoulder girdle, termed *épaulement*, is repeated over and over again before *port de bras* is added. Eventually the body will respond without conscious effort to the task of shaping itself in the exacting lines of classical form. Accompanying the subtle movement of the *port de bras* and *épaulement* is the practice of the refined usage of the head in relation to the total body design.

PORT DE BRAS

Port de bras is a term which refers to the carriage of the arms through various classical positions resulting in arm movement of a quality uniquely associated with balletic grandeur and elegance. In classical ballet, the arms have a number of movement designs which have evolved over the years to complement the movement of a given step. The *port de bras*, therefore, is as precise and exact in execution as are the legs in ballet steps. Diligent practice of *port de bras* emphasizes the preciseness of the movement which can be further augmented by a slow tempo.

While the Russian, French and Italian schools all agree on the five classical positions of the feet, they vary somewhat on the names and number of arm positions. The Russian school (Vaganova method) presents three arm positions plus a preparatory position; the French school (*Danse d'école*) establishes five arm positions plus the preparatory position; and the Italian school (Cecchetti method) teaches ten positions. Due to overlap of the total number of positions, all three schools combined make up ten different positions.

In view of the eclecticism of American ballet, the student dancer should be familiarized with the arm positions of all three schools. All arm positions are usually incorporated in the American classes whether or not they are specifically labeled with their original nomenclature.

Important as the correctness of the arm positions is, it is only part of *port de bras*. The actual movement of the arms as they "dance"

Arm Positions—Italian School

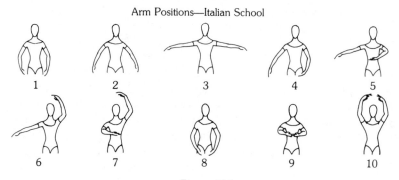

Figure 14.1

1 First position; 2 Demi-seconde position; 3 Second position; 4 Third position;
5 Fourth position en avant; 6 Fourth postion en haut; 7 Crossed fourth position;
8 Fifth position en bas; 9 Fifth position en avant; 10 Fifth position en haut

Arm Positions—Russian School

1 Preparatory position; 2 First position; 3 Second position; 4 Third position

*For arm positions in the style of the French School see Chapter 12, Figure 1.

through the positions is the more significant and difficult aspect of *port de bras*. As Vaganova readily points out, as soon as a complicated phrase of dance is presented to the student, the *port de bras* must be actually demonstrated rather than described. So subtle is the coordination of the arms with the rest of the body as it forms the classical steps, that only perfect demonstration of the *port de bras* on the part of the teacher and sensitive duplication on the part of the student can produce those results which are in keeping with the classical tradition.

The beginning student often feels great frustration in the attempt to coordinate the *port de bras* with the rest of the body as movement is formed into a dance phrase or *enchaînement*. This difficulty is overcome by practicing the entire *port de bras* of the dance phrase to the music used for the particular *enchaînement*. The *port de bras*, when practiced in isolation, helps to set the muscle patterns of the arms. At the same time, the inactive legs are kept from interfering with the muscular learning and its associated rhythms in the upper body. When the arms have sufficiently "motor-memorized" their respective pattern and rhythm of movement, the difficulty of arm-leg coordination is considerably lessened when the complete *enchaînement* is attempted.

The arms themselves are held in a specific manner as they form the various classical positions. The entire arm, from shoulder joint to fingertips forms a slightly rounded curve as opposed to a bent or straight arm line. The positioning of the parts of the arm in the classical *port de bras* are detailed as follows:

1. Beginning with the shoulder girdle, this entire area is held down and remains virtually immobile although the arm movement actually eminates from this vitalized area.

2. The elbow is ever so slightly flexed although it is never seen to form an angle. In addition, the elbow is lifted to ensure the softly curved line of the whole arm. This subtle lift in the elbow also counteracts the tendency to drop the elbow which detracts from the beautiful arm curvature desirable in the balletic technique. The muscles in the upper arm come into play as they lift the elbow itself. There is a slight suggestion of inward rotation in the upper arm. Visually, the upper arm and elbow are seen to be part of the curve of the whole arm.

3. The wrist actively holds the hand so that it too continues the curved line of the arm through the wrist to the fingertips.

4. The hand itself, while simply held, belies a touch of stylized elegance. All five fingers are relaxed but slightly separated. The fingers themselves are always extended seeking to lengthen the curve of the entire arm. The thumb and middle finger, however, form their own slight curve similar to a "C" shape. The middle finger is closest to the thumb and is thus slightly lower than the second, fourth, and fifth fingers.

Tension caused by the entire body during barre and center work is generally manifested in the hands. For the beginner, especially, it is a constant occurrence that the fingers stiffen and assume unorthodox designs. Shaking the hand will temporarily relax it so that it can resume its proper classical formation.

As was previously stated, the verbal description of the actual movement during the *port de bras* is nigh impossible with regard to rendering its kinetic subtleties. The precise demonstration of arm movement by the teacher and its careful duplication by the student is the surest manner of attaining a good foundation in *port de bras*. Let it suffice to say only that *economy of movement* as the arms move between positions is the rule of thumb. For example, the arms must maintain their specified soft curvature. In *port de bras,* the arm moves as a unit from the shoulder joint. The arms must pass through the positions forming the particular *port de bras* design with exactitude. Too much flexion of the wrist, elbow, or finger joints adds movement and destroys the classical purity of *port de bras* by rendering it, in the words of Vaganova, "excessively sweet."

There is no limit to the invention of patterns for *port de bras* exercises which consist of the ten different positions combined from the three great schools of technique. The single regulation upon which they all agree, however, is that the arms must pass through the "gateway" each time a new movement is formed. The "gateway" is the curved position of the arms in front of the body which corresponds to the French and Russian first position and the Italian fifth position *en avant.* The reason behind this rule directly related to the development of ballet in the procenium arch theatre. Because the dancer is choreographically presented most often facing the audience, the *port de bras* must include the forward movement of the arms through the "gateway" lest the body appear flat and two dimensional.

A related but more complex part of *port de bras* work is the specific movement of the shoulders, termed *épaulement*. In general, it has been traditionally and correctly adhered to that *épaulement* in its full use is not part of beginners work. The work is touched upon in this text merely as a theoretical presentation. Hopefully, it will serve to familiarize the student with the concept of *épaulement* prior to intermediate level work.

ÉPAULEMENT

Épaulement is the subtle placing of the shoulder girdle in relation to two basic body positions termed *croisé* and *effacé*. In beginning ballet, emphasis is necessarily laid on the square placement of the body in the *de face* position. Eventually, however, the body is carefully taught to break out of the two dimensional *de face* position which emphasizes the flatness of vertical and horizontal lines. *Épaulement* introduces the fullness of dimension in body positions. The body in *épaulement* departs from the *de face* flatness, and blooms into the perspective depth of the *croisé* and *effacé* positions. In the *battement tendu croisé* position the body is placed in the room diagonally rather than *de face*. The extended leg will cross the imaginary center line to the front or back. The *épaulement* in this case calls for the shoulder opposite the extending leg to slightly pull forward while the head inclines toward the opposite shoulder. In the *croisé* position, the arm design has several variations while the extending leg may be *pointe tendue*, *dégagé*, or *en attitude*.

In the *battement tendu effacé* position, the body is placed diagonally in the room rather than in the *de face* position. The extending leg opens to the front or back away from the imaginary center line of the body. The *épaulement* in the *effacé* calls for the shoulder opposite the extending leg to pull forward while the head inclines toward this shoulder. In the *effacé* position the arm designs consist of several variations while the extended leg may be *pointe tendue*, *dégagé* or *en attitude*. *Effacé* suggests that the diagonal positioning of the body in the room shades the side of the body farthest from the front of the room. This chiaroscuro effect particularly points up the beauty of depth dimension produced by the body *en effacé*.

All ballet from the barre exercises through the gamut of center dancing involves *port de bras* and *épaulement* along with participation of the head. Whereas the head positions are learned at the barre, the movement of the head through these positions is carefully practiced in the *port de bras* exercises. The Italian method lists five major positions of the head. They are as follows:

1. Erect
2. Inclined to either side
3. Turned to either side
4. Lowered
5. Raised

The Russian school which avoids *de face* dancing as soon as the necessary squared-off placement is learned at the barre, states as a general rule that when *épaulement* is used the head is always turned in the direction of the forward shoulder. Accordingly, the level of the head depends on the aesthetic of the particular step in question.

The French school according to Prudhoummen and Guillot uses the same five head positions found in the Italian School. It is furthermore pointed out that in actual dance movements, the five positions are rarely seen as precisely as they are taught. Rather, the head is always viewed at intermediate points between positions due to the combination of several positions.

ARMS AND HEAD AS INSTRUMENTS
OF EXPRESSION

Special and separate attention to the arms and head as well as the legs develop the body for classical ballet. The proper development of the *port de bras* and the head along with *épaulement* lends finesse to the expressive instrument that a dancer's body is meant to be. Good *port de bras*, head and *épaulement* movement renders a fullness to ballet dancing making it a truly harmonious and organic expression of man.

In terms of expression the head and especially the face are of the greatest significance and usually the most underdeveloped and neglected aspect of the ballet dancer. When an audience views a dancer, they do so as people observing and reacting to another human being. In daily life, people are conditioned to react to the upper body and especially the face of the person with whom they interact. This conditioned reaction naturally enough transfers to the dance theatre situation. Consequently, not only does the head in ballet dancing give the beautiful finishing touches to the body line but it serves a greater artistic purpose. The dancer's individuality of facial expression provides interest to the audience but it also establishes itself as a powerful instrument of expression for the dancer. The eyes, the cheek muscles, and the mouth are all effective in communicating the nuances of poetic intent as delineated by the choreographic direction. This ability to render nuances of artistic expression is indicative of the interpretive artist. Two contrasting examples of balletic facial expression are cited here as instances of the expressive potential of the face. Thousands have witnessed and succumbed to the tender, child-like face of Fonteyn's "Juliet," portrayed by this sublime artist even as she approached her fifth decade. By contrast, Suzanne Farrell in the neo-classic *Agon*, has often achieved a "coldness of expression" or rather, inexpression, that creates an aesthetic element in itself.

It is imperative the student understand that the face is an instrument of expression. Whether it expresses something specific or no particular thing—it is still there and unavoidably expresses something. That "something" had better be in keeping with the choreographic intent. The face of the dancer, as well as the man on the street, is capable of expressing body/mind conditions. And only at this juncture is the ballet dancer a creative artist as opposed to a technician!

PETIT ADAGE:
SPATIAL TRANSITION FROM BARRE TO CENTER

Immediately following the barre work, comes the initial center exercise called the *petit adage* or small slow movements. It consists of elements of the barre work such as various kinds of *petits battements, demi-pliés, développés, relevés* and *balancés* in various classical positions done with *port de bras*. These movements are usually done to a moderate tempo of 3/8 or 4/4 music. The purpose of *petit adage* is to aid the body in its transition from working at the barre to working unsupported by the barre in the center. The *petit adage* also aids the dancer in making the transition from working in a stationary place at the barre to working in center where the exercise may call for moving short distances as when the body transfers weight from one leg to the other. This center exercise ought never, on any level of the student's development, be spectacular in effort, complexity, or speed. The transition from barre to center, aside from indicating a spatial change for the dancer in the classroom, represents also a physiological and psychological change.

Physiologically the dancer must learn to rely on his acquired stability in the turned-out position. The dancer often sustains his balance at the barre through slight and not so slight muscular adjustment in the arm which rests on the barre. In the center, the dancer, unaided by the barre, must have the necessary stability to perfectly control his vertical position in space. The physiological adjustment to this new use of space in the classroom becomes, in time, a less conscious effort. However, it must be remembered that the premature addition of speed or design complexity in a *petit adage* exercise inhibits the student's satisfactory accomplishment of the exercise. In most instances an exercise too fast or too complex will nullify motor learning in that particular exercise.

The *petit adage* exercise also provides the student with help in making the psychological transition from the barre to the center. As a student continues the study of ballet, the barre work becomes concomitantly more correct as the student becomes confident in this newly acquired skill. Because of the countless hours already spent working at the barre, his security there is considerable due to the physical and in turn psychological support the barre offers him. While the student knows from the teacher's instruction that he must never physically use the barre for more than minimal balance and support, he nevertheless has a certain psychological and natural dependence on the barre. The beginning student has not had to brave the challenge of balletically moving through space since the barre work is essentially stationary. Consequently, consciously and unconsciously there persists a certain amount of both physical and mental insecurity. If the student's confidence in his correct execution of barre exercises is allowed to make a natural and pleasurable transition to a similar center exercise without interference of physical or mental insecurity, the objective of the first center exercise is met. Therefore, much of the content of the *petit adage* should reflect the objectives of carrying over from the barre work all positive values, such as confidence relative to technical ability, body stability which is rooted in the student's mental attitude as well as technical ability and pleasure in moving unsupported through limited space.

Another positive value that accrues to the performance of the *petit adage* exercise is the student's satisfaction derived from viewing his mirror image. This is usually the first instance in the class when the student legitimately views himself. The better he looks, the greater his self-image and self-esteem. Without this positive feedback that the student receives from an acceptable mirror image, his confidence and hence his progress is interfered with.

The technical success of the *petit adage* exercise depends, of course, on the adequacy of the student's barre work. If all the barre exercises are performed in keeping with the correct balletic technique, the center exercises should occur with considerable success and minimal interference from lack of balance. The control and aligned "pull up" in the torso, the correct amount of muscular contraction occurring in the buttocks which maintains the turnout in the moving legs and a minimal amount of tension in the throat area are only a few of the major body states underlying the exercise as it is executed. These "body states", i.e., aligned "pull-up", correct contraction deep within the hip area, and minimal tension, act as those major visible clues which, if present, indicate that the center exercise is being done properly. If these major "body states" are not fully present, such technical necessities as properly flexed and pointed feet, straight knees, well-shaped arm and head positions and movements will not properly develop or if already present, will disintegrate. The total impression the dancer should reflect in the *petit adage* is one of confidence in dancing an exercise which is geared to his level of accomplishment.

A sample *petit adage* suitable for an adult ballet student during the first six months of study would be as follows:

Using 16 measures of 3/8 time (or 2/4 time) begin in fifth position, right foot front. *Battement tendu plié, en croix* on 8 measures. Coordinate the front, side, back and side direction of the legs with the *port de bras* flowing from first position to second position, back to first position palms facing downwards and back through the gateway to second position. Using the next 4 measures, the right leg does *développé* to the front (*en avant*) and closes to fifth position. The left leg does a low and quicker *développé à la seconde* on the 5th measure; it presses into second position *demi-plié* on the 6th measure. *Relevé passé (battement retiré)* on the left leg on the 7th measure and close the right leg in 5th position back on the 8th measure.

In the second 8 measures of the exercise the arms maintain their second position through the 5th measure. On the 6th they move to the low preparatory position and without stopping they move to the high 5th position on the 7th measure as the legs form the *passé*. On the 8th measure they open softly to the second position. The exercise should be done immediately with the left leg. This exercise as all center exercises is most profitable when reversed.

There can be countless variations and degrees of difficulty in this exercise relative to the level of the class. However, its developmental purposes, as previously discussed, should remain the primary objective for both teacher and student rather than particular spatial design.

GRAND ADAGE
APLOMB AND ELEGANCE OF MOVEMENT

Adagio is an Italian word meaning at leisure or at ease. The French term, *grand adage,* has been derived from it to describe the series of slowly executed movements done in center work which are designed to develop balletic line, strength, grace, and balance. While the Italian term *grand adagio* is more commonly spoken in the United States, this chapter will employ the French rendering for the sake of linguistic consistency. The *grand adage* is especially demanding because the body is for the most part of the exercise supported on only one leg at a time. The *grand adage* section of the class involves the use of such movements as *pliés, relevés,* and *développés* in all directions and positions (i.e., *effacé, écarté, croisé* and *à la seconde; posés en promenade; arabesques* and *attitudes; grands ronds de jambe;* elaborate *port de bras;* and often slowly performed *terra à terre* steps. Vaganova points out that the *grand adage* ought to contain the most difficult *adage* movements relative to the level of the class.

From the point of view of movement analysis, the *grand adage* comprises the classical body positions and the flow of movement linking the classical body positions into movement phrases. Position and the flow of movement are inextricably intertwined and are the physiological substance of classical ballet.

The general term, *adage,* also refers to those movements in classical *pas de deux* where the woman is supported and aided by her male partner. However, the early years of ballet training are concerned only with the first usage of the term *adage* wherein the highly controlled movement skills necessary to the dancer are practiced at a very slow tempo. It is in this sense of the term that the following explanations relate.

GENERAL PURPOSES OF THE GRAND
ADAGE IN THE CLASSROOM

In ballet, the *grand adage* section of the class has essentially two purposes. First, slow movement is a fundamental part of the dynamics of dancing. The dancer must be able to dance slowly as well as at various faster *tempi*. Just as there is an almost infinite range of *tempi* for the musician to conquer, so must the technical facility of a dancer deal with a wide range of *tempi*.

Secondly, the *grand adage* provides the development of both tremendous muscular control and accuracy which are essential to performing slow movements with seemingly effortless fluidity. The ability to sustain the flow of very slow movement takes much practice over long periods of time. Only then are such movements achieved with both physical solidity and majestic elegance. But before fluidity and ease are an actual part of a dancer's technique, an appropriate ground work must be laid. Hence, there are more immediate objectives to be attained in *grand adage* practice for the beginning adult ballet student.

SOME SPECIFIC OBJECTIVES OF
GRAND ADAGE FOR THE BEGINNER

Through elementary *grand adage* practice, it is possible for the student to become intelligently attuned to the presence of his kinesthetic sense so that it can be of use to him in his development of classical line of positions and poses, in the development of efficient and pleasurable flow of movement between positions, in the development of balance of body weights in the classical positions, and with the transitory flow of movement from one position to the next.

Kinesthetic awareness provides a kind of "muscle memory" for the dancer whereby the body not only perceives the feeling of a certain classical position or balletic movement, but can later reproduce the position or movement by recalling the feeling associated with it. Kinesthetic awareness results from perceptions created by means of receptors located in the muscles, tendons, and joints. Hawkins summarizes this awareness as "sensory information resulting from muscle tension and spatial and temporal orientation (which) are integrated into a synthesized sensation that results in a kinesthetic perception."

In classroom work, the beginning student's three kinesthetically related objectives in practicing *grand adage* are the following:
1. The development and maintenance of the correct balletic *positions* in relation to efficient transfer of weight stemming from kinesthetic awareness.
2. The development of the *flow* of movement from one position to the next position by way of one's kinesthetic awareness.

3. The development of the ability to *balance* in the various positions and poses resulting from weight transfer as based upon kinesthetic awareness.

1. *Positions.* Without the classical line of the balletic position, a dancer has no ballet technique as such. Therefore, the development of kinesthetic awareness in relation to the balletic concepts of body positions and lines is essential. As related to kinesthetic perception, the slow tempo of *grand adage* practice provides the opportunity to painstakingly form correct body positions so that the actual positions reflect the student's conceptual understanding of what is correct.

Since the development of kinesthetic awareness is significantly related to motor learning, it is imperative for the ballet student to seek out the motor sensations of all the balletic positions and movements which comprise the classical steps. Each position, from the five classical positions of the arms and legs to an *attitude en relevé,* and each movement from a *demi-plié* to a *pirouette* has its unique kinesthetic sensations. Retention of these numerous, unique kinesthetic sensations ensures economy in learning, considerably reduces the need for repetition, more efficiently channels energy and provides greater muscular control with less effort. Lack or loss of the kinesthetic sensations associated with the classical positions and flow of movement in ballet are usually directly related to the lack of or loss of ballet technique in dancers during any given level of motor achievement.

The commonly used term "correct position" refers, of course, to adequate turnout, straight knees, properly aligned torso, correct arm and head positions, etc. that are unique to each balletic position or pose. Although all the elements of correct positions are introduced and constantly practiced in the barre exercises, they are often more difficult to attain with an *adage tempo* and in center work. Moreover, all correct positions and poses used in *adage* (i.e., extension in *à la seconde,* first *arabesque,* front *attitude,* etc.) are founded on the proper placement and alignment of the torso in its relations to the head, arms and legs. The "feeling" that the position is correct is due to the development of kinesthetic awareness that it *is* correct. The daily presence and the keen eye of the teacher hopefully reinforces the correctness or rectifies incorrectness of the student's kinesthetic awareness of his line. For example, kinesthetic awareness of the alignment of the torso begins the moment the student learns to "stand" in the five classical positions. At this time the torso, placed over legs which are rotated outward at the hip joint, begins to become sensitized to the feeling of that particular position.

2. *Flow.* In an *adage* exercise the dancer must slowly move from one correctly aligned classical position to the next, often transferring weight as the body moves through time and space. The traditionally correct position itself and the actual movement of "getting there" are the chief elements which contribute to the *adage* phase. For instance a common *adage* movement is *piqué arabesque* on the right, *demi-plié* on the right, *piqué attitude* directly back onto the extended left leg. The *piqué* action is the flow of movement which culminates in the position of *arabesque*. This position melts into the flow of movement of the *demi-plié* and on into the next *piqué* which is capped by the following position of the *attitude*. Thus, the *piqué arabesque, demi-plié, piqué attitude* can also be read as flow of movement, position, flow of movement, and position.

While the importance of the classical position in the ballet dancer's technique cannot be underestimated, the flow of movement or the "getting there" is perhaps of greater significance. The *quality* of the flow of movement determines the quality of the dancer. It is the "quality" that is so indefinable and illusive because it results from a wonderful mixture of motor skill and individual personality. It is the very visible difference so often observed when a technically capable student dances next to an artist. Both technician and artist perform the same steps with the same perfection of classical line, but the qualitative approach of the student and that of the artist markedly differs in the eye of even the most unschooled observer. Conversely, one occasionally sees the reverse of this in the naturally gifted student and the overly technical oriented professional.

In ballet, there is usually only one correct procedure and sensation for each individual motion for "getting there" or flowing from one classical position to the next. For this reason, the correct muscle memory, based on correct "feelings" provided by the kinesthetic perception must be meticulously attended to by the student as the flow of the movement is experienced.

While the kinetic concept of correct classical position is rooted and perfected in the barre work, the quality of the flow of movement is often a natural attribute in a student dancer. Where it is not a natural gift in the dancer, improvement of the quality of flow can be acquired with time, identification of it in others through careful movement analysis, self-observation and attentive practice thereon.

3. *Balance.* The third objective for the beginner in practicing *grand adage* movement is the exploration of the physiological and psychological problem of balance in relation to ballet technique and finding the adequate kinesthetic awareness to control balance once awareness is developed. Since ballet is based mostly on vertical balance of the torso, balance can be defined as body parts or weights equally arranged around the body's vertical axis or, in Metheny's terms, around the "line of gravity." The pelvis area is where the greatest body weight is concentrated and is the body's center of gravity which is constantly pulled toward the earth's center. This center of gravity in the body is supported by the legs through which runs Metheny's imaginary line of gravity. If all the parts of the body are properly balanced and counterbalanced in relation to the center line of gravity, balance will occur. In other words, the line of gravity stems from the top of the spine through the shoulder, hip, legs, and feet and onto the earth's center. As long as weights are equalized or counterbalanced around the line of gravity, the dancer can balance in any conceivable position. Hawkins further describes balance as a principle of weight compensation noting that ". . .whenever a body part moves from the line of gravity, an opposing part moves in the opposite direction so that balance is stabilized."

BALANCE AND WEIGHT SHIFTS
IN GRAND ADAGE

Acquiring the necessary skill in balancing is based on a steady progression of balancing feats provided by the gradually increasing demands on the body at barre and in the center exercises. The necessary skill to balance in *grand adage* is rooted, or course, in the barre work since it is there that the dancer first learns to balance his body anew in the unnatural and difficult balletic turnout. First he learns the necessary kinetic adjustments of balancing on flat feet and *demi-pointe* in first position. Secondly, from this relatively stable balletic position he learns the extremely subtle sensations of weight shifting in *battement tendu* when the body is constantly shifted from one to both legs. Thirdly, such simple steps as *glissade* and *pas de bourrée* teach the student to shift weight between turned-out legs as the body moves through space. When the dancer arrives at the *adage* section of class in the center and away from the barre, his body must tackle the larger problem of balancing in the three aforementioned ways in addition to the body's increase in the spatial range of arm and leg movements. *Grand adage* works by virtue of its slowness allowing the student to carefully learn to adjust his body weight to maintain adequate balance and alignment for the large intricate positions which the body forms. Precisely because of the slow tempo, the body can achieve accuracy of balance as well as position. For this reason it is most important for the student to work daily in *adage tempo* and with the traditional movements associated with formal *adage* i.e., développé, port de bras, classical positions involving *promenade, grand rond de jambe, arabesque, attitude,* etc. Although speed, as an element of *allégro* work, is a necessary part of learning to dance, it tends to unsettle both the accuracy of the aesthetic line of positions and the sureness of balance. *Grand adage* exercises serve to counteract these negative but normal tendencies since the slow *adage tempo* gives ample time for kinetic learning and kinetic correction of minor faults introduced in fast movement. At the same time, *adage* exercises provide an indispensable part of one's physical capabilities as a dancer.

PRACTICE

The practice of the *grand adage* section of class is most often included as the second or third exercise after barre work. For the sake of change in routine, however, it is occasionally done later in the center work. The duration of the *grand adage* depends on the option of the teacher and level of the student. It is generally 16 measures of 4/4 time (64 counts) or 16 measures of 3/4 time (48 counts). This provides musical time to perform the movement design of the *adage* on first one side of the body (using 8 measures) and then to convert it to the other side of the body (8 measures). As in all exercises at the barre, it is necessary to convert the *adage* to the opposite side of the body so as to bi-laterally develop and maintain the same muscular form, strength, and facility.

For more complex and memory taxing *grand adages*, the entire 16 measures is occasionally devoted to a single movement pattern to one side for one group of students. As the first group rests before converting the pattern to the other side of the body, a second group performs the *grand adage* on the first side. This second way of presenting the *grand adage* in the classroom is admittedly more for the intermediate and advanced pupils since it demands greater strength. Yet, the longer form finds justification for periodic use on the elementary level. The lengthy *grand adage's* beneficial qualities can be directed at the beginner on a scaled down basis.

The longer *adage* can make better use of music in that generally a substantial number of musical measures more fully develop a musical theme. Since the *grand adage* music is almost always fragmented from whole and often masterly compositions, a 16 measure passage is more ample time to convey musical wholeness, to say nothing of choreographic unity of the exercise. Albeit that the *grand adage* is merely an exercise to be done with the greatest technical perfection possible, the very character of *adage*, as traditionally evolved by the great teachers, demands that appropriate musical and aesthetic sensitivity be imparted to the student along with the stately movement designs. It is at such junctures in ballet instruction that the truly inspired teachers will bestow the best of their experience, ignite the student's potential artistry, and richly fulfill their own time-honored role of "passing on" the art of the ballet.

The long *adage* provides the possibility of combining a greater variety of movements such as *pliés, développés, posés,* and *balancés en attitude* and *arabesque, promenades, pirouettes, grand rond de jambe, port de bras,* etc. into the *adage* movement pattern. Not only does the number and variety of movements train the dancer's memory for dealing with longer and longer passages of movement, but the long *adage* also demands the controlled flow of movement between various and often uncommonly juxtaposed movements. This particular aspect of the long *grand adage* unquestionably provides the student with the opportunity for dealing with a choreographic challenge rather than a mere technical exercise. This leads us to a third quality provided by the long *grand adage*.

The notion of a "choreographic challenge" for the adult beginner may appear premature in view of the lengthy process that is associated with ballet study, but the long *grand adage* can be designed on a level concomitant with the beginning adults' knowledge and physical ability. The choreographic challenge is simply one more way of providing the adult beginner with a rich dance experience. Such challenges can only serve to spur the student on since "a choreographic approach" to an *adage* illuminates for them and puts within their technical reach a part of the ballet art which initially tantalized them and thus encouraged them to study in the first place. Without the personal experience that a student feels dancing is for one, all the correctly performed barre work and center exercises in the world will not sustain the emotional interest. Physical interest alone in ballet is merely the practice of exquisite calisthenics. Granted the great teacher and the inspired student are jointly involved in a realm stemming from exquisite calisthenics, but there is also one actually much higher and by nature perhaps more elusive. It is the realm of art, that realm which uniquely sustains the student's emotional interest. S. K. Langer has spoken of art as the formulation of feeling and that art expresses our "life of feeling." Thus it is for the dance student to personally find, form, and realize through the kinetic media of the body the emotional substrata that is this "life of feeling." The formulation of one's "life of feeling" is by way of kinetic expression, the creation and crystallization of one's very own "life of feeling." This experience, which is essentially aesthetic, is one's link to the creative aspect of the balletic art form. For the beginning adult, it is a deeply personal, complete and memorable experience. It is a happy, if only momentary, encounter with Martha Graham's famous uttering ". . . we are all born with genius, but most of us only keep it for ten minutes."

This "aesthetic" experience, intellectually examined by countless philosophers as a unique flowering of civilization, is precisely what seems to be grasped and dearly held by the young adult beginning dance classes. This precious and gossamer adventure envisions for the student, values and realities not necessarily part of the times in which we live. From this highly personal and aesthetic occurrence the adult ballet student derives some of the greatest enrichments in life. Surely this alone is justification for the presence of ballet study within the realms of higher education.

EXAMPLES OF GRAND ADAGE PRACTICE

One unique and memorable example of *adage* movement was used by the late Anatole Oboukhoff. Immediately following the barre, this amazing teacher would evolve an *adage* beginning with innumerable *battements tendus* in the various body directions to a march *tempo*. Without a pause the exercise would change *tempo* and a long series of *développés* in classical positions, *grands pliés,* and various *posés* revolving *en promenade* would follow. Then without pause the pianist would shift to an *allégro tempo* and the movement consisting of a variety of jumps and *pirouettes* would follow. Such is not the fare of beginning dancers or even the daily needs of the professional dancer. This general description of an Oboukhoff *grand adage* is included as a note of historical interest as well as an extreme example of the variation of approach to a *grand adage*.

Increased endurance is one of the benefits of this "ballet-length" type of *adage* for the developing student. Such a *grand adage* presents musical problems in that few ballet records have these *tempo* changes. If a pianist is available for class, such *tempo* changes are possible and provide an interesting challenge for the artistic side of the students' development.

Suggested Grands Adages With Emphasis on the Needs of the Adult Beginner

Even the very first *grands adages* performed by the beginning ballet student include the essential elements which comprise *adage* on all levels of difficulty. The following grand adage suggests the initial approach. It uses the elements of *plié, port de bras, développé,* and small *terre à terre* movements done *en face.* It specifically does not include the use of the *épaulement en croisé,* and *en effacé* positions, or turning movements of any kind.

This sample of *grand adage* has 8 measures of slow 4/4 time (*adagio*) before the movement is converted to the opposite side of the body. The body stands *de face.* The legs are in the first position during the introductory musical chords. All arm positions are labeled according to the Russian style unless otherwise stated.

Measure 1: Slow moving *port de bras* from the low preparatory position through first, third and second positions.

Measure 2: *Grand plié* on four counts. The *plié* can be comprised of two counts going down into the *plié* and two in coming up from it or three counts going down and one coming up. Both arms move as in the *grand plié* at the barre.

Measure 3: *Développé à la seconde.* With the right leg come to *passé* on count one, extend on count two and three and return to first on count four. Arms are held *à la second* and do not move on this measure.

Measure 4: Left arm repeats the *port de bras* of measure 1 as the right arm remains in the second position.

Measure 5: *Demi-plié, temps lié* forward on the right foot (arms prepare from the first to second), *rond de jambe à terre en dedans* the left, closing it in fifth position.

Measure 6: Bring the right leg to passé on three counts and close it front on the fourth count. Arms stay in second.

Measure 7: *Développé* the left leg *à la seconde* exactly as in measure 3. Arms also are as in measure 3.

Measure 8: Arms reverse the spatial pattern of the arms in measure 1 moving from second, through third, to first and preparatory. Legs *demi-plié* in first position on last two counts of the measure.

A more complex adult (intermediate level) version of this same *adage* is altered as follows:

Measure 1: is executed the same but in *relevé* and from fifth position.

Measure 2: Same as in the first version but *plié* is done from fifth position.

Measure 3: Same as in the first version with emphasis on correctness but with higher extension of the working leg.

Measure 4: Arm movement and *terre à terre* movement of measures 4 and 5 in the first version are combined.

Measures 5: Perform the *passé* as in first version allowing the body to revolve *en promenade*, turning counterclockwise on the left leg *(dedans)*. Arms are held in third position during the *promenade*.

Measure 6: Open this position to *attitude croisé derrière* as the arms do a full *port de bras* from third to the French third position. *Attitude en relevé* on the fourth count.

Measure 7: From the *attitude en relevé*, *demi-plié* on the supporting left leg, and extend the attitude leg back so as to form a fourth position *allongé à terre*. The arms open to second and execute a full *port de bras* as the upper torso stretches forward.

Measure 8: Slowly pull the body upright on the left leg. The right leg then executes a *rond de jambe à terre en dedans* and closes in the fifth position with a *demi-plié* and the body facing front. Arms perform the inverted *port de bras* of the 8th measure in the first version.

This second *adage* is really a movement design for an intermediate adult student whose strength and capacity for correctness are rooted in many months of previous work. It is included to demonstrate that like the elementary version, it is built on the same balletic movements which have been complicated by the addition of extension, *relevé*, positions revolving *en promenade,* and a greater use of spatial range. Similarly, the second version becomes a more advanced *grand adage* by substituting *grands ronds de jambe* for the two *ronds de jambe à terre,* by performing all *développés en relevé,* and by changing the *promenade en retiré* and *attitude* into a *pirouette en dedans* followed by a *pirouette en dedans en attitude.* In addition, to further develop this *grande adage* pattern into advanced level work, the musical tempo would become *adagissimo* to allow time for the movements of greater complexity and to provide greater challenges for the dancer.

AMBULATORY MOVEMENTS: WALKING AND RUNNING MOVEMENTS

The normal human movements of walking and running form a considerable part of choreographic material. In 19th century ballets both movements are performed in a highly stylized manner. In 20th century ballets, walking and running are often done in a more natural style. This change in the 20th century is due to the creation of more realistic ballets by such choreographers as Tudor, de Mille, Robbins, and Ashton. It is also due, in part, to the influence of the modern dance on ballet choreography. While modern dance invents its own highly stylized approaches to walking and running, it generally begins the instruction of technique in close accord with the more natural manner of walking and running.

GRANDE PROMENADE OF THE COURT

Grande promenade or grand walking is the term used in ballet to describe the walk. *Pas marché* or marching step is also traditional terminology applied to the walking movement. The *grande promenade* is a walk in very high style. It was first employed by name in ballet performances of the aristocrats of the French court who participated in the palace ballets. For the nobility, such stylized walking was fairly normal. In the main, the activities of these hothouse aristocrats were part of the royal design that encouraged the cultivation of an artificial and protocol-laden atmosphere which extended to the palace gates. Their lives were devoted to taking part in the pleasure-giving activities devised by court artisans for the delectation of the royal family. During the height of the reign of Louis XIV no part of court life was left ungilded according to the aesthetic concepts of the times. Thus, it was natural that courtiers consciously and unconsciously reflected in their body movement the exquisite external surroundings. The aesthetic environment within the palace walls consisted of the creations of the finest sculptors, painters, architects, musicians, poets, and dancing masters of the time. Personally the courtiers were attended and complemented by the prolific originality of the best talents of the time in clothing design and in hair dressing. One consequence of this abundance of contrived ingenuity at court resulted in a special way of moving the body. For example, imagine a courtier approaching the enormous gilded and glittering rooms of Versailles, attired in pounds of brocade, jewels, and hairpieces. Even the glorious staircases and doorways had not a foot of space unadorned as an intricate part of its design. One's feet touched floors of the most exquisite inlay of varyingly colored woods or marbles. Only those of highest birth might sit in the presence of the king and then only on backless chairs (the taboret). All gestures and greetings were in accordance with the prescribed court etiquette. The intimate language of the body thus developed its own expression in keeping with and reinforced by these artificial surroundings. Thus, the walking style of the nobles as they displayed themselves at court became refined in the extreme so that the ideal manner of their walk displayed an inordinate aplomb, a luxurious arrogance and a studied elegance.

From court histories, paintings, drawings, and the journals of various dancing masters, we know that the court ballets reflected the art and architecture of the time in their classical themes and stage designs. Likewise, baroque choreography incorporated the stylized comportment of the body. The ballets at the court of Louis XIV were the ultimate in the enthusiastic display of all that the late 17th century aesthetic could devise. The participating dancers in the ballets were generally burdened with glorious but weighty apparel. It was not uncommon for costumes to weigh fifty pounds so the dancers could not do much more than walk in intricate choreographic floor patterns. The walk or *grand promenade* thus played a large part in the early ballets and was presumably performed "to the hilt."

GRANDE PROMENADE

The remnants from this courtly walk are to be seen today in such ballets as *Sleeping Beauty, Nutcracker,* and *Swan Lake* (Acts I and III).

The *grande promenade* is also present in most *pas de deux* variations which are seen as choreographic pieces in themselves. While the costumes used in today's ballets, the bejeweled tutu and tunic, are abbreviated versions of courtly attire, they are still the height of elegance while they are designed to call attention to the beauty of the moving body as it *promenades.*

The ballet beginner is capable of attempting the *grand promenade* in the very first class. The normal mechanics of walking are already present so the particular style of the walk becomes the challenge. The student begins in the upstage left corner with the right foot pointed behind the supporting left leg. The arms are held in a well-rounded *demi-seconde,* the head is held high and the eyes must focus on a point across the room and slightly higher than eye level. The right leg takes the first step forward, becoming fully stretched as in *battement tendu* before it assumes the weight of the body. As the right leg takes the weight, it does so first through the ball of the foot and then through the heel. The left leg proceeds to take the next step by first stretching the leg forward and then assuming the transfer of body weight through the ball of the foot and then through the heel. The overall effect of the walk should be smooth and gliding and should appear comfortable in its air of elegance.

RUNNING

The ballet has special styles of running called *pas couru* and *pas de bourrée couru.* The manner in which these steps are often seen today dates from the ballets of the Romantic age when the dance evolved a choreographic style in keeping with the aesthetic tastes of the day. The appearance of *pas couru* and *pas de bourrée couru* as part of the dancer's vocabulary of movement resulted from the very essence of the Romantic dance. As was discussed in Chapter 6, the social reaction to the devastation wrought by the memory of the Napoleonic Wars resulted in a penchant for ballets depicting other-worldly subject matter so that gossamer fairies (*La Sylphide,* 1832), Wilis (*Giselle,* 1841), and mermaids (*Ondine,* 1842) were indeed box office dynamite. The most obvious choreographic device for portraying such filmily clad creatures as fairies and wilis' is a movement which is so swift and smooth that the dancer appears to be floating or flying through space. The ballet masters thus evolved a highly stylized technique of running which was practiced in the classroom for direct transfer into the ballets then currently being created.

PAS COURU

The *pas couru* consists of consecutive and small and rapid running steps. The step can be performed on the half toe and is performed foward, backward, or in a circle. It is performed as a movement in itself as Ulanova faultlessly demonstrated in the Soviet film version of *Romeo and Juliet*. *Pas couru* is also used as a step to gain momentum as when the running leads into *grand jeté*.

The dancer performs the pas couru on the balls of the feet and with the knees slightly bent. *Pas couru* is the swiftest locomotor movement in ballet's repertoire of steps. It is, unfortunately, often neglected in the American training.

PAS COURU FORWARD

The action of the run is concentrated in the hip joints while the pelvis is held firm. Due to the required quickness of the step, the degree of *plié* in the knees is held constant. The dancer attempts to make as many very fast small steps as possible while completely controlling the torso and *port de bras* movement. The dancer also attempts to cover as much space as possible in the allotted time. The *pas couru* is practiced by both men and women.

PAS DE BOURRÉE COURU SIDEWAYS

The beginner also learns another, more stylized form of running, the *pas de bourrée couru*. The step consists of small and quick consecutive steps in fifth position on the full or *demi-pointe*. Like the *pas couru*, its effect is one of smoothness, although it does not travel so swiftly.

The invention of the *pointe* shoe and the development of its use by Marie Taglioni gave special significance to the *pas de bourrée couru*. The technique of performing this step on full *pointe* and its growing popularity with choreographers in the early 19th century evolved its pedagogy and stimulated its choreographic usage to an extent that this movement is still essential today.

The beginner practices the *pas de bourrée couru* sideways, traveling across the room. It is begun and executed in a tightly held fifth position on *demi-pointe*. Space is never seen between the moving legs. Although the knees and ankles should appear absolutely taut during the movement, there is a slight flexing action in both so that movement can occur and so that it appears smooth and effortless.

The slight flexing action in the knees and ankles introduces a technical problem which can only be solved by the individual. It is important to remember that in the *pas de bourrée couru* the beautiful final effect is what counts. Because there are various shapes of legs (protruding knee caps, straight legs, hyper-extended legs), there are also appropriate and subtle mechanical manipulations in the knees and ankles for finding the best technical approach for each student. This is best left to the discretion of the teacher. Let it suffice to say that for some legs an equal amount of "give" in both knees works best. For others, the front leg should remain taut while the back ankle "gives." Alexandra Danilova, famous for her *pas de bourrée couru* as well as her exquisitely formed ballet legs, allowed the front knee to noticeably flex as she performed the step.

After the student has learned the *pas de bourrée couru* sideways on *demi-pointe*, it is then practiced moving forward, backward, and in a circle. While the beginning student must learn and practice the *pas de bourrée couru on demi-pointe*, it must be pointed out that the step is most beautifully executed on full point. For all practical purposes, *pas de bourrée couru* is a purely feminine step and is only done by male dancers in certain character roles.

The *pas de bourrée couru* is further discussed in Chapter 15 since its swift movement over the floor's surface places it in the category of *terre à terre* steps.

PAS DE VALSE

Pas de valse is a three-step running movement performed in 3/4 time. The first step is taken in a *demi-plié* while the second and third are on straight legs and *demi-pointes*. Each step must be taken forward accompanied by transfer of the body weight so that the dancer advances in space. The step is also done *en tournant*.

The *pas de valse* is akin to the mechanics of the "triplet" movement in modern dance. The difference in execution between the two approaches is that the *pas de valse* emphasizes the luscious and lilting quality of the waltz.

CHAPTER 15

Petit Allégro

Introduction

At the very core of ballet dancing reside the many steps which come under the heading *petit allégro*. Brisk, light movement, smoothly executed, characterizes *petit allégro* combinations. There are two kinds of *petit allégro* steps. Steps which are performed close to the floor, often emphasizing a horizontal line of movement, are termed *terre à terre* steps. *Petit allégro* steps which are based on jumping movement always emphasize the vertical line of movement.

Several classifications of *terre à terre* steps provide a meaningful structure for the study thereof. Included in the *terre à terre* category are those small steps which are performed with both feet close to the floor; small steps based on the *relevé* movement; small steps based on *piqué* movement; and small steps based on turns. Numerous *petit allégro* steps are rooted in jumping movement and will be discussed in Chapter 16. All *petit allégro* discussed in this chapter are generally considered suitable for the beginning levels of classical ballet.

The Petit Allégro: Terre à Terre Steps

Within the category of *terre à terre* movement are found some of the oldest steps in the ballet vocabulary. Occasionally bearing the same names today, they were movements derived by 16th and 17th century dancing masters from peasant and court dance forms. Refined versions of these steps by early choreographers were absorbed by the *danse d' école,* preserved and handed down to the present. These steps, as the generic name indicates, are performed with the feet close to the ground. Instead of springing from one position to another, the feet, in *terre à terre* steps, glide along the floor in complete or at least close contact. On occasion, a *terre à terre* step may employ some jumping movement. The degree of jump in a *terre à terre* step generally reflects the individual style or choreographic intent so that there is no set rule on the matter today. However, the general character of *terre à terre* steps suggests that they are designed to contrast with the movement of jumping steps and that their chief interest lies precisely in their non-jumping quality of movement. The spatial designs which these ancient movements create and their ability to connect other steps in the formation of movement phrases contribute to the richness of the classical technique.

FIVE BASIC STEPS

One of the first and most useful *terre à terre* steps taught in the training of a dancer is the *glissade*. It is primarily a connecting movement in that its unique shape causes it to be used as a preparatory movement for both small and large jumps. The *glissade* is also used to provide design contrasts when combined with vertical shaped steps such as *piqué* and *relevé*. Because of the ubiquitous presence of *glissade* in *allégro* combinations, the six variations of the *glissade* movement are described in their ascending order of difficulty. Each variation is distinct from the other depending on its starting and finishing positions and its direction of movement.

GLISSADE

Glissade devant is a sideways moving *glissade* initiated from the fifth position with the front foot. The movement ends with the same foot remaining front in the fifth position.

1. From a fifth position *demi-plié,* right foot front, slide or "glide" the right foot to the side direction as in *battement tendu à la seconde.*
2. The supporting left leg pushes against the floor so that the weight energetically transfers onto the right leg. This movement causes the right leg to return to a *demi-plié* position slightly after the left leg extends itself as in *battement tendu à la seconde* position.
3. Almost immediately the left foot glides along the floor and closes behind in a fifth position *demi-plié* as the right foot remains front.

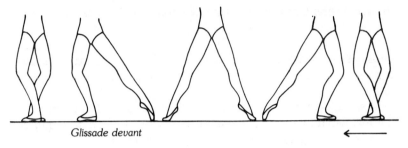

Glissade devant

Fig. 1. Glissade

For purposes of precise movement analysis, the *glissade* has just been described in several phases. However, the step begins and ends in the *demi-plié* so that the movement itself is actually in two segments. That is, the *glissade* movement is a combination of gliding the right foot and pushing with the left foot in the first segment. The second segment of the *glissade* movement is a landing on the right foot and a gliding or folding into the fifth position by the left leg. Whether the *glissade* travels sideways, forwards or backwards, it moves approximately the distance from the fifth position to where the leg extends in the *battement tendu*. At the moment the weight is about to be transferred from one leg to the other, both legs and feet are fully stretched at an elevation level which barely clears the floor. The basic and reoccurring fault in all the *glissades* is the inability to keep the heels firmly on the floor in the fifth position before and after the gliding movement. This is a problem especially common in the adult student. It is primarily due to lack of elasticity in the achilles tendon. The fault can normally be overcome with effort and careful practice. For a correctly executed *glissade*, the heels must acquire the ability to hold contact with the floor in the fifth position. In addition, any long term association with ballet study requires this particular technical ability to be mastered in the interest of injury prevention.

Glissade derrière is a *glissade* which travels sideways and is initiated by the foot in back. It follows the same procedure listed in the movement analysis of *glissade devant*, being the same movement except that *glissade derrière* is initiated and resolved with the same foot remaining fifth position back.

Glissade en avant is a forward moving *glissade* which begins and ends with the same foot in fifth position in front. It is accomplished by the same careful procedure as the two previous *glissades* except that the leg glides in a *battement tendu* to the front direction.

Glissade en arrière is a backward traveling step which begins and ends with the same foot in fifth position back. It is achieved by gliding the back leg from its fifth position into a *battement tendu* to the back direction.

Glissade changé is a *glissade* which alternates the fifth position of the feet when they close. There are two kinds, *glissade dessus* (*glissade* over) and *glissade dessous* (*glissade* under).

Glissade dessus travels sideways. The movement is initiated by the back foot which closes by changing to the front when it arrives in fifth position. Otherwise, it is performed the same as previously described *glissades.*

Glissade dessous also travels sideways. The step is initiated by the front foot which closes by changing to the back.

The basic *port de bras* associated with the *glissade* is a movement simple in design but often difficult to gracefully coordinate with the leg movement. The arms begin in the preparatory position thus complementing the *demi-plié*. As the legs glide into the *glissade* movement, the arms softly open to *demi-seconde*. They smoothly lower and return to the preparatory position as the step concludes. The head and eye focus are *de face* and only begin specific but optional *épaulement* movements at the early intermediate levels of study.

Simply as a matter of reference, the following stylistic and rhythmic variation of the *glissade* is included here. This is the *glissade précipitée*, also termed *glissade piquée* and *glissade pressée*. This *glissade* is done very quickly. It travels horizontally very little and occasionally one sees it done with a certain amount of vertical effort. It is particularly effective when used to precede a pose as in *glissade précipitée, piqué arabesque*. Done in the traditional manner, such a combination will take approximately the same time (two counts) as one of the six basic *glissades*.

PAS DE BOURRÉE

Pas de bourrée is the characteristic movement of a French 17th century folk dance called the *bourrée*. The *bourrée* itself probably originated in the Auvergne, a province in central France. The provincial *pas de bourrée* was adapted and refined by the early dancing masters for use in court dances. The step was further refined and stylized as 19th century ballet developed on a professional scale so that it comes down to us in various intricate forms.

Pas de bourrée almost always involves three steps or transfers of weight as the feet perform a simple weaving movement. As a *terre à terre* movement, the three steps comprising *pas de bourrée* are taken firmly and close to the floor. It is interesting to note the human mind at work in the development of ballet terminology. The etymological root of *pas de bourrée*, especially in the first sense mentioned above, provides such a case in mind. The conceptualization prior to verbalization of an essentially kinetic entity provides interesting speculation as well as fascinating research objectives for dance historians. The term, *bourrée* means "stuffed"; hence, it is possible that the *pas de bourrée* derives its name because the foot work in the step appears to have the quality of stuffing the feet into the floor. Etymologists have also suggested that *pas de bourrée* may mean "step of the peasant" since the term *bourrée* could derive from *bourrienne*, a French synonym for peasant or country person.

Not only is the *pas de bourrée* a charming movement in its own right having a wide range of styles and interpretations, but it also serves as an auxiliary movement. Auxiliary movements are those which can be used to give impetus to other steps while they also can link various steps or movement phrases. For example, they are used to form compound steps such as *grand renversé pas de bourrée en tournant*. Lastly, in classical ballet, *pas de bourrée* is often employed to travel short distances between steps instead of simply walking from one spot to the next.

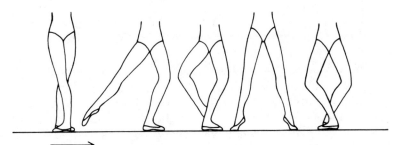

Pas de bourrée dessous

Fig. 2. Pas de Bourrée

The *pas de bourrée* with its three transfers of weight (stepping movements) is done in a precise pattern according to the dictates of any one of its many variations. Two basic kinds of *pas de bourrée* are listed by Vaganova. They include *pas de bourrée* steps which are executed with a change of feet. The two most common *pas de bourrée* with a change of the fifth position are *pas de bourrée dessous* and *dessus*.

Pas de bourrée dessous (*pas de bourrée* under) starts in the fifth with the right foot back. *Demi-plié* as the right foot initiates a preparatory movement opening in *battement tendu dégagé à la seconde*.

1. From the second position, the right leg moves in a *coupé* action *sur le cou-de-pied* in back of the supporting foot and the weight is immediately placed on the *demi-pointe* of the right foot.
2. The body moves sideways onto the left leg forming second position *demi-pointe*.
3. The left leg descends from the *demi-pointe en fondu* with a sinking-like action as the right leg draws inward closing in *demi-plié*, fifth position front.

Pas de bourrée dessus (*pas de bourrée* over) starts in fifth with the right foot front. *Demi-plié* as the right foot initiates a preparatory movement opening in *battement tendu dégagé à la seconde*.

1. From the second, the right leg moves in a *coupé* action *sur le cou-de-pied* in front of the supporting foot and the weight is immediately placed on the *demi-pointe* of the right foot.
2. The body moves sideways onto the left leg forming second position *demi-pointe*.
3. The left leg descends from the *demi-pointe en fondu* as the right leg draws inward closing in *demi-plié*, fifth position back.

The two forms of *pas de bourrée* which do not involve a change of feet are as follows:

Pas de bourrée devant (*pas de bourrée* in front) starts in fifth with the right foot front. *Demi-plié* as the right foot initiates a preparatory movement opening in *tendu battement dégagé à la seconde*.

1. From the second, the right leg moves in a *coupé* action *sur le cou-de-pied* in front of the supporting foot and the weight is immediately placed on the *demi-pointe* of the right foot.

2. The body moves sideways onto the left leg forming second position *demi-pointe*.
3. The left leg descends from the *demi-pointe en fondu* as the right leg draws inward closing in *demi-plié*, fifth position front.

Pas de bourrée derrière (*pas de bourrée* in back) starts in fifth with the right foot back. *Demi-plié* as the right foot initiates a preparatory movement opening in *tendu dégagé à la seconde*.

1. From the second, the right leg moves in a *coupé* action *sur le cou-de-pied* in back of the supporting foot and the weight is immediately placed on the *demi-pointe* of the right foot.
2. The body moves sideways on to the left leg forming second position *demi-pointe*.
3. The left leg descends from the *demi-pointe en fondu* as the right leg draws inward closing in *demi-plié*, fifth position back.

The following are some additional remarks in reference to the execution of various forms of *pas de bourrée*. As in all ballet steps, the various forms of *pas de bourrée* are also done conversely, i.e., beginning with the left leg. In addition, all four kinds can begin with the front or back foot. The distinctive element in each *pas de bourrée* is the front or back placement of the foot *sur le cou-de-pied* and its relationship to the front or back placement in the closing fifth position. As described above, the *pas de bourrée* begins with a *dégagé* action. The step can also be done by substituting the *dégagé* action with a *coupé* only from the fifth to the *coupe-de-pied*. The latter style (i.e., without the *dégagé*) is most commonly performed when the *pas de bourrée* is used as an auxiliary step. For example, the preparatory *dégagé* is superfluous in a movement phrase such as *grand renversé en dedans, pas de bourrée en tournant, pas de bourrée dessus, pirouette* from fourth.

Pas de Bourrée Piqué

The *pas de bourrée* previously described is historically the earlier style of execution. The movements within this *pas de bourrée* represent the soft and unemphasized steps of the French school as it influenced Russian ballet in the 18th century. Vaganova relates that it was the energetic Italian influence of the 19th century that changed the character of the *pas de bourrée* as it had been taught in the Imperial Ballet School.

The Italian approach brought a sharper movement quality to the legs in the *pas de bourrée* so that with each transfer of weight the free leg "snapped" to the *cou-de-pied* or *retiré* position. Today we inherit both styles of *pas de bourrée*, the softer French version and the more vital Italian interpretation which now has its special terminology, the *pas de bourrée piqué*. It is particularly effective when done *en pointe*.

Pas de Bourrée en Tournant

Once the student arrives at a more intermediate level, the *pas de bourrée en tournant* is introduced. This is the basic *pas de bourrée* step which can be manipulated to turn inward *(en dedans)* or outward *(en dehors)*. The leg initiating the first step of any of the four basic *pas de bourrée* steps so indicates the inward or outward turning direction which the *pas de bourrée* will take.

Pas de Bourrée Couru

The *pas de bourrée couru* is often called simply *bourrée*. This corruption of the terminology seems to have evolved on the basis of convenience. The shortened term *bourrée* also clearly distinguishes the movement with its traveling characteristic from the *pas de bourrée* based on three stepping movements. The *pas de bourrée couru* or *bourrée* is executed in fifth position, and less commonly in a parallel first position where the legs do not turn out and is on full or *demi-pointe*. It is comprised of an indefinite number of successive small, quick steps in any direction.

In the execution of *pas de bourrée couru,* the legs are uncompromisingly held together so that the right leg continuously hides the left leg from view. A tiny step is taken sideways by the right foot and immediately the left foot closes tightly into the fifth position. This stepping process precisely repeats itself for the duration of the amount of time allotted to the *bourrée*. Care must be taken to give the illusion that the *bourrée* is one smooth gliding movement instead of a series of tiny steps. A simple and slow *port de bras* usually accompanies classroom practice.

The mastery of this *pas de bourrée* (especially on full *pointe*) usually requires more practice than many steps so far introduced in this book. Its apparent simple structure is deceiving. While the individual elements of the *bourrée* step require no great feats of balance, the overall visual effect of gliding and smoothness is quite another matter. Futhermore, since the evolution of the point shoe, the *bourrée* has been a substantial part of the 19th and 20th century ballet vocabu- lary. Consequently, it must be daily practiced with particular attention to the preciseness of the fifth position.

Tombé Pas de Bourrée Dessous

One of the most kinetic and often used of movements involving the *pas de bourrée* by preceding the step with a *pas tombé* or falling step. The *pas tombé* is a preparatory movement which involves the body falling forward, sideways or backwards onto one leg in a *demi-plié*. The weight is transferred onto the leg which initiates the falling movement while the free leg launches into the succeeding and more substantial step. The *pas de bourrée dessous* is regular except that instead of closing in fifth position it ends in fourth position.

Tombé pas de bourrée is one of the special movement phrases in beginning ballet where the student can first experience and control the satisfying, yet difficult challenge which ballet technique presents. Up to now the student has constantly had to learn to hold, to control, to contract, to restrain, in the interest of correct execution. This step's freer flow of movement is a pleasurable change in the use of direction of energy. *Tombé pas de bourrée* is often favored by many teachers who use it toward the end of class as part of larger movement combi- nation. It allows the student to genuinely experience what moving "feels" like. It also serves to launch the body into even larger moving steps such as a *grand jeté*.

BALANCÉ

Balancé is a soft flowing *terre à terre* movement done in a triplet beat, usually 3/4 meter. The first version of the *balancé* the students learn is executing the rocking movements from side to side. The step is de- scribed as follows:

1. The right foot starts *sur le cou-de-pied* back. Step sideways with the right leg fully stretching into *pointe tendue* before it takes the weight and sinks into *demi-plié*.

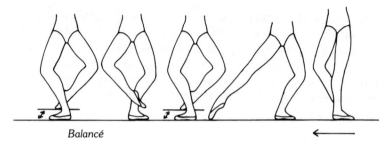

Balancé

Fig. 3. Balancé

2. The left foot steps some twenty inches behind the right foot into *demi-plié.*

3. The weight transfers back onto the right leg as it falls slightly forward into *demi-plié.* The step repeats immediately to the alternate side, beginning with the left leg. Careful visual analysis of *balancé* will reveal that the most ideal movement quality results when the legs maintain *demi-plié* throughout the three beats of the step. Only the moment before the first transference of weight does the leg initiating the step fully stretch as it is about to step sideways. This initial step establishes the spatial size of the step and it should be large. *Balancé,* because the muscles maintain a minimum amount of tension, should feel as muscularly fluent as it looks.

The simplest form of *port de bras* for the *balancé* begins in the preparatory position. As the first step is taken sideways the right arm moves to second position as the left moves to first position. This position is held through the remaining two steps. As the step is repeated alternately, the right arm moves to the first and the left arm to second position on the first step to the left. The head turns slightly to the right and then returns to center, coordinating its design with the arms and legs. Care should be taken to keep the head line, not allowing it to tilt upward. At first the step should be practiced with the head and torso completely *de face.* Shoulder and hip lines must stay parallel with the mirror or Wall 1. (Russian floor plan)

The preceeding is a very mechanical movement analysis of *balancé.* Only after the precise positions are understood and effortlessly achieved, should the student give in to "dancing" the step. When advanced dancers perform *balancé* they give in to the swaying movement of the step and pass slightly beyond the textbook positions of arms and legs. However, because of the comparatively high amount of muscular relaxation involved in *balancé,* the classical look can become shoddy or altogether lost unless the dancer's acquired sense of the academic line underscores the execution of the step. Consequently, strict attention to line is particularly important in the initial practice of all steps. As has been suggested, the *balancé* has a rocking quality. While the rocking movements are very clearly part of the work of the legs, the upper body moves smoothly and without visually transmitting the slight jarring from the transferal of weight.

Balancé can be reversed simply by taking the second transference of weight in front rather than in back of the supporting leg.

Each version of *balancé* is often used to travel sideways. In this intermediate level use of the *balancé,* the first of a series of *balancé* is regular while the second, fourth, sixth, etc., is done turning as well as traveling in the same direction as the first *balancé.*

In summary, while *balancé* is a desirable step in beginning ballet because of its simplicity in form and demand, its use also provides relief from the excessive tension of *allégro* steps. Its swaying movement provides the student with the kinetic experience of dancing. As the student advances, *balancé* is often employed as a preparatory movement for launching into large movement designs based on the *développé relevé.*

PAS DE BASQUE

Pas de basque derives its name from an area of Northern Spain known as the Basque country. *Pas de basque,* like *pas de bourrée,* is a clear cut example of a ballet step taken from folk dancing and adapted for court use. Nineteenth century ballet masters later refined and classified the step, elevating it to a new level of precision. While the term *pas de basque* refers to a specific locale, the basic movement design itself is found in other national dances. Traces of *pas de basque*-like movements are found in folk dance forms of Europe, the Balkans and the near East and attest to the step's pleasurable kinetic sensations. In the United States, *grand pas de basque* has been adapted from the ballet usage and is commonly taught in the jazz class as a "hitch kick." The Rockettes have developed this novel usage of *pas de basque* to a high degree of perfection at New York's Radio City Music Hall.

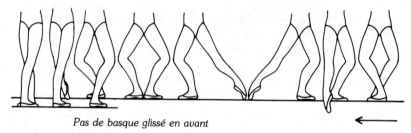

Pas de basque glissé en avant

Fig. 4. Pas de Basque

Pas de basque is essentially a sideways moving step executed in three counts. Like many *allégro* steps it can be done moving forward *(en avant)* or backward *(en arrière)* and from all directions of the body, i.e., *croisé, effacé, de face,* etc. *Pas de basque* is done in three basic ways as a result of its evolution within ballet technique. It is performed as a *terre à terre* movement *(pas de basque glissé, en arrière* and *en avant),* as a *sauté* movement *(pas de basque en avant* and *en arrière),* and as a very large movement calling for considerable elevation *(grand pas de basque),* performed *en avant* only.

The ballet student will begin by learning the *pas de basque glissé* since this *terre à terre* form is the easiest to master.

Pas de basque glissé en avant is a *pas de basque* gliding forward. It begins in fifth position, right foot front and is as follows:

1. On the first of three counts, *demi-plié* and brush the right foot forward and then around to the side, inscribing a 90° curve on the floor. (This is exactly one half of a *rond de jambe à terre en dehors.*) While still within the first count, press the weight onto the right foot and into *demi-plié* as the left leg extends itself *point tendue* in second position.
2. On the second count, brush the left leg forward, coming through the first position (forming *demi-plié* with both legs) and on to fourth position front as the right leg extends *pointe tendue* behind.
3. On the third count, the right foot closes to fifth position behind or *sur le cou-de-pied.* The step repeats alternately.

The *pas de basque glissé en arrière* is a *pas de basque* gliding backwards. It can be extremely awkward and for this reason is often not practiced. However, its matery has particular merit. As has been said elsewhere, it is difficult to manipulate the legs in steps where the legs move behind the body. This is due to pelvic construction, to lack of visual contact with the space behind and the simple fact that it is not so kinetically pleasing to move in this way. However, practice and mastery of *pas de basque glissé en arrière* is an excellent way to overcome a real or potential aversion to moving *en arrière*.

Pas de basque glissé en arrière is performed precisely in reverse of *pas de basque glissé en avant*. It begins in fifth position, right foot in back.

1. On the first of three counts, *demi-plié* and brush the right foot backward and then around to the side, inscribing a 90° curve on the floor. (This is exactly one half of a *rond de jambe à terre en dedans*.) While still within the first count, press the weight onto the right foot and into *demi-plié* as the left leg extends itself *pointe tendue* in second position.
2. On the second count brush the left leg backward coming through the first position (forming *demi-plié* with both legs) and on to fourth position in back as the right leg extends *pointe tendue* in front.
3. On the third count, the right foot closes to fifth position, in front or *sur le cou-de-pied*. Although *pas de basque glissé* is done *terre à terre*, it maintains a buoyant quality. This buoyancy is achieved by utilizing the concept and practice of *fondu* whereby the knees and insteps articulate to the fullest.

Pas de basque sauté en avant and *en arrière* are *pas de basques* moving forward or backward and follow the basic spatial pattern of *pas de basque glissé*. However, both include a jumping movement instead of a gliding one. The right leg makes the *demi-rond de jambe* movement to the second position several inches off the floor. The weight is transferred onto the right leg with a jumping movement. The step finishes the same as *pas de basque glissé*.

Grand pas de basque, although highly refined in the technical sense, can still be seen as one of the more spectacular folk movements which the Basques perform. It is similar in attack to *pas de basque sauté* except that the knees do not bend on the first count and the movement is larger.

1. The right leg inscribes a *demi-grand ronde de jambe en dehors en l'air* in front of the body and is immediately followed by a *demi-grand rond de jambe en dedan en l'air* by the left leg, starting from

its second position. Thus, while the body is still in the air the left leg is seen to momentarily overlap the right leg.
2. On the second count, the left leg lands forward of the right in a fourth position and takes the weight as the right leg stretches to *pointe tendue* behind.
3. On the third count, the right leg closes to fifth position behind. The step can immediately repeat on the alternate leg, but is not done in reverse.

The first *port de bras* for the practice of *pas de basque* corresponds to the breakdown of the leg movement given at the beginning of the discussion.

1. The arms move from the preparatory position to the first.
2. They open to the second position.
3. They resume the preparatory position. The head may remain *de face* or it can incline slightly to the right as the arms move to the second.

PAS DE CHEVAL

Just as the African imitated the leaping deer in dances and the gypsy imitated the charging bull in flamenco dancing, so too the 17th century court imitated its most honored animal, the horse. *Pas de cheval* or step of the horse is so called because the legs, in the most elegant manner possible, imitate those of a horse pawing the ground. For the beginner, *pas de cheval* is done as a *terre à terre* step. The step always begins and ends in fourth position with the right leg *pointe tendue devant*.

1. The right foot brushes inward toward the supporting leg to a height below the knee.
2. It then returns to the *pointe tendue* with a *développé* devant.

An accompanying *port de bras* coordinates with the leg design and begins in the second position of the arms. As the leg retracts and *développés* outward to the *pointe tendue devant*, the arms move to the preparatory position, through first position and then outward to second position. The head tilts slightly left (away from the working leg) at the beginning of the *pas de cheval* and then centers itself at the culmination of the movement.

Pas de cheval is initially practiced facing the front of the room *(de face)*. Later on it is often done *effacé* since this design is particularly pleasing. The *effacé* direction shows the dancer's well-arched insteps to advantage as the legs articulate the characteristic pawing movement. The step is also done with the left leg. It is only done to the front direction.

While *pas de cheval* is first learned as a *terre à terre* step, it is generally performed as a jumping movement. In this form of the step, the supporting leg executes one *temps levé* or *sauté* as the working leg retracts and extends to *pointe tendue devant*.

Perhaps the most delightful use of the *pas de cheval* is the 19th century ballet *Don Quixote* created by Petipa. In this variation of the step, the ballerina moves forward *effacé* performing a series of *pas de cheval temp levé* on full *pointe* as the working leg executes the pawing movements. Needless to say, this is exceedingly difficult and only mentioned here as a point of interest. The various forms of *pas de cheval* exemplify the notion that fundamental steps may seem pedantic in their academic setting but that the choreographic imagination knows no bounds.

In summary, it is important to remember that whenever *terre à terre* steps such as *balancé, glissade, pas de bourrée,* etc. are used as preparatory movements, they serve as the breaker of inertia. Consequently, preparatory steps should be executed as secondary in value, in attack, in spatial size and in visual interests as compared with the step for which they are a preparation. Only when executed as such do preparatory steps mesh with the wholeness of a movement phrase to develop in an *enchaînement* such elements of aesthetic verity as contrast, dynamism and harmony.

TERRE À TERRE STEPS
BASED ON RELEVÉ MOVEMENT

Relevé, a term in dance meaning "raised," is another of the basic ways of moving in ballet dancing. Its special quality is characterized by a vigorous usage of the leg where it is concentrated mainly in the articulation of the ankle joint. It has many specific applications. Essentially, *relevé* means the rising up of the body onto the *demi-pointe* or ball of the foot, or onto full *pointe*. The wide application of *relevé* calls for its simple use in the five classical positions to its more complex use in the classical poses of *arabesque* and *attitude*, in movements such as *pirouettes* in all positions, and in all *terre à terre* dancing.

Through the rich heritage of ballet technique, we have two approaches to the execution of the *relevé*. Both are relevant and useful for today's student dancer. First, the so-called French and Russian approach to *relevé* is characterized by a smooth and tenuous rise to the full or *demi-pointe*. The Italian School (Cecchetti method) teaches *relevé* to be performed with a slight springing movement which appears to display more openly the actual vigor and strength necessary in the movement.

Relevés on both feet and then on one foot must be done first slowly, consciously and consistently for many weeks at the barre before they are attempted in center.

Frankly, the *relevé* movement is a shock to the body, especially the spine and knees. Until the legs straighten properly and develop adequate supportive strength they cannot ward off the jarring effect inherent in a faulty *relevé* to themselves or to the vertabrae. Caution is of vital importance. Insofar as any jumping movement is the logical extention of the *relevé* kinecept, the body is vulnerable to jarring movements in jumps as well. The correctly executed *relevé* assures that the entire foot works in the raising and the lowering of the body. Correct motor habits in the execution of the *relevé* are the only insurance against chronic injury. Consequently, the careful and at first, slow and thoughtful practice of *relevé* at the barre is imperative.

Relevé practice at the barre consists of simple, rhythmic variations in first, second and fifth positions. First, facing the barre, they are practiced with simply rising from the flat foot to half toe. *Relevé* from the fifth position demands the use of the Cecchetti spring upward from *demi-plié*. At the height of the *relevé* in the fifth position the legs are tightly drawn together so that no space is visible between them. They likewise release from this position with a slight spring. Turnout during the *relevé* is maintained by the constant but gentle pressure produced at the top of the thigh bone as it rotates outward from the hip socket. Any loss of this pressure causes the turnout to be diminished. Sporadic efforts to increase the pressure produces clutching the barre and excessive nervous tension which in turn impair balance. Hence, the emphasis is on gentle but constant pressure. Secondly, *relevés* are introduced to the student combined with *demi-plié*. They are also done facing the barre on one leg at a time, with and without *demi-plié*. The free leg helps secure the turnout of both legs by being held or "locked" in the *cou-de-pied derrière* position and later in the *retiré* position.

In the center work for beginning ballet, *relevé* is most used in the *petit adage* exercise following barre work although it also appears in *terre à terre* combinations of steps. The most basic steps using *relevé* are *échappé*, *relevé passé en arrière* and *en avant*, and *relevé en arabesque*.

Relevé and the Problem of Balance

Any time a *relevé* is executed whether on both legs or in one of the beautiful positions such as *attitude* or *écarté* it should be remembered that the weight of the torso must be placed precisely over the legs or leg as the case may be. Too often, the central problem with *relevés* is that students are so involved in the flow of the dance movement they fail to move through the correct preparatory position where the weight is over the legs before the final position occurs. This, of course, presumes that the torso itself is properly aligned.

ÉCHAPPÉ RELEVÉ

Échappé is a term meaning the equidistant escape of the feet from the center line of gravity. That is, the legs begin in a first or fifth position *demi-plié* and "escape," springing outward to a second or fourth

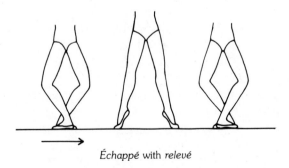

Échappé with *relevé*

Fig. 5. Échappé

position on *demi-pointe* while the knees and ankles straighten. The crucial point is that the escape of the legs begins from the heels pushing against the floor. The *échappé* step is completed as the feet begin the reversal of the movement by releasing first the ankles and then in the knees as the legs are drawn back to the beginning fifth position. Due to the nature of this step, the chief fault is generally the inability of the student to properly maintain the torso alignment. The pelvic area tends to release backward as the legs escape to their open position. Therefore, preliminary *échappé* practice done to a slow tempo while facing the barre can help the student consciously establish the appropriate habit for holding the spine in its proper alignment.

RELEVÉ PASSÉ EN AVANT
AND EN ARRÌERE

Relevé passé is a step rooted in and derived from the barre exercise *battement retiré*. Its great difficulty as the beginning student first attempts it, lies in the fact that the *relevé* is on one leg instead of two. This naturally demands greater strength and a modicum of balance. Not only can the *relevé passé* be an exciting and satisfying step in itself, but it is especially important because the body position of *relevé passé* is identical with that used in the *pirouette en dehors* and *en dedans*. Therefore, it is introduced to the beginning student early and practiced for months in preparation for *pirouette* work.

The *relevé passé* is done moving forward *(en avant)* and backward *(en arrière)*. Only *relevé passé en avant* is described in detail here.

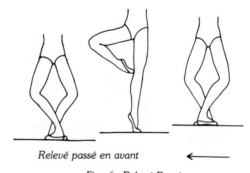

Relevé passé en avant   ⟵ ——

Fig. 6. Relevé Passé

1. Begin in fifth position with the right foot back. Press into *demi-plié* and with a push from both heels spring or *relevé* onto the half point of the left leg. The right leg likewise originates its *retiré* or *passé* position from the heels pushing down in the *demi-plié*. The right leg immediately flexes or retracts to the *retiré* position as the left leg arrives on *demi-pointe*.
2. With a slight springing movement the legs return to the fifth position *demi-plié*. The heels should land simultaneously as the right leg closes in front.
3. The movement is then repeated moving forward with the left leg and so on for a total of eight *relevés passés*. It is done in reverse by moving backward to form *relevé passé en arrière*. The *port de bras* is usually simple and held in second or fifth position in beginning classes. As control of the *relevé passé* develops, the movement is made richer by the addition of a variety of *port de bras* and a special rhythmic emphasis in attack.

RELEVÉ EN ARABESQUE

The *relevé en arabesque* is the rising of the body into perhaps the most characteristic and beloved body lines in the ballet art. *Relevé en arabesque* is a most intricate and difficult movement while it also has the notoriety of being universally the most ill-executed. Before the *relevé en arabesque* is presented here, a discussion of the *arabesque* is prerequisite.

Essentially the *arabesque,* whether perfect in the cool classicism of Fonteyn or stunningly flamboyant in the manner of Plisetskaya, is rooted in the *battement tendu en arrière* and the *grand battement en arrière* at the barre. Until both these exercises are done with a conscious effort for correctness in regard to the following points, the *arabesque* should not be attempted in center: i.e., the pelvis must not open unduly on the working side; the upper torso only slightly shifts forward in counterbalance to the lifted "arabesque leg"; and the *arabesque* leg extends with taut knee and foot while the back muscles hold the leg solidly in its space. In other words, the lifted leg must arrive at its desired height and resist the tendency to bounce or readjust its height.

The initial experience with the *arabesque* in center is based on simple exercises which include stepping onto a straight leg into the *ara-*

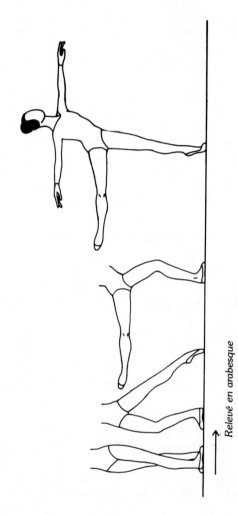

Relevé en arabesque

Fig. 7. Relevé en Arabesque

322

besque and immediately forming the position rather than "climbing" into it. Once the correct and immediate alignment of the arabesque can be produced at will, the student is ready to apply the relevé movement to the arabesque.

1. From the fifth position the student extends the right leg forward and falls (tombé) onto the right foot in a demi-plié allowing the body weight to move directly over the right leg.
2. From this demi-plié position the right leg then proceeds to straighten itself pushing the heel into the floor as it does so.
3. At the moment the right foot presses onto the floor to begin the relevé, the left leg lifts en arrière and is held for the desired amount of time by the back muscles, trained incidentally, through cambré exercises. As the legs form the lower part of the arabesque body line, the arms have a variety of positions which determine whether the arabesque is called first, second, third or fourth arabesque.

Final Word on Relevé Exercises

It is important to note that the relevé is the basis for leg strength in all dance forms, but especially so for ballet and modern dance. Unless the relevé is diligently practiced, the legs will never be developed enough to work on point or to execute the long series of jumps in allégro work. Point work and allégro steps are all based on the perfection of the simple relevé and most injuries during point work and allégro relate directly to laxness in the relevé. For example, the knees during point work often sustain injuries because they are not properly pulled taut or are not adequately held in line with the feet in the demi-plié which precedes the relevé. Likewise, landing from grand jeté onto legs not correctly strengthened through relevé movements generally causes injury.

TERRE À TERRE STEPS BASED ON
PIQUÉ MOVEMENT

Piqué, literally to prick, is a darting movement in ballet and is executed by stepping directly onto the full or demi-pointe of the working foot. The entire weight of the body is carried onto one leg as it darts in any given direction. The extended leg, the arms, torso and head are free to simultaneously form any desired balletic position. Each *piqué* normally represents one step advancing into space away from the starting point. Thus, the array of *piqué* movements includes *piqué sur le cou-de-pied; piqué retiré* or *piqué passé; piqué en arabesque* and *piqué en attitude; piqué à la seconde, croisé, écarté* and *effacé. Piqué* can also be a specific way of executing all forms of *pirouettes, pas de bourrée,* and classical poses.

Two objectives must be met before the *piqué* movement can be satisfactorily employed in classroom dancing. First, the working leg must be able to function as an "iron ramrod." Later, it intermittently goes in and out of *demi-plié* in the course of executing other adjoining steps such as successive *piqués* and *piqué balancé.* However, the first experience with *piqué* is more successful if the student concentrates on the idea of the leg being straight and strong as it moves to the *piqué.* Motor learning will occur sooner if the student kinesthetically "memorizes" the sensation of straightness in the working leg.

The second objective to be met in the initial experience with *piqué* is the problem of taking the weight of the torso as it is concentrated in the pelvic area and directly placing it over the *piqué* leg as it arrives at the climax of the *piqué* movement. This demands, of course, a combination of conceptual understanding and kinesthetic awareness. In this case, the mirror's reflection is a particularly helpful instrument since it is visually apparent to the student whether the hips are or are not directly over the working leg as the movement is executed. Likewise, the kinesthetic sensation of correct execution is more readily reinforced via the mirror's feedback.

PIQUÉ EN AVANT, SUR LE COU-DE-PIED

The practice of *piqué* is occasionally introduced at the barre within the context of one of the barre exercises. However, the adult beginner may successfully begin *piqué* practice in the center with the step *piqué en avant* or *piqué* moving forward. Traditionally the forward path of movement for each student in the class is a diagonal from the dancer's upstage left corner to the downstage right corner. *Piqué en avant* is executed as follows:

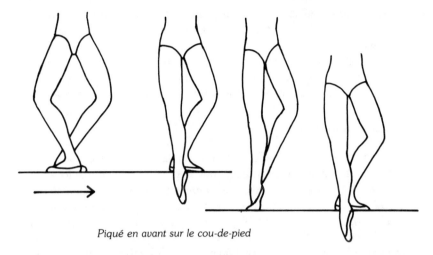

Piqué en avant sur le cou-de-pied

Fig. 8. Piqué

1. The dancer begins from fifth position, right leg front, in *demi-plié* facing the direction in which the body is to proceed. The arms are in *demi-seconde* or third position, French style.
2. From the *demi-plié* the right leg sharply extends front as in *battement tendu dégagé en avant*.
3. The body moves forward and directly over the right leg as the weight is transferred onto it. The left leg simultaneously moves quickly *sur le cou-de-pied en arrière*. It is necessary for the body to move into the *piqué* immediately and as one unit. In other words, if the body moves forward in sections, i.e., chest and head, then arms, then hips, then the other leg, rather than as a unified mass of bones and muscle, the movement will lack control. Control is prerequisite to balance, and since balance assumes the equal distribution of body weights around a center point, the *piqué* without control will not appear to be an effortless darting of the body into a balance. Rather, the result is effortful and awkward when the body attempts to meet its objectives without correct motor mechanics.
4. Coming out of the *piqué* movement demands equal attention from the dancer. The *piqué* step forward has already been taken in initiating the *piqué* movement. Now the dancer must remember to

stay in the new space while the left foot in *sur le cou-de-pied* directly lowers itself to the floor in a *demi-plié*. That is, the left foot lowers into the *demi-plié* directly under and thus fully supporting the concentration of weight in the pelvis.
5. The right leg maintains its turnout, straight knee and pointed foot and is thus in the proper position to execute the next *piqué*.

A Common Fault

As a series of *piqués* is performed moving diagonally across the room the hip of the *piqué* (working) leg may begin to slightly thrust forward and lead into the movement of the *piqué* leg. This is detrimental to the *piqué* as well as to the body placement in general. Therefore, effort must constantly be made to separate the work of the *piqué* leg from the placement of the pelvis. At all times both hip bones are parallel to the shoulder girdle and absolutely perpendicular to the path of *piqué* movement.

 Piqués in beginning classes are always practiced consecutively and in series of eight or sixteen as the student travels diagonally across the floor. They are done both forward and backward.

PIQUÉ EN AVANT EN RETIRÉ

Piqué en avant en retiré is performed in the same manner as the simpler *piqué en avant sur le cou-de-pied*. The only difference is that the free leg retracts with a snapping quality of movement into the *retiré* position. This positioning of the free leg into *retiré* demands slightly more energy than in the simpler *piqué* step. It is assumed that the student will make every effort to keep the hips well placed (parallel to the floor line) during the series of *piqués* and that the foot in *retiré* will not sickle. At first, the *piqué en avant en retiré* is done consecutively while traveling across the floor. On a more advanced level, *piqué en retiré* is reversed or done *en arrière* by initially stepping backward.

PIQUÉ EN ARABESQUE

As the student progressively develops the total battery of balletic skills, compound movements of considerable motor complexity are presented. The *piqué en arabesque* is a compound movement in that while one kind of motor effort is being used in the working leg and the spine, the remaining part of the body must assume a body position which is correct but not resultant from the same movement flow as on the working side of the body. In *piqué en arabesque* the leg projects a percussive quality while the rest of the body projects a lyrical line, seemingly devoid of tension. *Piqué en arabesque* should only be attempted after the simple *piqué* is correctly achieved and after experience with *adage* and *allégro* in center practice has become part of the student's daily class work.

The *piqué en arabesque* occurs via the same process as the previously described *piqué* movements. The chief difference is that the *arabesque,* being a complex position, must first be mastered at the barre *(grand battement* and *développé en arrière)* to insure proper placement and control when it is used in conjunction with the *piqué.* As the one leg goes into the *piqué* movement, the other leg immediately lifts to its desired height (45°é90°) *en arrière* and the arms and head assume one of the various traditional sets of arm positions. First arabesque is the body position most commonly associated with the *piqué en arabesque.*

The clear cut application of the concept of tension and relaxation (contraction and release), which modern dance creators have so beautifully expressed in their immeasurable contributions to dance, is directly applicable in all *piqué* movement, but especially in the *piqué en arabesque.* The flow of movement into the *piqué* is a movement of relative relaxation while the moment of balance at the climax of the *piqué en arabesque* is one of tension or contraction of the muscles "holding" the body in the arabesque position. This tension is considerably released as the body comes out of the *arabesque* and prepares for the succeeding movement. In keeping with the ballet aesthetic, this tension and its release is not visible to the observer although one may kinesthetically empathize its presence in the dancer and accordingly be affected by it.

PIQUÉ EN ATTITUDE

The *piqué en attitude* is approached and practiced in precisely the same fashion as the preceding description of *piqué* movement. The chief difference is, of course, the difficult body position of the *attitude.* Once the *attitude* can be correctly formed at will and without subtle adjustments of positioning, the *attitude* can be applied to the *piqué* movement. This tends to approach the intermediate level of adult ballet.

TERRE À TERRE STEPS
BASED ON TURNING MOVEMENT

Turning movements have always been a part of dancing, whether in the primitive ritualistic dance, folk dances, court dances or theatrical forms of dancing.

In ballet, there exists a large variety of turning movements variously called *tours* or *pirouettes*. These are performed on both legs as well as on one leg. Turns can be done singly as in *soutenu en tournant* or they can be multiple as in a triple *pirouette en dedans*. In addition, they are done consecutively as when *piqués tournés* and *chaînés* are performed traveling across the room. Turning movements cover a broad range from those which are easy to perform due to their simplicity to those extremely difficult to execute due to their motor complexity. The adult beginner, who is well into the material required in beginning ballet, practices such turns as *soutenu en tournant, piqué tourné, chaînés,* and the preparation exercises for the *pirouette*. These turns are always executed on the ball of the foot *(demi-pointe)* in beginning ballet.

There are also compound turning steps in intermediate and advanced ballet such as *emboîté, saut de basque, sissonne détourné* and *renversé*. These steps are first learned in the context of their spatial design. The turning factor is added only when the basic motor mechanics are accomplished without loss of vertical alignment and horizontal shoulder and pelvis placement. The compound turning steps as well as the multiple and consecutive turns elicit a kinetic brilliance when eventually executed on full point.

SPOTTING

Spotting is a term in ballet used to describe the subtle but necessary head movement which is an essential part of all *tours* and *pirouettes*. This head movement involves the dancer focusing on a chosen "spot" in front of him. As the body revolves on each turn, the head turns at the last possible moment and with the greatest possible speed resumes focus on the exact chosen "spot". In other words, for every revolution the body makes in *tours* or *pirouettes*, there is a corresponding "spotting" movement of the head.

Spotting has two purposes, one functional and the other aesthetic. Functional purpose: Numerous *tours* and multiple *pirouettes* without the aid of spotting would cause the dancer to become dizzy and therefore lose his or her equilibrium. That is, the dancer's loss of equilibrium is due to the unsettling of the endolymph fluid in the inner ear. If spotting is correctly performed, the endolymph fluid remains undisturbed and the dancer does not suffer from dizziness. Aesthetic purpose: Spotting lends to all turning movements in ballet an element of brilliance and excitement which is immediately empathized by the spectator. The movement quality of the dancer's spotting head in *tours* and *pirouettes* is similar to that of the head-snapping produced by the owl. The turn of the dancer's head while spotting should be as imperceptible and facile as the owl's head movement is from side to side. Spotting thus gives the impression that the dancer is spinning while forever facing the audience. Often the advanced dancer will finish a multiple *pirouette* with the last spotting movement totally apparent. This is visually exciting and legitimate while it underlines the impression that the dancer is fully in control of the turn.

Tours and *pirouettes* performed in place focus straight ahead on the mirror wall. *Tours* which travel across the room such as *soutenu en tournant* and *piqué tourné* focus on a point at the end of the path of direction. That is *piqué tourné* moving diagonally from upstage left focuses at a point downstage right.

Correct spotting involves the following kinecepts:

1. The focal spot should be on a *precise point* or area.
2. The focal spot should be straight ahead at *eye level*.
3. The eyes should actually *focus* on the spot and not just blurrily regard the general area.
4. The head must stay level and not tip forward, backward or sideways as it revolves while spotting. That is, the chin line of the correctly set head must remain parallel to the shoulder line, pelvis line, and floor line during the turn.

The last is generally the most common "spotting fault" to be found among adult beginners. While they seem to remember to focus directly ahead on a precise spot, the complex physiological coordination, especially for *pirouettes,* cause the set of the head to falter during the turn. This unfortunate occurrence sets off a chain reaction, i.e., faulty spot which leads to dizziness, loss of balance and control thus destroying the technical and aesthetic success of the *pirouette.*

SOUTENU EN TOURNANT

The *soutenu en tournant* or *soutenu* turn is the shortened Americanized usage of the term, *assemblé soutenu en tournant en dedans. Soutenu* translates as 'sustained'' so the description of the full nomenclature might read as "the legs assembling with a sustained quality while the body turns inwardly''. *Soutenu en tournant* is done on both legs and its mechanics are fairly easy for the body. Therefore, it is often the first to be learned. It is described as follows so that the turn will first be executed to the student's right or clockwise.

It is very important when initially attempting turns that the beginner obtains a solid motor experience of the sensation of turning. As a rule, right handed students perform turns *en dedans* better when turning clockwise. Therefore, the more facile direction for turning should be practiced first, followed by *en dedans* turns done counterclockwise.

1. The student begins in fifth position, left foot back. On count one, *demi-plié* on the right leg as the left leg does *battement tendu* to the side or second position.
2. On count two, execute a *demi-rond de jambe à terre* (90°) with the left leg and draw its foot into fifth position front, rising on half toe.
3. Still on count two continue the movement by turning on both feet *en dedans* (clockwise) to face the back of the room. Continue by pivoting on around to face the front of the room. The legs are still on *demi-pointe* and the left leg is in back.
4. Lower the heels to the floor maintaining fifth position.

The turn is then practiced to the left or turning counterclockwise. The *soutenu en tournant* practiced as such may be repeated in place or it may be combined with other *terre à terre* steps.

The *soutenu en tournant* is subsequently practiced as consecutive turns while traveling across the room from left to right. It is described as follows:

1. Facing front, step to the side in *demi-plié* on the right foot as the left slides in a *battement tendu* to second position.
2. Execute the *soutenu* as previously described.
3. Initiate the following turn by again stepping sideways into *demi-plié*, etc.

For the first attempt, the beginner is aided when doing the movement to three counts. As the step is assimilated into the kinetic sensations, it is easily done to two counts. In intermediate work it is often performed on one count. The preparation movements are made on "and" while the turn itself is accomplished on the accented beat.

The *soutenu en tournant* as described in this chapter accords with the French school due to the *demi-rond de jambe* in the step. This *demi*-circular movement aids the beginning student in the execution of the step. The Russian version of the step calls for the leg to directly draw into the fifth position instead of forming the *rond de jambe*. This is mentioned to point out that there are often several versions of executing a step. American dance is essentially eclectic and mixes Russian, French, English and Italian styles.

Eventually the *soutenu en tournant* is executed *en dehors* although it is more difficult for the body to maneuver.

PIQUÉ TOURNÉ

Tours which are executed on one leg are also referred to as *pirouettes*. The *piqué tourné en dedans* or *piqué* turn revolving inward, is generally the first *pirouette* learned in ballet. The turning movement involves the dancer stepping directly onto one leg "straight as an iron ramrod" while the other leg forms *sur le cou-de-pied*. It is executed as follows:

1. Face front in fifth position, *demi-plié* with the right foot front.
2. The right leg does *battement tendu dégagé* to the front direction (*devant*) and immediately swings in a *demi-rond de jambe* to the side direction (*de côté*).
3. *Piqué* onto the *demi-pointe* and turn to the right as it arrives in the side direction.
4. Simultaneous with the *piqué* action of the right leg, the other raises to *sur le cou-de-pied derrière*.

It is important to remember that the turning action occurs precisely at the same moment that *piqué* and the *cou-de-pied* take place.

The *piqué tourné en dehors,* meaning *piqué* turn revolving outward, is described as follows:

1. Face front in fifth position, *demi-plié* with the right foot forward. The left leg slides to the side as in *battement tendu dégagé.*
2. Swing the left leg forward in a generous *demi-rond de jambe* slightly *dégagé.*
3. The right leg begins to *relevé* from its *demi-plié,* pulling the *piqué* leg directly onto *demi-pointe* as well as directly under the concentration of body weight (pelvic area).
4. At the moment the *piqué* leg supports the weight, the right snaps *sur le cou-de-pied devant.*
5. When the turn is completed, the leg *sur le cou-de-pied* falls to the side again assuming the body weight in preparation for the *piqué tourné* to repeat.

The *turning action* occurs at the moment the weight is fully transferred onto the *piqué* leg.

THE ARMS IN SOUTENU EN TOURNANT AND PIQUÉ TOURNÉ

It will be remembered in the discussion of *piqué* movements that the concept of tension and relaxation was discussed. In *piqué* the body sustains a certain amount of tension during the moment of the *piqué* while the tension is considerably diminished as the body comes out of the *piqué* into the *demi-plié.* The same idea applies to the *soutenu en tournant* even though the weight is taken on both legs. In *piqué* and *soutenu en tournant,* therefore, the tension-relaxation concept can be spatially viewed as a body design which moves through space in a piston-like action of up-down-up-down or *piqué-plié-piqué-plié.* Let it suffice to say that the arm action for these turns must be purely mechanical in its correctness at the beginning, otherwise a stream of technical faults in the body alignment and placement will result from arms being allowed to enter into or assist the turning of the body.

The basic arm pattern or *port de bras* for *soutenu en tournant* and *piqué tourné en dedans* and *en dehors* is the constant and rhythmic opening and closing of the arms from second to first, second to first, etc. When the body is on the *piqué* or on both legs in *soutenu en tournant,* the arms are closed in first position and when the body is in the *plié,* the arms are in the second position. In other words, when the body feels and produces the necessary tension at the climax of the *piqué,* the arms and their associated muscles in the upper back likewise learn to "hold" in the first position. As the body releases into the *plié* the arms relax slightly as they open to the second. Thus, the arms and legs are coordinated during the turns. It is usually difficult for the ballet student to accept the fact that the correct way of moving in ballet is often mechanically the easiest and visually the most beautiful for the body to perform.

CHAÎNÉS

Chaînés, an abbreviated form of *tours chaînés déboulés,* translates as "a chain of turns which advance like a rolling ball". It is the term most used to describe a chain-like pattern of consecutive traveling *tours* which are executed on both legs. The step is described as follows:

1. Begin in the upstage left corner preparing to move diagonally to downstage right.
2. Point the right leg to the front direction *(pointe tendue à la quatrième devant).* The right arm is place forward in first position while the left is outstretched in second position.
3. *Demi-rond de jambe* the right leg from the front to the side direction and *piqué* onto it revolving one-half turn clockwise.
4. The left leg assumes the weight as it steps onto *demi-pointe* and completes another half turn, continuing on in a clockwise direction. This completes the first *tour.*
5. Subsequently, the right leg repeats the first half turn followed by the left leg taking the second half turn, etc.
6. As the right leg takes the weight on the first turn, both arms open to the second position. When the left leg takes the weight on the second half turn, the arms close in first position.

During the *chaînés,* the knees are absolutely straight. The legs must be close together whether on full or *demi-pointe.* The spotting head turns right with a snapping quality before the weight is taken on the left leg. The level of the chin and arms while opening and closing, must sustain a line parallel to the floor. The arms move in their opening and closing pattern, from the shoulder joint only. The shoulder girdle and upper back must not become involved in the arm movement since involvement will upset the body's verticality during the chain of turns.

PREPARATION FOR PIROUETTE EN DEHORS

Pirouette, meaning to spin or whirl is the term used to describe the most complex turning movements in ballet. The brilliantly spun *pirouette*, along with the elegant line of the *arabesque* and glamorous vigor of the *grand jeté*, is one of the hallmarks of the ballet.

Carlo Blasis records in his *Traite Elementaire, Theorique et Pratique de L'Art de la Danse* (1820) that Gardel and Vestris *fils* may be regarded as the inventors of the *pirouette*. These two dancers were active in Paris in the 1770's. Blasis credits Vestris in particular, with perfecting, diversifying and thus increasing the vogue for *pirouettes*. Since the time of Vestris, *pirouettes* exceeding three revolutions per step have been performed in various body positions, including *sur le cou-de-pied* (French and Russian schools), *retiré* (Italian school), *à la seconde, arabesque,* and *attitude.*

Specifically, the *pirouette* consists of one or more complete revolutions of the body while it is supported on one leg. The supporting leg is absolutely straight at the knee and is on *demi-pointe*. The balance must be flawlessly correct otherwise the turn will not occur or the dancer will prematurely fall out of the turning position. The spotting movement used by the head is also an organic part of the *pirouette*. The turning action itself is actually a result of a perfectly coordinated preparation consisting of a combination of *plié, relevé,* and special arm movements. The head and shoulders are not involved in the amassing of the necessary force for the turn.

Due to the motor complexity of the *pirouette*, long hours must be spent working on the preparatory exercises associated with it. As the college student approaches the intermediate level, the preparatory work for *pirouette* is feasible. The quarter turn preparation for *pirouette en dehors* is described as follows: The exercise uses four counts for each quarter turn and begins, standing in fifth position, right foot front. Hold the arms forward in first position.

Step I

1. Brush the right leg to the side as in *battement tendu à la seconde.* Arms open into second position.
2. Close the right leg to fifth position front in *demi-plié,* feeling the weight of the body on both feet. Simultaneously, close the right arm back to its initial first position.
3. The following movements occur simultaneously:
   a. *Relevé* onto the *demi-pointe* of the left leg.
   b. With the same pushing action from the *demi-plié* in fifth position, raise the right leg *sur le cou-de-pied* front.
   c. Move the left arm forward to meet the other arm, thus forming first position of the arms.
   d. At the precise moment of points a, b, and c, the entire body (excluding the head) makes one quarter turn to the right. The head, with the keen focus of the eyes, arrives a split second later.
4. Both legs lower into fifth position *demi-plié.* The arms retain the first position. The body now faces the right side of the room or 90° away from the front of the room.

Step II—Second Quarter Turn

Repeat the movements of Step I so that the second quarter turn finishes facing the back of the room or 180° away from the front of the room.

Step III—Third Quarter Turn

Repeat the movements of Step II so that the third quarter turn finishes facing the left side of the room or 270° from the front of the room.

Step IV—Fourth Quarter Turn

Repeat the movements of Step III so that the fourth turn finishes facing the front of the room and the body has completed 360° of revolution. The right leg closes in fifth position back at the end of the fourth quarter turn.

The exercise is now converted to the opposite leg causing the quarter turns to revolve to the left.

Half Turns

The exact same preparation is used to execute half turns to the right and left.

Whole Turns

The exact same preparation is used to execute whole turns to the right and left.

Double turns are also practiced from this preparation while multiple turns require more complex preparatory movements.

Similar exercises using second position and fourth position are also utilized in developing the strength and coordination necessary for good *pirouettes*. The exactitude of the body's positions during the exercise coupled with precise timing are essential to successful and beautiful *pirouettes*. If any element of the exercise goes askew, no matter how minor, the *pirouette* will be in jeopardy. Should the *pirouette* be incorrectly practiced, the ensuing and thus ingrained bad habits will result in a chain of technical ineptitude.

CHAPTER 16

The Petit Allégro:
Aerial Steps

Professionally geared ballet schools throughout the world generally teach children many *allégro* steps facing and holding on to the *barre*. This pedagogical technique is helpful, but not absolutely necessary for the adult. All *allégro* steps described here are done with the student facing the mirror while standing in the center of the classroom.

CHANGEMENT

Changement is one of the simplest jumping steps to be accomplished in *allégro* movement. Because of the ever-present effort required to maintain the turnout of the legs and proper alignment, however, this step demands considerable concentration. The technical approach to *changement* is as follows:

1. The student stands in fifth position, right foot in front. On the "and" count (musical upbeat), the legs move into a preparatory *demi-plié*. On the count of one (musical downbeat), both feet push away from the floor propelling the body on a vertical trajectory. The feet, as in all jumping steps, are fully pointed at the height of the jump. During the brief moment when the body is off the floor, the legs and pointed feet are tightly closed in the fifth position.
2. During descent, the right leg moves from the front to fifth position back, creating the change of fifth position which is the essence of the step.

The most general fault observed in *changement* occurs when the lower spine releases its firmly held alignment, causing the pelvis to move back of the vertical axis of the body. That is, when the body de-

337

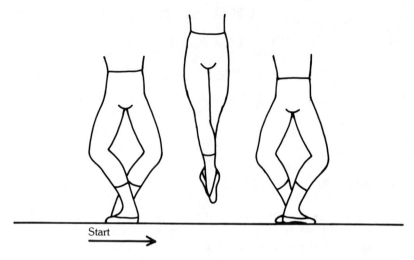

Start

Fig. 1. *Changement de pieds*

scends from the jump, the muscles controlling the lower spine relax, causing the lower back to release its vertical position while the upper torso counter-balances by "bucking" forward. This fault can be completely avoided if the student clearly understands and applies the concept of pressing the feet away from the floor in the jump and maintaining a well turned-out and correct *demi-plié.* It is also essential that the entire sole of each foot evenly support half of the body's weight.

The arms for *changement* are rounded in the preparatory position. At first, maintaining the satisfactory *port de bras* can prove to be difficult since the arms reflect much of the physical strain of correctly learning to perform the *changement.* Later on, however, the tension, particularly in the hands, tends to disappear as the step becomes easier to perform.

For the beginner, *changement* is done in a series of 8 or 16. The step is often incorporated with other jumping steps to form a classroom *enchaînement.* The eventual embellishment of *changement* with *épaulement* movement (subtle but precisely executed movements of head and shoulder girdle) gives to its relative simplicity of form visual interest and considerable style.

The eyes are focused straight ahead in *changement* since the classroom style of practicing this step, as well as most elementary *allégro* steps, coordinates with the *de face* positioning of the body. The central reason for dancing *de face* is for the purpose of artful display and expression. Therefore, from the very beginning of ballet training, whether the art is studied for a professional career or pleasure and the attainment of confident self-awareness, the ability to face the observing eyes of the teacher or the public is necessarily acquired. In addition, too often the effort and concentration involved in remembering and executing an exercise produces a glassy-eyed gaze on the face of the student. Often, too, the focus of the eyes drops to the floor instead of being directed straight ahead. Such faults concerning the focus of the eyes are as much a bad habit as rolling over on the arches and are equally difficult to erase once they become ingrained into the nervous system. More seriously from the audience point of view, an immobile face, glassy stare, or downward-cast eyes harms a performance far more than some technical impropriety. Consequently, it behooves the student to practice *changement* (and all succeeding *de face allégro* steps) with attention to the performance values of alertly focused eyes and a personable facial expression as well as those pertaining to technical demands.

Vaganova hints at the psychological attitude which is demonstrated by clear and intelligent focus of the eyes when she discusses a dancer's "aplomb" in relation to stability of the body. While she discusses the presence of physical aplomb as related to physical stability, it follows that the necessary psychological aplomb of confidence arises from that very physical stability. The absence of psychological aplomb is the antithesis of the popular image of a dancer on and off stage! Thus, eye-focus is the central expressive point for the entire face and throat area. Becoming aware of its expressive potential is of enormous importance to the student dancer.

SOUBRESAUT

A step technically related to *changement* but more advanced is the *soubresaut*. In *soubresaut*, which literally translates as a "sudden jump", there is no change of feet in the fifth position. The body springs upward and forward during the movement so that it begins the jump from one spatial point and ends in another. The legs are held tightly together and the feet are pointed during the jump. The landing is accomplished on both feet in fifth position *à terre*. The precise spatial directions of the horizontal traveling are indicated by whether the *soubresaut* is performed while traveling *en avant, croisé en avant* or *ouvert en avant.* The step is also done moving backwards in the various positions.

The *port de bras* plays an important role in *soubresaut* since the arms embellish the body line and impart a certain amount of dance quality to the simple jump. In a series of four *soubresauts croisés en avant,* right foot front, the arms gradually arrive at one of the various classical arm positions so that during a series of four *soubresauts,* the arms complete a *port de bras* moving from the preparatory position to third *arabesque* arms where the right arm arrives in first position, palm facing downward and the left arm extends diagonally upward to eye level, palm downward.

ASSEMBLÉ DESSUS AND ASSEMBLÉ DESSOUS

Assemblé is one of the first jumping steps within the general category of *allégro* movement which is introduced to the student. Although the step may seem inordinantly difficult to execute at first, the student has actually practiced it in part at the *barre.* For example, *assemblé* is performed precisely as the *battement tendu plié de côté* is done at the *barre* with the addition of a small jump made by the supporting leg. Consequently, a verbal and visual image of the similarities between the previously learned *barre* exercise and the *assemblé* will facilitate physical mastery of the step.

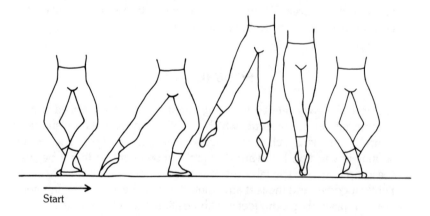

Start

Fig. 2. *Assemblé dessus*

Assemblé Dessus

The basic spatial and rhythmic form of this step is as follows:

1. On the "and" count both legs bend in a small preparatory *demi-plié* in fifth position, right leg back.
2. On the first count the right leg disengages from the fifth and brushes through *pointe tendue* to the side direction. Simultaneously, the left foot pushes off the floor to a full point so that the body is propelled upward in a vertical trajectory. The right leg forms a 25° angle with the vertically aligned left leg at the height of the trajectory of the *assemblé*. If the height of the working leg achieves a 45° angle, it is referred to in the French and Cecchetti methods, respectively, as *demi-hauteur* or *demi-position*, which indicates that the leg level is half-way between the *pointe tendue* and hip-height.
3. At the highest elevation point of the *assemblé dessus*, the legs quickly come together or assemble. The body then lands in fifth with the right foot front. Both feet must arrive in the fifth position at the same time and the body must not resist its natural inclination to land in the *demi-plié*. *Assemblé dessus* is profitably practiced when done in series of eight consecutive *assemblés*. The first *assemblé* will be initiated by the right leg, the second *assemblé* by the left leg, and so on.

Assemblé Dessous

The *assemblé* is also learned in reverse so that the body moves backward in space. The reversal of direction occurs when the right leg begins front in the fifth position and brushes side through the *pointe tendue*, closing back in the fifth position *demi-plié*.

Eight *assemblés dessous* are eventually added to the eight *assemblés dessus*. This basic *assemblé* practice, arduous as it is tedious, is absolutely necessary in the development of proper alignment for *assemblé* and for developing adequate strength in *allégro* movement.

In the *assemblé*, the *plié* serves to soften the shock of landing as it returns to the floor. The *plié* also improves the movement quality produced by the body as it lands. The "cushioning" effect of the *plié* or "soft landing" as it is often called, is not only aesthetically desirable but physiologically necessary in all jumping steps. That is, the cushioned landing protects the body's skeletal structure, especially the spine. The *plié* works protectively, adding to the cushioning effect that the intermittent cartilage along the spinal column provides for the bony vertabrae. In addition, the *plié* disseminates the shock of the landing through the legs and upward through the body so that the spine does not bear the entire responsibility. Mechanically, the *plié* is simply a necessity in ballet in that what goes up must *first* go down. Therefore, it is important to give much care to the correctness as well as the movement quality of the *plié* aspect of the *assemblé*.

Many teachers, some who still personally recall the classes of Enrico Cecchetti and Nicholas Legat, employ a combination of *assemblé dessus* and *dessous* with an extra *demi-plié* inserted between each *assemblé*. This particular *enchaînement* is unique in the way it is designed to teach the feet to point under the weight of the body and at the same time to resist the weight of the body in the spatial formation of the steps. *Assemblé* is, after all, a movement whereby the resistance to gravity and the pleasurable giving in to its downward pull is of the essence. The effort required to execute this *enchaînement* correctly is considerable, but over a period of time the legs develop the required strength and agility. Over the years this elementary *enchaînement* has proved to be so significant in the training of dancers, that many professionals continue to practice it in the maintenance of their technical skills.

When done in a series of eight, the steps must be worked so that each *assemblé* uses the same amount of effort to push off from the floor. Likewise, each landing in the series of *assemblés* should be precisely controlled according to the method of execution. As the body lands in fifth, there should be no shifting or adjusting between the weight-bearing legs and feet. In other words, the movement design of the step must clearly and economically reflect the physiological authority that is felt by the dancer performing the step. No indications of superfluous movement due to unsure balance must be allowed. Usually a clear mental image of the step, which is also verbally reinforced by the teacher, insures good execution even on the elementary level of study.

Following the basic concept of *en croix* directions, the *assemblé* is also done to the front direction (*assemblé en avant*) and the back direction (*assemblé en arriére*) as well as to the side directions (*dessus* and *dessous*) in the basic stages of ballet training. In more advanced work, *assemblé* is done in complex variations of the basic step where it is performed with the addition of beats or with a turn in the air.

The elementary form of the arm movement for the *assemblé dessus* and *dessous* is standard and simple. The arms begin in the preparatory position. At the moment the body is propelled vertically upward, the arms open to a *demi-seconde* position whereupon they return to the preparatory position as the body lands.

In beginning ballet, the head does not have any movements but continues the line of the spine. While it is not rigidly held in place, some conscious effort may be necessary to keep the chin from jutting forward during the ascent of the step. The eyes simply hold their focus straight ahead. Later, *épaulement,* which uses subtle shoulder and head positions, is added to the dancer's repertory of movements so that the *assemblé* takes on both stylistic and kinetic depth which helps to transform the precisely constructed movement pattern of *assemblé* into one of the many artistic components that comprise ballet dancing.

JETÉ, DESSUS AND DESSOUS

The term *jeté* is generically used to designate the various forms of a leap which is basically a jump from one leg to the other. The step derives its name from the French verb, *jeter,* which means "to throw". In all *jeté* steps, the leg which initiates the leaping movement brushes the floor as it begins the movement, so that the brushing movement gives the leg the appearance of being "thrown".

In beginning ballet, the *jeté dessus* and *jeté dessous* represent the student's first attempts with the movement of the leap. The student will recall from the study of *assemblé* that the qualifying term *dessus* indicates that the working leg in fifth or *sur le cou-de-pied* position starts from behind the supporting leg and ends in front of it, thus causing the entire body to move slightly forward. *Dessous* is the reverse in that the working leg in fifth or *sur le cou-de-pied* comes from the front of the supporting leg and ends behind it, thus causing the body to move slightly backward.

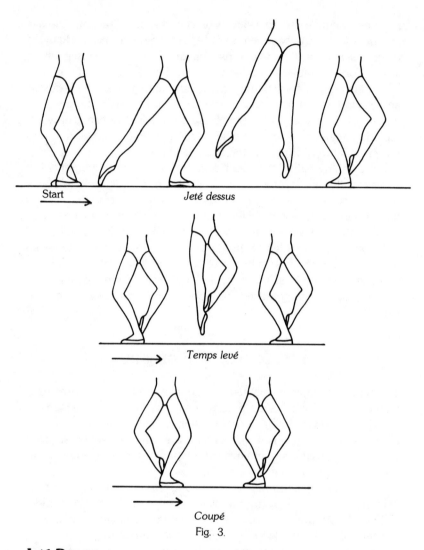

Start →

Jeté dessus

→

Temps levé

→

Coupé

Fig. 3.

Jeté Dessus

1. From fifth position *demi-plié* with the right foot back, the right foot brushes to the side direction using the *battement tendu dégagé* action. Simultaneously, the body springs with a vertical push of the left foot from *demi-plié* causing the foot and toes to point.

2. The body lands on the well turned-out right leg in *demi-plié*. The landing foot must arrive directly under the center of the body on each and every *jeté*. Simultaneously, the left foot arrives *sur le cou-de-pied* behind. From this landing position in the *demi-plié*, the body is ready to repeat the *jeté dessus* without an additional preparatory *plié* or it can immediately launch into a different step.

Jeté Dessous

1. From fifth position *demi-plié* with the right foot front, the right foot brushes to the side direction using a *battement tendu dégagé* action. Simultaneously, the body springs with a vertical push of the left foot from *demi-plié* causing the foot and toes to point.
2. The body lands on a well turned-out right leg in *demi-plié*. The landing foot must arrive directly under the center of the body on each and every *jeté*. Simultaneously, the left foot arrives *sur le cou-de-pied* in front.

It is imperative that the student does not allow the body to zig-zag through space during a series of *jetés*. Rather, the body moves straight forward or backward on each *jeté* and never from side to side. If the turnout is maintained in both legs, the body will move slightly forward or backward on each *jeté,* that is, the approximate width of the foot.

The body direction of the elementary *jeté dessus* and *jeté dessous* is strictly *de face*. Accordingly, the head position and eye focus relate to this *de face* positioning of the body in space.

The arms are held in the *demi-seconde* position when *jetés* are practiced consecutively. Eventually, the most simple variation of movement design of the head and arms is introduced to give a graceful quality to the consecutive repetition of the *jeté*. It is as follows:

1. As the *jeté dessus* lands with the weight on the right foot, the head and eyes move from their *de face* positioning to a point slightly to the right of center.
2. At the same moment of landing on the right foot, the right arm moves slightly forward to the first position (Russian style). The left arm retains the *demi-seconde* position.

The total result is that the step is imbued with a subtle coordination of movement and design involving the head, right arm, and right leg.

All three design elements are momentarily welded together as the facial awareness focuses outward and over the right arm. This upper body movement is underscored and punctuated by the kinetic downbeat of the weight landing on the right leg.

The same head and arm movement is repeated in the succeeding *jeté* onto the left leg. Care must be taken to maintain the same quality and quantity of energy flow on each *jeté*. Although the leg work has a percussive quality from the vigorous and rhythmical pushing off and landing on the floor, the arm and head movement must retain its gracious softness.

Two additional forms of *jeté* which are closely related to the above are *petit jeté en avant* and *petit jeté en arrière*. In these steps the working leg is "thrown" in the forward and backward directions, respectively, while the other leg finishes *sur le cou-de-pied* or in a low extension in the back or front directions, respectively.

For a variation in the practice of consecutive *jetés,* which also provides an excellent strength building device, the *jeté* is often combined with *temps levé,* on the landing leg.

TEMPS LEVÉ

The *temps levé* literally means time raised, that is, a hop on one foot without any transfer of weight from one leg to the other. Since *temps levé* is done in any position, it serves as a device to emphasize by repetition the spatial design of the position of an antecedent step. It is also an auxiliary step in that the hop allows for a more facile initiation of a succeeding step. This simple *enchaînement* combining *jeté* and *temps levé* is as follows:

1. *Jeté dessus, temps levé* on the right foot
2. *Jeté dessus, temps levé* on the left foot.

COUPÉ

In a more complex version, the *jeté dessus, temps levé* combination can be combined with *jeté dessous* and *temps levé* by inserting one *coupé* in between counts. In this combination of *jeté* and *temps levé,* the *coupé* serves to reverse the *sur le cou-de-pied* foot position so that the *jeté dessous* may commence.

Coupé, like the *temps levé,* is in itself not a step. Rather, it is an auxiliary jumping or *terre à terre* movement done as a preparation. While the *temps levé* does not involve a shift of weight from one foot to the other, the *coupé* is essentially the shift of weight from one foot to the other in preparation for some other step. The term *coupé* implies a cutting movement in that one foot "cuts" away the position of the other foot and itself assumes the position. For example, the right foot back *sur le cou-de-pied* takes the weight of the body as the left foot moves or "cuts" the front *sur le cou-de-pied.*

In its simplest form, *coupé* is merely a single shift of weight while the freed foot is usually positioned *sur le cou-de-pied.* Generally the supporting leg will maintain a *demi-plié* since the *coupé* is a preparatory movement and the *demi-plié* allows for immediate action.

PAS DE CHAT

Pas de chat, literally "step of the cat", is a basic ballet step suggestive of a cat-like movement as the name implies. Although there are several versions of the step, the simplest form is described here in accordance with the Italian or Cecchetti style. The step begins and ends in fifth position. *Pas de chat* travels in a sideways direction only. It is described thusly:

1. From fifth position with the right foot in back, thrust the right leg to the full *retiré* position. Simultaneously, *demi-plié* on the supporting left leg.

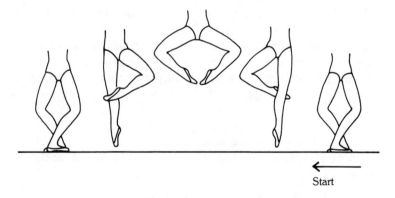

Start

Fig. 4. *Pas de chat*

2. From the *demi-plié,* spring diagonally upward to the right of center. Before the right leg has descended, the left leg "snaps" to a full *retiré* position so that during the *pas de chat,* both legs give the illusion of being momentarily suspended in air.
3. In the landing, the right leg is well turned-out as it arrives in *demi-plié* and the left leg appears to close in fifth position simultaneously with the right.

It should be clear during the practice of *pas de chat* that the position at the apex of the jump and the finish in fifth position are two moments which demand precision. That is, both legs must be in *retiré* at the same moment and the feet almost close at the same time in fifth. These two technical points render the correct symmetrical design to the execution of the step. The physical control necessary to execute the step as such gives the quality of the total movement a particular brilliance. Most importantly, however, is the internal rhythmic structure of the *pas de chat* which is attained when the legs are retracted in the *retiré* position and close in the fifth position. When done without the appearance of the simultaneous arrival at *retiré* and the fifth, the *pas de chat* has a lumbering quality due to the necessary, but all too obvious, shift of weight involved in the execution of the step. The noticeable shift of weight adds an internal beat which is unnecessary and contrary to the visual clarity the step should have. When performed as such, the step appears belabored and awkward.

The Cecchetti method teaches a diminuative version of the step which is usually done at a quicker tempo. In *petit pas de chat,* the feet form the spatial design by moving through the *sur le cou-de-pied* position rather than through the *retiré.*

Like the previous jumping steps, *pas de chat* is practiced in repetition, usually series of four or eight, traveling to each side. At first, the arms are held in a *demi-seconde* position. It is helpful to take advantage of the mirror's visual feedback regarding the design of the step by directing the focus straight ahead. Since *pas de chat* travels sideways, however, it is more appropriate to practice the step with the head turned in profile to the right as the body moves right. The right arm complements this head position by assuming the Italian first position while the left maintains the *demi-seconde.*

Strict reminders to be heeded when practicing the *pas de chat* are as follows:

1. The legs must maintain their turnout with special effort applied at the moment of the *retiré* position.
2. The heels must come down in each fifth position.

A simple combination for *pas de chat* is three successive *pas de chats* and one *changement*. More difficult, but necessary to practice for coordination and strength, is the combination of three *pas de chats* and one *assemblé*.

CHASSÉ EN AVANT

Chassé en avant or *chassé* moving forward is a simple jumping movement which is practiced on the elementary level in a repetitive movement sequence. That is to say, *chassé* is sequentially repeated a number of times and in so doing, the student progresses from one point in space to another.

While *chassé* can be done in various body positions and spatial directions, the beginning student will concentrate on practicing *chassé* moving forward, sideways and backwards only. It is introduced to the student in a diagonal line across the floor from corner 6 to corner 2. (Russian floor plan).

Chassé en avant begins in fifth position with the right foot front. When the left leg draws itself toward the advancing right leg, it gives the visual impression that the left leg is chasing the right leg out of its position. Accordingly, this illusory effect of chasing gives rise to its traditional French name, *chassé*.

1. Stand in fifth position, right foot front, facing the path to be traversed. *Demi-plié* and slide the right foot forward through the fourth position so that the weight transfers to the right leg.
2. At this moment the left leg is free to draw forward to meet the right leg as the body springs *en l'air*. The body must arrive at a level sufficiently elevated off the floor so that the feet and knees are fully stretched. For one instant, both legs are seen tightly held together in fifth position *en l'air*.
3. Having advanced forward in space, both feet land together in fifth position *demi-plié*. The right foot immediately initiates the slide into the next *chassés*. In this manner, the "chain" of *chassés en avant* progresses across the floor.

The *chassé en arrière* (backward) is performed precisely the same, but in the reverse direction. The back leg initiates the movement by sliding backward from its fifth to fourth position and so on.

Chassé is also done at the beginning with the body moving sideways or *de côté* through the second position. *Chassé* done sideways is perhaps the easiest of the three to master in that it basically resembles certain natural childhood play movements. In all the directional variations of *chassé,* once the initial momentum is established in a sequence of *chassés,* the chief problem is to remember to hold the turnout as the legs constantly pass through the fourth or second position and to point the feet when the body is *en l'air.*

Chassé en arrière represents a common difficulty to the student, as do all steps which move backward. The overwhelming feeling of awkwardness while moving backward is an acquired protective device. We do not easily move well when visual knowledge of space is denied us. Since we do not see the area of space we enter when we move backwards, such "blind" spots tend to create a certain amount of inhibition so that steps done *en arrière* are often not danced with full-out effort. Rather, the body attacks these steps with a certain timidity. Often such steps are diminutive in size and appear "marked" rather than danced.

Practice in moving backward in space with assurance and authority is the best preventive or cure for such psycho-motor problems. It is well-known that knowledge (in this case, kinetic awareness) reduces excessive anxiety, thus permitting an inner calm conducive to improvement of motor skills.

Start

Fig. 5. *Two chassés de côté*

The eye focus in these three versions of chassé is straight ahead for both the chassé en avant and en arrière. In chassé moving sideways, the focus corresponds to the sideways line of direction in which the body travels; thus, the head is turned in profile as the eyes focus at a point across the room where the sequence of chassés will take the body.

The port de bras for chassé is often the Italian style fourth position en avant throughout the repetitive sequence of chassé. This is standard classroom usage and desirable since a changing port de bras will invariably keep the body from attaining a solidly-held verticality while en l'air.

ÉCHAPPÉ SAUTÉ

The échappé sauté is a jumping step which starts from fifth position demi-plié, springs (escapes) into a demi-plié in second position and then springs back into the fifth position demi-plié. Échappé may also be performed by springing from the fifth position into the fourth position and back to the fifth position. When done to the second position, the échappé sauté may change feet in the closing fifth position. Échappé sauté is executed as follows:

1. From fifth position demi-plié, spring vertically into the air, fully extending the legs and land in second position demi-plié.
2. From second position, spring back into the air allowing the fully stretched legs to close fifth position demi-plié. The basic port de bras associated with échappé sauté begins with the arms in the preparatory position. They move up through first position and continue out to the second position corresponding with the legs as they land in second position demi-plié. They return to the preparatory position as the legs finish the step in fifth position. At first the eye focus should be straight ahead. Later when the échappé sauté is done with the feet changing the fifth position as they close, the head may be given a subtle but corresponding movement as follows: when the échappé sauté change begins with the right foot front, the head and eye focus moves slightly to the right of center as the body lands in the second position demi-plié. The head and eye focus return to center as the legs change and close to fifth position.

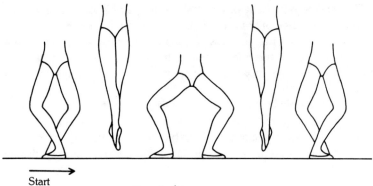

Start

Fig. 6. Échappé sauté

BALLONNÉ

The term *ballonné* suggests the bouce-like quality of movement associated with the step. The basic *ballonné* is appropriately taught to beginners after they are familiar with *assemblé* and *jeté*. *Ballonné* is later done in more complex body positions such as *effacé* and while moving from place to place.

1. The basic *ballonné devant* begins in fifth position, right foot front. The right leg begins the step with a *battement tendu devant,* fully brushing the floor with the working leg. At the same time, the left leg springs *en l'air* from the *demi-plié.*
2. The *ballonné devant* ends by landing on the left leg in *demi-plié* and the right foot comes *sur le cou-de-pied devant.*

In beginning ballet, the *ballonné* is usually practiced in repetitive sequence. When done in succession, the "chain" of *ballonnés* will travel across the floor. Care must be taken that the beginner does not attempt too much distance on each step since the student will lose placement and stability. After the first *ballonné,* each successive *ballonné* begins and ends with the working foot *sur le cou-de-pied.* The leg is actually executing the spatial design of *battement frappé* (minus its flexing action) during each *ballonné.* The term *battement frappé* is used to suggest that the mechanical action and spatial design are similar to the *ballonné* and, thus, helpful in describing it. The significant difference in *frappé* and *ballonné* lies in its rhythmical attack.

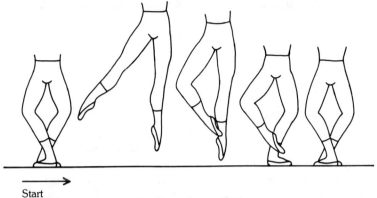

Start

Fig. 7. *Ballonné de côté*

The accent in the *frappé* action is usually outward while the accent in *ballonné* is invariably inward toward the springing leg. It is helpful to think in terms of the first *ballonné* in a series as beginning with a *battement tendu dégagé* with each successive *ballonné* executing a *battement frappé* with the working leg. An excellent practice plan for *ballonné,* after its introduction and initial attempts to perform it in place, is to execute it as follows:

Ballonné devant. The body moves on a diagonal line across the floor beginning from corner 6 to corner 2. The eye focus will be toward corner 2 at first, or in the line of direction. The arms are held in the Italian style third position. Eventually, change the head focus to the mirror or wall 1. This will facilitate learning to do the *ballonné* later in the *effacé* position. The *ballonné* may also be practiced with the working leg moving *à la seconde* while the body travels sideways (*de côté*). The head is then held in profile so that the focus is in the line of direction.

The chief problem in executing the *ballonné* well is having the necessary strength to spring the body off the floor. That is, the supporting leg must work sufficiently so that its foot becomes completely stretched and off the floor at the height of the elevation. *Ballonné derrière* simply reverses the direction of the working of *ballonné devant.* As in all the preceding steps described so far, consistent and careful practice is the only effective means of building strength and perfecting the step.

In intermediate work, the *grand ballonné* is added to the student's repertory of ballet steps. It is mechanically identical in its operation to the basic *ballonné*. It differs in that it is spatially large because the extended working leg lifts *devant* or *à la seconde* to waist level and retracts to the knee instead of *sur le cou-de-pied*.

EMBOÎTÉ

Emboîté, literally "boxed in" or fitted tightly together, is a small jumping step usually done in a series of two or more while traveling forward. The term *emboîté* refers to the closely-knit relationship maintained by one foot to the other during the step. In *emboîté*, the feet continuously change in the *cou-de-pied* position and come *devant* as the weight on the supporting foot alternates. The step is described as follows:

Begin in fifth position, right foot front. *Demi-plié* and spring into the air bringing the left foot forward *sur le cou-de-pied devant*. The left foot holds this position as the right leg lands in *demi-plié*. From this position, the step immediately repeats on the alternate side by springing onto the left foot and landing in *demi-plié* while the right foot comes forward of the left foot *sur le cou-de-pied devant*. *Emboîté* may also be danced *en arrière* by precisely reversing the position of the free foot to the *cou-de-pied derrière*.

Emboîté en tournant (boxed in while turning) is not generally considered a part of beginning ballet work since all turning movements

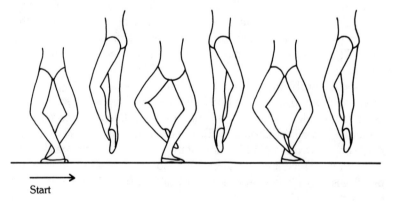

Start

Fig. 8. Emboîté en tournant

require the ability to "spot". However, *emboîté* is most often choreo-graphically used in its turning form rather than its elementary form. As a turning step, *emboîté* involves a half-turn of the body on each *emboîté*. Since *emboîté en tournant* is almost always done in a series of two or more, the visual effect is a turning progression of little jumps. In all forms of *emboîté*, special care must be taken to maintain the turnout.

SISSONNE

The adult student is generally ready to attempt the basic forms of *sissonne* after the material of a complete beginning class is familiar. Al-though not historically documented, the term *sissonne* may derive its name from the inventor of the step. The simplest form, the *sissonne simple,* is a spring from two feet that lands on one foot and does not travel. Both feet push from fifth position *demi-plié* into the air. While in the air, the legs are held fully stretched and together. At the moment of landing, one foot comes *sur le cou-de-pied, devant* or *derrière*. The step, literally a hopping movement, is repeated by springing from one foot and landing on the same foot.

The movement of the *sissonne simple* is also commonly referred to as *temps levé* in the Cecchetti method. Many teachers who essentially teach the Russian style additionally use the term *temps levé* for the sake of clarity. The meaning of *temps levé*, raised time or raised step, clearly describes the movement. Also, the usage of *temps levé* rather than *sissonne simple* alleviates possible confusion when the more substantial movement of the *sissonne fermée* and *sissone ouverte*, are introduced to the student.

Sissonne Fermée

Sissonne fermée, closed *sissonne*, is basically a spring from two feet in fifth position *demi-plié* and a descent from the spring into fifth posi-tion *demi-plié*. In the process of execution of *sissonne fermée,* the body travels forward (*en avant*), sideways (*de côté*), or backwards (*en arrière*) to a different place of landing. *Sissonne fermée en avant* is described as follows: Start from fifth position, right foot front; the focus is forward with the arms held in *demi-seconde*.

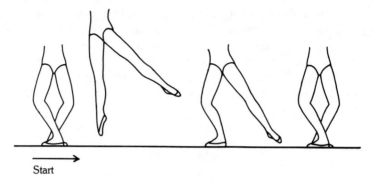

Start

Fig. 9. *Sissonne fermée en avant*

1. *Demi-plié* and spring from both feet upward and forward. The forward movement will cause the left leg to thrust back into a fourth position *en l'air*, i.e., the leg's position in *arabesque*.
2. The body will land on the right foot in *demi-plié* and as quickly as possible the left leg will close into fifth position. It is imperative that the legs close as quickly as possible. While it is illusion only, the visual effect of the step should be that the legs close simultaneously in fifth position.

Sissonne fermée de côté, sissonne closed, moving sideways, is described a follows: Start from fifth position, right foot front; the focus is forward and arms in *demi-seconde*.

1. *Demi-plié* and spring from both feet upward and sideways to the right. The spring will cause the left leg to thrust *en l'air* to a *demi-seconde* position of the leg.
2. The body begins to land on the right leg in *demi-plié* and the left follows by meeting the right leg, closing into fifth position. This step can be done beginning with either foot in front in the fifth position and executing the *sissonne* to either side.

Sissonne changée de côté is done precisely the same as *sissonne fermée de côté* except that the fifth position changes its front foot, *dessus* or *dessous*, at the finish of the step as the legs close into fifth position.

Sissonne fermée en arrière, closed *sissonne* moving backward, is performed precisely the same as *sissonne fermée en avant* except that the initial spring is upward and backward causing the front leg in the fifth position to thrust *à la quatrième en l'air.*

Sissonne Ouverte

Sissonne ouverte, open *sissonne,* differs from *sissonne fermée* in that the legs do not finish the step by closing in fifth position. As the landing takes place on the first leg, the other remains poised in the open position which was momentarily achieved during the jump. *Sissonne ouverte* can be done in the following ways: traveling forward *(en avant)* with the extended leg thrusting to the back in the *arabesque* position *(à la quatrième derrière)*; sideways *(de côté)* with the opened leg thrusting to the side *(à la seconde)*; backwards *(en arrière)* with the extended leg thrusting front *(à la quatrième devant)*.

What has been described for the *sissonne fermée* is substantially the basic kinetic material which applies to the numerous varieties of the *sissonne* movement. Each form of *sissonne* involves subtle changes of *épaulement,* changes of direction, and the embellishment of beats. There are also compound forms of *sissonne* which include turns and auxiliary movements. In addition, *sissonne* movements vary in size. Whether the *sissonne* is large or small depends on the amount of musical time allotted to it. For example, one measure of moderate waltz time will allow for the execution of a very large *sissonne* while a small *sissonne* can be accomplished on a quarter note.

The technical problem most common in the *sissonne fermée* or *ouverte* is the superfluous and unaesthetic involvement of the upper back in the step. This fault is characterized by the chest uncontrollably lurching forward in the *sissonne en avant* or collapsing in the *sissonne en arrière.* The *sissonne* movement is basically the work of the legs which spring the body *en l'air* as well as create the visual design. The spine should not visually reflect the action of the legs. Instead, the firmly held back is what gives solidity and authority to the *sissonne* movement.

In *sissone ouverte,* the leg which opens and establishes the position must retain the initial height of the leg for as long as the position is held. That is, the leg must not be allowed to "bounce" in the attempt to hold it in position. Establishing good motor habits by careful and knowledgeable practice of this particular aspect of *sissonne* will prove to be invaluable as the student progresses. A simple, yet helpful, combination of *sissonne ouverte en avant* and *assemblé derrière* can help ingrain an efficient motor habit. As the body springs into the *sissonne ouverte,* the extended leg must hold the position so that the following *assemblé derrière,* which acts to close the *sissonne's* open position, begins at the same height and place. The correct practice of this combination is designed to inculcate adequate muscular control in the back, which is necessary to avoid a bouncing, extended leg. Another problem the student encounters in mastering the *sissonne ouverte* and *fermée* is the maintenance of fully arched feet. The feet begin stretching the *pointes* as soon as they begin to leave the ground. The feet maintain the arched position and only relinquish their stretch gradually, as each portion of each foot meets the floor upon landing. The technical use of the feet in this manner contributes a refined and desirable quality to the flow of the movement. It also produces the desired balletic design of fully extended legs from hip to toe. This is especially significant in terms of the empathic-kinetic impact the movement has on the spectator. For instance, lack of technique exemplified by unstretched knees and feet gives the visual impression of devitalized and unfulfilled movement, and this same impression can be perceived by the spectator.

FAILLI

Failli is a simple, yet subtle, jumping movement with a fleeting quality. It is done in one count. The step involves a change of direction from *crosié* or *de face* to *effacé* or vice versa, and it is embellished with épaulement. Therefore, the step is part of the work of the student who approaches the intermediate level.

1. Begin *de face* in fifth position with the right foot front. *Demi-plié* and spring vertically upward with the legs held tightly together.
2. While in the air, turn the torso to the right of center from *de face* to *effacé.* The left shoulder moves slightly forward. At the same moment, the head turns slightly toward the left shoulder. At the highest point of the movement's trajectory, the left leg opens behind (*effacé derrière*) the body.

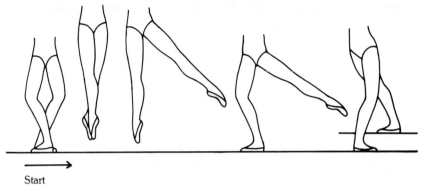

Start

Fig. 10. *Failli*

3. The descent occurs as the right leg lands in *demi-plié;* the left leg moves forward through the first position *demi-plié* and on to form the fourth position *croisé*. As the body descends into the fourth position *croisé*, the left shoulder stays slightly forward and the head remains inclined slightly toward the left shoulder.

   During *failli*, the arms execute a subtle breathing-like movement which resembles the inhalation-exhaustion quality of movement of the rib cage. In a small, quick *failli*, the arms open from preparatory position to *demi-seconde* and return to their original preparatory position. If the *failli* is done as a larger movement, they may move proportionately from the *demi-seconde* to a full *seconde* position and finish in the *demi-seconde*. While *failli* may seem kinetically easy at first attempt, the difficulty involved in perfecting the step indicates otherwise. The sensitive use of *effacé* and *croisé* body directions and the use of *épaulement* provide a subtle quality of movement which relegates *failli* to an intermediate level of ballet.

BATTERIE

A beginning adult class in ballet would not be complete from an educational point of view without some elemental experience of *pas batterie* or beaten steps. *Batterie* is a generic term applied to all movements in *allégro* where the legs beat together. In *allégro* work, *these percussive little movements result from the tautly held legs beating to-*

gether while the body is at the height of a jump's trajectory. Beaten steps add visual and rhythmic interest to allégro steps.

A less common form of *batterie* is occasionally displayed in nonjumping movements when one leg beats against the other. For example, in the *petit* or *grand adage, batterie* movements are executed with one foot vibrating in a beat-like action against the supporting leg. This is often done with the beating leg in the *cou-de-pied* position while the supporting leg is *en pointe.*

Vaganova lists three categories of beats:

1. *Pas batterie* includes any *allégro* step that is embellished with beats. This category includes such steps as: *assemblé battu, jeté battu,* and *échappé battu.*
2. *Entrechat* includes those steps which consist of interweaving movements created when the dancer jumps into the air and both legs beat by quickly crossing in front and behind each other before landing in fifth. The *entrechat* is done on more advanced levels with a consecutive accumulation of beats before the landing. Starting with the *royale,* this primary form of *entrechat* is followed by *entrechat trois, entrechat quatre, entrechat cinq, entrechat six, entrechat sept, entrechat huit, entrechat neuf,* and *entrechat dix. Entrechat* is generally done in place, although a series of *entrechat* may travel forward, backward, or diagonally.
3. *Brisé,* which includes several variations, forms the third category of beaten movements. The *brisé* is actually an *assemblé* movement done with beats and it may or may not travel in various directions. Due to considerable technical requirements, the *brisé* is not part of beginning ballet.

In accordance with the objectives of this book, only the *royale,* and the *entrechat quatre* from the *entrechat* category and the *échappé battu* from the *pas battu* category will be discussed.

ROYALE

Royale is the simplest form of beaten movement from the *entrechat* category and often the first beaten step to be learned, since *royale* is a *changement* embellished with a beat, it belongs theoretically in the category of *pas batterie.* However, it is also the precursor of all *entre-*

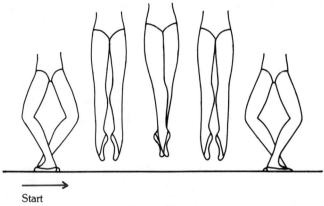

Start

Fig. 11. *Royale*

chat movements so that Vaganova has listed *royale* in the *entrechat* category. Since *royale* is essentially the *changement* step that has been previously learned, it is the wisest choice of beating steps to attempt in terms of a "sampling" experience. It will be recalled by the student that *changement* is a jumping movement from fifth position and, after the highest elevation point has been reached, the legs change position before landing in fifth position. In the *royale,* the straightened legs beat together one time at the highest point of elevation before the feet change position in the air. The beat must be felt on the inside of the thighs rather than on the calves and must never appear to be done solely by the feet.

The arms may be held in the preparatory position throughout a series of *royale.* At first the student will be so occupied in accomplishing the leg movement of the *royale* that the head and focus will simply be *de face.* Later, shoulder movement of *épaulement* will be added to give the simplicity of a series of *royales* greater visual interest and a softer kinetic quality. Visual interest is increased when the subtle turning of the upper body causes light to fall differently on its form, softening and shading the sculptured design presented by the body. *Épaulement* also produces an actual change in kinetic quality. The delicate oppositional pull that is present in all *épaulement* movement is natural to the counterbalancing tendencies inherent in the moving body.

It is necessary when first attempting the beating movement in the *royale* (and all other *batterie* steps) to experience the kinetic and tactile sensation associated with the step. As aids in identifying the kinetic and tactile sensation while attempting the step, the following two methods are used:

1. Stand facing the barre in fifth position with both hands on the barre. During each *royale,* allow the arms to support the weight of the body by pressing downward against the barre as the body springs into the air. During the jump, the legs are fixed in the air so that they can "beat" unencumbered by the body weight. Practiced in this manner, the student has time to place the beat high on the inner thigh area. It is also important during the actual beat that each leg exert the same force against the other so that the effort is not made by one leg while the other becomes passive. If this should happen, the passive leg will release its straight knee and bend under the force of the other leg, causing the step to be ineptly performed. Experience bears out that poorly executed steps invariably invite injury.

   Through the above approach to *royale,* the student can focus attention on identifying the kinetic-tactile sensations associated with the *royale* without having to deal with gravity, that is, landing before the correctly formed "beat" is executed and felt. Once the full sensation of "beating" is learned, it is more easily transferred to other steps such as the *assemblé* and *jeté.*

2. A less orthodox, but more elementary, approach to learning the sensations associated with beats is often helpful. It is as follows: From a supine position, roll upward so that the shoulders, elbows and hands are supporting the vertically aligned body. The legs are held together in fifth position, feet pointed and placed directly over the shoulder area. Change the fifth position of the legs in a small scissor-like action, allowing each change to form a beating together of the legs at a point above the backs of the knees. Not only does this method allow for experiencing the kinetic-tactile beating sensation without jumping, it has the advantage of supplying visual reinforcement to the student.

Royale is generally practiced in series of 8 or 16. It can be combined with *changement* and *grand échappé* for the intermediate beginner. All-out effort is needed for the practice of *royale* and its associated steps. For this reason, a series of *royale* and *changement* is that part of *allégro* practice generally saved for the closing moments of the class.

At this time, the last vestiges of energy can be used on such jumps without fear of debilitating the student for other movement.

ENTRECHAT QUATRE

The *entrechat quatre* done correctly allows the student to experience a touch of brilliance and virtuosity even on the beginning level.
  Start with fifth position, right foot front.

1. Form a *demi-plié*.
2. Spring, upward and slightly open the legs.
3. Beat the legs together, right leg in back.
4. Open the legs and finish in *demi-plié* fifth position, right foot in front. Impossible as it may seem to the student, these four separate movements of the *entrechat quatre* occur on one count of music.

ÉCHAPPÉ BATTU

Échappé battu is a beaten form of *échappe sauté* previously described. From fifth position *demi-plié* with the right foot front, spring into the air and land in second position *demi-plié*. From second position, spring again into the air and beat the right leg in front of the left

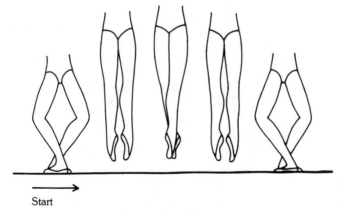

Start

Fig. 12. *Entrechat quatre*

leg before landing in fifth position *demi-plié* with the right leg in back. The tautly held legs should exert equal force in forming the beat. The dancer must strive to place the beat high in the leg. The arm movement for *échappé battu* is the same as for *échappé sauté*, described earlier in this chapter. Since the feet change in this step, the head response to *épaulement* movement in a series of *échappé battus*. That is, after arriving in the second position *demi-plié* on the first *échappé battu,* the head moves slightly to the left of center and the left shoulder moves slightly forward. This head movement is coordinated with the left leg coming front as the legs close the step fifth position.

Strictly speaking, *épaulement* movement does not come under the domain of basic material for the beginning student. However, as the student approaches the beginning-intermediate levels, where initial experience of *batterie* movements such as *royale, entrechat quatre,* and *échappé battu* occur, the concept of *épaulement* becomes relevant to the increasingly difficult movement material.

CHAPTER 17

The Grand Allégro: Leaps and Jumps

The technical information discussed up to this point represents a considerable amount of balletic material. The majority of beginning ballet college students will not have the opportunity to pursue the more difficult aspects of many of the exercises and steps due to limited time imposed by the academic structure. On the other hand they will often achieve a level of proficiency in ballet fundamentals which will allow them to experience certain aspects of intermediate work. While the more difficult material is generally executed with imperfect results, "the feeling of dancing" is an invaluable adventure for the career-minded student or the balletomane. Therefore, the beginning student is usually presented with the basic leaps and jumps of *grand allégro* work.

As the student begins to enter the intermediate levels of ballet study, the fundamentals are still practiced and become so instilled that they seem easy. The more demanding aspects of the exercises and steps become a fresh challenge. In time, the steadily perfected building blocks of technique begin to emerge as a sturdy foundation.

Concomitant with the progression of technical skills are the specialized activities of separate classes. The intermediate female dancer will be exposed to point work and the male dancer to special men's classes. Ultimately, the advanced levels of ballet will involve the study of partnering or *pas de deux*.

The *grand allégro* occurs during the last part of the ballet class in which the dancer is expected to expend the remainder of his energy. This closing portion of the ballet class emphasizes large jumping steps which are primarily designed to encompass as much space as possible. These are total body movements which cut through space in both horizontal and vertical thrusts of energy. They include such steps as *grand jeté, grand jeté en tournant,* and *fouetté en l'air.*

GRAND JETÉ

The adjective "grand" specifically indicates that the angle formed by the legs during the leap is 90° or greater. In the actual movement, two kinecepts are combined; that is, "big jumping step from one foot to the other" and "thrown movement" result in a large leap or *grand jeté*. The student approaches intermediate work when he is balletically equipped to meet the demands of the first attempts at *grand jeté*. Months of barre work must prepare and strengthen the feet, legs and back so that they can propel the body into the air and controllably sustain it as it lands. *Grand jeté* is not necessarily a part of beginning ballet work, especially for the adult, but it is occasionally introduced depending on the class's rate of progress.

To give the student the greatest possible kinetic experience, the *grand jeté* is often accompanied by three additional running steps, making a four count pattern. The pattern consists of a leap onto the right leg followed by three running steps on the left, right, and left foot.

During the moment of the *grand jeté* both legs are expected to be straight in the air while the three running steps are always in *demi-plié*. The leaping leg is "thrown" into the air as in a *grand battement* while the other leg pushes upward from its *plié,* through the foot, and then straightens as it leaves the floor.

Although the leap itself is straight-legged, it lands in a *demi-plié* position as the foot touches the floor. The landing must be quick and pliable, which demands strength and control. The landing in the *grand jeté* is always more difficult and potentially injurious than the ascendency of the leaping movement.

GRAND JETÉ DESSUS EN TOURNANT

The *grand jeté dessus en tournant* means a large leap executed with a turn. It is commonly referred to in the United States as *"tour jeté,"* this name being a grammatical corruption of the original terminology. While its full and correct execution is beyond the capability of the beginner, its mechanics and spatial pattern are introduced as the student approaches the intermediate level. It is described as follows:

1. Facing the front of the room, stand on the left leg, pointing the right leg behind. Arms are held as in second arabesque. Step back-

Fig. 1 *Grand Jeté Dessus en Tournant*

wards onto the right foot moving to *demi-plié*. Allow the body to rotate one half of a turn to face this new line of direction.

2. Sharply lift the leg front as in *grand battement devant*. The arms simultaneously move through the preparatory to the fifth position *en haut.*

3. Immediately push off the floor and *directly upward* through the *plié* of the right leg.

4. The body rotates another half turn in the air as the legs simultaneously exchange their positions in a scissors-like action.

5. The body lands on the leg which executed the *grand battement*. It must land silently in a *demi-plié* while the general body position is in first or second *arabesque*.

Second position *arabesque* is usually recommended for the landing position since the formation of these arms aid in maintaining square placement. The *arabesque* leg will have a tendency to bounce or drop completely upon landing. This should not be permitted because the step then becomes incorrect as well as heavy and awkward. Rather, the strength of the back must be used to hold the leg in its extended position.

GRAND FOUETTÉ

The *grand fouetté*, translated as "whipped in the air", is a large jumping movement on one leg while the other thrusts upward in a *grand battement* to the front direction. At the height of the jump and the *grand battement,* the torso rotates in the hip socket making one half turn. Due to the rotary movement of the torso, the body position becomes first *arabesque* which is also the landing position of the *fouetté.*

To execute *grand fouetté* follow the five point procedure for the *grand jeté dessus en tournant* but omit the change of supporting leg in point 4. Like the *grand jeté en tournant,* the *grand fouetté* is part of intermediate level ballet. The step is only mentioned here as some indication of the path of technical progression which must be pursued by the beginner who wishes to continue further in his study of ballet. *Fouetté* can also be executed with *piqué* or *relevé* movement instead of the *sauté.*

GRANDE SISSONNE

The *grande sissonne à la seconde* is the largest of the numerous varieties of *sissonne.* That is, the body covers the maximum space during the execution of the step.

Standing *de face* in fifth position, right foot front, move to a *demi-plié.* From both legs jump vertically, drawing the right leg to a *retiré* position as the left leg extends to a full height second position. The arms simultaneously pass from the preparatory position to the second, third or fifth position. The step is often compounded by closing back to the fifth position from the full-height second with a *sauté* movement. In this case the arms would move back to their beginning position.

Grande sissonne largely depends for its successful execution on massive strength. Not only must the criteria for the correct body positions be met, but the dancer must strive with optimum effort to jump as high as possible and to land as softly as possible. Consecutively performed *grandes sissonnes* are kinetically exciting for the dancer as he experiences this out-of-the-ordinary use of space. The tendency is often for the dancer to enjoy the feeling of the movement to the disparagement of meticulous technical care. Repetition of the step should therefore be limited and based on the relative strength of the class.

GRAND ÉCHAPPÉ

The beginning ballet student will accomplish this *grand allégro* move-ment sooner than the other four discussed in this chapter. It is per-formed in the same manner as the *échappé sauté* in *petit allégro* ex-cept that it moves through more space by the fact that it is a maximum effort jump. Due to the height achievable in the *grand échappé* the legs must be kept together in a tight fifth position as the body propels itself upward and only when the body descends do the legs open in second position. The arms follow the same pattern as in the *échappé sauté*.

General Comments on Grand Allégro

Due to the characteristic largeness of *grand allégro* steps, even the well-placed student has a tendency to execute them with excessive abandon and thus runs the risk of slipshod dancing. In particular, college students seem to enjoy uppermost the *grand allégro* section of the ballet class. The pleasurable sensations resulting from one's own leaps darting through space create an exalted feeling of self-propulsion. At such times one tends to forget that one is also prac-ticing a precisely controlled physical activity and of necessity must continue to adhere to the rigors of technical correctness. For this rea-son, the steps which comprise the early work in *grand allégro* move-ment are not usually compounded with additional steps other than auxiliary or linking movements. Rather, in early practice they are done successively in place such as a series of *grands échappés* or suc-cessively across the room such as *grands jetés* linked with *pas couru; grands jetés dessus en tournant* linked with *chassé; grands jetés fouettés* linked with *glissade; grandes sissonnes* linked with *coupé as-semblé*. Repetition as such allows for ideal motor learning in that the continuous sensations of good and bad technical habits can be more readily identified and retained or identified and corrected.

At the same time it would be wrong if the emphasis on technical ex-actitude were to imply that the enjoyment of *grand allégro* movement was inappropriate or even detrimental to the dance student. On the contrary, the positive physical excitement which accompanies *grand allégro* provides an important aspect of the student's dance and life experience. It quickly becomes apparent that all the months of effort at the barre and the center exercises have culminated in a highly specialized and formally systematized skill. Perseverance and patience and very hard work have opened up a new door. Such self-realization gives the professionally minded dance student fresh incentive to continue the arduous pursuit of excellence. It also teaches the student the rudimentary performing value of projecting his experience and expression of joy in movement to an audience. For the dance student with other career objectives in mind, the self-realization obtained through the study of ballet offers conceptual awareness of the process of achievement which is happily transferable to other endeavors.

INTRODUCTION TO POINT WORK

Even before the beginning of ballet study the female student is usually attracted by the prospect of dancing *sur les pointes*. The allure of the rather mechanical feat that dancing on point is, has always been a magical attraction for all ages of students. The glamour of the seemingly tiny satin shoes, the accomplishment of defying gravity by sustaining one's self on the very tips of the feet, the inevitable association of being close to the heart of the ballet when one arrives at the level of point work, all contribute to the enchantment which the student experiences. Indeed, one only has to watch a ballet performance once to draw the conclusion that this aspect of ballet techniques must not only be the most difficult but also the most beautiful. However, after the first point class, most students reëvaluate these initial impressions of point work, so great is their shock that so much beauty must of necessity be grounded in such misery! In most cases, this, happily is a temporary feeling. The first sensations of the hard shoe, the new stresses placed upon the foot structure and the raw blisters on the toe knuckles subside with a few more classes. Like all the other aspects of one's developing technique, it becomes understood that point work is just one more difficult skill to accomplish and the end result is its own sparkling reward.

POINT SHOES

After two years of continuous ballet classes the female student is theoretically prepared for point work. Some adult students may take less preparation depending on their degree of natural aptitude i.e., muscular coordination, leg strength, finely arched feet.

The preparation of proper fitting point shoes is prerequisite to the first class. The universally admired American-made point shoes come in varying shapes and strengths so that the adult beginner has point shoes available to her which will give the necessary support. As the total body strength develops, the dancer gradually works toward lighter and less restrictive shoes. In the United States point shoes are marked from 2 to 2 ½ sizes smaller than a street shoe. The point shoe should fit snuggly but must not allow the toes to overlap or the foot to be cramped. The shoes are worn with a small amount of lamb's wool wrapped about the toe knuckles. Each shoe is made with a drawstring which helps to secure its fit around the foot. The student must sew on her own ribbons and heel elastics according to the teacher's directions. Usually, each pair of point shoes comes with a brochure giving this and additional information.

Due to the materials in the point shoes' construction, they absorb the moisture from foot perspiration and must be dried out after each lesson. Care of point shoes consists of placing them in an airy place to dry after which the heels are folded inward and the ribbons are then wrapped around them.

It is difficult to precisely date the first appearance of point work although it was probably sometime between 1810 and 1820. It was not until after 1870 that the first blocked point shoes were designed, which is to say that for half a century a dancer had to use her own unaided powers to rise *sur les pointes* in her soft-soled satin slippers. A number of these shoes belonging to the early 19th century ballerinas can be seen presently in the museums and library collections of theatrical memorabilia around the world. With the exception of finely stitched darning about the toes of these shoes, they were identical with the party shoes of the day. Similarly, the shoes were tinted to match a costume as they would have a ball gown.

The interest aroused by the feat of point dancing insured its continued presence and caused changes to be made in the soft slippers so that they would facilitate the efforts of the wearer. As a consequence the structure of the point shoe has been continuously evolving wherever ballet exists and numerous versions of the hard soled, boxed toe shoe have been developed.

BASIC BARRE EXERCISES
SUR LES POINTES

From the beginning it is important for the dancer to think of the point shoe as being part of one's foot in the way a sock takes on the shape of the foot and feels a oneness with it. Too, it is most helpful for the student to adopt the mental attitude that she is in command of her shoes and not the other way around. Lack of a firmly established positive mind-set about point work can delay progress here as anywhere else. That point work is initially painful and that there will always be the threat of bothersome blisters is a foregone conclusion that one learns to accept if one is going to pursue the ballet art. If the student has had the proper prerequisite training and her feet are normally structured with an average or highly arched ankle and metatarsal, there should be minimal discomfort. On the other hand, if the student has very little or no arch in the ankle and metatarsal area, point work will be most difficult under any circumstance. Extremely uneven toes also render point work chronically difficult.

Relevés in First Position

The introduction to point work always begins with the student facing and holding onto the barre as the exercises are performed. From first position with all the toes flat inside the shoe, the knees taut and the thighs pulled up, the dancer slowly rises through the foot to the *demi-pointe* position and continues on up to the full *en pointe* placement of the feet. The movement is then completed by allowing the feet to retrace their path and lower back to the first position. This is usually done 4 to 8 times the first class. The same exercise is then done 4 to 8 times in the second position, again facing the barre.

Pliés en Relevé

The next exercise adds a *demi-plié* at the peak of the rising movement. The student rolls up through the half to the full point and executes a *demi-plié* while at the same time maintaining the turnout by pressing the heels forward. As the legs stretch out of the *plié,* the dancer attempts to hold the heels forward. The feet then lower back to the first position. This exercise is done 4 to 8 times and is then repeated in second position.

The purpose of this exercise is to stretch the top of the foot from ankle joint to the metatarsal so that the foot can learn to form the same shape in point shoes as it has learned to do in soft ballet slippers. If a student has a highly developed arch or an extremely flexible one, this exercise must be modified so that the ankle joint bends slightly, thus keeping the feet from stretching beyond what is technically required. At this juncture it is also important to resist the tendency to allow the body weight to sink into the shoes. The student must be ever mindful of pulling up and out of the shoes by using the muscular tension so carefully practiced in the early ballet classes.

Demi-plié Relevé

Another point exercise combines a simple *demi-plié* in first position and from the depth of the position, the dancer uses a springing action (Italian School) to rise on full point. Likewise, this is done 4 to 8 times in first and second position. As in all *plié relevé* movements it is mandatory that the heels are solidly on the floor in the depth of the *demi-plié.*

Sous-Sus

In the course of the first point classes, this *plié-relevé* is also done in the fifth position and is referred to as *sous-sus.* In this movement both legs must draw tightly together as the dancer springs upward from the *plié.* Adding a slight impetus to the upward effort, the step may also move forward, backward or sideways.

Échappé Sur Les Pointes

The logical development of the point exercises at the barre leads to *échappé* with the *relevé* being performed *en pointe.* Again, the technical rules require that the heels are solidly on the floor in the *demi-plié,* that the legs escape to the *relevé en pointe* with a springing action, that the knees and thighs are pulled taut and that the dancer pulls up and out of the shoes.

Relevé Sur Le Cou-de-pied

So far, the student has experienced rising to the points from both feet. Rising onto the point of one leg only is far more difficult, demanding considerable strength, proper vertical alignment and firm horizontal placement. The student stands on the supporting leg with the other *sur le cou-de-pied.* After four *pliés relevés* in this position she transfers the weight to the other leg and repeats the exercise. The shoulder girdle should not be allowed to move upward during the exercise as is the natural tendency but the strength for the movement should come from the *plié*.

Battement Retiré Sur Les Pointes

To increase the challenge the dancer next approaches the *battement retiré* which is combined with a *demi-plié* and a spring to *relevé en pointe*. This is first approached by repeating the movement 4 times on each leg changing the fifth positions, and then alternating the step from one leg to the other. When alternating the *retiré*, the body will move forward or backward depending on which foot begins the movement. Since the dancer is still facing the barre, 4 *battements retirés en pointe* forward and 4 backward are usually all the space allows.

As the student progresses these exercises are combined to increase their motor complexity. Shortly, the same exercises are executed simply and then in combination in the center of the studio after they are done at barre. Simple *port de bras* is added.

Barre en Pointe

In the next stages the student graduates to a full barre designed just for the development of point work. Ideally, a full class in soft shoes precedes this style of point class. The dancer moves through the complete barre from *pliés* in all positions, *battlements tendus, ronds de jambe*, etc. The exercises are all laced with movements such as *relevé* and *sous-sus*.

After some months to one year the dancer attempts simple steps on point or wherever in the classical movements a *demi-pointe* can be replaced by the full extension of the foot *en pointe*. Such material is based on *pas de bourrée, piqué tourné, pas de bourrée couru, battement retiré*, and *piqué arabesque*. Eventually, the entire vocabulary of ballet is performed on the points. In movements such as the *grand allégro* presents, the leaping and jumping movements, while not on point, are nevertheless done in point shoes and the whole problem of landing correctly and quietly is tackled.

Point Shoes and the Male Dancer

Occasionally, teachers will request male dancers with poorly formed feet to don point shoes and practice the most basic point exercises. It would appear that the technical results have rarely equaled the effort involved. However, for those male dancers planning to teach classical ballet and to choreograph in the classical style, such an attempt provides invaluable first hand experience of what is essentially the domain of the female with whose technical needs he will be dealing.

MEN'S CLASS

The earliest formal ballet classes for males date back to the days of Beauchamp when only men were officially allowed to participate in theatrical productions. It will be remembered that the female roles in ballets were traditionally done in travesty. As times changed and the ballet profession developed, women began to infiltrate the professional ranks and even proved they were capable of the same movements as were male dancers once their heeled shoes and voluminous skirts were modified. Technique classes were therefore opened to the female dancer and the classes became mixed in the early 18th century. Soon, however, pedagogical discoveries raised the level of technical expectations so that the differences between the male and female balletic physique became more pronounced. Ambitious dancers would often seek out ballet masters for private lessons to refine their special abilities. Great dance personalities likewise invested themselves in expanding the physical boundaries of the art as when Gaetan Vestris tutored his inimitable son, Auguste, and Noverre gave special work to his protegée, Le Picq.

With the development of government subsidized ballet schools came the inclusion of special classes for men since it was deemed necessary to develop the unique aspects of the male dancer's technique. In fact, from the beginning of training, the children's classes in these state schools have always been separated. Unfortunately, during the period of the Romantic ballet, the tradition of the separate male class died out except for those in Russia and Denmark. Today, however, men's classes may be found in many public and private ballet schools.

In men's class, great emphasis is placed on the maximum use of the male's strength. Due to the nature of the material covered, only high level intermediate and advanced dancers should participate in such classes. All aspects of ballet technique dealing with *tour de force* and *bravura* elements are studied since these are what distinguish him from the female dancer. Such steps are generally found in the areas of *pirouettes*, and the *petit* and *grand allégro*.

During a given men's class, the dancer will first practice the complete barre and center work. These exercises may be modified to an extent so that they prepare the dancer for the vigorous classical steps to come. These include such movements as: *grandes pirouettes à la seconde, double sauts de basques, tours en l'air, entrechat huit*, and other *petit* and *grand allégro* steps embellished with beats and maximum elevation.

Where separate men's classes are not offered, the male dancer in an intermediate or advanced class will be given one or two of the above movements to practice while the female members are donning their point shoes for an equally brief practice at the end of a general class. The male combinations are given at a slower tempo to allow for greater elevation and the music is often given a stronger beat to emphasize the masculine quality in turns. Thus, for a brief 15–20 minutes at the end of a class, many teachers give alternating specialized classical movements for the male and female contingents in the class.

The great 20th century teacher, Asaf Messerer, cautions that when classes are mixed, the combinations must be carefully built so that men and women can perform them equally well. Within a given combination, he suggests that women, for example, be given *pirouettes* if a *tour en l'air* is included or that a man be given *pirouettes* if *chaînés* are a part of the dance phrase. In other words, he advises that movements suitable to each sex can be devised so that both male and female have the opportunity to work on what is more exclusively his or her domain.

PAS DE DEUX

The study of the art of *pas de deux* or partnering requires that both dancers are thoroughly grounded in ballet technique and are working correctly on an advanced level. The woman must be strong on point and have good placement and balance. The man must have a particularly strong back and sufficiently developed shoulder and arm muscles so that he can execute his supporting movements without strain. The various forms of gymnastic exercises such as "push-ups" and "pull-ups" are recommended to train his torso accordingly.

Pas de deux has often been described as a conversation in movement between two people. Not only should it be a polite conversation, it can be, and often is, a dance of love. The common sharing in the creation of beautiful movement must be based on respect and trust in each other's work. The male should reflect the manly qualities of pride in his graceful partner and must exhibit an unselfish giving of his presence to show her at her best. The female, in turn, should respond by being considerate and helpful in the technical aspects. At the same time, she must let her partner sense that she trusts him with the support of her body. Her femininity should show itself by expressing that she is ever aware of her partner being the cause of her special aesthetic impact during the dance for two. If there is not perfect harmony between the dancers during practice it will effect their progress in partnering. Personality conflicts will hinder the appropriate flow of movement as well as interrupt the vital tactile relationship between the two dancers.

While it would seem ideal if the male dancer were at least five inches taller than his partner, it is not always necessary as many superb partnering relationships in the ballet world have demonstrated. Rather, it is the dancer's tightly knit understanding of each other's love of what they are about in a *pas de deux*, their mutual trust and respect for each other's artistry, and a caring and careful tactile relationship based on a highly developed sensitivity toward each other's ever-shifting body weights and masses.

The primary classes in *pas de deux* work concentrate on the male learning to feel the female's balance first on both points and then on one. He learns the correct placement of his hands at her waist and how to hold her hands to support her balance in *arabesques* and *attitudes*. He also learns how to prepare himself in *demi-plié* to elevate her in simple lifts. For the female dancer, the primary classes consist of learning how to rely on the support of her partner without being so physically dependent on him that he becomes the initiator of her movement. It is imperative that the girl recognize from the start that in *pas de deux* work she must still do her own dancing and that her partner is there to complement her work in providing the unique contribution of his maleness. Actually the girl needs considerable strength to balance on point while placing her hand in his. Not only must she be able to hold her own position, which is rooted in spinal strength, but she must be able to provide the proper amount of muscular contraction in the arm she extends to her partner lest the position disintegrate at the moment of contact.

Too often *pas de deux* is not actually rendered as a dance of two but is presented as a female soloist accomplishing amazing feats by means of a human crane. When this approach occurs between dancers, innocently or not, all possibility of art is lost and the dance itself becomes meaningless except for its shape of contrasting body designs and rhythms. The lack of human rapport renders the dance plastic geometry and interesting, only if this meets the choreographic intent at the outset.

Upon acquisition of the most fundamental kinecepts of partnering, the dancers attempt supported *pirouettes,* simple *promenades en pointe* where the boy revolves the girl on point while she holds a classical position such as first *arabesque,* and more of the simpler forms of lifts. Since it is assumed that the dancers already command fairly advanced techniques, their progress is often swift. As on each level of balletic development, progressively new and difficult challenges which are successfully met, unleash fresh aesthetic as well as personal insights for the dancers. While the *pas de deux* traditionally has been the highlight in many a choreographer's work and therefore the supreme delight for the audience, it is nonetheless the ultimate and revered reward for the dancers, whether in class or on stage.

REFERENCES

Beaumont, C., & Idzikowski, *A Manual of the Theory and Practice of Classical Theatrical Dancing, Cecchetti Method.* London: C. W. Beaumont, 1971. Lowe and Brydone Printers, Ltd.

Birdwhistell, R. *Kinesics and Context.* Philadelphia: University of Pennsylvania Press, 1970.

Blasis, C. Translated by Evans, M. *An Elementary Treatise Upon the Theory and Practice of the Art of Dancing.* New York: Dover Publications, Inc., 1968.

Bosanquet, B. *A History of Aesthetics.* New York: Meridian Books, 1957.

Bruhn, E., & Moore, L. *Bournonville and Ballet Technique.* Brooklyn: Dance Horizons, 1961.

Ellis, R., & DuBoulay, C. *Partnering.* London: Wyman & Sons, 1955.

Fisher, S. *Body Consciousness.* New York: Jason Aronson, Inc., 1974.

Grant, G. *Technical Manual and Dictionary of Classical Ballet*, Second Edition. New York: Dover Publications, 1967.

Hall, E. *The Silent Language.* New York: Fawcett World Library, 1963.

Karsavina, T. *Classical Ballet, The Flow of Movement.* London: The Dancing Times, Ltd., 1962.

Karsavina, T. *Ballet Technique.* London: Adam and Charles Black, 1970.

Kirstein, L., Stuart, M., Dyer, C., & Balanchine, G.*The Classic Ballet, Basic Techniques and Terminology.* New York: Alfred A. Knopf, 1973.

Langer, S. *Philosophical Sketches.* New York: Mentor Books, 1964.

Langer, S. *Problems of Art.* New York: Charles Scribner's Sons, 1957.

Lawson, J. *The Teaching of Classical Ballet.* London: Adam and Charles Black, 1973.

Lawson, J. *Teaching Young Dancers.* London: Adam and Charles Black, 1975.

Methany, E. *Movement and Meaning.* New York: McGraw-Hill, Inc., 1968.

Messerer, A. Translated by Briansky, O. *Classes in Classical Ballet.* Garden City, N. Y.: Doubleday & Co., Inc., 1975.

Prudhommeau, G., & Guillot, G. *Grammaire de la Danse Classique.* Paris: Hochette, 1969.

Sachs, C. Translated by Schonberg, B. *World History of the Dance.* New York: W. W. Norton & Co., Inc., 1965.

Sparger, C. *Anatomy and Ballet.* London: Adam and Charles Black, 1970.

Steen, E., & Montagu, A. *Anatomy and Physiology,* Vol. 1. New York: Barnes & Noble, Inc., 1972.

Vaganova, A. Translated by Chujoy, A. *Basic Principles of Classic Ballet.* New York: Dover Publications, Inc., 1969.

SUGGESTIONS FOR FURTHER READING

Gregory, J. *Understanding Ballet.* London: Octopus Books Limited, 1972.

Hawkins, A. *Creating Through Dance.* Englewood Cliffs, N.J.: Prentice-Hall, Inc., 1965.

H'Doubler, M. *Dance, A Creative Art Experience.* Madison: University of Wisconsin Press, 1966.

Guillot, G., & Germaine Prudhommeau. Translated by K. Carson. *The Book of Ballet.* Englewood Cliffs, N.J.: Prentice-Hall, Inc., 1976.

Mara, T. *The Language of Ballet, An Informal Dictionary.* Cleveland, Ohio: World Publishing Co., 1966.

Terry, W. *The Ballet Companion.* New York: Dodd, Mead & Co., 1968.

GLOSSARY

The technique of classical ballet has been evolving since the time when Louis XIV officially organized the theatrical dance under the auspices of the Royal Academy. Almost immediately a special terminology for ballet began to flower as dancers and dancing masters originated novel steps which needed verbal identifications. During this period of rapid technical growth they likewise elaborated on many previously named steps inherited from the Renaissance court ballets. Naturally enough, names of these steps were indicated in the French language or changed from their original Italian into French and have been traditionally maintained as such.

When the French-trained Carlo Blasis penned the *Code of Terpsichore* in the early nineteenth century, the basis of today's terminology was fairly well secured. Further technical development in France during the Romantic Age and in Russia during the lengthy tenure of the French ballet master Marius Petipa, added to the corpus of terminology. Consequently, today we have a building body of terms contributed by the historical French, Italian and Russian schools. The American modern dance also has had influence on ballet choreographers who in the process of absorbing its fresh choreographic ideas, often adopt the novel terminology which expresses their contemporary approach to movement.

As each age expects something different from its dance and dancers, steps themselves and a particular style of performing them are constantly in flux and are given to certain nuances of meaning which are in turn signified by their terminology. Detailed studies of the etymology of ballet steps and their concomitant styles of execution are imperative for the dance historian and important for the education of the ballet student but require a more lengthy approach than is here possible. This glossary is meant to be only a general guide and quick reference to the most frequently used terms in the ballet classroom. For a comprehensive compilation of the terminology, consult Gail Grant's *Technical Manual and Dictionary of Classical Ballet*.

A

Abstract ballet

An abstract ballet is one without a narrative. It has been epitomized in the works of George Balanchine.

Adage or Adagio

French and Italian words for slow movement. In ballet the terms refer to two kinds of slow movement: (1) Long series of slow movements performed in the center practice of class to achieve balance, control, strength and line. (2) Generally a duet or *pas de deux* for a male and female dancer which involves complex lifts and supports.

Air, en l'

Indicates leg movement or leg position is raised to the hip level.

Allégro work

Lively movements based on all jumping steps characterized by lightness, smooth transition between steps and brilliance of execution.

Allongé

A body position or movement extended to its maximum length.

Aplomb

A uniquely elegant poise assumed by the dancer who is in full control of the body's movements and its balance.

Arabesque

Perhaps the hallmark of ballet poses. The arabic inspired name for this position relates to the longest line the body can make from the finger tips of an outstretched arm to the toe tip of one leg extended behind the body. Numerous varieties of *arabesques* derive from the Italian (Cecchetti), French and Russian schools.

Arrière, en	Term indicates that a step moves backward.
Assemblé	A jumping movement whereby the body is propelled upward, the legs meet in the air, and land in fifth position. There are numerous kinds of *assemblés* done to all directions, while turning in the air, with beats, etc.
Attitude	Elegant pose on one leg with the other leg bent at the knee to the front or the back of the body; the arms take various positions. The *attitude* was borrowed by Carlo Blasis from a statue of the God Mercury created by the Renaissance sculptor Giovanni da Bologna.
Avant, en	Term used to indicate that a step moves forward toward the audience.
B	
Balancé	A rocking step done close to the floor. Smooth transition of weight between legs is essential.
Balancoire, en	Seesaw-like movement involving the torso and the legs.
Ballerina	Title given to principal female dancers usually denoting extraordinary achievement.
Ballet	From the Italian verb "ballare" (to dance). A theatrical form of dance created to express in movement the ideas and feelings of a choreographer; it is enhanced by appropriate music, costumes, lighting, and

	scenery and is meant to be seen by an audience.
Ballet blanc	Literally "white ballet." A term applied to ballets wherein the dancers are costumed in the long, bell-shaped white dresses like the one first worn by Taglioni in *La Sylphide.*
Ballet d'action	Ballet with a narrative expressed by the choreography.
Ballon	A quality of movement associated with jumping steps wherein the dancer seems to bound effortlessly, pose in the air, land, and rebound.
Ballonné	An *allégro* step done in a variety of poses and directions in which the dancer "bounces" on one foot while the other leg extends itself at the height of the jump and returns to the *cou-de-pied* position upon landing.
Ballotté	An *allégro* step wherein the body is "tossed" back and forth from one leg to the other. Requires considerable technique to execute properly.
Barre	Exercises practiced in the first part of the class during which the dancer uses a horizontal bar to maintain and perfect balance and placement.
Bas, en	Low. Indicates position of arms or head.
Battement	A beating action which originates with the opening and closing of the legs. Two general types, large

(grand) and small *(petit) battement* constitute most of the exercises at the barre. They are used in the center work exercises and contribute to the make-up of the construction of all steps. The most common *battements* include *battement tendu, battu, dégagé, développé, en cloche, fondu, frappé, glissé, retiré, serré, tendu, tendu relevé,* and the *grand battement.*

Batterie A term referring to all steps which include beats.

Battu Any step embellished with a beat; i.e., *jeté battu.*

Brisé A small beating step in which the movement has a "breaking" quality. Many kinds and styles of *brisé* have been handed down.

C

Cabriole Literally a caper. Elevation step which includes one or two beats and is performed in all body directions.

Cambré Stretching movements in the upper half of the body.

Center practice Middle section of the ballet class which is comprised of exercises done without the aid of the barre.

Chaînés A series of traveling turns which create a "chain" of movement.

Changement de pieds A jumping step in which the feet "change" the fifth position before landing.

Chassé
A movement in which one leg appears to be "chasing" the other. Commonly used as an auxiliary step.

Choreographer
One who composes ballets.

Choreography
The movement design of a ballet.

Coda
The finale of a *pas de deux* or an entire ballet.

Contretemps, demi-
Small, beating step used in preparation for moving sideways.

Corps de ballet
The dancers who perform in chorus as opposed to solo dancing.

Côté, de
Sideways.

Cou-de-pied
Area of the leg between the ankle and base of the calf.

Coupé
Small preparatory step in which one foot "cuts" the other away and replaces it.

Couru
Running.

Croisé
Crossed. One of the body directions.

Croix, en
Cross-shaped. Signifies that the working leg moves to the front, side, back, and side directions; for example, *battements frappés en croix.*

D

Danseur, premier
Leading male dancer. Counterpart of the ballerina.

Dedans, en
Inward, circular direction of movement.

Dégagé	Refers to one leg extending in an open position with the toes "disengaged" from the floor.
Dehors, en	Outward circular direction of movement.
Demi-hauteur	Half-height. Indicates a 45° lift of the leg or arm.
Demi-plié	Half bend of the knees. Essence of all jumping movements.
Demi-pointes	Standing on the balls of the feet.
Derrière	Behind. Movement, step or extension in back of the body.
Dessous	Under.
Dessus	Over.
Devant	Front. Movement, step or extension in front of the body.
Développé	A controlled upward and outward unfolding of one leg into one of the various positions.
Divertissement	Brief dances created to display the special qualities of one or more soloists.
E	
Écarté	Thrown apart. One of the directions of the body based on second position in which one leg is extended to the floor level or in the air. The body is placed diagonally in space, relative to the audience or front of the classroom.
Échappé	A jumping movement from fifth to second or fourth position in which

	the legs "escape" from each other at the height of the jump. Can be done with beats as in *échappé battu*.
Échappé sur les pointes	*Échappé* performed with a springing movement onto the balls of the feet or onto full *pointes* with the use of blocked shoes.
Effacé	One of the directions of the body in which its diagonal placement in space takes on a "shaded" effect from the audience's viewpoint.
Élan	Pertains to the energetic and stylish attack which a dancer gives to a movement.
Elevation	Elevation is the height a dancer can bound from a *demi-plié*. It is measured by the distance between the dancer's pointed feet and the floor.
Emboîté	A little jumping and turning step in which the feet stay "boxed" together. It is usually done in a series which travels across the floor.
Enchaînement	Combination of several steps fitted to appropriate music. Such movement comprises the last third of the class which is given over to full-out dancing practice.
Entrechat	A beaten jumping step in which the legs cross up to five times giving the appearance of "interweaving." In order of number of beats they are *entrechat trois, quartre, cinq, six, sept, huit, neuf* and *dix*.
Enveloppé	Inward folding of the leg from an extended position. Can include a *rond de jambe en l'air en dedans*.

Épaulé

One of the directions of the body determined by the placement of the "shoulders" within space.

Épaulement

Pertains to the movement of the upper torso as it is determined by the placement of the shoulders. Its use is essential for the elegant bearing of the dancer.

Extension

Refers to the dancer's ability to raise and hold the extended leg.

F

Face, de

Facing the front of the classroom or the audience.

Failli

A simple fleeting movement which usually links steps together.

Fermé

Term used to indicate that the legs come to a closed position at the end of a step.

Fondu

Sinking movement.

Fouetté

Whipping movement of the legs as in *fouetté* turns or of the torso as in *grand fouetté*.

Frappé

Striking movement.

G, H, J

Gargouillade

A "gurgling-like" step evolved during the Romantic era demanding considerable technical brilliance. Its form involves jumping, the *pas de chat* and single or double *rond de jambes* with both legs. It is rarely seen today, often referred to as a lost step.

Glissade

A *terre à terre* step used to connect other movements. Characterized by its gliding quality, it is performed in various directions and has several variations of form.

Haut, en

High. Indicates position of arms or head.

Jeté

Generic term for numerous jumping steps in which one leg is "thrown" outward in the process of execution.

L, M

Legato

Italian term meaning smooth or flowing.

Movement

Ballet involves seven basic kinds of movement. They are:
    élancer—to dart
    étendre—to stretch
    glisser—to glide
    plier—to bend
    relever—to raise
    sauter—to jump
    tourner—to turn

O, P

Ouvert

Term used to indicate that the legs finish a step in an open position.

Pas

A step compromising one or more transfers of weight. Also refers to a solo dance as in a *pas seul, pas de deux* (duet); *pas de trois* (trio); *pas de quatre* (quartet), etc.

Pas battu

Beaten step.

Pas couru

Running step.

Pas d'action	Those parts of ballets which carry the storyline by means of pantomime and dance.
Pas de basque	Ancient ballet step derived from folk dance movements of the Basque people in Northern Spain. Numerous variations exist.
Pas de bourrée	Ancient ballet step derived from the folk dances of the French farmer in the Auvergne region. Numerous variations frequent classroom work and the traditional repertory.
Pas de chat	Jumping step named for its "cat-like" movement quality. Russian version differs from the Italian.
Pas de cheval	Step in which the leg movements resemble a horse pawing the ground.
Pas de ciseaux	A jumping step in which the legs move in a "scissor-like" action.
Pas de valse	Waltz step.
Passé	An auxiliary movement where one foot "passes" the knee of the supporting leg. Sometimes the term is used to mean the *retiré* position of the legs.
Penché	Refers to the body "leaning" in any given position.
Piqué	Any movement performed by thrusting the weight directly onto the half or full *pointe* of one leg.
Pirouette	General term for turns on one leg.

Plié   Exercise which flexes the knees. The *demi-plié* permeates the corpus of ballet movement while the *grand plié* is used to develop strength and pliability in the legs.

Pointes, sur les   Body weight is supported on the very tips of the toes. Usage appeared in the 1820's in a somewhat awkward form but was soon perfected by Marie Taglioni.

Port de Bras   Carriage of the arms through the precise arm positions designated by the Italian, French, and Russian methods.

Posé   Same as a *piqué* movement.

Positions   The exactitude of classical ballet specifies basic body positions of which the Italian school has eight and the Russian and French schools claim eleven. The five feet positions were the earliest to be set, evolving from the Renaissance dancing masters. Precise arm positions were next codified, followed by specifications for holding the head, the hands, and the foot itself.

Promenade   Controlled revolving of the body on one foot.

Q, R

Quatrième, a la   To the fourth position.

Raccourci   The retracted position of the working leg during the execution of a *battement retiré*.

Relevé

The "raising" of the body onto the half or full point on one or both legs.

Renversé

An advanced movement whereby the body upsets and regains its balance during a turn.

Retiré

A retracted position of the working leg. Same as *raccourci*.

Rond de jambe

Round movements of the leg. They are practiced in every class at the barre where they are designed to exercise the rotation of the hip joint.

Rond de jambe en l'air

Rotation movements of the knee joints. Performed at the barre as well as in center work.

Royale

A jumping step with a single beat and change of legs. Also called a *changement battu*.

S

Saut de basque

A jumping step based on a traditional Basque folk dance movement.

Sauté

A step or position which has a "jump" added to it such as *échappé sauté* or *arabesque sauté*.

Sissonne

A jumping step said to be named for its French originator. Numerous forms of the *sissonne* comprise both feet pushing from the floor into a variety of positions which culminate on one or both legs.

Soubresaut	A sudden jump into the air which also propels the body forward or backward while the legs are firmly held together.
Sous-sus	An upward springing movement into fifth position on the half or full points.
Spotting	Special rapid head movements used during turns which prevent dizziness.

T, V

Taqueté	Staccato like movements on point introduced by the Romantic ballerina, Fanny Elssler.
Temps	Denotes timing. A part of a step where no shift of weight occurs.
Temps de cuisse	A traveling step comprised of a quick "thigh" movement and a *sissonne*.
Temps de flèche	This jumping step is characterized by a "bow and arrow" action in the legs.
Temps levé	A hop from one foot while the body assumes one of various positions.
Temps lié	A Russian exercise from the pre-Soviet days designed to perfect the transfer of weight from one position to another.
Tendu	Stretched positioning of the leg as opposed to the *plié*.
Terre, à	Ground level. The stretched or extended leg remains in contact with the floor.

Terre à terre	A term used to describe steps performed close to the ground.
Tombé	A preparatory movement in which the body "falls" forward, backward or sideways into a *demi-plié* on one leg.
Tour	Turn of the body as in *pirouettes*.
Tour de force	A special feat of technical skill used to display particularly brilliant abilities of a dancer.
Tour en l'air	A turn accomplished while the dancer is momentarily suspended in the air.
Tour jeté	Incorrect but commonly used term in America for *grand jeté dessus en tournant*.
Tournant, en	Indicates that the body "turns" while performing certain steps.
Turnout	Ideally each leg is rotated outward 90 degrees to provide maximum freedom of movement in all directions.
Variation	A solo dance within the choreographic structure of a ballet.

Author Index

Subject Index

403